THE INNS OF COURT
UNDER ELIZABETH I
AND THE EARLY STUARTS

1590–1640

Wilfrid R. Prest

The Inns of Court under Elizabeth I and the Early Stuarts

1590-1640

Longman

LONGMAN GROUP LIMITED
London
*Associated companies, branches and representatives
throughout the world*

First published 1972
ISBN 0 582 50831 2

For Cedar

Printed in Great Britain by
Hazell Watson & Viney Ltd,
Aylesbury, Bucks

Contents

Preface

'Of the nature and order of the inns of court . . . I must profess my unhappiness not to be able to write as I would, and they deserve . . . I humbly crave the learneds' pardon for it . . .'.

Edward Waterhous, *Fortescutus Illustratus* (1663), 526.

'A really good book on the inns of court has yet to be written . . .'.

Sir Frederick Pollock to Mr Justice Holmes, 1931:
The Pollock-Holmes Letters, ed. M. De Howe
(Cambridge, 1942), ii. 285–6.

The inns of court still occupy an historical no-man's land, the domain of antiquaries and domestic chroniclers. This book attempts a rescue operation, on a small but strategically important front. It aims to provide a reasonably comprehensive account of the composition, structure and functions of the late-Tudor and early-Stuart inns, relating developments within their walls to the wider world outside and covering a period long enough to highlight significant changes through time. Institutions are more than the sum of their human parts and this is not primarily a prosopographical study, although the first two chapters rely heavily on mass-biographical data. Some attempt has been made to take account of the activities and interests of the inns' common-lawyer members, but without in any way reducing our need for a general history of the early seventeenth-century legal profession.

I am most grateful for the help given by the staff of the following institutions: the Barr Smith Library of Adelaide University, the South Australian Public Library and the Victorian Public Library; the Bodleian Library, British Museum, Cambridge University Library, Essex and Northamptonshire County Record Offices and the Institute of Historical Research; the Folger Library, the Milton S. Eisenhower Library of The Johns Hopkins University, the Harvard Law School Library and the Henry H. Huntington Library.

The Masters of the Bench of the Honourable Societies of Gray's Inn, the Inner Temple, Lincoln's Inn and the Middle Temple kindly permitted me to consult the archives of the societies. I am particularly indebted to the librarians of the four inns, who eased my task in many ways; I hope their doyen, Mr A. W. Ringrose of Lincoln's Inn, will accept my thanks on behalf of his colleagues.

I gratefully acknowledge support for research in England from the Myer Foundation, the Australian Research Grants Committee and the Faculty Grants fund of The Johns Hopkins University. The editors of the *Journal of the Society of Public Teachers of Law* and *Past and Present* have kindly enabled me to reprint parts of articles which first appeared in their publications. I also thank Sir Francis Wogan Festing for allowing me to consult the diary of his ancestor, John Greene. I owe a particular debt of gratitude to Miss Irene Cassidy, my research assistant in London from 1968 to 1970, whose expert help did much to lessen the difficulties of working at a distance from the sources.

I cannot mention by name all those who have contributed to the emergence of this book from an Oxford D. Phil. thesis presented in 1965, but I thank them nevertheless. Christopher Brooks, Jim Main, Frank McGregor, Walter Richardson, George Rudé, Hugh Stretton, Lawrence Stone, Nicholas Tyacke and Robin Walker kindly read and commented upon various drafts; needless to say, the responsibility for errors of fact and interpretation which remain is entirely my own. I am also most grateful to the late H. E. Bell, Mrs Patricia Crawford, Dr D. E. Kennedy, Professor S. E. Thorne and the examiners of my thesis, Mr J. P. Cooper and Dr E. W. Ives, for their helpful suggestions; to my parents, for their moral and material support; and to all the friends and colleagues in Adelaide and Baltimore who urged me on. That has been the least of the kindnesses performed by my former supervisor, Christopher Hill; I only wish this book were more adequate recompense for his encouragement and inspiration.

Note. Dates are given in New Style, with the year commencing on January 1. Abbreviations, capitalisation and punctuation have been modernised in quotations from primary sources, but not in the titles of books. Unless otherwise indicated, all books cited were published in London.

Abbreviations

Additional	Additional MSS, British Museum
Al. Cant.	*Alumni Cantabrigienses . . . from the earliest times to 1900*, comp. J. and J. A. Venn, Cambridge, 1922
Al. Ox.	*Alumni Oxonienses: the members of the University of Oxford, 1500–1714*, comp. Joseph Foster, 1891–92
APC	*Acts of the Privy Council of England*, ed. J. R. Dasent, 1890–
Ath. Ox.	Anthony Wood, *Athenae Oxonienses*, ed. P. Bliss, 1813–20
BB	*The Records of the Honourable Society of Lincoln's Inn. The Black Books*, ed. W. P. Baildon and R. F. Roxburgh, 1897–1969
BIHR	*Bulletin of the Institute of Historical Research*
BM	British Museum
Bodl.	Bodleian Library, Oxford
Brerewood	Brerewood MS, Middle Temple Library
Cal. Com. Comp.	*Calendar of the Proceedings of the Committee for Compounding, &c., 1643–1660*, ed. M. A. Green, 1889–92

CMTR	*Calendar of Middle Temple Records*, ed. C. H. Hopwood, 1903
Cottonian	Cottonian MSS, British Museum
CRS	Catholic Record Society Publication
CS	Camden Society Publication *or* Camden Series, Royal Historical Society Publications
CSPD	*Calendar of State Papers Domestic*
CSPVen	*Calendar of State Papers Venetian*
CUL	Cambridge University Library
DBC	Report to Henry VIII on the state of the inns of court *c.* 1540 by Thomas Denton, Nicholas Bacon and Robert Carey, printed Edward Waterhous, *Fortescutus Illustratus* (1663), 543–46
D'Ewes, *Autobiography*	*The Autobiography and Correspondence of Sir Simonds D'Ewes, bart, during the reigns of James I and Charles I*, ed. J. O. Halliwell, 1845
D'Ewes, 'Secret Diary'	G. A. Harrison, 'The Secret Diary of Sir Simonds D'Ewes deciphered for the period January 1622–April 1624', Minnesota M.A. thesis, 1915
DLLA	*John Fortescue's De Laudibus Legum Angliae*, ed. S. B. Chrimes, Cambridge, 1942
DNB	*Dictionary of National Biography*, ed. Leslie Stephens, 1885–1900
DWB	*The Dictionary of Welsh Biography*, ed. J. E. Lloyd and R. T. Jenkins, 1959
EconHR	*Economic History Review*
EETS	Early English Text Society
EHR	*English Historical Review*
Ellesmere	Ellesmere MSS, Henry H. Huntington Library, San Marino
Foss, *Judges*	Edward Foss, *The Judges of England*, 1848–69

GEC	G. E. C[okayne], *Complete Peerage of England . . . and the United Kingdom*, 1910–
GI	Gray's Inn
GI Adm. Reg.	*Register of Admissions to Gray's Inn, 1521–1889*, ed. Joseph Foster, 1889
GIPB	*The Pension Book of Gray's Inn*, ed. R. J. Fletcher, 1901–10
Hargrave	Hargrave MSS, British Museum
Harleian	Harleian MSS, British Museum
HEL	Sir William Holdsworth, *A History of English Law*, 1922–52
HLQ	*Huntington Library Quarterly*
HMC	Historical Manuscripts Commission
IT	Inner Temple
IT Adm. Reg.	'Admissions to the Inner Temple to 1659' (typescript, Inner Temple Library, 1954)
ITR	*A Calendar of the Inner Temple Records*, ed. F. A. Inderwick, 1896–1936
Lansdowne	Lansdowne MSS, British Museum
LI	Lincoln's Inn
LI Adm. Reg.	*The Records of the Honourable Society of Lincoln's Inn. Admissions ... 1420 to A.D. 1799*, ed. Joseph Foster, 1896
LQR	*Law Quarterly Review*
MT	Middle Temple
MT Adm. Reg.	*Register of Admissions to the Honourable Society of the Middle Temple, from the Fifteenth Century to the Year 1944*, ed. H. A. C. Sturgess, 1949, vol. 1
MT Bench Book	*The Middle Temple Bench Book*, ed. J. B. Williamson, 2nd edn., 1937
MTR	*Minutes of Parliament of the Middle Temple*, ed. C. T. Martin, 1904–5
N & Q	*Notes and Queries*
OJ	William Dugdale, *Origines Juridiciales*, 1663

Petyt	Petyt MSS, Inner Temple Library
P & P	*Past and Present*
PRO	Public Record Office
Sloane	Sloane MSS, British Museum
SP	State Papers, Public Record Office
SS	Selden Society Publication
Stowe	Stowe MSS, British Museum
TRHS	*Transactions of the Royal Historical Society*

I

Dimensions

History and historiography

The early history of the inns of court was already obscure by the end of the sixteenth century; in a paper delivered to the Elizabethan Society of Antiquaries around 1600, Francis Thynne confessed that 'it is hard to know . . . the original of those inns of lawyers which we now have'. Because the inns are voluntary, unincorporate associations, without known founders and 'unhampered by charters or statutes', no formal documents exist from which their first establishment might be dated.[1] The earliest surviving records, the Black Books of Lincoln's Inn, commence in 1422. The first Black Book (1422–71) is devoted mainly to the financial transactions of the house, although it also contains a scattering of administrative and educational entries. These become much more prominent in the next two volumes, which cover the period 1471 to 1530, when the Black Books began to function as the minutes of the society's governing body, the masters of the bench. The minutes of the Inner and Middle Temple parliaments do not commence until 1505 and 1501 respectively, and the first twenty years' entries are sparse and cryptic, while there is a complete break in the Middle Temple records from 1525 to 1551. The bench minutes of Gray's Inn survive only from 1569, although a few fragments of an earlier volume are preserved in seventeenth-century sources.

The first literary description of the inns was the work of Sir John Fortescue, a member of Lincoln's Inn, who rose to be chief justice of the King's Bench before his attainder and flight to France in 1463. Fortescue wrote his treatise *De Laudibus Legum Angliae* (*c.* 1470) for

[1] Thomas Hearne, *A Collection of Curious Discourses* (Oxford, 1720), 110; *Selected Historical Essays of F. W. Maitland*, ed. H. M. Cam (Cambridge, 1957), 108.

the Lancastrian Prince Edward, son of Margaret of Anjou, in order to persuade the prince that English laws and government were totally superior to those of France. Only a few pages were devoted to the inns of court, but Fortescue depicted their virtues in glowing colours.[2] He began by claiming that, since the common law required a knowledge of French and Latin, it could not be taught at the universities of Oxford and Cambridge, where Latin was the only medium of instruction. Therefore legal training was provided in London, at the 'academy of the laws of England', comprising four greater inns of court and ten lesser inns of chancery, which served as preparatory schools for the inns of court. The students at the inns of court were virtually all noblemen's sons, since *pauperes et vulgares* could not afford the expense of residence. Tuition in dancing, music and other courtly arts was available, so many great men enrolled their sons there, 'although they do not desire them to be trained in the science of law, or to live by its practice, but only by their patrimonies'. The internal organisation and structure of the societies was not discussed, but their communal life was said to be exceptionally peaceful, despite the fact that they admitted as many students 'of mature age' as any French law school, Paris only excepted. Nor did Fortescue attempt to outline the methods of legal instruction, merely assuring the prince that they were 'pleasant, and in every way suited to the study of law, and also worthy of every regard'.

Tottel, the law publisher, brought out the first English translation of *De Laudibus Legum Angliae* in 1567, and this was followed by eight more English editions before the Civil War. Fortescue's didactic treatise enjoyed great popularity as an encomium of the common law, while his account of the inns was naturally regarded as the leading authority on the subject. John Stow and Sir George Buc, whose part-historical, part-contemporary descriptions of the inns were published in 1598 and 1615 respectively, both accepted Fortescue's claims for the high academic and social standing of the societies; indeed they tended to assume that the inns were still much as they had been when Fortescue described them more than a century before.[3]

This essentially a-historical attitude was fully shared by Sir William Dugdale, whose lengthy and immensely influential compilation *Origines Juridiciales* appeared in 1666, with further editions in 1671 and 1680. The second half of Dugdale's *Origines* consists of a series of extracts from the original records of the inns, arranged under subject

---

[2] *DLLA*, 117–21.

[3] Hearne, *op. cit.*, 2, 130; Caroline Skeel, 'The influence of the writings of Sir John Fortescue', *TRHS*, 3rd ser., 10 (1916), 77–114; John Stow, *A Survey of London*, ed. C. L. Kingsford (1908), i. 76–9; Sir George Buc, *The Third Universitie of England. Or, a Treatise of the foundations of all the colledges, ancient schools of priviledge, and of houses of learning, and liberall arts, within and about the most famous cittie of London*, printed as appendix to John Stow's *Annales*, ed. E. Howes (1615), 958–69.

headings and strung together with a minimum of explanatory comment. Most of the sources Dugdale used still survive, but were available only in manuscript until the end of the nineteenth century, when the societies began to publish calendars of their admissions registers and bench minutes. Unfortunately, few later writers felt any need to go beyond the extracts Dugdale had so conveniently transcribed and arranged. They therefore confined themselves to the domestic annals of the inns, making little attempt to connect these with the outside world. The highly favourable view of the inns which Dugdale took over from Fortescue went unquestioned, as did his assumption that benchers' orders and rules could be taken as statements of practice, rather than mere normative precepts.[4]

By attempting to relate the history of the inns of court to the historical development of the legal profession and the common law itself, Frederic Maitland and Sir William Holdsworth significantly enlarged the scissors-and-paste genre which even today draws a thin sustenance from the pages of *Origines Juridiciales*. But the two founders of modern English legal history did not break completely with the Fortescue–Dugdale tradition, for both still envisaged the societies as emerging from medieval obscurity in 'substantially their final forms'.[5] The decline and fall of the old educational system during the seventeenth century was seen as the first major break in their history, and even this did not much affect their constitution and internal organisation, which had been effectively settled from the time the inns first became distinct corporate bodies. Believing that the medieval societies were merely primitive replicas of the Tudor inns, Holdsworth felt no qualms about using the copious evidence of the sixteenth century to depict the state of the societies *ab initio*, complete with oligarchical government by the masters of the bench, hierarchical grades of membership, a collegiate way of life and a complex system of legal instruction by aural learning exercises.

This view survived unchallenged until 1959, when a new interpretation, emphasising change rather than continuity, was advanced by Professor S. E. Thorne.[6] Thorne's study of the fifteenth-century inns

---

[4] D. S. Bland, *A Bibliography of the Inns of Court and Chancery* (SS, supplementary ser., 3, 1965), sections B–F, gives a comprehensive listing of antiquarian histories; cf. William Herbert, *Antiquities of the Inns of Court and Chancery* (1804), vii: 'To give the substance of that expensive and interesting work [Dugdale] with the additional advantage of views of the places described, was the primary, and in fact, the only object here aimed at . . .'.

[5] F. W. Maitland, *English Law and the Renaissance* (Cambridge, 1901); *idem*, *Year Books of Edward II, Volume I, 1 & 2 Edward II, A.D. 1307–1309* (SS, 17, 1903), xviii, lxxx–lxxxi; W. S. Holdsworth, *Some Makers of English Law* (Cambridge, 1938), 46–9, and *HEL*, ii. 493–512.

[6] S. E. Thorne, 'The early history of the inns of court with special reference to Gray's Inn', *Graya*, 50 (1959); for a recent modification of the Thorne thesis cf. J. P. Dawson, *Oracles of the Law* (Ann Arbor, 1968), 36–8. Cf. Sir Ronald Roxburgh, *The Origins of Lincoln's Inn* (Cambridge, 1963), 31–3.

convinced him that there, 'just as at Oxford and Cambridge, teaching duties were only slowly grafted on to older institutions in which they had originally played no part'. The origins of the inns were not to be found, as Holdsworth thought, 'in a body of masters of the faculty of law, giving lectures and instructing their pupils'. The prototype inn of court rather emerged when a group of practising lawyers, whose business brought them regularly to London each term, clubbed together in order 'to rent a house, hire a cook and manciple, engage a servant or two and be assured of a bed and a reasonable dinner'. So, like the halls of the medieval universities, the inns began, sometime in the fourteenth century, not as schools or colleges but as clubs, offices and lodging houses, providing their small bands of members with food, shelter and companionship in an inhospitable urban environment.

Yet unlike the halls of Oxford and Cambridge, with which they had otherwise a great deal in common, the societies also came to function as teaching institutions. Just how and why this momentous development occurred is a matter for speculation. But while it seems likely that organised legal education was not provided much before 1400, an elaborate system of legal training had evolved by the middle of the fifteenth century. Meanwhile, after more or less uncharted wanderings, the societies of lawyers had finally settled in the sites off Holborn, Fleet Street and Chancery Lane, which they have occupied down to the present day. Once having become something more than lodging houses, they also began to acquire a corporate spirit, a sense of mutual pride and purpose, which finds its first expression in Fortescue's *De Laudibus Legum Angliae*.

Thorne's thesis has three great virtues. Instead of treating the inns as entities quite isolated from society at large, it places them firmly within an historical context, relating their development to the late medieval revolution in educational thought and practice which fostered the rise of collegiate teaching institutions throughout western Europe. It is based on a thorough examination of the surviving evidence, rather than merely hypothesising back from the status which the inns had achieved by the later sixteenth century. Above all, it insists that the inns have a history, not just a past, that they must be seen as dynamic organisms changing through time, not static entities essentially unaltered (or at most, corrupted) by the passing centuries.

Our conception of the origins and early history of the inns necessarily conditions our understanding of their later history. The orthodox assumption of essential continuity not only gives a false picture of the medieval societies, but also a foreshortening of perspective, a telescoped view of their later development. Above all, it neglects or pays insufficient attention to the transformation of the inns from small, inward-looking professional fraternities to large, complex, quasi-collegiate public institutions, between the end of the Wars of the Roses and the eve of the English Revolution. The main agent of this momentous change was their numerical expansion, to which we may now turn.

Membership and residence

As with population growth and price inflation, the expansion of education in Elizabethan and early Stuart England was part of a general secular movement throughout early modern Europe. Yet like the price revolution and the demographic upswing, its causes, scale and timing at both national and international levels are by no means firmly established. The wave seems to have begun in Quattrocento Italy, spread to the Low Countries and to Spain in the later fifteenth century, to France in the early sixteenth century, and to England by the 1550s, where the growth in numbers and size of educational institutions has recently been examined by Professor Stone.[7] Stone's dating of the English 'Educational Revolution' to the period 1560–1640 depends largely upon statistical evidence for a huge increase in the number of entrants to higher education during the later sixteenth century. Unfortunately, the admissions registers of the universities and inns of court are extremely fragmentary before the mid-sixteenth century, although relatively abundant and complete thereafter. So it is possible that the undoubted boom in the Elizabethan period was not really a new development, but merely the culmination of a long-term upward trend.

The problem hinges around our ignorance of the numbers of entrants to higher education before 1560. In the absence of complete records, it can only be overcome by extrapolation from those which do exist. Assuming that the surviving early records are reliable and that each house admitted the same proportion of the total number of entrants before as after 1550, a conjectural reconstruction of the missing inns of court data can be made.[8] The results of this obviously speculative venture set out in Figure 1.

The fifteenth century appears as a period of stability, if not stagnation, with admissions rarely rising above sixty a year, followed by a brief phase of sharp fluctuations in the early 1500s. Around 1530 a gradual but sustained upward movement begins, becoming a spectacular rise from about the middle of the century; by the 1550s admissions are nudging the century mark and by 1600 they have more than doubled, to an average of over 250 per annum. Although the upward trend peaks about the middle of James I's reign, there is a rally in the

[7] J. H. Hexter, 'The education of the aristocracy in the Renaissance', in his *Reappraisals in History* (1961), 45–70; Richard Kagan, 'Education and the state in Habsburg Spain' (Cambridge Ph.D. thesis, 1968), ch. 6, graphs 1–6; Lawrence Stone, 'The educational revolution in England, 1560–1640', *P & P*, 28 (1964), 41–80.

[8] I am grateful to Mr Peter Praetz of the Economics Department, University of Adelaide, for his expert assistance with the technical aspects of this undertaking.

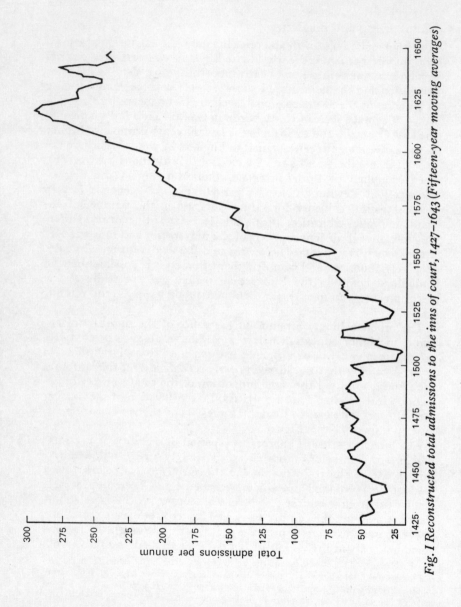

Fig. I Reconstructed total admissions to the inns of court, 1427–1643 (Fifteen-year moving averages)

1630s and very little weakening before the outbreak of the Civil War. Thus so far as the inns of court were concerned, the educational revolution was clearly an Elizabethan and early Stuart phenomenon; but its Henrician antecedents are equally apparent, even if the post-1550 expansion was of a different order of magnitude to anything which had come before.

Since the rate of annual admissions to the inns quadrupled between 1500 and 1600, it may seem self-evident that the size of their residential population must also have risen fourfold over the same period. Unfortunately, as we shall now see, the relationship between the number of admissions and the number of resident members at the inns was by no means straightforward. Fortescue claimed that each inn of court had at least 200 members. This figure is generally taken at face-value, but is difficult to reconcile with the few contemporary estimates available after 1550. Although admissions apparently remained stable through the fifteenth and early sixteenth centuries, then increased very rapidly between 1550 and 1575, a survey undertaken for the privy council in 1574 shows Gray's Inn with 220 members, the two Temples just under 200 each and Lincoln's Inn only 169.[9] One explanation for this anomaly is that Fortescue's figures were ridiculously exaggerated. However, an equally plausible solution is suggested by James Whitelocke's comment in another paper read to the Society of Antiquaries:

> For the inns court there are not at this time [i.e., *c.* 1600] any more in commons amongst us, when there are most, than 200, or 10 or 11 score, which is very seldome, and I suppose Fortescue meaneth only those that at that time were as residents and students in those houses *at some times or others.*[10]

The distinction made here is apparently between the total number who might use the inns over a given period of time, as against the number actually present at any point within that period. Given a high turnover of short-term residents the former would obviously be much larger; and indeed the domestic arrangements of the societies were designed to cater for just such a situation.[11]

Going back to Fortescue, we find that the early records of his own house include several lists of members, the last of which, dated 1454–5, names no less than 245 individuals. Yet a levy imposed only twelve years later was clearly based on the assumption that a maximum of 140 residents would be available to contribute, and the sum actually raised indicates that payments were secured from perhaps only half that number. The Elizabethan antiquary and lawyer, Sir John Ferne, claimed to have sighted a list of members of one of the houses compiled during the last year of Henry V's reign, which included 'scarcely

9 *DLLA*, 118–19; SP 12/95/91 (printed *ITR*, i. 468–9).
10 Hearne, *op. cit.*, 130 (my italics).
11 Cf. below, p. 12. *OJ*, 142–3.

threescore' names; when the admissions statistics of fifteenth-century Lincoln's Inn are compared with those for the later sixteenth century, this seems a much more likely estimate of the normal population of each late-medieval inn than the figures usually cited from Fortescue.[12]

The same essential distinction between numbers resident at a particular time and the total resident over a given period helps to clarify an apparent discrepancy between the 1574 figures cited above and those given by another official census carried out in 1586. The 1574 statistics probably represent the actual numbers resident on a specific day during term; the same would seem to be the case with the 1586 figures, except those for Gray's Inn. Here a total of 356 members during term was claimed, as against only 200 at the other three houses. Gray's Inn certainly did not admit sufficient entrants between 1574 and 1586 to produce a 75 per cent increase in its population over this twelve-year period; but some working lists from which the final totals were calculated have survived, and they show that the Gray's Inn figure was based on a count taken in Hilary term 1586 of 'the gentlemen fellows of this inn as generally happen to be in residence during term and vacation'. So, the total of 356 clearly represents the maximum number of potential Gray's Inn residents, any of whom might be sighted at some point or other in the course of a year, but hardly all at the same time. Another paper in the same group of manuscripts puts the number of commoners at Gray's Inn during Michaelmas term 1585 and Hilary term 1586 at 274 and 256 respectively.[13] These figures were probably compiled on much the same basis as those for the other houses, and the margin of numerical predominance which they give Gray's Inn is entirely within the bounds of probability.

Whitelocke's own estimate, which dates from about 1600, is slightly lower than that given by Sir Edward Coke, who put the size of each house in 1602 at between 240 and 260 members; it is not clear whether Coke meant actual average attendance or total individual attendance – probably the former.[14] Similar problems are encountered when one tries to make sense of the few scattered figures which can be extracted from the records of the inns themselves. In 1521 nearly 160 members of the Inner Temple were said to have accompanied the newly called serjeants of the house in procession to Westminster Hall; but in 1547 only 105 members of Lincoln's Inn contributed towards the expenses of a stand at the coronation of Edward VI. The Lincoln's Inn benchers claimed in 1605 that there were usually 140 persons 'and above' in commons every term; however in 1610 arrangements made for paying the chaplain's salary by compulsory levy presupposed that at least 200 members would be present over the course of each term. And in November 1641, when the political situation had already begun to

---

[12] *BB*, i. 45–6, 52; John Ferne, *The Blazon of Gentrie* (1586), 95.
[13] Lansdowne 106, ff. 92–7 (printed *BB*, i. 456–8); Lansdowne 47, ff. 113–22.
[14] *Le Tierce Part des Reportes del Edward Coke* (1602), sig. Divv.

depress attendance, the benchers complained that, whereas there were usually 220 to 260 members in commons every week during term time, numbers had now dropped off to 140 or 160 per week at the most.[15] The only other information from our period relates to the two Temples; in 1609 the Middle Temple bench stated that there had been 260 members 'or nearly' in commons in the middle of Easter term, while in 1613 no less than 353 individuals paid levies towards the cost of a masque produced at the beginning of that year. But this latter figure, like the assessment of nearly 300 Inner Templars for the 'barriers' staged at the investiture of Prince Charles in 1616, almost certainly includes contributions collected over the course of several terms.[16]

These fragments of data are hardly comprehensive, nor can they easily be checked against other forms of evidence. The admissions registers themselves provide little help. Because membership of an inn of court was a 'character indelible' retained for life, each member was a potential resident from the day he was admitted until his death.[17] But it cannot be assumed that all entrants listed in the registers automatically came into residence immediately after joining the societies, or indeed that they ever came into residence at all. While the usual age at admission seems to have been between sixteen and twenty years, it was common for youths to be enrolled at the inns before going up to university, especially if they were planning a career at the bar and wanted to gain two or three years seniority before coming into residence.[18] A few even more premature admissions have been noted; for example, Christopher Yelverton entered Gray's Inn in 1607 at the tender age of five, while Anthony Wrothe, an infant of twelve months, was admitted to the Inner Temple with his three-year-old brother Peter in 1630.[19]

These cases were probably exceptional, but the number of premature admissions during our period is unknown, since the registers do not list the ages of entrants, nor the dates when they first came into residence. We have a slightly better idea of the proportion of honorific admissions, although these are not formally identified as such, and some so admitted did subsequently come into residence or take part in the activities of their house. Most honorific admissions were made at the Lent and August readings, as a mark of respect to a man's office, rank or person. Middle-aged dignitaries – aldermen, ambassadors,

15 *ITR*, i. 63; *BB*, i. 284, ii. 88, 134, 361.
16 *MTR*, ii. 509; MT MS, unclassified, 'A note taken . . . upon the first roles for the Maske); IT MS, Accounts Book, 1606–48, f. 117.
17 Brerewood, 27. Membership could only be lost by expulsion, or, exceptionally, voluntary 'disadmittance': cf. *ITR*, ii, 109, 167.
18 Cf. *The Nicholas Papers*, ed. G. F. Warner (*CS*, 1866, n.s. 40), xii–xiv, and see below p. 134.
19 M. F. Keeler, *The Long Parliament 1640–1641* (Philadelphia, 1954), 403; *IT Adm. Reg.*, 431; cf. R. C. Black, *The Younger John Winthrop* (New York, 1966), 4, for Adam Winthrop, admitted to the IT aged 30 as a professional student.

clergy, courtiers, merchants, peers, physicians and politicians – admitted on these occasions may generally be assumed to have had no more than nominal further connections with the inn they joined. But this was not necessarily so in the case of their sons and servants, or office-holders in the legal bureacracy and civil lawyers.

The crux of the matter is that the inns kept no residence records as such. So unless independent biographical evidence survives, it is usually impossible to discover if or when a member came into residence, how long he stayed, and when, if ever, he returned. The admissions registers can therefore give only a rough indication of the number of potential residents admitted over a given period and their distribution between the four houses. Nearly 13,000 admissions are recorded between 1590 and 1639, but over six per cent of these may be discounted as purely honorific. Dual admissions and migrations from one inn to another, which might misleadingly inflate the total, were commonplace after the Restoration but still prohibited in theory and apparently rare in practice before the Civil War.[20] On the other hand quite a few cases of *bona fide* members who escaped the admissions registers altogether have come to light and there was also a small number of entrants whose admissions were possibly, but not definitely, honorific.[21] These anomalies may have cancelled each other out; we can only proceed on the assumption that they did, which leaves a final net total of 12,163 non-honorific entrants and potential residents admitted during the fifty years before the Long Parliament, or an average annual intake of just over 240 entrants to the four houses.

This latter figure is somewhat artificial, since enrolments fluctuated widely from year to year and were by no means evenly distributed; as the following table shows, Gray's Inn admitted nearly twice as many more entrants than any other house over the period and actually increased its share of non-honorific admissions from 34 to 41 per cent between 1590 and 1639. The Middle Temple, with only 23 per cent overall, was a poor second and its share decreased markedly after 1610. The Inner Temple and Lincoln's Inn came close behind, with about a fifth of the total intake each; neither showed much gain or loss during the period as a whole.

These statistics do not provide an infallible guide to the relative size of the inns, or their rates of growth, since the turnover rate, or average

[20] Dual or multiple admissions noted include Sir Robert Crane (IT and LI), Fulke Greville (GI and MT), Sir Dudley North (GI and IT), Sir William Pennyman (IT and GI) and John Winthrop (Ll and IT).
[21] Unrecorded entrants noted include Sir John Reresby and William Strachey (GI), Isaac Coe (LI), Edward Borlase and William Dryden (MT): cf. S. G. Culliford, *William Strachey 1571–1621* (Charlottesville, Va., 1965); *BB*, ii. 327; *MTR*, ii. 615; cf. also Egerton 2981 (Heath and Verney papers, iv), ff. 24–24ᵛ. Inaccurate transcriptions from the original registers to the modern printed versions do not generally present a problem; however, W. H. Cooke, *Students admitted to the Inner Temple 1574–1660* (1878) is unreliable.

TABLE I   *Non-honorific admissions, 1590–1639: decennial totals and percentages*

| Decade | Gray's Inn | | Inner Temple | | Lincoln's Inn | | Middle Temple | | Total |
	Number	%	Number	%	Number	%	Number	%	
1590–99	684	34·1	432	21·5	397	19·8	495	24·7	2,008
1600–09	780	34·2	411	18·0	431	18·9	661	29·0	2,283
1610–19	1,068	38·9	492	17·9	577	21·0	612	22·7	2,749
1620–29	1,158	46·3	421	16·8	441	17·6	483	19·3	2,503
1630–39	1,079	41·2	473	18·1	539	20·6	529	20·2	2,620
Total 1590– 1639	4,769	39·2	2,229	18·3	2,385	19·6	2,780	22·9	12,163

length of residence, was not necessarily constant throughout our period and the same at every inn. Generally speaking, entrants to the societies who had no ambitions for a legal career were unlikely to remain in residence as long as would-be barristers and other 'professional' members. The (admittedly scanty) biographical data indicates that about two years was the typical period of residence for the 'non-professional' student, and the judges' orders of 1574 suggest three years as the outside maximum. Of course individual exceptions abounded, and in any case we do not know the ratio of professional to non-professional entrants during our period. But the proportion of non-professionals certainly increased with the admissions boom in the second half of the sixteenth century, and Gray's Inn probably attracted a disproportionate share of non-professional entrants, thanks to its aristocratic image and reputation.[22] So while Gray's Inn was indeed larger than the other houses, the discrepancy would not have been quite so marked as the figures tabulated above might suggest.

The concept of residence also presents some difficulties. The word itself was rarely used by the inns; their residential requirements were usually expressed as an obligation to 'continue in commons' for so many weeks of term or vacation, or months of the year. While being in commons was the main criterion of residence, some members nevertheless preferred to 'frequent inns and victualling houses or live privately in chambers', despite the benchers' efforts to make them come

[22] Cf. Black, *op. cit.*, 23, 27; R. C. Bald, *John Donne* (Oxford, 1970), 54–8; below, p. 38; Essex R.O., D/DP A17; *Memoirs of Sir John Reresby*, ed. Andrew Browning (Glasgow, 1936), 3–6; *The Memoirs of Sir Hugh Cholmley* (1769), 36–9; *OJ*, 312.

into commons.[23] The benchers saw attendance at commons as basic to the survival of the inns as corporate bodies; thus in 1611 the Middle Temple bench claimed that without 'the holding together in commons [of] the companie of this fellowship in their publique hall . . . a companie so voluntarily gathered together to live under government could hardly bee termed a society . . .'. But the proliferation of exhortations and orders in the same vein seems sufficient evidence of their ineffectiveness.[24] At the same time, the fact that commons were provided on a weekly basis, with half-commons for those spending only a few days in town and 'repasts' for members requiring no more than a couple of meals, points to a rapid turnover of temporary residents, most of them probably country lawyers making a short business trip to London during term.

The other hallmark of residence was the possession of a chamber (or rather, a part-chamber, except for benchers). But newly admitted members were not always able or willing to obtain a chamber in their house. The official records of chamber transactions at Lincoln's Inn and the two Temples during the 1620s (when pressure on the available accommodation was relatively slack),[25] show that well over half the entrants in that decade never formally acquired a house chamber at all.

TABLE 2　　*Recorded admissions to house and/or chambers of non-honorific entrants, 1620–29*

Inner Temple		Lincoln's Inn		Middle Temple	
House	Chambers	House	Chambers	House	Chambers
421	183	441	208	483	229

Most chambers were held on a lease of one or more lives; leases could be assigned to another member during the lessee's lifetime for a purchase price negotiated between the two parties and an entry fine of between £1 and £5 paid to the house. When the lease expired through the death of the lessee or the last of the lives under which it was originally granted, the chamber reverted to the inn. A new lease was then arranged, and the incoming lessee paid to the house both the entry fine and the purchase price, which varied according to the amenities, condition and size of the chamber. At Gray's Inn leases were sometimes granted for a period of years and thus not necessarily voided by the lessee's death; both there and at the Inner Temple

[23] *BB*, ii. 251. LI MS, Vacation Commons 1629–35, contains the only surviving lists of commoners for our period, other than a single sheet in the unclassified MT MSS, which gives the names of fifty-four students in commons on 8 April 1630.
[24] MT MS, Minutes B, f. 236; cf. *BB*, ii. 89, 207; *GIPB*, i. 105, 190, 256–7; *ITR*, ii. 26, 122; *MTR*, i. 377, ii. 668.
[25] Cf. D'Ewes, *Autobiography*, ii. 82; *BB*, ii. 125, 259; *GIPB*, i. 324–5; *ITR*, ii. 151. No comparable records survive at GI.

lessees often paid an annual rent as well as an entry fine, rather than making an outright purchase of the lease.

Students sometimes temporarily occupied a room during vacations or at other times when its owner was absent; such *ad hoc* arrangements were not formally registered because the house received no financial benefit. Private sales and transfers made without paying an entry fine to the house were naturally forbidden, but occurred nevertheless. Thus the official records of chamber transactions are not entirely comprehensive. Yet it is clear that a sizeable proportion of students and barristers did not find accommodation within the four societies.

Londoners, who comprised about ten per cent of the members admitted during our period, could always live at home, while others might have friends or relatives in town who would be willing to put them up. The rest constituted a floating population, housed in neighbouring lodgings and tenements. Some of these were recognised annexes, like Fulwood's and Bentley's Rents near Gray's Inn; others, like Lincoln's Inn Grange, had no such semi-official status, being 'a receptacle for all sorts of strangers whatsoever'. Nearby inns, such as the Antelope in Holborn and the Black Spread Eagle in Fleet Street, also provided accommodation, and many students simply took rooms in a private house; one of the arguments advanced during the Protectorate against levying a general subsidy on the two Temples was that 'diverse gentlemen of those societies have chambers abroad in the city and suburbs'.[26]

Although the rulers of the inns disapproved of members living out, 'as forraignors rather than as fellowes associated together', no effort was made to enforce the judges' orders of 1574, 1584 and 1591 prohibiting the admission of more entrants than could be housed within the societies. As a result, the demand for chambers in the later sixteenth and early seventeenth century far exceeded the supply. In 1583 the Inner Temple benchers were told of two students who had allegedly 'continued there by the space of foure yeres and could never as yet gett any chamber in the house by reason of the scarcitie of them'. The situation was not much better when Lewis Bagot was admitted to the Inner Temple twenty years later. Bagot was obliged to entreat his fellow countryman from Staffordshire, Sir Walter Aston, 'to helpe mee to a chamber, whose answer was hee knew of none that were voide', but promised that Lewis might use his own when he 'went into the cuntrye'.[27]

[26] Cf. K. H. Haley, *The First Earl of Shaftesbury* (Oxford, 1968), 24; Black, *op. cit.*, 24–5; HMC, *Var. Coll.* iii. 89; PRO, Req. 2/203/30; M. E. Finch, *The Wealth of Five Northamptonshire Families 1540–1640* (1956), 26; *GIPB*, i. 118–19; *BB*, ii. 2; *ITR*, ii. 372.

[27] MT MS, Minutes C, f. 204; *BB*, ii. 257; *GIPB*, i. 324–5; *OJ*, 312, 316; *GIPB*, i. 62; IT MS, Petyt, Letters to treasurers and benchers, 7; Folger Library MS, L. a. 63–4; cf. *Letters of Philip Gawdy . . . 1579–1616*, ed. I. H. Jeayes (1906), 2–3.

The position may have eased slightly during the next decade; yet George Radcliffe, who was admitted to Gray's Inn in February 1611 and came into commons at the end of that year, lodged at 'an honest ould widdowes house' in Holborn until the Easter vacation of 1613, which he spent in the chamber of a kinsman at Gray's Inn, 'now in his absence'. After this experience, Radcliffe told his mother that he found 'lying abroade . . . both chargeable and inconvenient', and suggested that for £20 'together with what my good friends will lende me' he could buy 'a faire chamber'. Next month he wrote again on the same subject: 'I am now about a chamber: it is a faire chamber, butt will coste me much. Sende me worde when I shall have money towardes it . . .'.[28]

Radcliffe was not alone in finding 'house rent pretty smart in the citty', but a chamber at an inn of court was unlikely to be cheap. Besides the bare purchase price, which might run to nearly £200 by the end of our period, there was the entry fine to the house and the cost of furnishings; Justinian Pagitt compiled a list of *necessaria* for his new chamber at the Middle Temple in 1634 which included chairs, tables, bedstead, curtains, closestool, cupboards, desk, 'a wheele for bookes' and a pair of globes. So even when chambers became more readily available, as they apparently did in the 1620s, the capital outlay necessary to acquire one must have deterred many students, especially those who had no intention of remaining at the inns for more than a year or so.[29]

Once a member was formally admitted to a chamber, there was still no guarantee that he would occupy it. All those below the bench who possessed house chambers were supposed to be in commons for at least eight weeks each year, on pain of forfeiting their lease. In practice little notice was taken of less than a year's absence, and even longer periods of discontinuance were frequently overlooked. Much depended on the demand for chambers at the time and the status of the individual concerned; in 1617 a member of the Middle Temple was dispossessed because he had not been in commons for the last sixteen years, but in 1621 the benchers allowed a thirty years' absentee to keep his room. Dispensations were also readily granted for foreign travel, sickness, absence on business of state and so forth.[30]

The only other residential obligations were based on the need to

---

[28] *The Life and Original Correspondence of Sir George Radcliffe*, ed. T. D. Whitaker (1810), 65, 67, 76–7, 87, 92–3.
[29] Anon., *The Way to be Rich, According to the Practice of the Great Audley* (1661), 16; HMC, *Buccleugh*, iii. 370; IT MS, The Booke of the Generall Admittances into Chambers . . . 1554–1667, f. 288; *MTR*, ii. 823; *Cal. Comm. Comp.*, 1200; Harleian 1026, ff. 91–91v. A survey of 1574 (*ITR*, i. 468–9) suggests that about 20 per cent of the inns' resident membership were without chambers; this proportion probably continued to rise until at least *c.* 1610.
[30] See Appendix 2 below and *GIPB*, i. 154; *BB*, ii. 95, 104, 141, 243; *ITR*, i. 149; *MTR*, i. 166, ii. 530, 600, 638, 663.

ensure that sufficient members would be at hand for the readings and other learning exercises in Lent and August vacations. At Lincoln's Inn and the two Temples all entrants were supposed to be in attendance during each learning vacation, for at least two years immediately after they had first come into commons, or pay a twenty-shilling fine per vacation. However, this requirement could be avoided by buying a special admission. The proportion of new entrants with special admissions varied widely and inexplicably from one inn to another; by the 1630s more than 90 per cent of those joining the Middle Temple were specially admitted, as against only a quarter of the Inner Temple entrants and less than a tenth of those at Lincoln's Inn.[31]

TABLE 3 *Special admissions, number and percentage of total, 1590–1639*

Decade	Inner Temple		Lincoln's Inn		Middle Temple	
	Special	% Total	Special	% Total	Special	% Total
1590–99	63	14·6	42	10·6	252	50·9
1600–09	85	20·7	50	11·6	413	62·5
1610–19	135	27·4	41	7·1	492	80·4
1620–29	137	32·5	51	11·6	433	91·7
1630–39	122	25·7	40	8·9	449	84·9
Total	542	24·3	224	9·4	2039	73·3

Of course, it must not be assumed that all students with special admissions avoided learning vacations, while those generally admitted invariably fulfilled their formal obligations. Lists of members attending vacations at Lincoln's Inn between 1589 and 1596 and again from 1609 to 1611 show that the rate of absenteeism among generally-admitted students was between 30 to 50 per cent, although some

[31] Differences in fees charged for the various types of admissions do not completely account for the wide variation in the recorded proportion of special admissions at the three houses concerned. The fines payable by absentees from vacations were the same at Lincoln's Inn and the Middle Temple; the penalty at the Inner Temple is unknown; LI MS, Black Books V, f. 466v *et seq.*; *MTR*, i. 150, ii. 812.

recorded as absentees may actually have missed only part of their vacations.[32] The residential obligations of candidates for the bar and newly called benchers and barristers, which varied a little from house to house, were slightly more expensive to evade than those of the freshman student, but on the other hand they affected less than 20 per cent of the entrants admitted during our period.

It should also be noted that the four terms of Michaelmas (approximately seven weeks), Hilary, Easter and Trinity (about three weeks each), plus the Lent and August learning vacations, took up less than six months of the year; the rest was mean vacation, when the numbers in residence dropped sharply, 'none but students for the most part keeping commons'.[33] Moreover the inns always harboured a large and shadowy population of non-members; domestic staff, personal servants, lawyer's clerks, seminary priests, 'bankrupts and debtors, which make here their subterfuges from arrests' and sundry 'gentlemen of the country . . . forriners and discontinuers', whose presence threatened to turn the houses from '*hospitia* to *diversoria*', according to the judges' orders of 1614.[34]

It should now be clear why the size of the societies as residential institutions during the late sixteenth and early seventeenth centuries cannot be precisely determined. The inns were not organised on the lines of a modern university, with a fixed annual enrolment, a uniform pattern of attendance during the academic year and a standard annual turnover of students. They operated more like residential clubs or hotels, catering for a fluid, heterogeneous population of semipermanent guests and short-term transients. The lack of hard evidence, the problems of definition and the instability of their residential population defy all attempts at precise measurement. About the most one can say, following two well-informed contemporary estimates, is that the four societies probably accommodated around 1,000 members during term time by the beginning of the seventeenth century, although the total number resident and passing through in the course of a single term may have been up to a third or perhaps half as many more.

This certainly represents a vast increase since Fortescue's day, although by comparison with a modern university or industrial corporation the early Stuart inns of court seem almost microscopic institutions. Indeed it is clear that even the contemporary universities easily outstripped them, both in annual admissions and total enrolment. As early as 1577 William Harrison put the joint student enrolment of Oxford and Cambridge at 3,000, and Stone's statistics show that admissions to the four inns never reached more than two-thirds

[32] LI MS, Black Books V, ff. 501–503v, 519–521; VI, ff. 473–477v.

[33] Cf. *Handbook of Dates for Students of English History*, ed. C. R. Cheney (1961), 65–8 and references there cited; D'Ewes, *Autobiography*, i. 218; *BB*, i. 460–2.

[34] IT MS, Miscellanea 31, p. 24; Thomas Powell, *The Arte of Thriving* (1635), 177, 180–5; *GIPB*, i. 70, 214; *ITR*, ii. 228; *MTR*, ii. 789.

of the yearly intake of either university.[35] However, the individual houses of court were as big as any but the very largest university college. In 1621 only five of the sixteen Cambridge colleges claimed more than 200 members, including dons and servants. In a world where personal and social life still centred largely around the family, functional human groups of this size presented unusual problems of adjustment for their members and of management for their rulers.[36]

Architecture and topography

While the expansion of the inns affected practically every aspect of their activities and organisation, its most immediate and striking impact was on their physical appearance. When Elizabeth came to the throne in 1558, all four societies had been settled on their modern sites for at least a century. But their outward form and shape had changed hardly at all since the lawyers first took up residence, in buildings which they inherited from previous tenants. Most of these (except the halls, chapels and the Temple Church) were of timber construction, two or three storeys high, with large rooms running across each floor, divided by wainscot partitions into bedchambers and studies. Ditches or mud walls marked the boundaries of each house; the buildings within, grouped loosely round a central courtyard, were surrounded by fields and orchards. From Gray's Inn north to Highgate village was open country, and rabbits could still be caught in the coney garth at the back of Lincoln's Inn. Even the two Temples, hemmed in on three sides by houses and shops, looked out across green fields to the Thames and the clear expanse of Southwark marshes beyond.

The first major building erected by the lawyers was the Old Hall of Lincoln's Inn, completed in 1492. The red brick gatehouse of Lincoln's Inn on Chancery Lane was finished about 1520, while at the Inner Temple a series of timber buildings, erected in the 1530s and '40s, completed the quadrangle formed by the Temple Church, the cloisters and the hall. The Middle Temple gatehouse to Fleet Street, identified by Dugdale in 1666 as the oldest building of the house, was begun about 1520, and in 1528 a river wall was built along the southern boundary of both Temples.[37]

---

[35] Stone, 'Educational revolution', Table III.

[36] William Harrison, *The Description of England*, ed. G. Edelin (Ithaca, 1968), 70; David Masson, *The Life of John Milton* (1881–94), i. 113–14; cf. Peter Laslett, *The World We Have Lost* (1965), ch. 1.

[37] For a convenient summary of building activity see *OJ*, 146–7, 187–9, 231–6, 272–3. See also H. H. Bellot, *The Inner and Middle Temple* (1902), chs. 2, 12, 13, 16; Francis Cowper, *A Prospect of Gray's Inn* (1951), ch. 1; W. R. Douthwaite, *Gray's Inn, Its History and Associations* (1886), chs. 5–8; W. H. Spilsbury, *Lincoln's Inn* (1850); J. B. Williamson, *History of the Temple, London* (1925), pt. II, *passim*; Royal Commission on Historical Monuments, *An Inventory of the Historical Monuments in London*, vols ii and iv (1925, 1929).

The pace of construction quickened after 1550 and hardly slackened for the next ninety years. The extension and rebuilding of the inns soon alarmed Elizabeth's government, anxious to contain London's sprawl and particularly concerned by catholic proselytising among the junior members of the societies. In 1574 they were ordered to cease constructing new sets of chambers and to admit no more students than could be accommodated in the existing buildings.[38] But since most of the societies' revenues were derived from admission fees and chamber entry fines, while many benchers had a personal financial stake in continued expansion, it is not surprising that these commands were tacitly ignored.

Much of the capital and initiative for the new buildings erected during our period came from private members. Individuals and syndicates were permitted to erect sets of chambers at their own expense; these eventually reverted to the inn, but not until the builders and their descendants had enjoyed the right of nominating the occupants for a number of years or lives. With rising admissions there was a keen demand for accommodation and private chamber building could be a lucrative business.[39] But from the early 1620s, or slightly before, as the pressure on chambers eased a little, members showed less willingness to venture their capital on speculative chamber building; thereafter most new accommodation was put up at the expense of the house concerned.

Buildings not promoted by members were financed by a combination of short-term loans, levies and appropriations from general revenue. These sources were tapped both for the construction of new chambers and for major additions and replacements to the existing communal buildings. Between 1555 and 1560 the hall of Gray's Inn was rebuilt with a gallery, a hammer-beam roof and stepped gables in the Flemish style, while in 1624 the chapel was enlarged to accommodate the overflow congregations attracted by the sermons of Richard Sibbes. The Inner Templars added 'a great carved skreen' to their hall in 1574, and joined with the Middle in expensive renovations to the Temple Church during the 1630s. At Lincoln's Inn the kitchens were replaced in 1557, a gallery added to the Old Hall in 1565, and a new chapel costing some £3,500 was completed in 1623.[40] The Middle

---

[38] *OJ*, 312; these orders were re-issued ten years later, and the command against overcrowding was repeated again in 1596: *ibid.*, 316; *GIPB*, i. 62.

[39] Cf. George Fulwood's attack on benchers involved in chamber-building, *GIPB*, i. 118. For evidence of speculators attempting to keep up prices by leaving chambers vacant, cf. *ITR*, ii. 106.

[40] Sir John Summerson questions the traditional attribution of Lincoln's Inn chapel to Inigo Jones in *Architecture in Britain 1503 to 1830* (1953), 95; cf. *BB*, ii. 209, 211; William Martin, 'Some London topography in stained glass, c. 1623, in the chapel of Lincoln's Inn', *Proc. Soc. Antiquaries*, 2nd ser., 28 (1916), 140–6; Nikolaus Pevsner, *The Buildings of England . . . The Cities of London and Westminster* (1962), 294.

Temple hall, begun about 1562 and finished some twelve years later, was the only structure of comparable expense and size erected during this period. Covering an area of one hundred feet in length and forty in breadth, with a magnificent oak roof executed by a master-carpenter borrowed from Sir John Thynne at Longleat, a large gallery and an ornate screen, it still stands as a monument to the material well-being and social aspirations of the Elizabethan inns of court.[41]

The great rebuilding of the inns between 1550 and 1640 was not merely a matter of expanding accommodation to cope with a steadily growing membership. Many of the buildings erected at the inns during this period would have equally graced an Oxford or Cambridge college, and indeed the Middle Temple hall served as a model for the new hall built at Trinity College, Cambridge, in the early seventeenth century.[42] While all the early Tudor work had been executed in rough-cast and timber (except at Lincoln's Inn, where bricks for the hall and gatehouse were dug from clay-pits on the site), the Elizabethan and early Stuart buildings were predominantly brick and stone. This change made for greater comfort, durability and uniformity. It also allowed new buildings to rise to five or six storeys. During the Elizabethan building boom extra chambers were piled indiscriminately on existing structures and new courts, each side comprising several separate blocks of chambers, sprang up around the original nuclear quadrangles. By Charles I's reign, however, the benchers had begun to show some concern for the overall architectural development of the societies, and with the reduction in private building were better placed to control standards and styles of construction.

As early as 1615 the benchers of the Middle Temple decided that in future no new building projects by members would be authorised and any new buildings were to be erected at the expense of the society. In 1629 the Inner Temple parliament resolved to demolish a row of sixteen chambers put up some twenty years before by Edward Heyward, because they were of 'weak and unseemlie' construction, as well as blocking the view of the gardens and river. Two years later the length of a new building at the Inner Temple was deliberately restricted, in order to give 'a better ornament and prospect' to the hall.[43] John Bayliffe, the under-treasurer of the Middle Temple, who supervised the construction of a large six-storey chamber-block on Middle Temple Lane between 1637 and 1640, proudly described the finished building as being 'the gracefulest for situation, the best for convenience, the fairest for beautie and unformitie'. And in 1630, determined to prevent further 'disorderly building', the benchers of Gray's Inn decided to engage 'an able and sufficiente architecte' who was 'to

---

[41] John Buxton, *Elizabethan Taste* (1963), 62; Royal Commission on Historical Monuments, *Inventory*, iv. 148–51.
[42] Summerson, *op. cit.*, 113.
[43] *MTR*, ii. 592; *ITR*, ii. lxxv–lxxvi.

make a module of all this house how the same shall bee hereafter builded'.[44]

Grounds and gardens also came in for a good deal of attention. A 'faire walke under the trees' was made at the back of Lincoln's Inn in 1553, and between 1562 and 1568 the mud wall around the back garden was replaced in brick. While Francis Bacon was master of the walks, the garden of Gray's Inn was fenced and planted with roses, elms, beeches and sycamores, and a mound with a summerhouse, topped by a carved and gilded griffin (the newly adopted emblem of the house) was raised in the centre. The fields of the Inner Temple were enclosed with 'a stronge bricke wall' in 1601, and then transformed into 'large and lovely walks . . . ornyfied with beautiful bankes, curious knotts and bedds of fragrant flowers, and sweet herbes of sundry scentes and sortes'. Around them stood 'strong and stately rales of carved timber worke', with posts bearing 'the twelve celestiall signes, verie lively and artificially cutt'.[45]

These architectural and topographical changes were both demanded and allowed by the growth of the inns between 1550 and 1640. The pressure of increasing numbers necessitated additional accommodation and encouraged members to meet that demand by private building; more members meant more revenue for the societies, which permitted increased expenditure on public works. At the same time, the manner in which additional accommodation was provided and existing amenities improved points to a changing view of the functions and status of the inns. The benchers' architectural taste, at least as evinced by the Middle Temple hall and Lincoln's Inn chapel, remained profoundly conservative. But the shift from timber to brick, the growing concern for order, proportion and regularity, the conversion of fields and orchards to formally laid-out gardens, all suggest a conscious attempt to transform the former lawyers' hostels into the semblance of aristocratic, collegiate institutions, 'the nurserie for the greater part of the gentry of the realme'.[46]

[44] MT MS, unclassified, 'John Bayliffe the accomptantes answers . . .' (1642), f. 17; *GIPB*, i. 292.
[45] *BB*, i. 312, 335, 341–2, 350; IT MS, Miscellanea 32, f. 12v; *ITR*, i. 444.
[46] Lansdowne 115, f. 107v.

II

The Quality of Membership

Motives and status

There is no single explanation for the general expansion of higher education in post-Reformation England. Internal peace and political stability, a rising population, the prosperity of gentry, merchants and yeomen, the spread of protestantism, the enthusiastic propaganda of writers like Sir Thomas Elyot and Richard Mulcaster, all played an important part. But two particular reasons help account for the growth of the inns of court. Their geographical location made them ideally suited to introduce young men to the exciting world of London, already the mecca of ambition and talent, the kingdom's administrative, commercial, cultural and political hub.[1] The inns provided convenient communal accommodation midway between City and Court. For most young gentlemen who wished to spend some time in London, an inn of court was the logical place to stay, unless parents wished their sons to 'take lodgings in private houses, eat their meat in ordinaries and make their acquaintance with such men as they can find by chance'. It was obviously preferable that they should be accommodated 'with much better lodgings in those societies, where it is probable they will find their friends, and can never miss men of good manners and good conversation'.[2]

The inns were also the main gateway to a career in the common law. Erasmus had observed that there was no better way for an Englishman to attain fame and wealth than by becoming a common lawyer, and by the beginning of Elizabeth's reign the law had virtually

[1] F. J. Fisher, 'The development of London as a centre of conspicuous consumption in the sixteenth and seventeenth centuries', *TRHS*, 4th ser., 30 (1948), 37–50.
[2] *A Collection of Several Tracts of . . . Edward, Earl of Clarendon* (1727), 327.

replaced the church as the career open to talents, the ladder on which able young men could climb to power and riches. Public peace and private affluence, a booming land market, soaring prices, and an expanding commercial economy were the main ingredients of the lawyers' prosperity and the attractions of a legal career: 'Litigation bred lawyers, and lawyers litigation.' The university-trained civil lawyers, confined largely to practice in the Chancery, the Admiralty Court, the Court of Requests and the ecclesiastical courts, gained no commensurate benefit from these developments. In 1573 Gabriel Harvey, then a young fellow of Trinity Hall, the Cambridge centre for legal studies, gave this gloomy but realistic assessment of the civilians' prospects:

> The common law, to speak praecisely, is our civil law, and the civil law taketh place only in a few matters and meddleth in but a few cases. And it mai be in time also, that the common lawiers will handle the matter so (as I have heard saie a great number of them alreddi go about), that even those few cases too maie daily be more and more abridgid. . . .[3]

Besides their purely litigious functions, common lawyers acted as accountants, brokers, financiers, entrepreneurs and land agents; the barrister's sphere of operations was far less restricted than it is today, partly because the responsibilities of attorneys and solicitors were equally ill-defined and partly because of the lack of other professional men of affairs.[4] Of course the law was a lottery, for lawyers as well as litigants; while a few barristers or serjeants could perhaps demand £10 for a single appearance in Westminster Hall and expect to clear £400 in three weeks of term, there were also professional failures supported from the poor-box of their inn and 'soliciters and pettifoggers an infinite number', whose incomes and mode of life kept them at the level of the yeomanry, or even below it.[5] But patronage and patrimony

---

[3] David Knowles, *The Religious Orders in England* (Cambridge, 1953), iii. 5n; R. H. Tawney, 'The rise of the gentry, 1558–1640', *Econ. H.R.*, 11 (1941), 20–1; Lawrence Stone, *The Crisis of the Aristocracy* (Oxford, 1965), 191, 240–2; Christopher Hill, *Intellectual Origins of the English Revolution* (Oxford, 1965), 227; *The Letter Book of Gabriel Harvey, A.D. 1573–1650*, ed. E. L. Scott (*CS*, n.s. 33, 1884), 164. R. A. Marchant, *The Church Under the Law* (Cambridge, 1969), 3–4, suggests that the decline of the civilians after the reformation has been exaggerated, but Dr Marchant's evidence relates mainly to their undoubted revival under Charles I.

[4] Harvey, *Letter Book*, ed. Scott (1884), 164. Cf. Whitaker, *Life of Radcliffe*, 129; *Liber Famelicus of Sir James Whitelocke*, ed. John Bruce (*CS*, 70, 1858), 14–30; 'Correspondence of Lady Catherine Paston 1603–1627', ed. Ruth Hughey (*Norfolk Rec. Soc.*, 14, 1941), 76; *The Oxinden Letters 1607–1642*, ed. Dorothy Gardiner (1933), 7–8.

[5] Harrison, *Description of England*, 173–4; Sir Henry Ellis, ed., *Original Letters, illustrative of English History*, 3rd ser., iv. 53–7; Anon, *The iust lawyer* (1631), 18–19; *Diary of . . . the Rev. J. Ward . . . (1648–1679)*, ed. Charles Severn (1839),

played a part in this lottery; nor was it only the younger sons of mere gentlemen, or boys like George Vavasour, with 'nothing else to trust to but his learning' who took to the law.[6] Sir Edward Coke, who died one of the richest men in England, was the only son of a prosperous and respectable Norfolk barrister, while the extended legal dynasties of Croke, Finch, Hare, Littleton and Yelverton continued to be represented at the inns, consolidating family fortunes founded generations back.

As noted in the last chapter, the societies also admitted many members who had no intention of following a legal career. During the late sixteenth and early seventeenth centuries a stay at the inns was part of the conventional gentlemanly education and it seems to have been generally accepted that young men, whether or not destined for the bar, should acquire some knowledge of the law while they were there. In a highly litigious society men of means had an obvious need for a modicum of legal skill, which might enable them to deal with the suits of avaricious neighbours and troublesome tenants. While gentlemen might not wish or need to practise the law, 'yet ought they to have the knowledge therein for the better furtherance of their neighbours just causes, to give unto them good counsel freely, to make an end of debates and stryfes'.[7] Moreover, as Sir Humphrey Gilbert explained, 'noble men and gentlemen should learne . . . to put their owne case in law, and to have some iudgement in the office of a justice of the peace and sheriffe; for thorough the want thereof the beste are often tymes subiecte to the direction of farre their inferiors'.[8]

When it was customary for 'gentlemen of the best quality' to join the inns, 'though with no intent to study the law as a profession', gentlemen of somewhat lesser breed and those who wished to pass as gentlemen naturally followed suit. Just as a nineteenth-century industrialist might send his son to public school for processing into the figure of a gentleman, so merchants and yeomen of Elizabethan and early Stuart England achieved the same object by entering their sons at one of the inns: 'Whosoever studieth the lawes of the realme . . . he shall be called master . . . and shall be taken for a gentleman'.[9]

The serious law students; the sons of the gentry, sent with the hope

---

292. Most contemporary estimates of lawyers' earnings are probably much exaggerated; cf. Whitelocke, *Lib. Fam.*, xiv and L. B. Osborn, *The Life, Letters and Writings of John Hoskyns, 1566–1638* (New Haven, 1937), 68.

[6] *GIPB*, i. 228; *BB*, ii. 358; Thomas Dekker, *The Seven Deadly Sinnes of London* (1606), in *Illustrations of Old English Literature*, ed. J. P. Collier (1866), ii. 30. H. H. Cooper, 'Promotion and politics among the common-law judges of the reigns of James I and Charles I' (Liverpool M.A. thesis, 1964), chs. 4–5.

[7] *DLLA*, 119–21; Clarendon, *Tracts*, 327; B.L., *The Institucion of a gentleman* (1555), sig. Diiiivvv.

[8] *Quene Elizabethes Achademy*, ed. F. J. Furnivall, EETS, extra ser., 8 (1869), 6.

[9] *The Diary of John Evelyn*, ed. E. S. De Beer (Oxford 1955), v. 358; Sir Thomas Smith, *De Republica Anglorum* (1583), 27.

that they would pick up sufficient legal expertise to free them from servile dependence on their inferiors and fit them for the service of the commonwealth; the place-hunters, fortune-seekers and social climbers – all mingled together at the schools of dancing, fencing and music scattered around the inns, to acquire the non-academic accomplishments which befitted the role of the gentleman.

Fortescue emphasised that besides providing for practising and would-be lawyers, the societies also attracted well-born youths who neither needed nor desired to embark upon a legal career. Although this claim is difficult to verify from the surviving evidence, there is no reason to doubt Fortescue's word, especially since the time is past when the Lancastrian period could be dismissed as a sterile interlude of civil chaos, mercifully cut short by the advent of the first Tudor in 1485. Yet while we may no longer regard Skelton's 'noblemen born,/to learn they have scorn' as an adequate summary of the period's cultural and educational achievements, the general 'use of the inns of court as finishing schools, devoid of any intention of legal practice' cannot be dated much before the middle of the sixteenth century.[10]

Until the end of Henry VIII's reign hardly any laymen with an inns of court background appear in public life; the few prominent exceptions, such as Thomas Cromwell, Sir Thomas Wriothesley and Sir Henry Wyatt, were either infants or middle-aged when they joined the inns, so their admissions may be regarded as almost certainly honorific.[11] A trickle of well-born entrants whose careers were made outside the common law began in the second and third decades of the sixteenth century; but the major influx coincided with the admissions boom which began around 1550 or shortly before. Nor was it until Elizabeth's reign that the societies clearly acquired the public status of 'seminaries and nurseries wherein the gentrie of this kingdome are bredd and trayned upp'.[12]

Once the inns had come to be known and regarded as 'honourable societies', the presence of men who could not claim hereditary gentility was bound to be seen as an anomaly, especially since attitudes towards upwards social mobility seem to have hardened in the later years of Elizabeth. Proposals to ban those whom Blackstone later termed 'obscure and illiterate persons' from studying or practising the common law were no novelty. But we now begin to come across more generalised complaints about the intrusion of the lower classes into institutions supposedly reserved for their betters, and demands

---

[10] *DLLA*, 118–19; J. E. Neale, *Essays in Elizabethan History* (1958), 231. Cf. Joan Simon, *Education and Society in Tudor England* (Cambridge, 1966), Pt I *passim*, esp. 9, 13.
[11] Sir William Worcester's complaint (*c.* 1450) that 'men of noble blood' desert arms 'to learn the practice of law', quoted J. R. Lander, *Conflict and Stability in Fifteenth-Century England* (1969), 144, is no evidence for the attendance of non-professionals at the inns.
[12] Cf. Lansdowne 140, f. 107v; *ITR*, ii. xiv.

for positive measures to exclude them.[13] Fortescue's account of the inns, with its stress on the exalted social standing of their membership, helped provide some apparent justification for the view that the societies had always been, as they now claimed and seemed to be, academies for the aristocracy and gentry, to whose select company the sons of merchants and yeomen had no right of admission.

If these opinions were taken at face value we should have to believe that the social quality of the inns' membership was already much diluted by the end of the sixteenth century and that it continued to decline thereafter. Yet every other indication is to the contrary. Although only two sons and heirs of peers were admitted during the ten years before the Long Parliament, as against no less than twelve in the last decade of the sixteenth century, the total number of entrants from peerage families nearly doubled over the same period, from sixteen between 1590 and 1599 to twenty-nine between 1630 and 1639. Nor do the admissions registers show the *proportion* of lower-class entrants at any of the four houses increasing before the Civil War, although the *number* of low-born entrants doubtless rose as the total intake expanded.[14]

The views of critics who castigate the ambition and worldly success of the lower orders as symptomatic of a general social malaise, and look back from the evils of the present to the happy state of some previous golden age, must always be approached with scepticism. In 1586 Ferne asserted that 'our auncient governours in this land did . . . provide that none should be admitted into the houses of court . . . except he be a gentleman of blood', and claimed to have seen a list of members from the 1420s, whose heraldic arms showed all to be perfect gentlemen by descent: 'whereas pitie now to see the same places . . . altered quite from theyr first institution'. Sir George Buc, James I's master of revels, claimed that the inns received the sons of 'the best or better sort of gentlemenne of all the shires of England', yet nevertheless protested against the fallacious notion that 'the sons of graziers, farmers, merchants, tradesmen or artificers can be made gentlemen by their admittance or matriculation in the butterie role, or in the steward's book of suche a house or inne of court, for no man can be made gentleman but by his father'. Buc also appealed to certain 'ancient orders and customs' by which all but the sons of gentlemen by birth were strictly excluded from membership.[15] Yet no such rules appear in the surviving records of the inns, and Fortescue states explicitly that it was economic considerations which prevented those

[13] Cf. Paul Lucas, 'Blackstone and the reform of the legal profession', *EHR*, 77 (1962), 456–96, and references there cited, esp. 462–3.

[14] Stone, *Aristocracy*, 793; the figures for all peerage representatives come from the admissions registers; see below, p. 30.

[15] Ferne, *The Blazon of Gentrie*, 92–5; Buc, *Third Universitie*, 968; E. W. Ives, 'Some aspects of the legal profession in the late fifteenth and early sixteenth century' (London Ph.D. thesis, 1955), 113–15.

The Quality of Membership

other than the nobility (broadly defined) from sending their sons to the inns of court. Moreover, Dr Ives has shown that while most Yorkist and early Tudor lawyers did come from gentry families, the profession also included a fair sprinkling of merchants' and yeomen's sons. On these grounds alone it is impossible to believe that the aristocratic purity of the inns survived until the later sixteenth century, when it was suddenly and rudely defiled by the intrusion of the commonalty on the make.

The earliest known proposals to restrict admissions to the inns (as distinct from the legal profession), on social grounds were not motivated by any desire to preserve the societies as enclaves of the well born; on the contrary, the Rev. William Day in 1566, like John Stockwood thirteen years later, feared that unless positive measures were taken to prevent the gentry deserting the church for the law, 'all pregnant wittes [would] go to the innes of court'. Nor did the rulers of the inns show much concern about the purported inrush of poor men's sons. In February 1601 the Inner Temple benchers decided that henceforth no person was to be admitted 'unless of good parentage and no evil behaviour', and in 1614 their colleagues at the Middle Temple determined to expel any members who were servants, unless their master was a nobleman or gentleman of standing. However, there is no indication that either resolution was ever actually invoked against a would-be or current member.[16] Some nine months after James I's accession, the benchers received the king's 'expresse comaundement . . . that non be from henceforth admitted into the socyete of any house of court that is not a gentleman by discent'. The immediate motivation and timing of this edict remain a mystery. However James's decree had no discernible effect on the benchers' admissions policies; indeed neither before nor after 1604 is there anything to suggest that persons who could not produce evidence of hereditary gentility were refused admission to the inns of court.[17]

The notion that birth was the sole or prime criterion of social status naturally appealed to snobs, traditionalists, and impoverished younger sons clinging to their tattered gentility. But it had little value as a description of the social realities. Sir Thomas Smith's observation, that gentlemen were made good cheap in England, was more to the point. New riches took little time to become old family, especially around London and the home counties; the title of gentleman was not yet a mere courtesy, but even the Court of Chivalry increasingly disregarded the hereditary criterion, and those who could afford and desired to pass for gentlemen adopted the style without worrying whether their families had borne arms for three generations.[18] It would have been impractical and embarrassing for the benchers to have enforced the 1604 order, even if they had shown any great enthusiasm for the idea, which they did not. Since status largely depended upon 'port' or outward show, especially in the relatively anonymous and socially fluid environment of London, there was no urgent reason for the inns to exclude men of bourgeois or small farmer stock whose fathers could afford to support them in the manner of gentlemen.

Income and social origins

So, like the proverbial doors of the Ritz hotel, the inns remained open to all sorts of men, rich and poor alike, as long as they could foot the bill. In practical terms this meant that they were considerably more exclusive than the universities, since no scholarships were offered to needy students and no formal opportunities existed for poor men's sons to pay their way by working as menial servants.[19] If a young man whose father could not afford to keep him at the inns was unable to obtain financial support from friends or relatives, he was effectively debarred from membership. The only possible expedient to supplement a meagre parental allowance was taking casual attorney's work, as recommended by Thomas Powell in his careers handbook for impoverished country gentlemen with large families. Powell suggested that a mere gentleman's son might be sent to an inn of chancery and entered as a clerk in a prothonotary's office to learn the practical side of the law. After twelve months or so he could move on to an inn of court, where with a few years of study he 'may attaine to the imployment of some private friends, for advising with and instructing of greater counsale, whereby he shall add both to his meanes and knowledge'. But Powell admitted that this course was not practicable until a student had acquired some knowledge of forms and procedure; meanwhile 'the common lawyer is to be bred onely upon the purse'.[20]

The accepted minimum cost of maintaining a student at the inns was about £40 a year during our period; it could be slightly less or a

[18] G. D. Squibb, *The High Court of Chivalry* (Oxford, 1959), 174–5; Stone, *Aristocracy*, ch. 2.
[19] Cf. the description of the Middle Temple, *c.* 1540, in Cottonian Vitellius C. ix, ff. 312–19, printed *OJ*, 193: '. . . there is no lands nor revenues belonging to the house, whereby any learner or student myght be holpen out and encouraged to study, by means of some yearly stipend or salary; which is the occasion, that many a good witt, for lack of exhibicion, is compelled to give over and forsake study . . .'; see also *The Diary of John Manningham of the Middle Temple*, ed. John Bruce (*CS*, 99, 1868), 81 and HMC, *Var. Coll.*, iii. 89, for students supported by a patron's 'exhibicion'.
[20] Thomas Powell, *Tom of all Trades* (1633), 3–4, 24–5; cf. Ellis, *Original Letters*, 2nd ser., iii. 168–70.

great deal more, depending upon personal circumstances and tastes.[21]
The major costs were probably not the house fees charged for pensions and commons (although admissions charges, chamber entry
fines, rents and furnishings all demanded substantial cash payments),
but the necessary incidentals to residence: a fashionable wardrobe,
dinners and suppers in town, fees to dancing academies and fencing
masters, miscellaneous expenses for gaming, drinking, plays, the
maintenance of a personal servant and so forth. These were the items
where economies would have been most effective but were possibly
most difficult to achieve, given the pressures of youthful snobbery. Sir
John Holles put out £30 a year to maintain his younger brother
Thomas at Gray's Inn between 1599 and 1605; Thomas claimed that
this was 'scant allowance', to which his brother replied that it was
indeed 'too short for a mongrel course betwixt a student and a revel-
ler' but quite sufficient for 'such as intend that business [i.e. study]
only, in such equippage as thereto belongeth'. Simonds D'Ewes received £10 a quarter while he was a student at the Middle Temple in
the early 1620s and found it hard to make ends meet; his allowance
was raised to £100 a year when he was called to the bar, freeing him,
as he said, from the 'continual want, or short stipend, I had for the
last five years groaned under'. Young Edward Hyde was allowed £40
a year at the Middle Temple in the late 1620s; his uncle, the bencher
Sir Lawrence Hyde, who thought this too little, tried to persuade
Edward's father to make it £50 and 'bestow on him a suit of satin for
a revelling [or dancing] suit', to accompany 'those divers sober fine
gentlemen that are students and yet revellers'. So Owen Salusbury's
plea to his father in 1635, that he could not live at Gray's Inn on £10
a quarter, was probably quite genuine. By contrast Edward Heath,
who came up to the Inner Temple in 1625 when his father had just
been made attorney-general, had £80 a year, plus occasional parental
subsidies towards his tailor's bills: in 1630 he received £24 from Sir
Robert for a new cloak and suit, plus £13 for a length of green velvet.[22]

Variations of income level between different parts of the country

---

21 Thomas Lodge, *An Alarum against Usurers* (1584), 5; Essex R.O., D/DP A17;
PRO, C142/429/145; Yorks Arch. Soc., MS 178, p. 17; *APC, 1615–16*, 628; *ibid.,
1617–18*, 256–8; *CSPD, 1634–35*, 373; *Winthrop Papers*, ed. A. B. Forbes (Boston,
1929–47), iv. 206; *Life of Radcliffe*, ed. Whitaker, 92. The cost of a university
education varied according to the student's rank and pretensions, but the minimum seems to have been between £10 and £15 per annum: H. F. Fletcher, *The
Intellectual Development of John Milton* (Urbana, 1956–61), ii. 78–9; the larger
sums noted by J. T. Cliffe, *The Yorkshire Gentry from the Reformation to the
Civil War* (1969), 75–6, were for gentlemen's sons entering as fellow commoners.
22 HMC, *Portland*, ix. 15; D'Ewes, *Autobiography*, i. 232; G. Davies, 'The date
of Clarendon's first marriage', *EHR*, 32 (1917), 407; *Calendar of Salusbury Correspondence 1553–circa 1700*, ed. W. J. Smith (Cardiff, 1954), 154: Egerton 2983,
ff. 14, 23.

and within each rank of society make it impossible to say below what social rank the cost of maintaining a young man at the inns became prohibitive. Yeomen 'of abilitye' were commonly supposed to find no difficulty in sending their sons to the inns for a year or so, and Thomas Wilson claimed that many yeomen were worth £300–£500 per annum 'and some twise and some thrise as much'. Yet in Elizabethan Norfolk a wealthy yeoman was merely a man drawing more than £100 yearly from his lands, while the average income of the Devonshire yeomanry was estimated in 1630 at between £40 and £100.[23] Much would obviously depend on the proportion of a man's income which could be devoted to educational expenses; yet it seems unlikely that any but the most prosperous small farmer or citizen could have found £40 or £50 a year to maintain a son at the inns of court.

The evidence of entrants' social origins provided by the admissions registers helps to corroborate these conclusions. Unfortunately, the Middle Temple records alone provide details of the parentage and rank of members admitted over the full period 1590 to 1639: at the other houses this information is not consistently supplied until the first or second decades of the seventeenth century. Another difficulty is that the registers of the inns, unlike the college and university records of Oxford and Cambridge, do not explicitly indicate the sons of plebeians or yeomen; lower-class entrants were either gratuitously promoted to the rank of gentleman or listed only by their father's name, without any designation of rank. Moreover, besides, and sometimes instead of, parental degree or rank – peer, knight, esquire, gentleman – a number of occupational classifications were used, such as clergyman, lawyer, alderman, merchant or citizen. Since these categories of rank and occupation were not mutually exclusive, it seems likely that the proportion of bourgeois and professional men's sons admitted during our period was slightly higher than the records indicate, as barrister fathers, for example, usually appeared under their courtesy rank of esquire, rather than their occupational title.

Table 4 (*a*) divides the entrants admitted between 1590 and 1639 into four groups according to their own or their father's ranks as stated in the admissions registers: (i) peers, baronets, knights and esquires; (ii) gentlemen; (iii) common and civil lawyers, clergy, doctors, merchants and citizens; (iv) unclassified and unspecified. The last category comprises all entrants listed by name alone, plus those whose fathers, where named, are similarly unidentified by rank or occupation, together with a handful of entrants, mostly the sons of house servants, who do not clearly fit into any other group. Where a rank is given for both the entrant and his father, only the father's rank

---

23 George Whetstone, *A Mirour for Magestrates of Cyties* (1584), 75; cf. H. J. Carpenter, 'Furse of Moreshead', *Trans. Devonshire Assocn. for the Advancement of Science*, 26 (1894), 172, 174–5; Mildred Campbell, *The English Yeoman* (New Haven, 1942), 216–20.

has been counted; where an entrant or his father is identified both by rank and occupation, only the occupational classification has been used. The sons of lawyers and merchants who are not so described by the registers but can be identified from other sources have been included under category (iii). Table 4 (*b*) is compiled on the same principles, but covers the three decades 1610 to 1639, when the admissions registers provide a more nearly complete listing of entrants by parentage and rank.

TABLE 4   *Recorded social rank of non-honorific entrants, 1590–1639, number and percentage*

	(*i*) Peer-esquire		(*ii*) Gentlemen		(*iii*) Bourgeois and professional		(*iv*) Other and unspecified		Total
(a) Whole period									
Gray's Inn	1,917	40·2	2,166	45·4	321	6·7	365	7·7	
Inner Temple	529	23·7	1,451	65·1	232	10·4	17	0·8	
Lincoln's Inn	1,009	42·3	1,171	49·1	157	6·6	48	2·0	
Middle Temple	1,487	53·5	1,031	37·2	232	8·3	30	1·0	
Total	4,942	40·6	5,819	47·8	942	7·8	460	3·8	12,163
(b) 1610–39									
Gray's Inn	1,563	47·3	1,389	42·0	241	7·3	111	3·4	
Inner Temple	512	36·9	710	51·3	153	11·0	11	0·8	
Lincoln's Inn	964	61·9	462	29·7	102	6·5	29	1·9	
Middle Temple	903	55·6	560	34·5	144	8·9	17	1·0	
Total	3,942	50·1	3,121	39·7	640	8·1	168	2·1	7,871

It will be seen that category (i) entrants account for some 40 per cent of the grand total and over half of the total in Table 4 (*b*). Categories (iii) and (iv) remain fairly stable at just over one tenth of all entrants for both periods covered, while the proportion of those listed merely as gentlemen is nearly half for the full period 1590 to 1639 and about two-fifths for the last thirty years. Assuming that all category (i) and say two-thirds of category (ii) entrants were from the landed classes proper and did not misrepresent their rank, no more than a quarter of the members admitted to the inns during our period could have come from non-gentry or non-peerage families. Even this estimate is almost certainly over-cautious, but because the accuracy of rank attributions in the registers cannot easily be tested, it seems necessary to allow for a large margin of error. Much the same result would be achieved if every member from an urban area were transferred to category (iii); on this basis Stone classified 25 per cent of the Middle Temple entrants during the 1630s as bourgeois and professional. But we may doubt whether all those listed as town dwellers should be automatically categorised as non-gentry, since it seems likely that the number of country gentlemen maintaining houses in provincial towns was at least as great as the number of non-gentry who lived in the countryside and called themselves 'gent'.[24]

The tables suggest that the social composition of the four inns was remarkably uniform; the only seeming exception is the disproportionate under-representation of category (i) entrants at the Inner Temple and the corresponding over-representation of category (ii). But this anomaly may be more apparent than real, since before the middle of our period the Inner Temple records make little distinction between the parental rank of entrants, instead labelling almost every new member as *'generosus'*.

These figures suggest a striking contrast between the social composition of the inns and the Elizabethan–early Stuart universities. Stone has estimated that less than half the undergraduate population of Oxford and Cambridge during this period was of gentle birth, while the proportion of peers', knights' and esquires' sons was quite minute.[25] A further index of the social exclusiveness of the inns is the high proportion of elder to younger sons among their members; as the following table shows, of those whose order of birth is clearly specified in the admissions registers, 5,540 were described as eldest sons, only sons or sons and heirs, as against only 1,834 second or younger sons. The proportion of entrants whose family position is not stated in the admissions registers declines sharply during the last two

24 Stone, 'Educational revolution', 59–9; cf. W. G. Hoskins, *Provincial England* (1963), 86–7; J. E. Neale, *The Elizabethan House of Commons* (1949), 176–7; J. F. Pound, 'The social and trade structure of Norwich 1525–1575', *P & P*, 34 (1966), 61–4.
25 Stone, 'Educational revolution', 57–68.

TABLE 5 *Birth order of non-honorific entrants admitted 1590–1639, number and percentage*

	Gray's Inn		Inner Temple		Lincoln's Inn		Middle Temple	
Elder, only, son and heir	2,210	46·3	654	29·3	885	37·1	1,791	64·4
Younger son	339	7·1	208	9·3	364	15·2	923	33·2
'Son'	842	17·7	161	7·3	303	12·7	4	0·2
Unspecified	1,378	28·9	1,206	54·1	933	35·0	62	2·2
Total	4,769	100	2,229	100	2,385	100	2,780	100

decades of our period, enabling the predominance of elder sons (3,041), over younger sons (983), 'sons' (515) and unspecified entrants (584) to be seen even more clearly.

We need hardly add that the use of quantitative evidence from a pre-statistical age is always a risky undertaking, and these figures must be treated with as much or more caution than those cited in the previous chapter. Administrative failures did occur in the compilation of the original registers, and the room for conscious and unconscious error in the social classification of entrants was obviously considerable.[26] The most we can hope is that a combination of literary and statistical data provides a reasonably dependable approximation of the social composition of the societies during our period.

Regional origins

While membership of the inns of court was largely restricted to a numerically small élite of English society, the inns were at the same time national bodies, recruiting their members from all over England and Wales. The geographical origins of entrants admitted between 1590 and 1639, whose own or father's place of residence is specified in the admissions registers (10,917 out of 12,163 non-honorific admissions), are set out in Table 6. Every English county is represented, from Yorkshire (648) and Kent (617), to Rutland (33), Cumberland and Northumberland (32 each). There were also sizeable Irish and Welsh contingents (407 and 526), besides two lonely Scots.

[26] Thus two yeoman's sons, Robert Callis and William Denney, were both admitted to Gray's Inn as 'gents' in the 1590s. Social downgrading was also possible; Ellis Wynn was entered at Gray's Inn as the son of 'John Wynn gent.' in 1616, five years after his father became a baronet: *GI Adm. Reg.*, 90, 97, 145.

TABLE 6 *Regional origins of members admitted 1590–1639*

County	Gray's Inn	Inner Temple	Lincoln's Inn	Middle Temple	Total
Bedfordshire	61	15	47	18	141
Berkshire	37	20	49	81	187
Buckinghamshire	38	58	37	47	180
Cambridgeshire	29	12	33	16	90
Cheshire	92	42	44	14	192
Cornwall	3	13	62	78	156
Cumberland	20	6	4	2	32
Derbyshire	68	49	23	15	155
Devon	10	162	101	213	486
Dorset	6	17	20	174	217
Durham	38	3	13	2	56
Essex	175	67	160	104	506
Gloucestershire	25	54	67	113	259
Hampshire	39	40	86	89	254
Herefordshire	32	25	12	53	122
Hertfordshire	58	37	59	40	194
Huntingdonshire	17	2	9	17	45
Kent	313	98	80	126	617
Lancashire	176	2	15	8	201
Leicestershire	73	36	23	32	164
Lincolnshire	261	44	94	29	428
London	392	193	175	195	955
Middlesex	123	54	49	59	285
Norfolk	226	57	168	39	490
Northamptonshire	87	27	38	131	283
Northumberland	19	1	1	11	32
Nottinghamshire	36	13	15	14	78
Oxfordshire	42	38	43	35	158
Rutland	20	5	4	4	33
Shropshire	52	67	108	20	247
Somerset	14	50	91	145	300
Staffordshire	31	60	15	36	142
Suffolk	249	56	79	35	419
Surrey	72	75	41	49	237
Sussex	103	84	17	78	282
Warwickshire	36	36	29	89	190
Westmorland	21	5	1	6	33
Wiltshire	32	32	126	130	320
Worcestershire	23	51	19	75	168
Yorkshire	387	99	102	60	648
IRELAND	188	46	91	82	407
SCOTLAND	2	–	–	–	2
WALES	208	99	143	76	526
Total classifiable	3,934	1,950	2,393	2,640	10,917

The largest single group were the Londoners, who have been counted separately; together with the Middlesex men they made up just over 11 per cent of the classifiable total. This was in part the obvious result

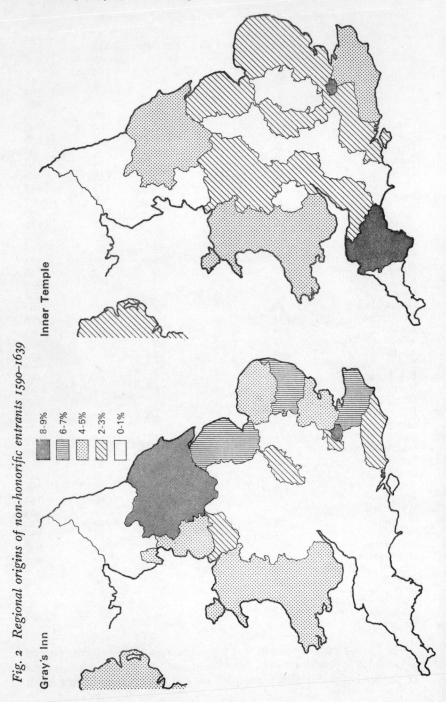

Fig. 2 Regional origins of non-honorific entrants 1590–1639

Gray's Inn

Inner Temple

8-9%
6-7%
4-5%
2-3%
0-1%

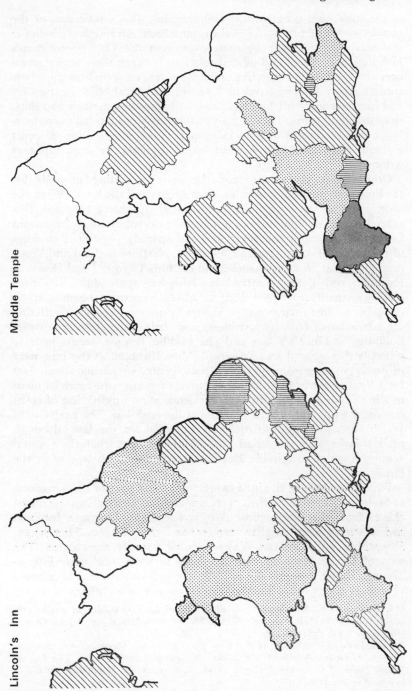

Middle Temple

Lincoln's Inn

of the inns' own geographical situation, but also a reflection of the populousness and prosperity of the capital itself. Although the societies jealously guarded their independence from the City government's jurisdiction, personal and official relations between their senior members and the London merchant oligarchy were close and on the whole cordial. Many lawyers lived in London, held legal office in the City and intermarried with London mercantile families, as they had done since medieval times. These traditional connections tended to counterbalance the cultural and social gap between young inns of court gallants and staid citizenry so often depicted by contemporary writers.[27]

Otherwise it is evident that the main recruiting grounds for the inns were the home counties, East Anglia and the South West, the most populous and economically advanced regions of England. Distance from London alone does not seem an overwhelmingly important factor, for although the backward and sparsely populated counties of the far north – Cumberland, Durham, Northumberland and Westmorland – sent very few members to the inns, Cornwall and Devon at the other end of the country were both well represented. Irishmen had been attending the inns since the fifteenth century; the once-strong prejudice against their presence, shown by numerous orders restricting the admission of Irish-born students and their segregation in separate buildings at Lincoln's Inn and the Middle Temple, seems to have virtually disappeared by our period. Most Irishmen at the inns were probably younger sons of the catholic gentry preparing themselves for a legal career in their native country; even after the establishment of King's Inns at Dublin in 1542, residence at an English inn of court remained a prerequisite for practice at the Irish bar. The majority of Welsh entrants were also probably intended for the law, although their parents may have had the additional hope that they would acquire a socially desirable English accent during their stay at the inns.[28]

While members of the inns came from every part of the kingdom, each house showed a distinct regional bias. Gray's Inn recruited chiefly from the North, East Anglia and Kent. Lincoln's Inn also had a strong East Anglian connection, while Devon, Hampshire, Shropshire, Wiltshire and Wales were all strongly represented. The men of Devon, 'innated with a genius to study law' according to Thomas Fuller, comprised the largest group next to the Londoners at both Temples; but while the Inner Templars were otherwise drawn

[27] S. Thrupp, *The Merchant Class of Medieval London* (Chicago, 1948), 258, 260–3; Whitelocke, *Lib. Fam.*, 4, 76–7; E. M. Symonds, 'The diary of John Greene (1635–59)', *EHR*, 43 (1928), 385–6.
[28] C. E. Bedwell, 'Irishmen at the inns of court', *Law Magazine and Review*, 5th ser., 37 (1911–12), 268–77; *APC*, 1627–28, 408–9; Thomas Carte, *The Life of James, Duke of Ormonde* (Oxford, 1851), ii. 84–5; A. H. Dood, *Life in Elizabethan England* (1964), 98.

fairly evenly from the Midlands, Yorkshire, Wales and the Eastern shires, the Middle Temple catchment area was primarily the South and South West -- Cornwall, Dorset, Gloucestershire, Somerset and Wiltshire. Northamptonshire, a county notorious for its puritanism, was also far more strongly represented at the Middle Temple than at any other house. Edward Bagshaw, a follower of Lord Montagu of Boughton and stepson of the pious judge Sir Augustine Nicolls, claimed at his Middle Temple reading in Lent 1640 'alliance to three judges more, all of them readers of the Middle Temple and all Northamptonshire men, where from my childhood I have lived'.[29]

As Bagshaw's boast suggests, the regional connections of each inn were based upon family and neighbourhood ties with particular houses. These loyalties were naturally strongest among families with a legal tradition. Hence the dynastic names repeated over and again in the admissions registers: Bacon, Finch, Yelverton at Gray's Inn, Croke, Hare, Littleton at the Inner Temple, Hyde, Montagu, Pagitt at the Middle Temple, Ayloffe, Clarke, Kingsmill, Rokeby at Lincoln's Inn. Sir Ralph Rokeby, a bencher of Lincoln's Inn and secretary to the Council of the North until his death in 1596, claimed in the family chronicle which he compiled towards the end of his life that 'there hath been a Rokeby continually a lawyer and governor of the benche' of Lincoln's Inn from Henry VI's time. Again, in 1589, Sir Christopher Yelverton boasted that his family's links with Gray's Inn went back 'two hundred years agoe at the least'.[30]

Sentiment and tradition were reinforced by more mundane considerations. Richard Atkins, the grandson of a Welsh judge, was naturally 'sent to Lincolnes Inne, the place where the family of my father's side had anciently been'. But Lincoln's Inn, like the other three societies, offered dispensations from, or substantial reductions of admission fees to the sons of benchers and senior barristers of the house. These concessions were often extended to more distant relatives, as well as the sons and kinsmen of judges and serjeants. If an entrant were unable to claim kinship with a sufficiently distinguished past or present member to obtain a concessional admission, there might still be a family friend or relative at one of the inns who would be prepared to stand as manucaptor or surety for the young man's debts to the house, help find him accommodation and generally 'give direction both for the course of his study and choice of acquaintance'. Family attachments once made were generally durable and the co-

---

[29] Cf. D. Brunton and D. H. Pennington, *Members of the Long Parliament* (1954), 6–7; Thomas Fuller, *The Worthies of England*, ed. John Nichols (1811), i. 283; T. K. Rabb, *Enterprise and Empire* (Cambridge, Mass., 1967), 102, n. 1; Edward Bagshaw, *A Just Vindication of the Questioned Part of the Reading* . . . (1660), 15: the three judges were Sir Henry Montagu, Sir Sydney Montagu and Sir Francis Harvey.

[30] T. D. Whitaker, *An History of Richmondshire* (1823), i. 168; *GIPB*, i. xviii.

hesiveness of county society naturally strengthened and multiplied the effects of a single family's connections with a particular inn.[31]

Among the other considerations influencing the choice of an inn, variations between the nominal admission charges of the four houses were probably not of great significance, because the amounts actually charged fluctuated considerably from one individual to the next.[32] But the fact that Gray's Inn offered a general admission at £4, which provided virtually the same benefits as a special admission elsewhere, helps to explain why that society attracted nearly twice as many more enrolments than any other house during our period. Another reason for the popularity of Gray's Inn was perhaps its reputed connections with court and government circles through such famous alumni as Lord Burghley, Sir Francis Walsingham, Sir Francis Bacon and Sir John Finch. Burghley and Bacon kept up their association with Gray's Inn after they had attained high political office, and the latter's disgrace in 1621 had no perceptible effect on the society's enrolments. Gray's Inn clearly had a more aristocratic tone than the other houses; no less than twenty-three eldest sons and heirs of peers from families ennobled before 1604 were enrolled there, as against only seven at the other three inns. Another advantage was its pleasant situation on the edge of open country, away from the crowded and unsavoury alleys which surrounded Lincoln's Inn and the Temple.[33]

The differing religious alignments of the four houses were another important variable. Puritan-minded parents were doubtless attracted by the presence of Richard Sibbes as preacher at Gray's Inn from 1617 to 1635; but Lincoln's Inn, the society of William Prynne and Henry Sherfield, Thomas Gataker and John Preston, maintained the longest succession of puritan preachers and the leading reputation as a hotbed of militant puritanism. In 1641 the pious Lady Brilliana Harley congratulated her son Edward on his move from the Temple to Lincoln's Inn, 'because theare is a better preacher'. This was Joseph Caryl, who may also have been one reason why in 1635 John Pym sent his second son Charles to Lincoln's Inn instead of the Middle Temple, which he had attended himself and where his eldest son was placed in 1629.[34]

Some families seem to have shown no strong preference for any inn, while a few others, like the Wynns of Gwydir, were apparently deter-

31 *The Vindication of Richard Atkyns* (1669), 3; *The Autobiography of Sir John Bramston*, ed. Lord Braybrooke (CS, 32, 1845), 103; *MTR*, ii. 718; IT MS, Petyt, Letters to treasurers and benchers, 24; *ITR*, i. 169; *The Earl of Strafford's Letters and Dispatches*, ed. William Knowler (1739), i. 1; SP 16/447/82; D'Ewes, *Autobiography*, ii. 182, 184.

32 *GIPB*, i. 49, 271, 276; *ITR*, i. 223, 234, 251, 423, ii. 70; *BB*, i. 438, ii. 152, 252, 270; *MTR*, i. 171, 176; *OJ*, 201.

33 *GIPB*, i. 48; Conyers Read, *Mr Secretary Cecil and Queen Elizabeth* (1956), 30–3, 115; John Nichols, *The Progresses . . . of James I* (1828), ii. 735; Stone, *Aristocracy*, 691; cf. Mathew Carter, *Honor redivivus* (1655), 153.

34 *Letters of Lady Brilliana Harley*, ed. T. T. Lewis (CS, 58, 1854), 127, 130; *Long Parliament*, Keeler, 317–18; *MT Adm. R.*, 79, 123.

mined to distribute their sons between all four houses.[35] And besides adolescents finishing their formal education or preparing for a legal career, there was also a substantial minority of older entrants – benchers' clerks admitted by their master's favour, men who had acquired posts in the legal bureaucracy and needed to join the inn where their office was situated, attorneys seeking to advance their incomes or social standing or both – for whom local and familial ties presumably had less importance than for most younger students and their parents. But even if modified in particular cases by differences in fees, social standing, situation and religious temper, the paramount importance of family connections remains beyond dispute.

A more crucial question is whether the regional bias of each house merely reinforced the local loyalties of its members, or whether the inns rather helped to develop a sense of nationalism within the dynastic and legal framework of the Tudor and early Stuart state. Nationalism is a cultural, not a constitutional phenomenon. While the Tudors managed to impose the rule of London on the country at large, administrative and political centralisation alone could hardly break down deepseated provincial loyalties. Yet Mr Harding's claim that the inns 'only intensified local divisions' is unfounded.[36] The regional attachments of the societies never became so pronounced as to direct all entrants from one locality to a particular inn at the expense of the rest, nor were the social contacts of members confined to fellows of their own society. There is no evidence that the members of each inn felt an exclusive provincial commitment or identification, comparable to that shown by the different national groups at medieval European universities, or even by the undergraduates and fellows of some Oxford and Cambridge colleges.

On the contrary, just as in modern developing countries education is consciously harnessed to propagate an awareness of nationhood, so the inns of court and universities served a similar role in early modern England, simply by bringing together the young men who would eventually inherit the natural magistracy of the nation, and exposing them to a wide range of common experiences. For this purpose it did not much matter whether students learned a great deal of law or logic; the important thing was the opportunity to mingle with their fellows from all over the realm, and thus to catch a glimpse of the wider world which lay beyond the bounds of their own parish or county. As Clarendon maintained, by 'spending some time [with] the nobility and best gentry of the kingdom', students at the inns would inevitably come 'to know the general state of the kingdom and the humour of the people'.[37] Besides the benefit of a vicarious national Grand Tour, young inns of

---

35 *Calendar of the Wynn (of Gwydir) Papers 1515–1690*, ed. John Ballinger (Aberystwyth, 1926), 12, 39, 61; cf. HMC, *Var. Coll.*, iii. 89.
36 Alan Harding, *A Social History of English Law* (1966), 250.
37 Clarendon, *Tracts*, 327.

court men had free access to the rich social, religious, political and intellectual life of London, already a strong counter-force to parochialism. Thus the inns were truly

> schools of civility and chivalry, as well as law. For the country gallant is here principled to his after improvement; here by reading both books and men, here by knowing wisdom and folly, he after becomes a luminary in the counterey firmament, an oracle of the justice bench, a worthy representative to parliament . . .[38]

Here indeed lay their major contribution to the quality of English life during the century before the Civil War.

Social tensions and the exodus of the gentry

So far the congruity between the public image of the inns as 'honourable societies' and the actual social quality of their membership has been emphasised. But there is another side to the picture. Ben Jonson's dedication of *Every Man out of his Humor* (1605) to 'the noblest nurseries of humanity and liberty, in the kingdome – the innes of court', is followed by the significant rider 'I understand you, gentlemen, not your houses'.[39] The influx of well-born amateur students in the later sixteenth century did not curtail the existing functions of the inns as associations, clubs and schools for would-be and practising lawyers. While the benchers welcomed the social cachet derived from their presence, little effort was made to absorb the newcomers into the societies, which continued to be operated and organised primarily for the benefit of their professional membership. Left very much to their own devices, the young gentlemen tended to form a group apart from the career lawyers and law students, an ornamental but essentially irrelevant appendage, 'whose lyves' (as Sir John Finch explained at Gray's Inn in 1634) 'ar not to benefitt your selves by any degree or title the house can give you, but com hither to honor it'.[40] It is doubtful whether the young gentlemen themselves desired any closer association with the inns' professional activities. The status of common lawyers in Tudor and early Stuart England was not high, and while barristers may have been better regarded than clergymen or physicians, this was despite rather than because of their vocation. Most counsellors had some claim to gentility in their own right, yet practice of the law was unlikely to elevate and might well depress their social status. Claims that 'the profession or science of the law be more noble, more necessary and more meritorious than any other' and that 'the

[38] Edward Waterhous, *A Discourse and Defence of Arms and Armory* (1660), 134.
[39] Cf. P. J. Finkelpearl, *John Marston of the Middle Temple* (Cambridge, Mass., 1969), 78.
[40] Sloane 1455, f.10v.

dignitie of this profession doth accordingly dignifie all the professors thereof' had by no means superseded the traditional view that 'gentlemen who have skyll in the lawes to whom fortune hath not granted large meanes to live otherwyse than by the fruicte of theyr learning, al such may reasonablye take monye for ther counsel, . . . so to take as in taking they may also geve to whom they take'. Customary sneers at the lawyer's reputed avarice, mendacity and lack of polite (that is, classical) learning had a strong social connotation; and because the roles of attorneys and barristers were not yet clearly differentiated, the latter still attracted some of the odium which by the end of the seventeenth century had been largely transferred to the former.[41]

So the young gentlemen had every incentive to adopt attitudes and patterns of behaviour which would clearly distinguish them from the common lawyers with whom they were nominally associated. Hence the aggressive insistence on their own gentility, fully echoed by the poets and dramatists whom they patronised; hence also the competitive aping of court modes in dress and taste, the cult of wit, the incessant versifying (for private circulation, not mercenary publication), even perhaps the obsessive drinking, gaming and womanising.[42] The pressure to deny any personal identification with the practice of the law extended even to practising lawyers; thus young Edward Hyde took care not to mix unnecessarily with his fellow barristers, 'very seldome using, when his practice was at its height, so much as to eat in the [Middle Temple] hall'.[43] These manoeuvres could obviously impose heavy demands on a student's economic and psychological resources. Contemporary satirists made much of the gap between the means and pretensions of the young inns of court gallant – always short of money, despite and because of his extravagant expenditure on clothes and women. The resulting tensions appear in much of the poetry produced at the inns during our period, and may also be discerned in the curious mixture of makebelieve and worldly cynicism which characterised the courts of the princes elected by the junior members at Christmas time. They could also be vented on a personal

---

[41] Stone, *Aristocracy*, ch. 1; E. W. Ives, 'The reputation of the common lawyer in English society, 1450–1550', *Univ. of Birmingham Historical J.*, 7 (1959–60), 130–61; J. H. Baker, 'Counsellors and barristers', *Cambridge Law J.*, 27 (1969), 214–29; Sir John Davies, *Le premier reporte* . . . (Dublin, 1615), sigs. 9–10; B.L., *The Institucion of a gentleman* (1555), sig. D iiiirrr.

[42] Cf. John Carey, 'The Ovidian love elegy in England' (Oxford D. Phil. thesis, 1960), ch. 13; Francis Lenton, *The Innes of Court Anagrammatist* (1634); I.P., *A Handful of Honesty* (1623), ded. epistle; John Ford, *The Lover's Melancholy* (1629), ded. epistle; Richard Brathwait, *A Spiritual Spicerie* (n.d., [1638]), 426–9; Brian Melbancke, *Philotimus* (1583), epistle ded.; Bodl. MS. Don. c. 24, f. 63; *The Memoirs of Sir Hugh Cholmley*, 36–8; *Memoirs of Sir John Reresby*, ed. Andrew Browning (Glasgow, 1936), 3–5; *Private Memoirs . . . of John Potenger, Esq . . .*, ed. C. W. Bingham (1841), 32.

[43] *The Life of Edward, Earl of Clarendon . . . written by himself* (Oxford, 1761), 60.

target; thus Nashe depicts a 'mother's darling', who 'having played the waste-good at the innes of court' so that he can no longer support his 'collidge of whores', 'falles into a quarelling humor with his fortune, because she made him not king of the Indies, and swares . . . that nere such a pesant as his father or brother shall keep him under'. Similar frustrations may well have exacerbated conflicts between the benchers and their subordinates in the early seventeenth century.[44]

The practising lawyers who ruled the inns were not indifferent to the claims of birth and breeding. On the contrary, the heraldic crests which adorned the halls of the four societies, and the seating rules for Lincoln's Inn chapel, which ranked members in order of seniority 'excepte they be such persons of ranke and quality as noblemen or knights', while excluding 'persons of meane quality' altogether (as they were also excluded from Gray's Inn walks), point to a highly developed sense of social distinctions.[45] But while gratified to receive the sons of the landed classes, the benchers were unwilling to restrict admission to gentlemen of the third head. Indeed throughout our period they continued to permit even plebeians whose origins could not be disguised under a satin cloak to enter the inns, thereby provoking on at least one occasion explicit protest from the junior members.

In June 1617 some sixty barristers and students of the Middle Temple signed a petition of grievances against the bench, which included a complaint that

> whereas by the auncient fundamentall institucions of this kingdome the inns of court weare erected and have so continued till of late tymes, nurseries for the gentrye (and which ys more for the nobilitie of this lande) . . . the glorye of this societie is faded by the swarmes of attorneys which are nowe admytted . . . whereby the gentlemen of the societye are outeaten in the hall and eaten owt of their chambers of the house . . .[46]

From the mid-sixteenth century onwards orders forbidding the admission of attorneys and solicitors and prohibitions against members practising as attorneys were in fact issued at frequent intervals by the benchers and the judges. The main motive was apparently to give institutional substance to the emerging distinction between *officium ingenii* and *officium laboriis*, or what are now known as the upper and

---

[44]Cf. Carey, *op. cit.*, 335–66; Additional 22603, ff. 11–11v; cf. CUL MS, Dd. 5.14, Thomas Wateridge, 'Jocosa Seria' (1611–14), f.71v: 'Mr Edward Barnet of the Middle Temple, being otherwise a man of good conceyt and one that hath taken paines in the lawes of the land . . . was taken with a phreneticall melancholicke-humour, talkinge of serjeants that should breake open his chamber dore with a holberd for a debt of but 40s . . .'; *Works of Thomas Nashe*, ed. R. B. McKerrow (1910), i. 170; see also below, pp. 100–14.

[45] *OJ*, 184–6, 223–30, 238–41, 300–9; *BB*, ii. 242, 346; *GIPB*, i. 306; *ITR*, i. 253.

[46]MT MS, unclassified, 'Articles exhibited on the behalf of the gentlemen of the Middle Temple, whereof they desire reformacon for the societie'.

lower branches of the legal profession. Before the Civil War this dichotomy was by no means clearly defined; while attorneys were in general less esteemed and less well born than barristers and serjeants-at-law, their respective spheres of professional activity were by no means precisely demarcated. Barristers still could and did deal directly with clients, drawing up briefs and pleadings themselves; attorneys had not lost all rights of appearance in the Westminster courts and students frequently worked as or for attorneys both before and after call to the bar.[47]

Moreover, the attorneys hardly constituted an homogenous economic and social group. Besides the Marralls and Tangletons, 'scrambling ignorant petti-foggers, leane knaves and hungrie, for they live upon nothing but the scraps of the law', whom we often encounter in contemporary plays and pamphlets, they included such respected and relatively substantial men as Elias Ashmole, Thomas Blount, the friend of Selden and Anthony Wood, Bartholomew Cox, four times lord mayor of Wells, and Francis Swanton, son of a Middle Temple bencher and clerk of assizes on the Western circuit. While the inns wanted no truck with disreputable elements, a prosperous attorney who set his sights on 'an innes of court, an old rich widdow and the stewardship of leetes' had a good chance of realising his ambitions, if not necessarily in that order: a survey ordered by the benchers of the Middle Temple in 1635 revealed that some thirty-two members, including several barristers, were practising as common attorneys.[48]

Since many benchers must themselves have had close professional and even personal ties with individual members of the lower branch, it is hardly surprising that attempts to banish attorneys from the inns were unsuccessful until long after the end of our period. In fact the main pressure for their removal came from the judges, who were obviously less influenced by these pressures and could afford to take a more detached view of the profession's long-term interests. The benchers' reluctance to exclude attorneys may also have derived from an unwillingness to accept the financial consequences of any restrictions on entrance to the societies, which would inevitably reduce income from admission fees and chamber entry fines. These considerations did not much concern the judges or the junior members, who were entirely preoccupied, although for different reasons, with the social stigma arising from the presence of 'inferior and ministeriall persons'.[49]

The Middle Temple petition of 1617 also attacked the benchers for

[47] H. H. Bellot, 'The exclusion of attorneys from the inns of court', *LQR*, 26 (1910), 137–45; Baker, 'Counsellors and barristers', 222 ff.
[48] J. O. Halliwell, *Books of Characters . . . from the Reign of James I . . .* (1857), 216–18; Michael Birks, *Gentlemen of the Law* (1960), ch. 6; *Somerset Assize Orders, 1629–1640*, ed. T. G. Barnes (*Somerset Rec. Soc.*, 65, 1959), xxxiv–vi; *MTR*, ii. 387.
[49] *OJ*, 317.

admitting 'their owne livery servants, whoe although they are become fellowes of the societie, doe yet nontheless continue their servants in ordinarye, to the utter and perpetuall dishonor of this societie and the name of an inne of courtman'. The admission of bencher's clerks, as well as house butlers and stewards who had retired from active employment, had been a common practice almost from the beginning of the societies' recorded history.[50] There is no previous evidence of opposition to the custom, and the Middle Temple protest was not foreshadowed by a sudden increase in the number of former servants admitted to membership. However, it emphasises again the junior members' sensitivity to any real or imagined slight on their social position.

Under the later Stuarts the inns gradually ceased to play the part of academies and finishing schools for 'gentlemen of the best qualitie' and largely reverted to their former role of associations for practising and would-be lawyers. The gentry had begun to drift away even before the Restoration. In 1658 William Higford noted with disapproval that

> some of our gentry and nobility . . . when their sons leave the universities, omit the innes of court, and send them across the seas. Travail is a necessary accomplishment of a gentlemen . . . but what is it to be conversant abroad and a stranger at home? These innes of court are vertuous and fruitfull seminaries for youth, where they study the known lawes of the land, and other noble exercises.[51]

Five years later Edward Waterhous confirmed that the inns were now 'thought mean lodges for nobility and the eldest sons of gentry, who all goe abroad to travel, leaving the younger brothers or gentlemen's sons of smaller fortune to inhabit them: so that the young inns of court men of our age, are such as mostly study to profess the law, and by it become great and rich . . .'. Clarendon's *Discourse Concerning Education*, written after his last exile from England in 1666, made a vigorous defence of the inns as proper places for 'noble and generous persons' to attend after university and before the Grand Tour.[52] But here, as in many other respects, Clarendon's words represented the attitudes of a past era and his voice went unheeded. The scale and speed of the aristocratic exodus should not be exaggerated; admissions to the inns during the later seventeenth century fell off far less rapidly than university enrolments, and the stated social origin of entrants who joined the societies in the first decade of the eighteenth century were not remarkably different from those recorded during the last thirty years of our period, although the proportion of entants

---

[50] Cf. *LI Adm. Reg.*, 15 (William Elyot), 17 (John Boteler) *et seq.*; see also below, pp. 80–81.
[51] William Higford, *Institutions: or Advice to his Grandson* (1658), 58–9.
[52] *Fortescutus Illustratus*, 537; *Discourse* (cited from A *Collection of Several Tracts*, 1727), 313, 327.

from mercantile and professional families had increased substantially and there were very few representatives of the peerage. The proportion of entrants called to the bar also rose steadily in the later seventeenth century.[53]

TABLE 7   *Recorded social rank of entrants 1700–9, number and percentage*

	(i) Peer-esquire	(ii) Gentlemen	(iii) Bourgeois and professional	(iv) Other and unspecified	Total
Gray's Inn	85 42·5	67 33·5	43 21·5	7 3·5	220
Inner Temple	220 44·0	166 33·5	116 23·5	– 0·0	250
Lincoln's Inn	111 44·4	95 38·0	43 17·2	1 0·4	250
Middle Temple	131 51·4	56 21·9	64 25·1	4 1·6	255
Total	547 45·2	384 31·7	266 21·9	12 0·9	1,209

While Locke thought it self-evident that heirs to landed estates would need to know some law, he believed this knowledge could as well be imparted by a tutor as acquired at the inns.[54] In George II's reign a treasurer of the Middle Temple looked back nostalgically to the days when the societies had been regarded as 'places designed for the education of the sons of the gentry and nobility', adding a saving clause which differs significantly from the panegyrics of the early Stuart period: 'nor is the same notion yet wholly eradicated out of the minds of our gentry'.[55] By 1758, when Blackstone delivered his first course of lectures at Oxford, 'the universal practice for the young nobility and gentry to be instructed in the originals and elements of the law' during a brief stay at the inns was so much a matter of ancient history that Blackstone thought it had fallen into disuse by the end of Elizabeth's reign.[56]

The retreat of young gentlemen students from the inns was part of a general post-Restoration reaction to the ideals and practices of the

[53] Lucas, *op. cit.*, 465–7; cf. Evelyn, *Diary*, v. 358; G. E. Mingay, *English Landed Society in the Eighteenth Century and After* (1963), 131–2.
[54] *The Educational Writings of John Locke*, ed. J. L. Axtell (Cambridge, 1968), 295.
[55] *Master Worsley's Book on the History and Constitution of . . . the Middle Temple*, ed. A. R. Ingpen (1910), 117.
[56] William Blackstone, *Commentaries on the Laws of England* (Oxford, 1765–69), i. 25.

'educational revolution'. In addition to the decline of humanist and Protestant zeal for learning as a means of secular and spiritual advancement, the economic squeeze on middling landholders made it more difficult for the gentry to meet the expenses of university or inns of court residence, especially if they also wished to give their eldest sons the benefits of a Grand Tour with a private tutor and an entourage of servants.[57] It was also difficult to argue that young gentlemen should be sent to the inns to acquire an elementary knowledge of the common law, when the societies had ceased to provide any form of legal instruction and when the law itself no longer occupied a central place in the world of intellectual or political discourse. The inns still retained some of the prestige which the well-born young amateur students had brought them more than a century before, and while they were now regarded as largely, if not wholly professional institutions, both the internal organisation and external orientation of the profession had been transformed since the mid-sixteenth century. The upper branch was now clearly distinct in function and status from the lower, and the professional dealings of barristers were subject to a complex code of etiquette designed to eliminate at least the more flagrant malpractices. The professional ideal, no longer framed merely in terms of narrow technical expertise, envisaged counsel as a disinterested advocate, serving the public good by pursuing his own and his clients' private ends. This happy neoclassical conjunction helped free the lawyers – or at least the upper branch – from a good deal of the moral and social disrepute under which they had previously laboured. Now the barrister's robes tended to elevate rather than depress a gentleman's status, and the inns continued to serve the landed classes by providing younger sons with a respectable alternative career to the church and the army. Equally important, their elder brothers were freed from the necessity of knowing (or pretending to know) sufficient law to avoid undue dependence on their social inferiors.

[57] Cf. H. F. Kearney, *Scholars and Gentlemen* (1970), ch. 9; Stone, 'Educational revolution', 73–5; *idem*, 'The ninnyversity', *New York Review of Books*, 28 Jan. 1971, 21–9.

III

Ranks of
Membership

From clerks to students

The hierarchical organisation of the Elizabethan and early Stuart inns of court mirrored the society of which they were part:

> How could communities,
> ... and brotherhoods in cities, ...
> But by degree, stand in authentic place?

The membership structure of each inn resembled a three-layered pyramid. At the apex stood the benchers, the self-perpetuating oligarchy of senior members who ruled the house. Next came the barristers, the main professional element, and below them the mass of inner-barristers or students, a mixed group of prospective lawyers and young gentlemen with no plans for a legal career. According to Coke each inn had at least twenty benchers, around sixty barristers and between 160 and 180 members below the bar. These figures probably give a reasonably accurate picture of the relative proportions at the beginning of the seventeenth century. By the late 1630s there were said to be no less than forty-eight full benchers at Lincoln's Inn, while the Middle Temple was credited with thirty-seven benchers and 189 barristers; but these probably included a good many men who were rarely, if ever, in residence.[1]

---

[1] Much of the argument advanced below and in the first section of the following chapter has recently received independent support from an important article by A. W. B. Simpson, 'The early constitution of the inns of court', *Cambridge Law J.*, 28 (1970), 241–56. Coke, *Le tierce part des reports . . .*, sig. Divv; LI MS, 'The Middle Temple Manuscript on Lincoln's Inn' (transcribed by W. P. Baildon), 145–7; Brerewood, 72–9.

The hierarchical structure of the societies was echoed and emphasised in every aspect of their organisation and daily life. Members sat down for meals in hall at tables ranged according to rank and were served in order, from the benchers down. Each rank had its own costume; benchers wore knee-length gowns tufted with silk and velvet, barristers a long black grogram robe with two velvet welts on the long hanging sleeves, students plain, sleeveless black gowns with a flap collar, topped by a round black cloth cap.[2] Within the walls of the houses barristers had few more privileges than students; although sitting at separate tables in hall they ate the same food, paid for their wine (which the benchers received free) and took no part in the government of the house except during vacations, when they ruled as delegates of the bench. The eight senior barristers at Lincoln's Inn were permitted to keep their law clerks in commons as benchers were, while the four senior barristers of the Middle Temple enjoyed the privilege of having breakfast sent to their chambers.[3] But all remained under the disciplinary control of the bench and were expected to continue taking an active part in the learning exercises, even after they had finished serving their post-call vacations.

The origins of this hierarchical system cannot now be traced with any certainty, but clearly go back at least to the mid-fifteenth century. Fortescue does not discuss grades of membership, but the report of Thomas Denton and his colleagues to Henry VIII gives an elaborate description of the way in which 'the whole company and fellowship of learners is divided and sorted into three parts and degrees'. This account makes it clear that in theory the ranks were a function of the learning exercise system. Thus the benchers are described as 'suche as before time have openly read . . . to whom is chiefly committed the government and ordering of the said houses, as to men meetest, both for their age, discretion and wisdomes . . .'. The barristers were those who 'for their learning and continuance, are called by the said readers to plead and argue . . . doubtful cases and questions, which amongst them are called motes'. Lastly 'all the residue of learners are called inner-barristers, which are the youngest men, that for lack of learning and continuance, are not able to reason and argue in these motes'.[4]

Since the learning exercises were not finally organised on a formal and compulsory basis until the 1440s or '50s, it seems unlikely that the ranks of membership as described above could have existed, except in very rudimentary form, much before that time. This supposition is strengthened by the early records of Lincoln's Inn, which until the 1480s normally distinguish only between fellows (*socii*) and clerks,

[2] *OJ*, 278; W. N. Hargreaves-Mawdsley, *A History of Legal Dress in Europe until the end of the Eighteenth Century* (Oxford, 1963), 92–4; J. H. Baker, 'The origin of the bar gown', *Law Guardian*, 49 (June, 1969), 17–18.
[3] *BB*, ii. 31; *MTR*, ii. 480.
[4] *DBC*, 544.

although the actual terms barrister and bencher first appear in 1455 and 1441 respectively.[5] Apart from sitting at a separate table and having the right to keep a clerk in commons (also shared by some barristers), the benchers do not appear to have enjoyed any special privileges or pre-eminence during the first fifty years of the society's recorded history. The terminology of the first Black Books fits well with Thorne's thesis of the purely professional origins of the inns; the fellows were presumably the practising common lawyers who made up the bulk of the societies' membership, and the clerks their professional servants, who probably included a number of young men learning the law as apprentices to the practitioners.

The division between clerks and masters or *socii* was reflected by the domestic arrangement of the house. The clerks sat separately from their masters in hall and paid a lower rate for meals; in return they waited on the rest of the company, like the servitors and sizars of Oxford and Cambridge. But its chief importance may well have been to distinguish those who were regarded as full members of the society and hence could participate in the management of its affairs from those who played a merely passive and subordinate role.[6] By the end of Henry VIII's reign this distinction could not have retained any practical significance, for the government of the inns had clearly passed into the hands of the benchers, and by the beginning of our period even the institutional forms of the old system were virtually defunct.

Law clerks and junior students no longer sat together, although at the Inner Temple there was still a separate group of students known as clerks commoners, who occupied a table to themselves under the supervision of their abbot. A few traditionalists like Sir Thomas Lucas, whose father had served as solicitor-general to Henry VIII and who himself became a bencher in 1568, admitted their sons to clerks commons for sentimental reasons: 'in that commons my father admitted me first and there also wolde I have hym to be . . .' wrote Sir Thomas to his colleagues on the occasion of his son's admission in 1592. But the clerks commoners did not still receive their food at a reduced rate and the only other relic of their former status, an elementary form of learning exercise known as clerks commons cases, had become mandatory for all students seeking call to the bar.[7] The situation at Gray's Inn was similar; although the benchers made several attempts to revive

---

[5] Cf. *BB*, i. 11, 26.

[6] *BB*, i. xii–xiii; cf. the editor's claim that clerks were merely junior fellows. This may have been true by the end of the fifteenth century, but note the distinction between admission as fellow or clerk ('*in socium sive clericum*') and the separate lists of clerks' and fellows' sureties in 1440–1441: *BB*, i. 9, 10. In 1466 'all being summoned who were of the said society' included bar and bench, but not clerks: *ibid.*, 41. *DBC*, 546; *OJ*, 193.

[7] *ITR*, i. 232, ii. 26, 42; IT MS, Petyt, Letters to treasurers and benchers, 38; *OJ*, 158.

the 'third table' by offering free admission to anyone who would join up as a clerk commoner, the institution had vanished altogether by the eve of the Civil War.[8]

The rise of the barristers

The main public function of the inns of court today (as for several centuries past) is to confer the minimum qualification for audience in the higher courts upon those of their members who are called to the bar. The origins of this valuable monopoly are unknown. Lawyers have usually seen it as a right delegated to the rulers of the four inns by the judges, but they cannot say when or why that act of delegation occurred. Like the social contract, it is a theoretical necessity, not an ascertainable historical fact.[9]

Barristers are still called to the bar of their inn, not to the bar of any law court. This is a relic of the time when the rank of utter-barrister was merely an internal promotion, which did not of itself entitle the holder to practise as counsel in the superior courts. The principals of the inns of chancery could also 'call to the barr to moot such of the companions that shall appear . . . able to moot', and there were still barristers at the inns of chancery in Elizabeth's reign. But by the time Fortescue wrote *De Laudibus Legum Angliae* the hospices of the men of the court had become differentiated into greater and lesser inns, and it was the barristers of the *hospicia majora*, the inns of court, who eventually gained the right of audience, while the *hospicia minora*, the smaller and less prestigious inns of chancery, came to be dominated by attorneys and other 'ministeriall' practitioners.[10]

The earliest definite identification of call to the bar of an inn of court with the right of audience in the higher courts occurs in 1547.[11] In 1559 the judges ordered with the benchers' assent, that no barrister under ten years standing in his house could appear at the bar in Westminster Hall; in 1574 the probationary period was put at five years after call (or two years for those who had performed an inn of chancery reading), and further reduced to three years in 1614. By the 1630s it seems to have become little more than a formality; one lawyer complained that nowadays there was only a convention that barristers

---

8 *GIPB*, i. 136, 271, 277; the term 'clericorum' is preserved in some mysterious lists, possibly pension rolls, entered in GI MS, Admittance Book, ff. 126 ff.

9 Cf. *Halsbury's Laws of England*, ed. Lord Simonds (3rd edn, 1952), iii. 1–6; all previous accounts have been superseded by two important articles of J. H. Baker, 'The status of barristers', *LQR*, 85 (1969), 334–8 and 'Counsellors and barristers', *Cambridge Law J.*, 27 (1969), 204–29; see also Simpson, *op. cit.*

10 H. H. Bellot, 'Some early law courts and the English bar', *LQR*, 38 (1922), 168–84; Sir Cecil Carr, *The Pension Book of Clement's Inn* (*SS*, 78, 1960), xvii–xix, 218–20.

11 *Tudor Royal Proclamations*, ed. P. L. Hughes and J. F. Larkin (New Haven, 1964–69), i. 371–2, 408–9; Sir Charles Ogilvie, *The King's Government and the Common Law 1471–1641* (Oxford, 1958), 77–8.

should not 'weare a barre gowne openly at any barre in Westminster Hall to practise the law' immediately after call, whereas 'heretofore they were wont (for the space of two yeres at the least after such theire call to forbeare both the gown and the practise'.[12]

Mere barristers were still unable to appear in the 'palladium of the coif', the Court of Common Pleas, which remained the exclusive preserve of serjeants-at-law until 1846, while the Star Chamber was monopolised by serjeants and readers until its abolition in 1641. Nor was there any equality at the bar, even among barristers of equal seniority; most judges had favourites whom they allowed to 'move' before other counsel were heard. But while the concept of an unqualified 'right of audience' has little meaning in the context of the Elizabethan and early Stuart legal system, it is clear that, by the end of the sixteenth century, call to the bar of an inn of court was generally recognised as being the basic prerequisite for practice in the central courts, not merely a step up on the inns' own membership ladder.[13] And even before the probationary post-call period had been effectively eroded, newly called barristers were under 'no special restraint' for 'giving council in their chambers or practising in the circuits', keeping manorial courts or drawing conveyances and pleadings.[14]

The rise of the utter-barristers seems to have been primarily the result of a vast increase in the amount of common law litigation during the sixteenth century and the inability of the benchers and serjeants to cope with the demand for legal services. The stages of the barrister's transformation from moot-man to counsel are still obscure, but the process did leave some trace on the records of the inns. While the names of members called to the bar were listed in the Black Books of Lincoln's Inn from 1518 onwards, the other houses did not follow suit until after the middle of the century, and no regulations setting out specific conditions for call to the bar appear before the beginning of Elizabeth's reign.[15] So long as the rank of utter-barrister had meaning only within the societies there would have been little need for such lists and regulations; but as it acquired a professional significance and the numbers seeking call simultaneously increased, the desirability of fixing more or less uniform qualifications for call and recording the names of those who had so qualified must have become apparent.

[12] *OJ*, 311–12, 317–18; Stow, *Survey*, i. 78; Brerewood, 12.
[13] H. Lévy-Ullmann, *The English Legal Tradition*, ed. F. M. Goodby (1935), 80; W. C. Bolland, 'Two problems in English legal history', *LQR*, 24 (1915), 393; William Hudson, 'Treatise of the Court of the Star Chamber', in *Collectanea Juridica*, ed. Francis Hargrave (1791–2), ii. 26–7; W. Notestein, F. H. Relf and H. Simpson, *Commons Debates, 1621* (New Haven, 1935), vi. 157; Baker, 'Counsellors and barristers', 215–18.
[14] IT MS, Miscellanea 31, p. 24; Baker, 'Counsellors and barristers', 218–20.
[15] The earliest orders are concerned solely with when calls shall be made and by whom; the only qualifications mentioned are reports on the candidates' fitness from a reader or examination of his ability by the whole bench: *BB*, i. 100, 179, 360; *ITR*, i. 187, 225 and cf. Williamson, *Temple*, 116–17, 188–90.

The major expansion in the number of barristers seems to have begun shortly after Elizabeth's accession. Sir Christopher Hatton, who attended the Inner Temple for a brief period in the early 1560s, complained in 1586 that 'there are now more at the barre in one house than there was in all the innes of courte when I was a younge man'.[16] The number of recorded calls at Lincoln's Inn remained fairly stable between 1520 and 1559, but then doubled during the 1560s and doubled again over the next twenty years. By this time figures are available for all four houses. They show that the upward movement continued, despite a setback in the 1620s, right up to the eve of the Civil War.

TABLE 8   *Recorded bar calls, 1510–1639*

Decade	Gray's Inn	Inner Temple	Lincoln's Inn	Middle Temple	Total
1510–19			18*		18*
1520–29			27		27
1530–39			8		8
1540–49			16		16
1550–59			24		24
1560–69		7*	54		61
1570–79	21*	29	63	37*	150
1580–89	73	62	105	85	325
1590–99	93	92	101	94	380
1600–09	89	89	97	108	383
1610–19	107	78	123	155	463
1620–29	55	88	147	111	401
1630–39	101	142	148	120	511
Total calls 1510–1639	539	587	931	710	2,767
Total calls 1590–1639	445	489	616	588	2,138
Total admissions 1590–1639	4,769	2,229	2,385	2,780	12,163
Ratio calls to admissions 1590–1639	1:10·9	1:4·8	1:3·7	1:4·7	1:5·9

* indicates total for part-decade only.

16 Foss, *Judges*, v. 423.

As these figures indicate, Clarendon's suggestion that less than one student in a hundred was ever called to the bar is misleading; at the Middle Temple, Clarendon's own house, slightly more than one entrant in five between 1590 and 1639 became a barrister.[17] Gray's Inn, the largest house in terms of admissions to membership, called the least number of barristers created during our period, while Lincoln's Inn called more barristers than any other society, both absolutely and in relation to the number of entrants admitted during the half-century from 1590. There is no obvious explanation for these disparities; but it is hardly surprising that the social prestige of Gray's Inn and its connections with court and government circles apparently attracted a disproportionately large number of young men with no interest in a legal career, while the seemingly most professionalised society should also have had the strongest reputation for puritanism.

The rapid expansion of calls during the late sixteenth century aroused some fears of overcrowding and a dilution of professional standards. Hatton complained that too many 'unmeete men verie rawe and younge men which are negligent and careless' were becoming barristers, while in 1602 Lord Keeper Egerton 'exhorted them that have authority to admit to the bar, to have care to name those that are literate, honest and religious and . . . not have calls by the dozens or scores'.[18] But the authorities' attempts to limit the numbers of barristers called were entirely ineffectual. In 1596 the judges ordered the inns not to create more than four barristers in any one year; this limit was raised to eight in 1614, despite a portentous warning that an 'over great multitude in any vocation or profession, doth but bring the same into disrepute'. Yet as Table 8 shows, the inns took no notice of either restriction, and by 1630 the judges had clearly given up hope of enforcing a maximum ceiling: their orders issued that year were almost an exact replica of those for 1614, but entirely omitted the clause regulating the number of calls to the bar. The few self-denying ordinances made by the individual houses were also ineffective.[19]

There was little personal incentive for the benchers to enforce a quota on entrance to the profession so long as plenty of work was available for the men at the top. Moreover call to the bar was by no means an inevitable prelude to practice as counsel at the Westminster courts, or indeed anywhere else. Although 2,138 barristers were called by the four inns between 1590 and 1640, Mr Cooper's list of practising counsel from the reigns of James I and Charles I includes only 489 names.[20] Admittedly this is based mainly on the published law reports from

[17] Clarendon, *Tracts*, 327: between 1590 and 1639 2,780 non-honorific admissions are recorded at the Middle Temple; 535 of these entrants were eventually called to the bar.

[18] Baker, 'Counsellors and barristers', 220–3; *Les Reportes del cases in Camera Stellata 1593 to 1609*, ed. W. P. Baildon (1894), 133.

[19] *OJ*, 316–17, 320–1; *ITR*, ii. 26; *MTR*, i. 416; GI MS, Order Book, f. 248v.

[20] Cooper, 'Promotion and politics . . .', 200–14.

the period, and therefore omits a good many men who practised mainly in Ireland or the provincial conciliar courts, as well as those who made only occasional or unreported appearances in Westminster Hall. We know so little about the organisation and structure of the early Stuart legal profession that it is impossible to estimate how many barristers would have to be included in these categories, or in other ancillary groups, such as those who never rose beyond 'keeping courts of manors, leets and barrons, swanimootes of forrests, Stannaries, Cinque Ports etc.', or were attached to central and provincial courts as legal bureaucrats, practised mainly as attorneys, or never formally practised at all.[21]

Until these basic questions are clarified there is no way of telling how many men were entering the upper branch of the legal profession in the early seventeenth century or how much work was available for them; the fact that calls continued to rise throughout our period and the absence of literary evidence to the contrary suggests that the profession was not overcrowded, but this assumption still awaits thorough investigation.[22] In any case more barristers meant more revenue for the houses from fines and compositions for vacations forfeited after call; and even if the benchers had actively supported limitations on the numbers called, it is doubtful whether they could have resisted the pressure from junior members, especially when reinforced by the urgings of their backers and patrons.

By 1590 the four inns had each laid down a broadly similar set of qualifications for call to the bar. The main academic elements were attendance at either four or six learning vacations immediately before call and participation in a given number of moots both abroad at the inns of chancery and within the parent house of court.[23] The judges were content to leave the benchers free to determine the course of pre-call exercises, but did make some effort to standardise the length of membership necessary to qualify students for the bar. Their orders of 1596 required that only those of 'convenient continuance' were to be called, but two years later the inns were specifically enjoined to call no barristers of less than seven years continuance in membership. This was little more than endorsing current practice, except as far as Gray's Inn was concerned, where six years had been the previous minimum. The period was raised to eight years in 1630, but with no apparent effect, since the Inner Temple had insisted on eight years since at least the 1580s, and the other houses continued to demand only seven years continuance.[24] There were exceptions to the seven year

21 Powell, *Tom of All Trades*, 26–7; *The Oglander Memoirs*, ed. W. H. Long (Newport, 1888), 165.
22 Cf. Stone, 'Educational revolution', 56; cf. M. H. Curtis, 'The alienated intellectuals of early Stuart England', *P & P*, 23 (1962), 39.
23 *BB*, ii. 103, 109; *GIPB*, i. 131, 308–9; *ITR*, i. 346, 431, ii. 207; *MTR*, i. 280, 394; ii. 605.
24 *OJ*, 313, 316.

rule. At Gray's Inn those students appointed to supervise the organisation of vacation moots were eligible at five years continuance, and in all the houses members who had spent two years or more at an inn of chancery were occasionally allowed to count this time towards their required seven years membership. Neither dispensation would have affected many students; but in addition the benchers frequently called men whose continuance fell below the prescribed minimum and who could claim no right to exemption on the grounds just mentioned.[25]

Without comparing the dates of admission and call of all 2,138 barristers created during our period, it is impossible to say exactly how many were called prematurely. An examination of calls made in the opening years of each decade indicates that the overwhelming majority of barristers had in fact completed at least seven or eight years as members, while some had even greater seniority.

TABLE 9 *Continuance of barristers called in first year of each decade 1590–1639*

Years of membership	Gray's Inn	Inner Temple	Lincoln's Inn	Middle Temple
Less than seven	18	2	7	8
Seven	8	5	41	20
Eight	16	31	13	21
More than eight	12	46	5	25
Unknown	5	7	1	1
Total	59	91	67	75

Note. Where less than ten barristers were called in the initial year of a particular decade, the sample was extended to subsequent years until at least ten barristers were included. As seniority was observed in calls of two or more barristers, all barristers in group calls were included, even if this resulted in obtaining more than ten names.

Gray's Inn was the only house where premature calls comprised a substantial fraction of the total: of the fifty-nine calls noted, no less than eighteen were early. However, most of those called under seven years (eight at the Inner Temple) lacked only a few days or weeks continuance. Normally only the benchers' minuted decision to call certain individuals survives, rather than the actual dates on which these students were formally sworn in and proclaimed as barristers (which

25 *GIPB*, i. 285, 291; BB, ii. 240.

was often several months later), so these figures may well exaggerate the number of premature calls.[26]

It is rarely possible to discover why given individuals were called before they had attained the minimum continuance. Timothy Turner, later Charles I's solicitor-general in Wales, was admitted to Gray's Inn from Staple Inn on 8 March 1607, and called to the bar on 30 October 1611; but Turner may have added three years continuance at Staple Inn (from which no records survive) to his four at the parent house. Irishmen not intending to practise in England and Englishmen going to Ireland were often treated very leniently; for example, Lawrence Parsons, admitted to Gray's Inn on 4 February 1607, was called to the bar five years later, when he took up the post of attorney-general in Munster.[27]

The sons of benchers, both past and present, could also usually count on indulgent treatment in this respect. William Snygge, the son and heir of Sir George Snygge, baron of the Exchequer, was called to the Middle Temple bar by his father's request in October 1613, when he had only six years and five months standing in the house, although the benchers resolved that their action in this case should not create a precedent. At Lincoln's Inn the sons of three judges and past benchers, Sir John Glanvile, Sir Henry Hobart and Sir William Jones, all received similarly favoured treatment, possibly without any explicit request from their fathers.[28]

At Gray's Inn and the Middle Temple, where readers still retained some limited right of calling to the bar, most premature calls seem to have been made at readings and were obviously a personal favour from the reader to the student concerned.[29] At his Lent reading in 1611, Sir Francis Eure of Gray's Inn called Nathaniel Finch and John Potts, both lacking seven years continuance but both sons of Eure's colleagues and fellow-benchers. Eure had himself been called with only three years continuance, at the summer reading of Francis Aungier in 1602; this call was confirmed by pension in February 1603, 'because he was sonne & is brother to the Lord Ewry & was called to the barr by Mr Aunger . . . & alsoe hath performed the exercises for that calling'.[30] Eure was very well treated, but perhaps no better than his rank required.

The most effective way of becoming a barrister, with or without ful-

[26] For examples of barristers called but not published or sworn until achieving full continuance, see *BB*, ii. 299, 309; *ITR*, ii. 88, 107.

[27] *GI Adm. Reg.*, 118; *GIPB*, i. 195; F. E. Ball, *The Judges in Ireland 1221–1921* (1926), i. 330.

[28] *MTR*, ii. 424, 569, 571, 573; *BB*, ii. 131, 201, 213.

[29] This loophole was closed when the bench appropriated all rights of call to themselves, at Gray's Inn after 1629, at the Middle Temple after 1610: *GIPB*, i. 187, 226, 233, 290, 292; *MTR*, i. 364–5, ii. 527, 536; *OJ*, 312.

[30] *GIPB*, i. 161. Francis was the second son of William, second Lord Eure, who was succeeded by Ralph, third Lord Eure, in 1594: *GEC*.

filling the formal qualifications, was, however, to obtain an office, preferably in the London-based legal bureaucracy, although an assizes clerkship would do as well. Thus Richard Willis, the eldest son of Lord Thomas Coventry's secretary, entered the Middle Temple in 1617 '& for the first foure yeeres kept constantly at study, & in commons, neither parted with his chamber'. Then he married and left the society; but after his wife's death in 1629 Willis decided to 'renew his former studdyes, for the better fytting of himselfe for a prothonotaries place in Wales', to which, with the clerkship of the Carmarthen circuit, he had gained a reversion two years before. Here the rank of utterbarrister would evidently carry a certain status, so Willis sought and received this 'badge of favor', with Coventry's support, in June 1629.[31]

But it was more usual for office-holders to be promoted in recognition of the dignity of their place than for the call to be regarded as a qualification for office. At the Inner Temple after 1597 office-holders were usually appointed 'associates of the bar', placed at the upper bar table in hall, and freed from the learning exercises which utter-barristers were normally supposed to perform. Among those who became associates during our period were Thomas Corie, who bought the chief prothonotary's place in Common Pleas for £10,000 in 1638, Sir Henry Croke, who was described as master of the Pipe Office when he was called at the request of his father, the judge Sir John Croke, in 1617, John Keeling, coroner and attorney in the King's Bench from 1631, together with sundry examiners in Chancery, attorneys of the Star Chamber and so forth.[32]

Any discussion of the conditions governing call to the bar which did not attempt to consider the role of patronage would be sadly incomplete. There are about thirty known cases between 1590 and 1640 for which concrete evidence exists of a patron's intervention on behalf of a candidate for call.[33] These must represent only the tip of the iceberg, despite the standing orders of the judges and individual houses against calls made 'by letters or for any reward'.[34] Even the formal preliminaries to a general call of barristers would have tended to encourage the intrusion of patrons and outside backers. All students who believed themselves eligible went in a group with cap and gown to visit each resident bencher and formally request his approval of their

---

[31] MT MS, unclassified, 'Various Papers 1643' (*sic*), Thomas Lord Coventry to treasurer and benchers, 19 June 1629; W. R. Williams, *The History of the Great Sessions in Wales, 1542–1830* (Brecknock, 1899), 193; *MTR*, ii. 752. Cf. *ITR*, ii. 97: Mr Brocke's call considered, 'to enable him for a place of good account, which he is in hope of when he shall be himself qualified'.

[32] *ITR*, i. 419, ii. 27, 43, 82, 102, 121, 199, 244, 248.

[33] GI MS, Order Book, f. 209v; *GIPB*, i. 111, 329; IT MS, Petyt, Letters to treasurers and benchers, 4, 9–11, 16, 18, 21, 28, 44–6, 60, 77; *MTR*, i. 401, 423, 424; ii. 523, 742, 842. No cases of patronage in calls at Lincoln's Inn have been found.

[34] *OJ*, 314; *BB*, i. 360, 401, ii. 45; *ITR*, ii. 101; *MTR*, i. 234.

call; the bench then met in conclave and voted on the individual candidates.[35]

Nevertheless, in only a tiny fraction of the known cases where patronage was a definite factor were there attempts to circumvent or override the prescribed requirements for call. Generally speaking the patron – whether bishop, courtier, judge, peer or even monarch – seems merely to have brought a candidate for the bar to the attention of the bench and requested his call as a personal favour. Would-be barristers may sometimes have felt impelled to obtain a patron's backing, not because they feared rejection, but simply to display their connections with the great and powerful. Thus in 1602 Richard Vennard, not satisfied with gaining the support of Sir Christopher Yelverton and Sir Edward Coke for his call to the bar of Lincoln's Inn, asked them to persuade Robert Cecil to procure the queen's assent, 'humbly desir[ing] that it might grow unto him by her majesty's favour'. Unfortunately neither Cecil's nor the queen's response has survived; but Vennard did not receive his call.[36]

In a world where no one could lightly reject Burghley's counsel to 'keep some great man thy friend', attempts at preventing recourse to patrons were inevitably little more than pious gestures. Yet it is important not to exaggerate the role of nepotism and patronage in undermining the formal criteria of 'learning and continuance'. The benchers' continual insistence that no man would be called until he had fulfilled the proper qualifications cannot be discounted as empty rhetoric. So far as the inns' educational standards were concerned, the fatal step was not the acceptance of patronage in calls to the bar, but rather the establishment of precise and detailed requirements for call – so many moots to argue, so many vacations to serve, so many years continuance. As a result, the aural learning exercises, already threatened by the advent of the printed text, came to stand in the way of a lucrative career at the bar, and were thus bypassed if possible or performed, if at all, in the most perfunctory manner. But this was hardly avoidable, once what had originally been no more than an internal promotion was transformed into a specific professional qualification, without any attempt to revise the conditions under which it was granted.

[35] D'Ewes, 'Secret Diary', 176; *BB*, ii. 397; IT MS, Miscellanea 29, f. 11v.
[36] HMC, *Hatfield*, xi. 25; *BB*, ii. 103; cf. Vennard's sneers at 'a man that had the name of law to his profession . . . for with much intreaty and with tears, hee got the certificate that he had long enough combatted with slender commons to write Esquire at Lincolne's Inne . . .': *An Apology: Written by Richard Vernon* (1614), in *Illustrations from Old English Literature*, ed. J. P. Collier (1866), iii. 5; also Benjamin Rudyerd's claim that ' "Mathon" [John Davies] hath got the barr and many graces, by studdyinge, noble men, newes and faces': quoted J. L. Sanderson, '*Epigrames p[er] B[enjamin] R[udyerd]* and some more "Stolen Feathers" of Henry Parrot', *Review of English Studies*, n.s. 17 (1966), 252.

From readers to benchers

While the rank of utter-barrister acquired a professional significance during the sixteenth century, it was still closely connected with the learning exercise system, which continued to provide the specific criteria for call to the bar. The rank of reader or bencher, which Dr Ives has shown to be the crucial step in the careers of early Tudor common lawyers, was meanwhile diminishing in professional importance and fast losing its former dependence on the performance of learning exercises.

Henry VIII's commissioners had informed their master that the benchers of the inns of court 'are such as have *before time* openly read'.[37] Two readings were held each year, one in Lent, the other in August. The Lent reading was reserved for double readers, who were 'those that have read once in the summer vacation and be benchers'.[38] So if their account were correct, only one barrister a year from each inn had the opportunity to deliver his reading and be promoted to the bench. But even at the beginning of the sixteenth century this was not strictly the case. At Lincoln's Inn a new sub-category of membership had already evolved, that of associate to the bench. This carried all the privileges of full membership of the bench, except for a vote in the government of the house, without any prior obligation to read. Moreover, the rule that barristers could come to the bench only after they had read was relaxed, to the extent of allowing men to be promoted several years before they were called upon to read. Nevertheless Dr Ives suggests that these expedients did not impair 'the traditional association of call to the bench with the first reading'; in other words, the principal qualification for promotion to the bench remained essentially as described by Denton, Bacon and Carey.[39]

Holdsworth discerned no significant changes in the membership structure of the inns during the sixteenth and early seventeenth centuries. So far as promotion to the bench was concerned, the great watershed, in his view, came with the restoration of Charles II. King's Counsel and other lawyers in receipt of Court favour then began to be elected benchers *ex officio*, without having first delivered a reading. Serjeants-at-law were increasingly chosen from among the ordinary barristers, rather than the benchers alone, which lessened the status of the bench and further reduced the incentives to undertake the expense of money and time associated with a reading. The doom of the system was finally sealed when readings were abandoned altogether in the later seventeenth century.[40]

---

[37] *DBC*, 544 (my italics).
[38] *Ibid*.
[39] E. W. Ives, 'Promotion in the legal profession of Yorkist and early Tudor England', *LQR*, 75 (1959), 350–1.
[40] *HEL*, iv. 263–72; *ibid*., vi. 478–94.

Yet if the classical model described by Denton, Bacon and Carey was not universally adhered to even at the beginning of the sixteenth century, it seems possible that the importance of the Restoration as a major turning point has been somewhat exaggerated. Contemporary accounts and the pronouncements of the benchers themselves do give the impression that the 'traditional association' between membership of the bench and reading was maintained well into the seventeenth century. But in practice the crucial distinction between reader and non-reader had become very blurred by 1640.

At the end of the sixteenth century the Middle Temple alone still restricted full membership of the bench to men who had previously read.[41] Since only two readings could be held each year, an insistence on reading as the indispensable prerequisite for call to the bench imposed a firm upper limit on the number of benchers who could be elected over any given period. The result is shown in Table 10; between 1590 and 1639 only eighty-one benchers were called at the Middle Temple.

TABLE 10   *Calls to the bench, 1590–1639*

Inn	Benchers	Associates	Readers	Non-readers
Gray's Inn	102	12(3)	84	18
Inner Temple	96	13(4)	79	17
Lincoln's Inn	98	24(3)	78	20
Middle Temple	81	18(3)	81	0

Note. The bracketed numbers represent associates raised to the bench before 1640, who are therefore counted twice, as benchers and as associates.

At the other houses, where no such restriction applied, the numbers called were considerably higher: 96 at the Inner Temple, 98 at Lincoln's Inn, 102 at Gray's Inn. If every Lent reading at the Middle Temple had been a double reading, a maximum of fifty new benchers could have been created. But as a Middle Temple bencher pointed out in the 1630s, this 'antient use' had become impracticable: 'If that course should now be observed, the number of utter-barristers being so great, many others would not live to read at all, or be very old ere

[41] In 1625, when plague forced cancellation of the Autumn reading, Robert Berkeley who had been due to read was pre-elected to the bench 'to read next in course to Mr Malett when time shall serve': *MTR*, ii. 701. Thomas Malett read in Lent 1626, Berkeley in Autumn 1626. No other men were elected direct to the bench before reading until the Civil War, although Sir Sydney Montagu, who was made associate bencher in 1616 and elected to read in 1620 but did not do so, is included in a list of full benchers compiled *c.* 1639: MT MS, unclassified, 'Names of the masters of the bench . . .' (box labelled 'Wine Accounts').

they attain thereto.' The last double reading at the Middle Temple was given in 1611 by Richard Swayne; between 1590 and 1611 another ten double readings had been performed, of which two were serjeant's readings accompanied by the single reading of an utter-barrister. But plague and the death of an elected reader caused the cancellation of ten more single readings, so a total of only eighty-one single readings were held and thus the same number of benchers called.[42]

It would seem logical to expect that when fewer benchers were created, those who did gain this promotion waited longer for call than their counterparts at the other houses. However, while there was a much wider spread of years between admission and call to the bench among benchers elected at the Inner Temple, Gray's and Lincoln's Inn than at the Middle Temple, the *average* number of years' continuance of Middle Temple benchers was not significantly greater.

TABLE 11   *Average years of continuance of benchers called, 1590–1639*

	Admission to Bench		Bar to Bench	
(i) *Whole period, 1590–1639*	years			years
Gray's Inn	25·0			17·4
Inner Temple	23·9			15·2
Lincoln's Inn	24·9			16·2
Middle Temple	26·4			17·1
(ii) *1590-99 and*				
1630-39	*1590s*	*1630s*	*1590s*	*1630s*
Gray's Inn	24·2	26·3	16·4	19·6
Inner Temple	20·5	25·3	11·5	16·8
Lincoln's Inn	23·0	25·7	14·6	17·3
Middle Temple	23·4	28·3	15·9	19·9

The explanation is that although insistence upon reading as the sole qualification for membership of the bench imposed a rigid limit on the number of barristers who could become benchers, Middle Temple barristers were more easily able to avoid reading. Well over a hundred Middle Temple barristers who were called upon to read refused to do so, as compared with only about forty at the other three houses put together.[43] So while one could not become a Middle Temple bencher

[42] Brerewood, 25; cf. *OJ*, 314, 316, 319. The lists of Middle Temple readers in *OJ*, 218–30 and *MT Bench Book*, 10–14, 86–114 are neither very reliable. For median ages of benchers at call, see below, p. 112.
[43] The Middle Temple records do not distinguish fines for refusal of inn of court readings from fines for refusal of inn of chancery readings: both appear

except by reading, well over half of those barristers who by seniority became eligible to read declined, and thus forfeited the chance of promotion.

Their motives doubtless varied, but the attractions of this alternative were considerable. It is significant that while barristers frequently refused to become benchers, only one instance of a barrister being denied promotion to the bench appears in the records of any house during our period. This was at Gray's Inn, where Christopher Molineux petitioned the queen in 1598, complaining that he had been refused call although several of his contemporaries had already joined the bench; the benchers responded with a detailed personal attack on Molineux, who was said to be 'not sufficiently learned in the lawes', 'unfit to governe in the said house . . . by reason of his want of discretion', too poor to afford a reading and 'not sociable'. But while personal factors may have played a negative role in other cases which we do not know about, academic or professional standing as such were not important criteria. At the Middle Temple as elsewhere, seniority was the key; once a barrister had reached the head of the seniority queue he could normally expect an automatic invitation to the bench. (Men were sometimes advanced before their contemporaries if they received a major external preferment or were strenuously pushed by an outside patron; Sir Edward Coke's premature promotion to the bench of the Inner Temple in 1590 probably owed as much to the recordership of Norwich which he gained the same year as to recognition of his outstanding jurisprudential talents, while Francis Bacon's meteoric progress through the ranks of Gray's Inn – admitted 1576, bench 1586 – undoubtedly depended on the influence first of his father, the lord keeper, and then his uncle Lord Burghley).[44]

The financial and intellectual demands of a reading might easily seem disproportionate to the benefits accruing from membership of the bench, especially since serjeants and judges were no longer chosen exclusively from the benchers' ranks (although they were usually promoted to the bench *pro forma* before leaving the houses). Roughly two-thirds of the benchers elected during our period received no further professional preferment for the rest of their careers; and the benchers' traditional right of pre-audience in the courts was being

---

as '*pro non legendo*' (e.g. MT MS, Minutes C, f. 78). But a comparison with the other houses, each supplying at least two inn of chancery readers to the Middle Temple's one, shows that between fifteen and twenty barristers at each inn were fined for failing to give an inn of chancery reading at all, or performing it too perfunctorily. No less than 124 Middle Temple barristers were fined *pro non legendo*, so it seems reasonable to suppose that at least 100 had refused to read in their own house.

[44]*GIPB*, i. 123; cf. *ibid.*, 72. According to Robert Ashley's autobiography, in 1614 the Middle Temple benchers passed him over in the election of readers, on account of his poverty, '*licet in eorum omnibus exercitiis versatissimus*': Sloane 2131, f. 20.

undermined 'by reason of the favours and kinship of judges'.[45] Moreover, at the Middle Temple the fines exacted for refusal to read were
very low, rarely above £10, as compared to £50 or more at the other
houses. So many barristers declined the honour that in 1595 all those
who had 'put by their readings' were gathered together at a separate
table in hall, the *'mensa seniorum magistrorum de la utter barr –
Anglice*, the Auncients' table'. The ancients did not enjoy all the
domestic perquisites of full benchers, but had the important privilege
of exemption from 'moots and exercises in the house' – no mean advantage for busy lawyers. Nor were they regarded as academic or
professional failures: 'It is no disgrace for any man to be removed
hither, for by reason of the great and excessive charge of readings,
many men of great learning and competent practice, and others of less
learning but great estates, have refused to read and are here placed'.[46]

There was still the problem of men who lacked sufficient seniority
or learning to read but had received some honour or office which
elevated them above the status of mere barristers. The solution was
to make them associates of the bench, with all the privileges of full
benchers, other than a voice in the government of the house. Four
of the eighteen associates called during our period subsequently read
and became full benchers, but owed their initial promotion to external preferment: the recordership of London in the case of Sir
Henry Montagu, the place of solicitor-general to Queen Henrietta-
Maria in the case of Sir Peter Ball. Sir Francis Moore and Sir Walter
Pye seem to have been called associates not on the strength of any
specific office they held but due to the influence of their patrons, Lords
Ellesmere and Buckingham respectively. The remaining associates
were all office-holders: Sir Henry Calthorpe, the queen's solicitor;
Sir George Carew, master of the Court of Wards; Thomas Crump-
ton, chief prothonotary of the Common Pleas; Sir Thomas Fleetwood,
attorney-general to the Prince of Wales; Gregory Donhault, master
in Chancery; Sir Robert Henley, master of the King's Bench office;
John Goldesburgh, second prothonotary of Common Pleas; Sir Sidney
Montagu, master in the Court of Requests; Richard Moore, master in
Chancery extraordinary; Robert Napper, chief baron of the Exchequer in Ireland; James Pagitt, baron cursitor of the Exchequer and
Sir Benjamin Rudyerd, surveyor of the Court of Wards. These men
were all called in direct response to their promotions; the same is
probably true of the two other associates created during our period,
William Mann, who was a secondary in the King's Bench and Fabian
Phillips, a justice of North Wales, but no direct chronological link
can be established in their case.[47]

---

[45] Brerewood, 29.   [46] *MTR*, i. 338; *OJ*, 204.
[47] Sources: *DNB*; Williamson, *MT Bench Book*; Foss, *Judges*, v, vi; G. E.
Aylmer, *The King's Servants The Civil Service of Charles I, 1625–1641* (1961);
Al. Ox.; *Al. Cant.*; Ball, *Judges in Ireland*; Williams, *Sessions in Wales*.

The system of bench recruitment at the other houses was far less closely tied to the academic exercise of reading: instead of readers being chosen as benchers, some benchers were chosen as readers. Only at Gray's Inn were any readers still selected from below the bench, and even there prospective readers were usually called to the bench as probationers some years before they were due to read. These 'assistants to the reader' sat at the bench table and attended pension meetings, but had no formal say in the affairs of the inn.[48] Those who refused to read when their time came were liable to be fined and demoted; in 1617 the penalty for failure to read after election as an assistant was raised to automatic expulsion, a drastic sanction which was never actually invoked. And while huge fines were sometimes imposed on recalcitrant assistants, these exemplary penalties were rarely, if ever, paid in full.[49]

Benchers and assistants to the reader were elected, usually in order of admission to the house, from among the ancients, a rank of membership similar only in name to the ancients of the Middle Temple. The Gray's Inn ancients were barristers of eight to twelve years standing who had not yet been called to read, senior barristers who had refused to read, the sons of judges and peers, and various other dignitaries, such as officers of the central legal bureaucracy, whom the inn wished to honour. While the Middle Temple ancients were a recent creation, Simon Segar's post-Restoration chronicle of Gray's Inn includes a list of ancients stretching back as far as 1514 (whereas his list of bar calls does not begin until 1574).[50] Promotion to this 'Grand Company' (apart from honorific and *ex officio* appointments) depended on seniority; calls were made every four or five years by pension order and twenty or thirty barristers promoted together. The newly elected ancient, unlike his namesake at the Middle Temple, was not freed from all academic obligations, being required under bond to serve nine consecutive learning vacations after his call. Although this requirement could be evaded by a cash payment of £3 per vacation, it seems to have been rigorously enforced, even to the extent that ancients who were M.P.s gained no relief when the Commons were in session.[51]

Gray's Inn elected 102 benchers between 1590 and 1639, eighteen of whom read neither before nor after call. Of these, all but six had been called on account of their offices and were formally excused reading, or never asked to read. When Sir Dudley Digges obtained the reversion of the office of master of the Rolls in 1630 for a down

[48] *GIPB*, i. 104, 184. Gray's Inn benchers were still strictly known as readers; for clarity, the term bencher is used throughout.

[49] Thus in May 1615 Thomas Ellis was fined £100 for refusing to read; by November 1616 his fine had been reduced to £10: *GIPB*, i. 218; GI MS, Order Book, f. 314.

[50] Harleian 1912, ff. 190 *seq.*, 207ᵛ *seq.*

[51] *GIPB*, i. 262.

payment of £5,000 and the promise of the same amount at the death of Sir Julius Caesar, his only connection with Gray's Inn was his honorific admission to the house in 1618 by the Prince of Purpoole. But Digges immediately had himself re-admitted to Gray's Inn and was called to the bench with full voting rights five days later. Digges never attended any pension meetings and took no part in the government of the house, let alone performed a reading.[52] Another purely honorific appointment was that of Sir William Pennyman, who had entered the Inner Temple in 1623 but became a bencher of Gray's Inn in 1638 when he purchased a place in Star Chamber worth £2,000 a year, with its offices at Gray's Inn: Pennyman did at least attend a few benchers' meetings before the outbreak of the Civil War.[53] The six non-readers who were not officers included Sir Richard Hutton, who was called to the bench as a serjeant-elect in 1603, Thomas Hetley and Sir Nathaniel Finch, who became serjeants and left the house five years and one year respectively after becoming benchers, Henry Dewell and Sampson Eure, whose readings were cancelled because of plague and Sir Euble Thelwall, a master in Chancery and principal of Jesus College, Oxford, who was raised from associate to full bencher in 1624 'as a token of the kind acceptance of the house for the care and charge he undertooke in the buylding and contryvinge the chappel this last vacacon'.[54]

While nearly one in five of the benchers elected at Gray's Inn during our period read neither before nor after call, collectively the benchers did make an effort to preserve at least part of the 'traditional association'. In February 1613 they even declared that only such 'as are to reade or suche as are assistant to the reader shall be assotiated to the readers' table', a statement of intent which could have carried little weight in the light of their previous practice. Nor did it prevent the election as associate the following year of Sir Richard Williamson, a master of Requests and one of the legal members of the Council of the North, or of three more associates before 1640. If non-readers were called to the bench it was vital that they should not be allowed to take precedence over any readers called subsequently, for this would deny the primacy of the reading as the major learning exercise and the most important determinant of a member's status within the house. But however clear in theory, the distinction between reader and non-reader was exceedingly difficult to maintain in practice.[55]

On one notable occasion it was overthrown by the direct intervention

---

[52] Bodl. MS, North, c. 4, f. 11; Aylmer, *King's Servants*, 72–3; *GIPB*, i. 299.
[53] *GIPB*, 333; *DNB*; Lucy Hutchinson, *Memoirs of the Life of Colonel Hutchinson* (Everyman edn, n.d.), 54.
[54] *GIPB*, i. 163, 233, 246, 266; for Eure and Finch see Harleian 1912, ff. 179ᵛ seq.
[55] Cf. *GIPB*, i. 148, 203, 209, 241, 278.

of the crown. John Wright, clerk of the House of Commons from 1613 to 1640, was called as an associate bencher in 1622 on condition that he would take place after all those who had read or would read in the future. Although no court favourite (he had been arrested and imprisoned along with Sir Edward Coke and Sir Edwyn Sandys at the close of the 1621 parliament), Wright somehow managed to secure a royal letter requiring him to be given precedence 'according to the antiquity of his tyme and callinge to the bench', or in other words, seniority as if he had read.[56] This command, delivered to the bench as they sat at dinner on 29 January 1623, was received with considerable dismay; the benchers managed to postpone an answer for a week, sending messages through Sir Julius Caesar and Sir Thomas Edmondes to excuse their procrastination and discussing the matter at four separate pension meetings. But these tactics were in vain, and on 5 February Wright was permitted to take his precedence as from his date of call, 'which place', the minutes carefully added, 'was assigned to him *ex gratia* by reason of his Majesty's letters'. In 1629 Wright was elected treasurer of the society, thus gaining a voice and vote in pension for the rest of his life.

The benchers had here been forced to compromise a principle under irresistible external pressure. But on other occasions the initiative for compromise came from the bench itself. Thus the pension order which James I contested on Wright's behalf was accompanied by a rider preserving the seniority of six benchers called on previous occasions who had not read – Sir Euble Thelwall, Sir George and Sir Thomas Ellis, both members of the Council of the North, Francis Curle, the auditor of the Court of Wards, and John Gulston and Thomas Waller, prothonotaries of the Court of Common Pleas.[57]

At the Inner Temple and Lincoln's Inn the bench was recruited entirely from members who had not read. At neither house was there a senior group of utter-barristers corresponding to the ancients of Gray's Inn, and readers were always chosen from benchers, not vice versa. Both societies had standing orders which provided that benchers who refused to read in their turn should be fined and demoted, but these rules were laxly enforced and benchers who did not read were generally accorded the same rights and status as those who had.[58] Just as at Gray's Inn, the majority of non-readers held office in one of the conciliar courts or the bureaucracy which serviced Westminster Hall.

Most also escaped their reading without penalty, although the rulers of Lincoln's Inn were more likely to exact payment for this

---

[56] GI MS, Order Book, f. 314; *GIPB*, i. 252; *Commons Debates for 1629*, ed. Wallace Notestein and F. H. Relf (Minneapolis, 1921), xxv.

[57] *GIPB*, i. 253–4, 255, 287; GI MS, Order Book, f. 345v; cf. *ibid.*, ff. 330, 359v; *GIPB*, i. 271.

[58] *ITR*, i. 146, 248; LI MS, Black Book V, f. 422v.

privilege than their colleagues at the Inner Temple, and three members of Lincoln's Inn were demoted from the bench altogether for failing to read. Edward Abdy asked to be excused his reading when his turn came up in 1608; this was refused and Abdy suffered demotion to the rank of associate, petitioning unsuccessfully for restoration to the bench in February 1609.[59] Ughtred Shuttleworth became a bencher in 1630 and was chosen to perform the Lent reading of 1634. But he was by then 'liveing in remote and unknown parts' (probably Lancashire) and made no reply to the summons; whereupon the benchers, preferring, as they put it, 'the publicke good and governement of this house before the particuler respects of anie one man's person', ordered that Shuttleworth be 'putt from the bench'. Finally John Baber, the recorder of Wells, who had been raised to the bench in 1639, was fined £40 and demoted in February 1641 for his refusal to read.[60]

The other seventeen non-readers from Lincoln's Inn escaped with nominal fines or no fines at all. Sir Roger Owen, the son of a judge, a member of the Council of the Marches, M.P. for Shropshire from 1601 to 1614, and a leading spokesman for the opposition in the Addled Parliament, was specifically dispensed from reading when he was called early in 1611, without having to pay for the privilege. Among those less fortunate were William Ravenscroft, clerk of the petty bag in the Chancery office, who was called from associate to full bencher in January 1621 'upon the mocion and at the request of Sir James Ley', then a bencher, attorney-general of the Court of Wards and chief justice elect of the King's Bench. Ravenscroft was given precedence over all other benchers except double readers, although his own reading was excused: 'And the said William Ravenscrofte, to shewe his thankfull acceptacion of this favour . . . offred to adde xxx li. more to the xx li. hee hath alreadie paid towardes the building of the chappell'.[61] Another was Sir Edward Clerke, who became associate in 1619 on being appointed master in Chancery extraordinary and was called to the bench in 1626, presumably in recognition of the knighthood he had just acquired. Sir Edward was dispensed from all exercises, and while not granted precedence in respect of his knighthood, did gain the right to reckon his seniority from the date of his call, which meant in effect that he took precedence over all benchers called after him, whether or not they subsequently read. For these favours Clerke paid £20 outright and loaned £50 to the house to be repaid at the rate of £10 a year.[62]

Clerke got off more lightly than the Welsh judge Sir Peter Mutton,

59 *BB*, ii. 110, 119.
60 *BB*, ii. 310, 354, 356–7; 'The household and farm accounts of the Shuttleworths', ed. John Harland (*Chetham Soc.*, 41, 1856), pt. 2, app. i, 305.
61 *BB*, ii. 137, 212, 219–20.
62 *Ibid.*, 264; *DNB*; Foss, *Judges*, vi. 9.

who pleaded 'infirmitye of body' when his turn to read came, but was nevertheless fined £10. Besides James Clark, John Giles, Thomas Thyrwhit and Edmund Walmsley, all of whom apparently died before their reading was due, most of the remaining non-readers seem never to have been called upon to read.

The twenty-four associate benchers elected at Lincoln's Inn included fifteen men who cannot be positively identified as office-holders. Some of these must actually have held offices, although no evidence of the fact has come to light; among the rest were such distinguished figures as Sir Roger Owen and Sir William Sidley, both later called as full benchers, Sidley 'in respect of his worthines, great readinge, learninge and experience', Michael Dalton, the author of two standard texts for local governors, and Sir Francis Russell, fourth earl of Bedford, the builder of Covent Garden Square and one of Pym's aristocratic friends. The relatively high proportion of non-office-holders among the associate benchers of Lincoln's Inn helps to explain why that society elected more associates than any other inn during our period.[63]

No Inner Temple benchers were directly fined for refusing to read and none were demoted from the bench. Of the seventeen non-readers among the ninety-six benchers called at the Inner Temple between 1590 and 1639, ten were office-holders and promoted as such. Of the remainder, John Clough and Paul Wright probably died soon after their call, Sir Charles Caesar seems to have owed his promotion to acquiring a knighthood and John Selden to his intellectual eminence, William Littleton left the house as a serjeant-at-law within two years of his call, while neither Sir Ralph Hare nor George Wilde ever seems to have been asked to read. In addition thirteen associates were called, all office-holders, four of whom subsequently became full benchers without having to read.

No fixed scale of promotion for office-holders seems to have existed at the Inner Temple or the other houses, perhaps because the status of officers varied somewhat according to fluctuations in the business of the court to which they were attached. Ability and personality may also have played a minor part; Richard Brownloe, the very competent and longlived chief prothonotary of Common Pleas from 1590 to 1638, was promoted to the bench of the Inner Temple in 1591 and continued to attend parliament meetings until only a few years before his death. But Brownloe's far less eminent successor, Thomas Corie, never rose above the rank of associate bencher. There were some vague upper and lower limits. In 1626 Thomas Willis was called to the bench on condition that he leave his clerkship of assizes, an office evidently felt to be unfitting for a bencher; three years later, having purchased the position of clerk of the crown in Chancery for a reported payment of £6,000, Willis was called to the bench uncon-

[63] BB, ii. 29, 168; LI MS, Black Book V, f. 484; *DNB*.

ditionally.[64] Barons of the Exchequer, masters of Requests, masters in Chancery, recorders of London and legal officers of the crown or royal family were almost invariably called to the bench on their appointment, if they were not already benchers. The offices held by associate benchers were not necessarily less lucrative or even less prestigious; thus besides George Farmer, third prothonotary of Common Pleas and John Keeling, coroner in the King's Bench, the Inner Temple associates during our period include the chief clerks of the Court of Wards, Hugh Audley and Richard Chamberlain, Sir Henry Croke, master of the Pipe Office and Samuel Wightwick, assistant chief clerk of the King's Bench. In fact, as this recital suggests, the main difference between associates and full benchers was simply that the associates were predominantly administrators rather than advocates.

This survey of promotion to the bench suggests that the changes Holdsworth attributed to the later seventeenth century were already well in evidence during the fifty years before the Civil War. In three of the four inns reading was no longer an essential prior qualification for call to the bench. Double readings had ceased altogether by 1640; barristers were generally called before they had read and a substantial minority who never delivered a reading enjoyed the same privileges as readers, including seniority as from their date of call. Most non-readers were office-holders; those who did not reach the status of full bencher were elevated to the position of associate, a rank which had emerged at Lincoln's Inn in 1505 but was not firmly established at the other houses until after Elizabeth's accession. According to Dr Ives the first Lincoln's Inn associates were elected to overcome 'a difficulty in maintaining an adequate number of benchers'; this was certainly not the main reason for promotions to that rank during the period with which we are concerned.

The supersession of the original clerk–fellow dichotomy by the tripartite hierarchy of bench, bar and student in the course of the fifteenth century seems to have stemmed largely from the development of the learning exercise system. But the changes discussed above came as a response to external demands and pressures. The rise of the utter-barristers, their transformation from learners to lawyers, was affected by the expansion of common-law litigation during the sixteenth century. And as bar and legal bureaucracy grew in numbers and wealth, it was increasingly difficult to limit membership of the bench to those who had previously performed a reading. Thus the rank of bencher tended to become rather an accolade of professional success than a degree of learning which of itself entitled the holder to important professional privileges. These developments reflected the

[64] *ITR*, i. 373, ii. 155, 179, 211, 247; cf. *GIPB*, i. 166: Ralph Ewens promoted ancient 'in respect of his good places of service . . . and when it shall appere that suche officers have had higher places it shall bee furder considered'.

growing irrelevance of the learning exercise system to the business of learning and practising the law. But although the learning exercises themselves were virtually defunct by the end of the seventeenth century, the internal membership structure which they initially defined has survived, with minor modifications, down to the present day. The benchers retain their standing and authority at the inns, although they no longer claim pre-eminence in the courts by virtue of their rank alone; the barristers, on the other hand, despite their professional status and responsibilities, remain as powerless within the societies as their moot-men predecessors more than four hundred years ago.

IV

Administration and Government

Centralisation

Holdsworth was merely endorsing a truism when he claimed that the medieval inns of court showed 'no signs of democracy'; since the origins of the benchers' present hegemony cannot be traced to any specific charter or grant, it must be explained as a prescriptive right, legitimated by usage time out of mind.[1] Yet however effective as a rationalisation of the *status quo*, even a superficial survey of the evidence casts this orthodoxy into doubt. Its proponents rest their case largely on the purported absence of any democratic remnants from the earliest period of the inns' history: thus the chaplain of Gray's Inn argued in 1901 that

> if the members below the grade of the benchers had in the latter part of the fourteenth century a share in the government, or a franchise . . . it is at least not easy to imagine how, in the case of Lincoln's Inn by 1422, and in the others by the end of the fifteenth century, they had lost it so completely that not even a ritual custom survived as its memorial.[2]

Until the last twenty years of the fifteenth century, however, Lincoln's Inn was ruled not by the benchers, but by an executive of four 'governors', who held office for a year at a time. It is true that after 1427, when the names of Lincoln's Inn readers first became available, the governors were practically always chosen by rotation or co-option

---

[1] *HEL*, ii. 417; cf. *BB*, i. iv; *ITR*, i. xxxvi; *MT Bench Book*, xvii. But cf. Hastings Rashdall, *The Universities of Europe in the Middle Ages* (Oxford, 1936), iii. 169 n.2, and Simpson, 'Early constitution', *passim*.
[2] *GIPB*, i. xiii.

from the members who had performed or were about to perform a reading, the group which by the mid-fifteenth century had come to be known collectively as the bench.³ But while all entrants were supposed to swear an oath of obedience to the governors '*pro tempore existentibus*', their duties were mainly administrative and their power by no means absolute. On several occasions major decisions affecting the entire society are recorded in the Black Books as having been sanctioned by general meetings of all members, or of the barristers meeting with the governors and benchers, 'all being summoned who are of the said society, as well at the bench as at the bar, to communicate, understand, ordain and do what should be good . . . by their common consent and sole and spontaneous wish and authority'.⁴ Of course it is possible that the attendance and 'common consent' of members below the bench were no more than a formality, like the compulsory attendance of gild members at the quarterly Courts of Assistants of the sixteenth-century livery companies.⁵ But even if that were so, it is difficult to understand how such a practice could have originated under a totally autocratic form of government.

Until the last two decades of the fifteenth century the Black Books frequently list orders made 'by the society' or 'ordeyned by the felyshippe of Lincolnesynne', rather than by the governors alone. The exact significance of the terminological difference is again obscure; but in other contexts 'the society' seems to have meant just that – the whole body of members, or the *socii* as distinct from the *clericii*, and not just the benchers or governors acting as the collective embodiment of the entire membership.⁶ Moreover, as suggested above, the membership structure of Lincoln's Inn during the early fifteenth century had not yet evolved into a rigid three-tiered hierarchy defined by the learning exercises. Lincoln's Inn was hardly a primitive democracy at any stage of its recorded history, but the society does not seem always to have been as oligarchical in government and hierarchical in structure as it later became.

The first major change in the balance of power within the house appears to have come around 1480, when orders in the Black Books begin to be consistently recorded under the joint authority of the benchers and governors, while references to consultation or participation by the junior members cease altogether. The governors had apparently lost all independent authority by the beginning of Henry VIII's reign, although appointments to the office did not finally cease until 1574. Just how and why the benchers were able to gain full control is unclear, but it seems reasonable to suppose that their take-over was connected with the crystallisation of the learning exercises

³ Cf. S. E. Thorne, *Readings and Moots at the Inns of Court* (*SS*, 71, 1952), xii.
⁴ *BB*, i. 4, 28, 41–2.
⁵ Cf. George Unwin, *The Gilds and Companies of London* (3rd edn, 1938), 221.
⁶ Cf. *BB*, i. 2, 3, 9, 11, 12, 18–19, 46.

as a compulsory and continuing form of legal instruction. Apart from the need for firm direction from above to keep the system operating smoothly, the division of members into graded ranks of learners and teachers emphasised the high status of the bench and must have encouraged élitist attitudes among those who had risen to the top of the academic ladder.

The manner and timing of the benchers' access to power must have varied somewhat from one house to the next. As late as 1540 Thomas Denton and his colleagues (on whose report Holdsworth mainly relied for his account of the fifteenth and early sixteenth-century inns), described the governing bodies in the following terms: 'Pension, or parliament in some houses, is nothing else but a conference and assembly of their benchers and utter-barristers onely . . . and these together . . . treate of such matters as shall seem expedient for the good ordering of the house'.[7]

Barristers continued to attend parliaments at the Inner Temple until at least 1580, and throughout our period 'parliaments of attendance' were still held at the Middle Temple on the last Friday of each term, when all barristers in commons were supposed to be present, on pain of forfeiting 3s. 4d. '*pro con consultando*'. By the 1630s and probably long before this custom was only an emasculated relic of more democratic days; for, as the author of the Brerewood manuscript explains, the barristers were merely informed of 'all new made rules' and 'may not consult (but must consent) when they meet there'.[8]

As admissions expanded rapidly during the later sixteenth century, the societies came to play a larger role in the upbringing of the governing classes and also entered into a closer relationship with the government itself. Before Elizabeth's accession their contacts with the central authorities had been intermittent. But the influx of new members after 1550 filled the houses with a substantial proportion of England's future ruling class and made them prime targets for the catholic missionary priests who began to arrive in London from the mid-1570s on. It was largely to counter this threat that the state began to show a growing interest in the societies' affairs. The judges acted as the main formal channel of communication; their powers were ill-defined, but they were considered 'to best knowe the orders and formes of those houses'. Between 1559 and 1640 at least sixteen sets of 'judges' orders' were issued to the inns.[9] Some dealt mainly with

[7] *DBC*, 546; cf. *OJ*, 196.

[8] *ITR*, i. 305; Brerewood, 9 (*OJ*, 201); cf. *MTR*, ii. 600; Bagshaw, *A Just Vindication of the Questioned Part of the Reading . . .*, 14.

[9] *APC*, *1629–30*, 145; cf. *BB*, i. 455. Most of the judges' orders were transcribed by Dugdale from the records of the inns: *OJ*, 311–21. See also *GIPB*, i. 60–2; *MTR*, i. 364; *GIPB*, i. 169–70, 172, and IT MS, Petyt, Letters to treasurers and benchers, 4, 9, 50, 51, 55; IT MS, Miscellanea 31, pp. 23, 25; *APC*, *1623–25*, 19–20; Hargrave 311, ff. 241v–242v; *MTR*, ii. 836.

such technical matters as the performance of learning exercises and were frequently prepared in consultation with the benchers. Others included much broader issues and were promulgated at the command of the crown or the privy council or both. The crown and its agents also showed no reluctance to intervene directly in the societies' activities. Although Elizabeth's ministers were preoccupied with safeguarding religious conformity, their surveillance tended to strengthen the benchers' position; the government naturally supported the centralisation of power at the inns (and the extension of the benchers' authority over the inns of chancery) with the aim of creating a command chain which would effectively implement its religious policies.[10] Oligarchy and hierarchy went together; as the benchers' power within the societies was reinforced, the internal grades of membership became more sharply differentiated. These developments were hardly unique to the inns, but rather exemplified a general tendency affecting virtually every corporate body in Tudor England.[11]

Under Elizabeth's successors, who were generally less concerned with combating popery than with maintaining the authority of government at both local and national levels, explicit reinforcement of the benchers' position within the societies became more frequent, if not necessarily more consistent or effective. During the early seventeenth century the state's relationship with the inns, as with the City government and the chartered trading companies, was marked by occasional clashes of interest or jurisdiction on particular issues; but the early Stuarts nevertheless made every effort to bolster the dignity of the benchers vis-à-vis their subordinates, 'for that all government is strengthened or slackened by the observing or neglecting of that reverence and respect which is to be used towards the governors of the same'.[12]

Bureaucratisation

The earliest Black Book of Lincoln's Inn covers the half century from 1422 to 1471 and is reproduced verbatim in the first fifty pages of W. P. Baildon's published calendar. By the end of the sixteenth century the Black Book entries for a single year rarely occupy less than five printed pages, despite substantial abbreviation and omissions. Moreover the Black Books were no longer the sole all-purpose register of the society's affairs; since 1573 admissions had been entered in a separate register, which was soon supplemented by a Red Book for chamber

[10] H. H. Bellot, 'The jurisdiction of the inns of court over the inns of chancery', *LQR*, 26 (1910), 384–99; cf. M. H. Curtis, *Oxford and Cambridge in Transition 1558–1642* (Oxford, 1959), 41–5.
[11] Cf. Unwin, *Gilds and Companies*, 217.
[12] *OJ*, 318 (1614 judges' orders); Valerie Pearl, *London and the Outbreak of the Puritan Revolution* (1961), 70–1.

transactions and a White Book for interim decisions and memoranda. The diversification and expansion of administrative records was a phenomenon common to all houses under Elizabeth and the early Stuarts, reflecting the growing complexity and volume of their daily affairs.

Before the great expansion of membership which began around 1550, most of the routine chores necessary for the day-to-day running of the inns were performed by the members themselves. At Lincoln's Inn the collection of payments towards the house rent and fuel for the fire in the hall had been entrusted, from at least 1422 onwards, to the pensioner and collier, two unpaid officers chosen from members below the bench. After 1455 they were assisted by a treasurer, who supervised the society's finances and eventually emerged as its formal head and spokesman. The chaplain's stipend was paid from members' dues collected by the dean of the chapel, who, like the marshal appointed to superintend activities in the Christmas vacation, was always a bencher. In addition to these honorary member-officers the inn employed a number of full-time servants, headed by the chief butler and steward. The butler was major domo and chief functionary of the bench; his duties ranged from an assortment of purely clerical tasks to oversight of the junior servants and supervising the service of meals in hall. The steward was exclusively concerned with the provision of commons, the management of the kitchen and the collection of payments for commons. The same basic pattern was found at the other houses, with minor variations; for example, pensions were collected at the Inner Temple by the treasurer or chief butler, while the office of keeper of the Black Books, instituted at Lincoln's Inn some time before 1513, had no parallel elsewhere.[13]

The main change in these arrangements during our period was a general reduction in the responsibilities of member-officers and a corresponding rise in the number and importance of salaried officials. The most striking instance was the delegation of most of the treasurers' duties to full-time administrative assistants, who had originally been merely servants of individual treasurers, but became regular employees chosen and paid by the inns. By 1640 little real power remained in the treasurers' hands and only at the Inner Temple did they still normally hold office for longer than a year; elsewhere a desire to spread the patronage and prestige of the treasurership more equally among a greater number of benchers had led to the annual appointment of treasurers and the assumption of their erstwhile duties by the under-treasurers.[14]

---

13 See the introductions to the first volumes of the printed records, especially *BB*, i, and Thorne, 'Early history', 79–82.
14 Holdsworth's statement (*HEL*, xii. 21) that the annual appointment of treasurers was not uniform practice until the eighteenth century is technically correct, although Gray's Inn adhered to annual appointments from 1622 until

At Gray's Inn the position of under-treasurer was not formally established until 1639, with the appointment of Thomas Teasdale, an ancient, to 'collect all pensions personall and reall, fines, moot failes, bolt failes and other revenues ... and to account to the treasurer'.[15] A permanent under-treasurership was instituted at Lincoln's Inn in 1622; the incumbent's chief task was to receive all revenues previously collected for the treasurer, to whom he rendered a termly account.[16] The first under-treasurer of the Middle Temple had probably been appointed as early as Henry VIII's reign, but the office did not become firmly established until the election in 1591 of Richard Baldwin, who had previously been employed as a butler. Baldwin remained under-treasurer until his death in 1619, when he was succeeded by John Bayliffe, who served until 1654. In 1625 Nicholas Hyde, then treasurer of the Middle Temple, was relieved of the 'trouble of receiving anye monies into his hands', and henceforth Bayliffe alone was responsible for gathering the Middle Temple's income. He also recorded admissions to the house and to chambers, kept a list of learning exercises performed by students, wrote up the parliament minutes, supervised building work and compiled the accounts presented each year in the treasurer's name. In return he received a yearly salary of £20, free board and lodging for himself and a servant, a poundage of one shilling in twenty on all revenues collected and various other allowances, including 'any ould cast table clothes and linen ... and things of what kind so ever within his charge and custodie, past employment and use to the house'.[17]

At the Inner Temple treasurers were not restricted to a year's term of office until after the Restoration, and the under-treasurers appointed during our period seem to have held a markedly lower status than elsewhere. Among those who served as treasurers for more than a year between 1590 and 1640 were Sir Edward Coke, Sir Julius Caesar, Sir Thomas Coventry, Sir Robert Heath and Sir Edward Littleton, all men of considerable general ability and experience. Another was John Hare, the industrious clerk of the Court of Wards, who initiated the practice of entering house accounts in a separate ledger. Hare was sufficiently proud of his innovation to add an explanatory note on the fly-leaf of the first account book, pointing out that previously accounts

---

the Civil War, following bench resolutions to that effect in 1617 and 1622; *GIPB*, i. 225, 249–50. At Lincoln's Inn treasurers were elected annually throughout our period, as they were at the Middle Temple from 1621 onwards; *MT Bench Book.* xxiii–xxiv.

[15] *GIPB*, i. 299, 323, 336.

[16] *BB*, i. 358–9, 383, ii. 102, 198, 238–40. In the later seventeenth century the under-treasurer's responsibilities were assumed by the steward (who emerged as the major administrative official) and chief butler: *BB*, iii. x, xiv; *HEL*, xii. 36.

[17] Williamson, *Temple*, 162, 220; Brerewood, 32; MT MS, Minutes C, f. 202; Minutes B, f. 19v.

'were kept uppon loose papers soone loste . . . but henceforth shall always appear in this booke' – as indeed they did.[18] The Inner Temple treasurers also relied heavily upon the chief butler, who performed much of the work, including clerical tasks and revenue collection, which was handled elsewhere by the under-treasurers.

Other officers whose duties were considerably diminished or eliminated during this period included the pensioners and colliers of Gray's and Lincoln's Inns, the receiver of admission monies at Gray's Inn, the stewards of the reader's dinners and drinkings at Lincoln's Inn and the two Temples and various functionaries appointed for the period of Christmas commons.[19] The only new position created for members was at Lincoln's Inn, where from 1609 onwards a bencher was appointed as master of the library, mainly to receive the levy paid by newly-called barristers and benchers towards the purchase of books.[20] Otherwise the inns chose to lessen the duties entrusted to co-opted members and increase the responsibilities of their paid servants, particularly the butlers and under-treasurers.

The servant problem

While the benchers retained ultimate control over the societies' affairs, they necessarily relied very much on the industry and integrity of their servants. Unfortunately the inns' employees were given little incentive to place their masters' interests before their own. Following normal contemporary practice, their cash wages were relatively insignificant; most also received free food and accommodation, but they were all forced and indeed expected to derive the greater part of their income from tips, fees, and allowances of provisions.[21] The task of ensuring that they did not exceed their entitlements was rendered well-nigh impossible by continued inflation and the breakdown of rules against the employment of married men. Meanwhile the size of the inns' domestic establishments expanded alarmingly. In the early sixteenth century the Middle Temple had employed only eight servants: a steward and manciple, three butlers, two cooks and a laundress. By the 1630s the society still supported the steward and his manciple (now renamed the 'paniarman'), as well as five butlers, three washpots, two scullions, two cooks, two turnspits, 'an old woman to

---

[18] *ITR*, i. 195, ii. 78, iii. lxxvi, 112; IT MS, Accounts Book 1606–1648, f. ii; H. E. Bell, *An Introduction to the History and the Records of the Court of Wards and Liveries* (Cambridge, 1953), 26–8.

[19] *GIPB*, i. 20, 229; *BB*, ii. 261, 393, 396; LI MS, Black Book VI, f. 336v; *MTR*, ii. 691; *ITR*, ii. 228; Williamson, *Temple*, 208–14; W. R. Prest, 'Some Aspects of the Inns of Court, 1590–1640' (Oxford D.Phil. thesis, 1965), 127–37.

[20] *BB*, ii. 117.

[21] Cf. Aylmer, *King's Servants*, 182–3, 433. For servants' wages and allowances, see GI MS, Ledger A, f. 26; IT MS, Accounts Book 1606–1648, ff. 2 *seq.*; LI MS, Black Book V, ff. 465 *seq.*; *BB*, ii. 122–3; *MTR*, ii. 733–5; *OJ*, 214.

wash the dishes', a gardener, a porter and the laundress not to mention the under-treasurer and his man, an unknown number of deputies and servant's servants, and the house musicians.[22]

In 1617 sixty barristers and students of the Middle Temple denounced the bench for ignoring complaints about the 'dishonest behaviour' of house servants and claimed that 'all owr officers are permitted to contract and to sell their places to owr great greavance and oppression'.[23] A resolution of 1553 prohibited such sales, but the Middle Temple benchers knowingly permitted this rule to be broken at least once during our period. Considering the general contemporary acceptance of venality of office and the demand for the available servants' places, both at the Middle Temple and elsewhere, it seems likely that the rule was simply abandoned as impracticable.[24] The first charge is initially less convincing, if only because most evidence about servants' dishonesty comes from the benchers' minutes; but it possibly refers to a specific occurrence of which we now have no knowledge, for the benchers did often show a somewhat ambivalent attitude towards their employees' misdeeds. Besides the constant and inevitable peculation of junior servants, for which there is an abundance of generalised evidence, examples of more serious frauds occasionally come to light.[25] In 1597 the chief butler of Gray's Inn was demoted for embezzlement and the chief butler of Lincoln's Inn was expelled in 1623 for a similar offence. In 1630 the steward of Gray's Inn was found to be allowing certain members to take commons without putting their names on the weekly roll; these fortunate individuals received their meals at a discount, while their money went straight into the steward's pocket. Yet the steward's punishment was merely a reprimand and a £10 fine (suspended after a month), which suggests that the benchers of Gray's Inn were resigned to accept the habitual dishonesty of their servants as a simple fact of life. That was certainly the assumption underlying the inns' accounting procedures and the reports of the numerous committees set up to investigate kitchen management.[26] Many of the servants dismissed for no stated cause during our period had probably been discovered expropriating house funds; in the light of the Middle Temple petition and the hardened attitude which the benchers doubtless acquired through their professional experience of such matters, it would be naïve to imagine that the few cases noted above comprised the full extent of the problem.

[22] *OJ*, 196; Williamson, *Temple*, 365; cf. *MTR*, ii. 698.
[23] MT MS, unclassified 'Articles exhibited on the behalf of the gentlemen . . .'.
[24] *MTR*, i. 91, 334, ii. 473, 491; cf. Aylmer, *op. cit.*, ch. 4; IT MS, Letters to treasurers and benchers, 20, 41–2; *BB*, ii. 85–6; *ITR*, i. 362–3, 435, 444.
[25] *BB*, ii. 183–5, 231, 288; *GIPB*, i. 282, 303; *ITR*, ii. 18–19, 197–8, 213; *MTR*, ii. 659, 734–5.
[26] *GIPB*, i. 133–4, 293–4; *BB*, ii. 241; LI MS, Black Book VI, ff. 349ᵛ, 356, 359; *ITR*, i. 427, ii. 40.

The servants' financial dependence on fees and gratuities paid by members inevitably weakened their reliability as agents of the bench. An Inner Temple bencher complained in the 1630s that whereas the butlers had once performed their duties without fear or favour, they were now 'negligent and loath to offend the gentlemen by reason of Christmas commons'. Like their counterparts at the other houses, the Inner Temple butlers earned most of their income as croupiers at the annual Christmas gaming sessions. Since the members in residence over Christmas could exclude individual butlers if they wished, the butlers naturally hesitated to inform the bench of breaches of house rules by junior members during the year, for fear of the consequences when Christmas came around. Indeed the failure of attempts to regulate Christmas commons was due in no small part to the servants' reluctance to abandon this traditional source of income, and their consequent cooperation with members who assembled at Christmas in defiance of the bench.[27]

The malfunctions of the commons system were a related problem. Throughout our period stewards were continually running into debt with the tradesmen who victualled the houses; at Lincoln's Inn the steward and butler together were dunned for £544 in 1608 and in 1621 the steward's guarantors were called upon to pay a total of £900 owing to the baker, brewer and chandler. The steward of Gray's Inn owed more than £200 in 1635 and left large undischarged debts when he resigned four years later.[28] As these liabilities accumulated the quality of food provided by the tradesmen naturally tended to decline, and members were less eager to come into commons. The proportion of overhead costs borne by those who did take commons therefore increased, necessitating rises in the weekly tariff, which depressed attendance still further. Inefficient kitchen management and rising food prices were obvious contributory factors, but much of the difficulty stemmed from the lax collection of members' payments by the butlers and stewards. In 1632 the Inner Temple steward was said to be owed no less than £2,400 for arrears of commons; members of the Middle Temple had run up commons' arrears of more than £400 by 1639, and in 1641 the steward of Lincoln's Inn claimed £800 in outstanding commons payments.[29] Yet the servants seem to have felt little urgency about hounding members for their money or preventing debtors eating commons; in the long run losses were usually made up by the inns (or their own guarantors) and there was also the risk of verbal or physical assault if they pressed too hard. The combination of the 'remissness or fearfulness' of the servants and the lackadaisical

---

[27] IT MS, Miscellanea 31, p. 50; *ITR*, ii. 132; *MTR*, ii. 877. However, efforts were made to compensate butlers for their loss of Christmas earnings: *BB*, ii. 291–2; *GIPB*, i. 327–8; *ITR*, ii. 219; *MTR*, ii. 804. See also below, pp. 105–9.

[28] *BB*, ii. 113, 226, 233; *GIPB*, i. 324; *ITR*, ii. 157; *MTR*, ii. 571.

[29] *GIPB*, i. 242; IT MS, Miscellanea 31, p. 47; *BB*, ii. 359; *MTR*, ii. 882.

or recalcitrant attitude of members kept the commons system in a state of perennial crisis.[30] As food prices soared to unprecedented heights during the personal reign of Charles I, the benchers were forced to pay out large subsidies in order to maintain this essential service; but their commands and entreaties for members to come into commons and pay their bills promptly had little effect, and it was not until after the Interregnum, when prepayment for commons became the general rule, that a solution to these difficulties became possible.[31]

For all this, it would be wrong to portray the servants of the inns as uniformly corrupt and negligent. Many came to the societies as young men, often following their fathers into service, and remained until they were pensioned off or even admitted to membership, with a grant of free commons and a chamber for the rest of their lives. When Thomas Parry retired from Gray's Inn in 1610 after more than thirty years as a butler, his son Nicholas was admitted to the reversion of the fourth butler's place; Nicholas became steward of the house in 1626, resigning this place in 1639 to become a butler again. Ten years later he was appointed chief butler, keeping that office until 1676.[32] William Guy was taken on as under-cook in 1582 and promoted to chief cook in 1604, leaving the post of second cook free for his nephew John, who had entered the inn's service in 1590 and was paniarman from 1602 to 1604. When William died in 1620 John again succeeded him, with the proviso that fifty shillings a term from the profits of his office were to be paid to William's widow; and on John's resignation in 1653 he was granted the right to take free commons in the house until his death.[33] The societies also contributed to the maintenance of servants during periods of sickness and occasionally paid burial charges or placed their sons in apprenticeships, while dependants who petitioned for financial support were rarely turned away empty-handed.[34] Of course the benchers had a strong moral and social obligation to provide this sort of care and the servants doubtless regarded it as no more than their rightful due. Yet in con-

---

[30] *BB*, ii. 151, 179, 269; GI MS, Order Book, f. 372; *ITR*, ii. 40; *MTR*, ii. 689.

[31] Recorded losses on commons reimbursed from general house funds reached more than £135 at Lincoln's Inn for the financial year 1638–9 and over £107 at the Inner Temple in 1636–7: *BB*, ii. 349; *IT MS*, Accounts Book 1606–1648, f. 255. For subsidies at the Middle Temple, see MT MS, unclassified, 'An account of apparells 1620–1624'; for evidence of financial difficulties at Gray's Inn, see *GIPB*, i. 333, 335, 338–9. For prepayment of commons 'as in other houses', see *ibid.*, 455–6 (1667).

[32] *GIPB*, i. 42, 193, 273.

[33] *Ibid.*, 159, 165, 238, 406; cf. Leonard Stone, 'Nicholas Parry and Simon Segar', *Graya*, 34 (1951), 79–89.

[34] *GIPB*, i. 100, 102, 234; *BB*, ii. 29, 136, 146, 354; *ITR*, ii. 168; *MTR*, i. 288, 365, 426–7; for admissions to membership, see above, pp. 29, 43. Pensions to dependants were frequently deducted from the wages of the incoming servant, as compensation for the payment which would otherwise have been made to induce the previous holder to relinquish his place.

junction with well-established family ties, such cradle-to-grave paternalism must have helped counteract the baneful effects of low cash wages, especially for those who had worked up from the bottom of the servants' hierarchy to the exalted position of chief butler or steward.

In April 1642 a committee of six benchers was named by the Middle Temple parliament to investigate a series of objections made by Robert Henley, an associate of the bench, against the last four accounts of the under-treasurer John Bayliffe. Both Henley's accusations and Bayliffe's original defence have disappeared, but a seventeen-page supplementary rebuttal, in which the under-treasurer answered charges not covered in his first reply, has survived in the Middle Temple archives.[35] This document illustrates the inadequacy of visualising relations between the inns and their servants solely in terms of the cash nexus, while also raising some important questions about the general administrative role of the masters of the bench.

Bayliffe, the fifth son of a Wiltshire family of minor gentry, became under-treasurer in 1619 after nine years' practice as a barrister and in the 1630s was described by the compiler of the Brerewood MS as 'a discreete and painfull officer to the whole house to the honour of the same'.[36] Whether or not Henley's charges were justified is impossible to say, but Bayliffe certainly reacted to them as if his whole life's commitment had been called into question: 'It hath mightily greeved your accomptant (even to make him wearie of his life) after soe long service, and many yeares experience of his faithfulness, to bee forced att last to plead for his integritie . . .'.[37] Denying that he had purloined timber from a demolished building for his own purposes, Bayliffe pointed out that all such material for which no further use could be found had been granted him by parliament: moreover, he 'came not to serve the house for such ends, viz. to sharke, defraude and cozen (leaving such practice to those of baser metell and coarser claye) but to doe his best . . . to beautifie and adorne the place'. Why else should he have left the bar,

> wherein he was well entered and whereof hee had such opportunities and encouragements putt into his hands to proceede . . . to become a servant and underling when hee needed not? But that hee saw whilst every one was busie and sollicitous to looke after his owne profitt . . . the house in the meane time, which received and harbored them all, was neglected and like to fall about theire eares; which to

---

[35] *MTR*, ii. 923; MT MS, 'John Bayliffe the accomptante's answers to the exceptions of Mr Henley . . .'. For Henley, see Aylmer, *King's Servants*, 305–8, 419.

[36] *MT Adm. Reg.*, i. 79; *Wiltshire Visitation Pedigrees*, ed. G. D. Squibb (Harleian Soc., 1954), 13; Brerewood, 32. For Bayliffe's later clashes with Henley and ultimate dismissal on the grounds of 'long neglect' and old age, see *MTR*, ii. 957, 969, 972.

[37] MT MS, 'John Bayliffe the accomptante's answers . . .', f. 7.

prevent, hee is persuaded, God putt into his hart, to change the course he was entering into . . . to become an instrument . . .[38]

The zeal of men who regard themselves as divine agents is frequently offensive to those with more mundane motivations. Bayliffe probably had only himself to blame for charges that he 'tooke too much upon him; that hee had too greate power, overruling the masters of the bench and not conforming to the treasurer; thereby giving the gentlemen occasion to bee discontented and complaine . . .'. The under-treasurer's self-righteous tone was unlikely to mollify his opponents, however valid his arguments. Moreover, after asserting, quite un-exceptionably, that 'next after the governors, to the officers and servants it belongeth, whether the society itselfe either stand or fall, prosper or decline', Bayliffe went on to wonder aloud why 'soe little heed hath bene taken in the choice of servants', and attacked the benchers' failure to ensure that bonds were obtained from all employees: 'Till this bee rectified, and they reduced to better attendance and conformitie to order in their severall places as they are entrusted, little good hee is persuaded cann bee expected or hoped for to the societie'.[39]

Despite the disarming assertion that his supposed excessive power was 'none at all, but accordinge to the orders and usages of the howse and under the masters of the bench', Bayliffe maintained that it was his duty to acquaint the benchers with their own orders and 'informe them aright'. Worst of all, he expressed sympathy with the dissident junior members: 'it bee incident to younge men newly gotten to theire libertie to bee humerous and soe apt to bee discontented and to complaine (which superior wisdome should regulate)', and in any case 'it was not at this time altogether without ground, but rather . . . upon good cause and reason'. Insisting that he had done everything possible to uphold the authority of the bench, Bayliffe turned the blame back to the benchers themselves:

> Where can obedience bee but under governors? What looseth the bonds of it, but misgovernment? And howe can that bee but by oppression, injustice or wronge? All these being rectified by superiors, the faster the knott of obedience; but being comitted, continued or not reformed, strike sore at government.

The only way to prevent further challenges and to 'establish your government in perpetuitie' was

> with a lovinge, faire and grave carriage . . . to settle among your-selves (the governours) in unanimitie and constant resolucion but this one principle, viz. joyntly as one man to endeavour (for *vis unita fortior*), two may doe somethinge and a three-fold sword is not easily broken, but what cann one doe? Division in this case is alto-gether destructive to advance the common good and publique

[38] *Ibid.*, f. 9. [39] *Ibid.*, ff. 10–13.

honor of the societie, without looking awaie towardes selfe ends or particularities. This is what will make you to bee in deed, *tutelares non titulares praesides*.[40]

The management problem

Bayliffe's imputations of disunity and factionalism are impossible to test, for very little can be now learnt about the conflict of arguments and personalities from which many decisions recorded in the benchers' minutes must have emerged. Indeed everything possible was done to conceal and minimise such conflicts. The formal bench meetings were held *in camera*, their procedure designed chiefly to reduce debate and discord to a minimum. The treasurer acting as chairman controlled the agenda. Once an item was put to the meeting, each bencher was supposed to speak in reverse order of seniority, 'and thereupon the most voices prevail'.[41] The minutes scrupulously record only decisions taken, not arguments or votes cast pro and con. Decisions affecting individuals were privately notified to the persons concerned; those involving the society in general were screened or announced in hall. The aim of presenting a picture of monolithic unanimity to the outside world may not have been fully achieved at the time, but the internal politics of the bench remain a closed book for the modern historian. Even when one can be reasonably sure that the benchers were seriously split on a certain matter, the alignments of individuals and the precise points in dispute are entirely unknown. It is a natural supposition that such men as Bacon, Coke, Egerton and Ley would have exercised an influence among their colleagues at the inns commensurate with their personal and professional standing; but again there is only a little indirect evidence to support this assumption and nothing to show exactly how and when that influence was used.[42]

Bayliffe's other criticisms boil down to a broad charge that the benchers were ineffective (if not positively harmful) as policy-makers and administrators, because their self-interest too often outweighed whatever concern they may have felt for the overall welfare of the society. The benchers' contact with and control over the daily life of the houses were indeed uneven. No formal attention was paid to the academic progress or personal welfare of junior members, while the monotonous, quasi-ritualistic repetition of standing rules and orders for performance of exercises, attendance at vacations, payment of commons and so forth suggests that their efforts to regulate the basic

---

[40] *Ibid.*, ff. 14–15; for student-bencher clashes, see ch. v below.
[41] The only contemporary account of a bench meeting is in Brcrcwood, 8–9 (printed with slight variations in *OJ*, 201). Note however that the treasurer did not preside at Lincoln's Inn: *BB*, iii. 181, 311. See also *ibid.*, ii. 118, 290; *GIPB*, i. 294; *ITR*, i. 395; *MTR*, ii. 600, 604–5, 848.
[42] Cf. *ITR*, ii. 7; *GIPB*, i. 227.

domestic and educational functions of the societies may often have been less than successful. Explicit and well-publicised policies were continually eroded by half-hearted and inconsistent enforcement, arising partly from the unreliability of the servants but mainly from the benchers' susceptibility to pressures exerted by colleagues, friends, kinsmen and patrons. Besides a natural reluctance to disappoint or offend those who requested individual exemptions from particular requirements, the benchers often seem to have been privately in two minds about the merits of the policies which they publicly professed to uphold, especially when these were originally imposed by some external authority, such as the judges or privy council. The failure during our period to exclude attorneys and Roman Catholics from membership must certainly be ascribed in part to the indifference or passive resistance of at least a significant minority of benchers. Similarly, the presence on the bench both of men who had not performed a reading and those who had personal experience of the objective weaknesses of the learning exercise system, may well have inhibited attempts to prevent any slackening of the inns' academic and residential requirements.[43]

While the benchers were not conspicuously successful in sustaining consistent policies in these and other fields, they showed little reluctance to exploit their authority on their own behalf, or to impose obligations upon junior members which they themselves were unwilling to accept. Thus it was at best somewhat unreasonable to expect utter-barristers faithfully to serve their quota of learning vacations after call, when the benchers who were also supposed to attend those vacations were frequently *in absentia*.[44] The rulers of the inns enjoyed many privileges, usually including first choice of chambers, held without payment and in single occupancy, free or reduced admissions for sons and close relatives, free wine in hall, the rights to be in commons or not as they pleased, to have meals brought to their chambers, to keep a clerk in commons at a nominal charge, to use a private common room and a separate cubicle in the communal privies. Junior members were constantly exhorted to show due deference to the masters of the bench and without their permission no barrister could appear in court against a bencher of his own inn.[45] Although heavily subsidised from house funds, which is to say at the expense of the members in general, these privileges normally seem to have aroused little resentment. Whether they represented good value for money is another question.

[43] See below, pp. 133–6 and ch. VIII.
[44] LI MS, Black Book V, f. 374; *BB*, ii. 338; *ITR*, ii. 21, 211; *MTR*, ii. 590.
[45] *BB*, i. 417, ii. 40, 45, 119, 120 (cf. 338), 331; *GIPB*, i. 93, 196, 211, 229, 236–7, 308, 332–3; *ITR*, i. lxxvi, ii. 49, 58–9, 96, 131, 184; *MTR*, i. 108, 257, ii. 473, 666, 708, 758; *OJ*, 209–12; Roger North, *Lives of the Norths*, ed. Augustus Jessopp (1890), iii. 45–6.

Only a minority of benchers seem to have taken any active part in the government of the inns. The attendance records of the formal bench meetings at Gray's and Lincoln's Inns over the fifty years before the Long Parliament, as summarised in the following table, suggest that on average no more than or just over half of those entitled to attend were actually present.

TABLE 12   *Average attendance at bench meetings, 1590–1640* (to nearest whole number)

Year	Gray's Inn	Lincoln's Inn
1590	12	14
1595	9	17
1600	12	16
1605	11	16
1610	15	16
1615	14	18
1620	15	18
1625	10	15
1630	10	15
1635	15	21
1640	11	16

Estimates of bench numbers: *Gray's Inn*: 21 (1599: *GIPB*, 143–4; list of bench chambers). *Lincoln's Inn*: 32 (1612: *BB*, ii. 147–8); 27 (1618: *ibid.*, ii. 203–4); 27 (1621: *ibid.*, 226); 48 (1630s: MT MS on LI, f. 48).

Comparable figures are not available for the two Temples, but the situation there was probably similar. The frequency of bench meetings increased during our period, but still varied considerably from house to house; in the 1590s the Middle Temple parliaments were only convened five times a year, although eight or nine councils was already the annual norm at Lincoln's Inn. By 1640 the benchers of each house assembled at least two to four times a term, but while even sixteen meetings a year hardly represented an intolerable burden, attendance was not compulsory, except possibly at Lincoln's Inn. Nor were there any quorum requirements, despite the fact that decisions sometimes had to be postponed for lack of numbers, or the absence of individuals particularly concerned with matters under review.[46] It is true that other opportunities were available to transact house business; thus many routine administrative chores – for example dealing with members who had not paid their dues – were apparently handled at high table during dinner.[47] Unfortunately no record

[46] *BB*, ii. 105, 206, 295; *ITR*, ii. 7; *MTR*, i. 367.
[47] Cf. *MTR*, ii. 906, for a bench meeting in the Temple garden; for bench table meetings at the Temples, see Williamson, *Temple*, 481, and cf. *OJ*, 198, for a reference to the Middle Temple butler recording bench-table orders.

of these occasions has survived, but it may be doubted whether those who did not bother to attend formal bench meetings showed much more interest in the affairs of their house at other times.

Individuals and small *ad hoc* committees were frequently appointed at Lincoln's Inn, much less often at the other houses, to deal with matters which could not be easily settled at bench meetings and to carry out various commissions, such as reporting on the repair of buildings, checking wasteful practices in the kitchens, interviewing prospective preachers and so on. These assignments seem to have been fairly widely distributed, although newly called benchers tended to be given a disproportionate share of the burden, along with a small group of more senior men who were evidently particularly competent or conscientious. While standing committees were rare, what seems to have been intended as a permanent body, responsible for all matters concerning chambers, was operating at Lincoln's Inn during the later years of James I.[48] An even more ambitious experiment had been made there in 1600, with the establishment of a group of committees:

> for a more especiall care and vigilant eye to be had upon the whole estate of this fellowship, as well for religion, learning and maners, as for dyet, mayntenance of buildinges and walkes and for bringing into the treasorye all such standing and casuall profittes as do or shall belonge to the said howse.

Four small committees were set up, to meet at least twice a term 'for conference upon their said severall affaires', but no more is heard of them after their initial establishment.[49] The same fate befell a committee of ten benchers appointed by the Middle Temple parliament in response to a petition from John Bayliffe in June 1641, 'to take care *ne quid respublica societatis detrimenti caperet*'. This was apparently envisaged as a permanent executive or steering committee; its members, three of whom constituted a quorum, were to 'propose and determine from time to time what they shall conceive to be best for the general good and government of the society', reporting directly to parliament 'that thereby it may be put into execution'.[50] These initiatives suggest some dissatisfaction with existing administrative arrangements; their failure is perhaps further evidence of a widespread indifference to such matters.

The other means by which benchers could become personally involved in the affairs of their house was through co-option to an office such as the treasurership. But, as we have seen, the offices filled by members were being stripped of their major administrative responsi-

[48] *BB*, ii. 181.
[49] *BB*, ii. 66; one further reference to the 'overseers for diett' occurs two days after the committees were first appointed: *ibid.*, 67. Another similar experiment in 1611 also failed to get off the ground: *ibid.*, 142.
[50] *MTR*, ii. 908–9.

bilities during this period, and in any case there were far fewer offices than benchers. At the Temples the only posts normally filled by benchers were the treasurerships and the two auditorships (of the annual accounts); at the other inns there were also the offices of dean of the chapel and master of the walks (both held for an indefinite period of years), and at Lincoln's Inn the mastership of the library (usually held by the dean of the chapel for the time being) and the keepership of the Black Books. If the opportunities for administrative involvement were limited, so were the incentives. The treasurership was a prestige position and the treasurers' powers to set admission fees, allocate chambers, compound arrears of fines and appoint servants offered many opportunities for 'pleasuringe a frende', as one former treasurer put it.[51] Otherwise there were few rewards, in terms of status, patronage or cash, for undertaking chores which would necessarily cut into the time a man could devote to his domestic and professional commitments. Unlike the fellows of a college or the governors of a chartered trading company, the benchers had neither an economic dependence on the inns nor a strong personal stake in their welfare. While carrying considerable benefits within the societies, membership of the bench did not by itself confer great professional privileges, and a bencher could not expect to advance his legal career by any contribution he might make to the administration of his house. Nor did the inns usually evoke the kind of unquestioning loyalty which might still have impelled men to active participation, regardless of conflicting demands.

Yet most institutions, whatever their formal structure, tend to be administered by a small group of activists, whose colleagues are generally grateful to be relieved of the responsibility. If many or most benchers were unable or unwilling to devote much time to the societies' affairs, there were still those like Sir Francis Bacon, William Hakewill, John Hare, William Ravenscroft and Sir Euble Thelwall, who evidently found real satisfaction in shouldering the burden. John Bayliffe's indictment of the collective apathy and selfishness of the bench is not contradicted by the evidence surveyed above, but it remains doubtful whether the history of the societies would have been significantly different if the benchers of our period had shown a greater sense of communal responsibility.

Let us follow up this point with a brief glance at the financial affairs of the societies. Since they enjoyed virtually no endowed revenue, the inns relied on members' current payments for the bulk of their income. Financial arrangements were originally very simple; each major recurrent expenditure was covered by a specific tax or levy, and

[51] *BB*, ii. 127. The treasurer's authority varied slightly from house to house and was sometimes exercised subject to the veto of the whole bench: *GIPB*, i. 232; GI MS, Order Book, f. 266v; *MTR*, ii. 473–4, 848; *ITR*, ii. 72; LI MS, Black Book VI, f. 85.

whatever remained over after these charges had been met became part of the 'stock', which could be devoted to occasional expenses or carried over to the following year. Well before the end of the sixteenth century, however, returns from various forms of non-appropriated revenue – mainly admission fees, fees for the purchase of chambers, fines for academic delinquencies and exemption from expensive offices like the stewardships of the reader's dinner – had far outstripped the balance transferred to stock every year from the appropriated payments. Yet the societies still failed to enjoy a comfortable affluence based on substantial annual surpluses of income over expenditure.

The surviving accounts for our period do not at once reflect this fact. Between 1590 and 1640 the Lincoln's Inn treasurer's accounts show a consistent credit balance at the end of each year's transactions, ranging from a high of £315 4s. 7d. for the financial year 1604–5 to a low of £5 15s. 7d. in the financial year 1631–2. The Inner Temple treasurer's accounts begin in 1606 and record only three deficit balances before 1640, the largest being of £41 3s. 11d. in the financial year 1639–40.[52] But it would be a mistake to suppose that the Inner Temple operated at a profit except in these three deficit years. Whenever the credit balance carried forward from one set of annual accounts exceeded the balance remaining at the end of the next, a loss had in fact been made on that second year's operations, which were actually being subsidised from accumulated capital. Just over half of the surviving accounts for the Inner Temple and Lincoln's Inn show such a loss; and while no comparable data exists for Gray's Inn and the Middle Temple, we do know that by the late 1630s both were forced to raise cash loans or levy aid rolls from their members in an effort to remain solvent.[53]

Why did the societies incur debts and continued operating losses when their actual and potential income was steadily rising with the expansion of their membership? In the first place, expenditure rose as fast or almost as fast as income, thanks to inflation, the malfunctioning of the commons system, increasing numbers of servants and benchers, and the latters' increasingly expensive tastes: food and drink consumed by the Middle Temple bench cost the society more than £80 in 1640–41, not an entirely insignificant sum when set against a total expenditure of £967 odd for that financial year.[54] Masques and similar presentations, which were more elaborate and numerous than ever before, required subsidies from house funds to supplement the payments of the individual participants and the proceeds of special

---

[52] Summaries of the annual treasurer's accounts for the Inner Temple and Lincoln's Inn are printed in *BB*, i., ii. *passim* and *ITR*, ii. 23 *et seq.*
[53] For aid rolls and debts between 1637 and 1640, see *BB*, ii. 342; *GIPB*, i. 327; *ITR*, ii. 247–8, 254; *CMTR*, 154; MT MS, unclassified, 'A briefe collection . . showing the state of the treasurie', f. 1.
[54] MT MS, 'A briefe collection . . .', ff. 6–8.

levies on the whole membership. But the chief drain upon resources was building and maintenance costs. While most buildings erected during Elizabeth's reign had been financed by private members and speculators, the societies themselves took over the greater part of this work in the early seventeenth century. Subscriptions for chambers in new buildings rarely covered construction costs. Yet blocks of chambers were at least partially self-financing and could yield substantial long-term revenues; no tangible returns whatever came from the large investments in communal buildings undertaken in the late sixteenth and early seventeenth centuries.

In the second place, while expenditure kept pace with income over our period as a whole, both fluctuated widely and unpredictably from year to year. A harsh winter or a plaguy summer depressed income from admissions and chamber entry fees, as did lax enforcement of the standing orders and negligence in the collection of dues and fines. Patterns of expenditure were somewhat less erratic, but varying outlays on buildings, masques and arrears on the commons accounts still caused large yearly fluctuations. This inherent instability might not have been very important if the benchers had been able to ascertain the financial position of the societies at a given time. But like most contemporary individuals and institutions, the inns clung to the medieval charge-and-discharge method of accounting, which was designed primarily to minimise fraud rather than to depict annual profits and losses. Hence rational economic management and detailed forward planning were out of the question.[55]

In any case the benchers felt no need for such subtleties. Even getting in the accounts presented considerable difficulties; Edward Pelham, a bencher of Gray's Inn who served as a pensioner in 1586–7 and dean of the chapel in 1590–91, still had not rendered any accounts whatsoever by 1596. Nor was Pelham a solitary delinquent; in October 1594 the accounts of no less than five Gray's Inn pensioners remained outstanding.[56] Because they were not intended to facilitate year-to-year comparisons, the accounts were compiled with little attention to consistency, either in the classification of items of income and expenditure, or in the period of time covered, which was usually a year but might be anything from three months to six years. For the same reason, no conscious effort was made to consolidate all the different accounts returned, although in practice the downgrading of many member-officers and the concurrent rise of the under-treasurers did work towards that end. Otherwise the only real advance before the Civil War was the gradual substitution of English for Latin and arabic numerals for roman letters.

So it is hardly surprising that financial matters were handled on an *ad hoc*, hand-to-mouth basis, or that the benchers suffered from a chronic shortage of ready cash. As debts accumulated or a major

[55] Cf. Stone, *Aristocracy*, 278–80.   [56] GI MS, Order Book, ff. 206v, 214, 220v.

outlay became necessary, special efforts would be made to reduce overheads, bring in arrears and tighten up on the collection of dues and fines; in addition an aid roll might be levied, or fresh loans raised, until the temporary crisis had subsided. In the short run this response was neither irrational nor unsuccessful. After all, the societies did manage to survive a general financial crisis in the late 1630s and the serious difficulties of the Civil War period, while still accumulating substantial capital assets in the form of new and renovated buildings.

In the long run, however, the uncertainty which bedevilled the inns' finances must have encouraged the commutation of their academic and residential requirements into fixed cash payments, which gave higher and more easily predictable yields than the casual revenues obtained from exercise fines and chamber leases. The process of conversion began before the Civil War, gained impetus during the difficult years of the mid-1640s and reached its conclusion around the end of the seventeenth century. As a result the Hanoverian inns of court existed in a state of comfortable prosperity, despite much reduced enrolment, and could even afford to create their own endowments by judicious investment in East India stock and 3 per cent annuities.[57] Yet the benchers are no more to be praised or blamed for achieving a final solution to the inns' financial problems in this fashion, than for creating those problems in the first place; both resulted from an interplay of circumstances and events which remained essentially beyond their control.

[57] *HEL*, xii. 15–26, 35–7.

V

Discipline and Disorder

The scope of discipline

Until the last twenty years of the fifteenth century, members of Lincoln's Inn seem to have been subject to no disciplinary restraints, other than those necessary to safeguard the peace of the whole community and maintain the performance of learning exercises.[1] But as the benchers gained control over the society in the half-century from 1480 to 1530, they sought to impose a general discipline and instil respect for their own authority. Thus members were punished for encouraging quarrels between their fellows, prohibited from shooting bows and arrows within the house, and admonished not to wear their shirts hanging out of their doublets or to speak 'lowde and hyghe at meyle time'.[2] The offences most frequently reported in the Black Books for this period, other than assaults and brawls, were disobedience or insolence to the bench and moral misdemeanours. The first recorded punishment for sexual misconduct was inflicted in 1478 upon a member who had entertained a woman in his chamber 'at the forbidden time'. After a rash of similar offences in the late 1480s, the bench decreed that anyone caught fornicating in his room would be fined £5, although the penalty was reduced to £1 if the act were committed in the garden or Chancery Lane. Amorous adventures further afield were also discouraged, and gaming totally prohibited, whether inside or outside the house.[3]

[1] Cf. *BB*, i. 3, 4, 43–6.
[2] *Ibid.*, 97, 110, 140, 181, 189–90, 193, 205.
[3] *Ibid.*, 71, 110, 134, 152; Cf. *ITR*, i. 46; *MTR*, i. 73; *BB*, i. 66, 76, 89–90, 139, 218, Cf. the first order against gaming (1431), which merely banned dice play in the house after 9 p.m.: *ibid.*, 4.

But from the 1530s the gradual expansion of membership and the lack of proctors or tutors made it increasingly difficult for the benchers to continue policing the personal lives of their subordinates. Attempts to regulate extramural behaviour ceased altogether during the second half of the sixteenth century and by the beginning of our period barristers and students were perfectly free to attend plays or sermons as they chose, to drink in taverns ('the inns-a-court man's entertainment', according to Bishop Earle), and patronise dicing houses or stews at their pleasure. Occasional orders against gaming inside the house continued to be issued until the early seventeenth century, but these prohibitions were largely relaxed during James I's reign. The judges' orders of 1614 expressly sanctioned gaming at Christmas time, so long as only members in commons took part and all profits went to the butlers of the houses; henceforth only gaming in the public rooms of the societies was subject to any form of control. More stringent bans on women visitors were adopted in the sixteenth century, although the main motive seems to have been the preservation of the good names of the societies rather than the extirpation of vice. As early as 1534 the benchers of Lincoln's Inn ordered that no woman should henceforth be entertained in any members' chamber, 'bycause the same ys thoght to be to the great disworship of the house'; and only two cases of 'a lewd woman in the night' are reported after 1550, both at the Inner Temple. Drunkenness, the other great vice of the age, was not punished at all, unless combined with more serious misconduct; thus in 1632 the Inner Temple benchers listed among various 'great offences', which must be checked, 'else government would fail', the crimes of 'coming into hall in boots, cloak and sword, striking therein, coming in drunk'.[4]

While fines were still exacted for failure to attend vacations or perform learning exercises, no other notice was given to the academic progress of junior members. The times had indeed changed since three Middle Templars, going out as serjeants-at-law in 1503, thanked the fellowship in their farewell speech for 'binding them to study by good rules ordained by the company, which restrained them in their youth from their dislike to study'. The new permissiveness was aptly characterised by George Whetstone in 1586, addressing himself to the younger members of the inns:

> It is verie wel knowen that these famous houses are the first intertayners of your lybertie. For notwithstanding in your governments there are many good and peaceable orders, yet your chiefest discipline is by the purse. Those that are disposed, studdie lawes; who so liketh, without checke, maye followe dalliance.[5]

4 John Earle, *Micro-cosmographie* (1628), 13; *ITR*, i. 211, ii. 80, 102; *MTR*, i. 248, 272, ii. 514, 533; *GIPB*, i. 36, 285; *OJ*, 318; *BB*, i. 237, 287; IT MS, Miscellanea 31, pp. 40–1.
5 *MTR*, i. 8; Whetstone, *A Mirour for Magestrates*, ded. epistle.

But as the benchers ceased to supervise the moral welfare of junior members or their behaviour outside the inns, they became correspondingly more anxious to maintain their own authority in the societies. Compulsory attendance at daily services in the Temple Church and chapels of Gray's and Lincoln's Inn was introduced, with the government's encouragement, early in Elizabeth's reign. The benchers were simultaneously devoting much attention to regulating the dress of their subordinates. Sporadic attempts in this direction began in the 1530s, although an account of the Middle Temple written around 1540 emphasised that 'they have no order for apparel, but every man may go as he listeth'.[6] That anomaly was redressed in 1557, when a set of eight orders, dealing mainly with apparel, was promulgated simultaneously at the four inns, after consultation between their respective rulers. All members other than knights or benchers were forbidden to wear velvet caps or light coloured clothes of any description, to wear 'studie gownes' outside the inns, to carry swords or rapiers while in commons, or to have beards of more than three weeks growth. No significant additions or amendments to these requirements were made by the Elizabethan judges' orders and Elizabeth's various sumptuary proclamations, leaving the benchers free to define and control 'excesse of apparel' as they thought best.[7]

The ban on beards lapsed as the fashion became general in the early years of Elizabeth's reign, but the rulers of each house acted separately to combat novelties which they found particularly objectionable – ruffs, white doublet and hose, velvet facings or wings on gowns, lawn caps and so forth. By the end of the century, however, the benchers had largely concentrated their efforts on compelling caps and gowns to be worn in commons, and excluding such courtier-like appurtenances as boots, cloaks, hats, long hair, spurs and swords. Whereas the 1557 orders forbade gowns to be worn outside the inns (perhaps with the hope that if students were less readily identifiable, clashes with the townspeople might be minimised), by 1600 gowns were officially required to be worn at all times, in town as well as at the inns, except when members were travelling to and from the country. But this rule was impossible to enforce, so in practice members were left free to dress as they pleased except when they assembled *en masse* in the public buildings of the societies, at meals and learning exercises in hall, and church or chapel services.[8]

During James I's reign some direct support was received from the king, himself a firm believer in the strict enforcement of sumptuary rules as a means of maintaining social order. James was responsible

[6] *BB*, i. 231, 261; *OJ*, 197; *ITR*, i. 142, 178.
[7] *Ibid.*, 310, 312–16; Hughes and Larkin, *Tudor Royal Proclamation*, ii. 187–92, 454–62; iii. 3–8; cf. *Statutes at Large*, 24 Hen. VIII, c. 13.
[8] *BB*, ii. 8, 46; *GIPB*, i. 147–8; *ITR*, i. 438–9; *MTR*, i. 297.

for two sets of orders issued to the inns via the judges. The 1614 judges' orders, which 'proceedeth first from his Majesties especial care and commandment', repeated the existing prohibitions on boots, cloaks, hats or weapons being brought into hall, adding that 'an outward decency in apparel is an ornament to all societies and containeth young men within the bounds of civility and order'. A second set of orders, issued by the king in 1623, commanded that 'the ancient way of wearing caps should be carefully observed' and boots 'laid aside in the inns of court, as ill befitting gown men'.[9]

'Theis thinges were patiently heard but the vacation following totallye brooken', according to Simonds D'Ewes, who was present at the announcement of the last order in the Middle Temple Hall.[10] It is not clear whether this was the normal sequence of events, although the Middle Temple benchers had encountered considerable resistance against their attempts to enforce dress regulations in the preceding decade. The fact that orders about apparel and recorded offences against them fell off substantially in the 1620s and '30s does however suggest that the benchers were gradually giving up their battle against the tide of fashion. Sir Richard Weston's farewell speech at the Inner Temple in 1634 certainly showed signs of a more realistic approach. Weston urged his former colleagues not to neglect 'distinction of times & persons' or 'fashions of the present':

> gentlemen that come not to study, but to stay here for a time, being persons of quality and rank . . . conversing much abroad & at court; if they should be held to such strictness of cutting the hair etc. they might seem strange where they go . . . but for students and barristers, they not to be allowed that liberty.[11]

Weston's differentiation between professional and non-professional members was an important practical concession, even if it preserved in principle the benchers' right to dictate the outward appearance of their subordinates. But this right, like the whole edifice of sumptuary legislation bequeathed by Elizabeth to the early Stuarts, did not survive the fall of the old régime. After the Civil War junior members were required merely to wear gowns in the public buildings of the societies. Since the gown had been largely discarded by laymen after the first quarter of the seventeenth century, it was now simply a distinctive professional badge or uniform, as consciously anachronistic as Charles II's professed concern to restore the societies to 'their ancient discipline and primitive institution', by reissuing in 1664 the 1630 judges' orders,

---

9 *OJ*, 318–19; IT MS, Miscellanea, 31, pp. 25–7.

10 D'Ewes, 'Secret Diary', 173–4; cf. Greene, 'Diary', 386–7.

11 IT MS, Miscellanea 31, pp. 36–7; cf. the hostile reception given by the lord keeper and lord privy seal to a long-haired barrister who appeared before them in 1632, and their admonition to 'governments in the inns of court to reform it in younge gentlemen . . .'. University College MS, Ogden 7/11 (I am indebted to Dr J. H. Baker for this reference).

complete with the old bans on long hair, cloaks, boots and swords.[12]

The other major disciplinary innovation of the sixteenth century is more difficult to trace, since it cannot be related to any specific policy decision like the 1557 apparel regulations. No community is ever entirely indifferent to breaches of the peace among its members; but while assaults and brawls at the late medieval–early Tudor inns were punished as they occurred, the benchers seem to have been prepared to accept a high level of interpersonal violence within the societies. Their successors gradually came to take a much more serious view of the matter; instead of merely levying punishment after the event, they showed themselves determined to suppress violence, not so much for humanitarian or moral reasons, but because it was felt to be a slight on their authority.

Here again, as with the regulation of apparel, the rulers of the inns were largely following the central government's lead. Professor Stone has pointed to the decline of casual violence among the aristocracy in the late Elizabethan–early Stuart period; whereas early Tudor governments lacked the resources and self-confidence to check the individual bellicosity and gang warfare of the peerage, their reluctant tolerance gave way to an attitude of severe disapproval under Elizabeth and James. The actual drop in aristocratic violence traced by Stone owed as much to a complex of independent cultural, demographic, religious and technological changes as to the stiffening pressure exerted by central and local authorities. But at the inns, as throughout the nation at large, casual private violence came to be regarded as an intolerable challenge to government. The theoretical basis of this outlook (hardly novel in itself) was summarised by Sir Thomas Smith in 1583:

> For as much as the prince who governeth the scepter ... hath this in his care and charge, to see the realme well governed, the life, members and possessions of his subjectes kept in peace and assurance: he that by violence shall attempt to breake that peace and assurance, hath forfeited against the scepter and crowne of England.[13]

The first serious attempts to lower the level of violence at the inns began after the middle of the sixteenth century. While a privy council directive of 1525 against members carrying weapons was apparently ignored by the benchers, their own joint orders of 1557 prohibited members in commons from wearing rapiers and swords. This ban was repeated two years later by the judges, who in addition forbade members to go through the town with weapons borne after them.[14] In

---

[12] *BB*, ii. 420, iii. 110, 249, 443–9; *GIPB*, i. 388–9, ii. 80; *MTR*, iii. 1097, 1105, 1234, 1366, 1364; MT MS, unclassified, William Morice to Clarendon, 15 May 1663.
[13] Stone, *Aristocracy*, ch. 5; Smith, *De Republica Anglorum*, 50–1.
[14] John Bruce, 'An outline of the history of the Court of Star Chamber', *Archaeologia*, 25 (1834), 380; *OJ*, 310–12.

1561 the Inner Temple parliament decreed that assaults on house servants would henceforth incur an automatic penalty of loss of chamber, discommoning and a £2 fine, and from 1565 'shooters with guns' were also liable to be fined. Lincoln's Inn followed suit with severe mandatory punishments for assaults on servants or fellow members in 1588, while all four houses moved to control the election of lords

TABLE 13. *Recorded penalties for acts of casual violence, 1460–1639*

1460–79	LI:	Exp (R), £6/3/4.
		Exp (R), £2 (pardoned); 2 × Exp (R), £2;
		2 × Exp (R), 6/8.
1480–99	LI:	2 × Exp (R), 1/8; 3 × 3/4; 2 × 1/8; 1/–; 2 OOC.
1500–19	LI:	Exp (R), 3/4; 2 × 13/4; 2 × 6/8; 12 × 3/4; 2/6;
		6 × 1/8; 1/–.
	MT:	£3/13/4*.
1520–39	IT:	OOC
	LI:	£1/2/6*; 5 × 10/–; 6/8; 1/–; 2 × OOC.
1540–59	IT:	£3/13/4.
	LI:	£2; £1; 10/–; 6/8; 5/–; 3 × OOC.
1560–79	LI:	2 × Exp; Exp (R), OOCh, £13/6/8 (compensation)
		& £2/13/4; OOCh, £2; £1.
1580–99	GI:	17 × Exp (R) & fines unspecified; Exp (R), £1.
	IT:	Exp; 2 × Exp (R).
	LI:	4 × Exp; 2 × £10; £6/13/4; £3/6/8 & compensation
		unspecified.
	MT:	2 × Exp; Exp (R), £10 (reduced to £3/6/8);
		Exp (R); public submission.
1600–19	GI:	Exp (R).
	IT:	Exp; Exp (R); 2 × £3; 2 × OOC.
	LI:	Exp; 2 × Exp (R), £5.
	MT:	Exp; Exp, (R) on apology; £5.
1620–39	GI:	Exp.
	IT:	Exp; Imprisoned (R); petition of submission.
	LI:	Exp; Exp (R), £13/6/8 (£3/13/4 paid, balance
		suspended on good behaviour); Exp (R) £5;
		2 × £10; £5; 2 × £3/6/8; £2.
	MT:	4 × Exp; Exp (R), £5; £10; OOCh, £5; £5;
		£2/10/–; £2.

Key. Exp = expulsion.   OOC = out of commons.
        (R) = readmitted.   OOCh = out of chamber.
        * Penalty for various offences including act of violence.
        Each penalty is separately listed.
        Thus 2 × Exp (R), £2; means two members expelled, later
            readmitted and fined £2 each.
        (Fines were usually accompanied by suspension from commons.)

of misrule and the traditional marauding of their followers on Candlemas Night.[15]

Penalties for acts of casual violence within the societies also escalated
sharply in the later sixteenth century. Even allowing for a three- or
fourfold decrease in the value of money between 1500 and 1600, it is
evident that the scale of fines imposed had at least doubled by the
beginning of James I's reign, while permanent expulsion had also become a standard punishment. At the same time unarmed assaults
were no longer regarded as venial offences, but punished almost as
severely as assaults with a weapon.[16]

The early records give only a bare factual account of offences and
penalties levied; for example, in 1523 Edward Griffin of Lincoln's
Inn is ordered to be 'owte of commens for that he did stryke Mr
Tankerett with his fyste'.[17] By the late sixteenth century the entries
have grown longer, more detailed and much more sententious; thus
in 1580 the Inner Temple benchers prefaced their decision to expel
William Parry for an armed assault with the explanation that, because of 'the offence done thereby to this house in committing so
horrible a fact inexcusable, some example should be made in show
of the utter misliking thereof'.[18] Again in 1606 a gentleman of Lincoln's
Inn was expelled, because 'he hath in the backsyde of this house
stroke and beaten George Lutwich, the chief butler, with a cudgell,
whereby one of his ribbes was broken, which misdemeanour and evill
example ys not sufferable in the government of this house'.[19]

Table 14 is a very imperfect attempt to chart the incidence of interpersonal violence within the societies from the late fifteenth to the late
seventeenth centuries. It is based mainly on the benchers' minutes,
which are not complete before 1569, and in any case do not list all
acts of violence. Some incidents undoubtedly escaped the benchers'
attention, and others must have been recorded only in sources which
no longer survive, such as the bench table minutes; there seems no
other way to explain the remarkable dearth of offences listed in the
Gray's Inn pension order book, for example.[20] But it would be reasonable to expect that, as the benchers' tolerance of casual violence
diminished rapidly in the later sixteenth century, a constantly higher

[15] *ITR*, i. 212, 234; *BB*, ii. 8, 16; *GIPB*, i. 67–8; *MTR*, i. 126, 168, 272, ii. 148–9;
MTR, i. 311, 318, 326, 328, ii. 575; Williamson, *Temple*, 361–2; Birch, *Charles I*,
ii. 311, 313–14; MT MS, unclassified, copy of commision to examine and try riot
in the Middle Temple, 15 Feb. 1592.

[16] Cf. *GIPB*, i. 217, 238; *BB*, ii. 294, 326; *MTR*, ii. 758, 760.

[17] *BB*, i. 205.

[18] *ITR*, i. 308–9.

[19] *BB*, ii. 101, cf. *MTR*, ii. 673–4.

[20] Cf. *MTR*, i. 383 for offence listed in the 'libro pantarie' rather than the parliament minutes. A few 'cupboards' or informal bench meetings at Gray's Inn were
minuted in the pension order book, but probably only a small proportion of the
total held.

proportion of offences and punishments would appear in the most formal records of the societies, simply because such matters were no longer regarded as mere administrative routine. So while the table is certainly defective, it probably becomes significantly more accurate from the late sixteenth century on.

TABLE 14   *Recorded acts of interpersonal violence (internal),*
1422–1679

Period	Gray's Inn	Inner Temple	Lincoln's Inn	Middle † Temple	Total
1422–39	–	–	O	–	O
1440–59	–	–	O	–	O
1460–79	–	–	3W, A	–	3W, A
1480–99	–	–	2A, 3X	–	2A, 3X
1500–19	–	O	4W, A, 8X	X	4W, A, 9X
1520–39	–	X	6W, 3A	O	6W, 3A, X
1540–59	–	X	3W, 3A, X	O	3W, 3A, 2X
1560–79	O	O	2W, 2A, X	O	2W, 2A, X
1580–89	O	2W	3W	2X	5W, 2X
1590–99	2X	W	2W, X	2W	5W, 3X
1600–09	O	W, X	2W	X	3W, 2X
1610–19	A	W, 2X	W	2W, A, 2X	4W, 2A, 4X
1620–29	X	O	W, 3A, 3X	3W, A	4W, 4A, 4X
1630–39	O	2A	5A	A/W[1], 3A	10A, 1A/W
1640–49	O	O	O	O	O
1650–59	O	O	O	O	O
1660–69	O	O	A	O	A
1670–79	X	O	O	A	X, A

Key. O = no assault etc., recorded.
W = assault etc., with weapon (rapier, sword, dagger, knife, cudgel, staff).
A = assault etc., without weapon.
X = assault etc., unspecified.
– = no records survive.
† = gap in records 1525–51.
[1] Striking servant with scabbard (1631).

The main developments in the later sixteenth and early seventeenth centuries appear to have been: (*a*) a sustained decline in the ratio of armed to unarmed and incompletely described offences down to

1629; (b) a complete cessation of armed offences after 1629 (or 1631); (c) an effective break with the tradition of endemic casual violence after 1640, only three offences being recorded over the next forty years. However, (d) even allowing for improved reporting towards the end of our period, the incidence of unarmed and unspecified offences appears to have risen during the sixty years before the Long Parliament; so that while the benchers evidently succeeded in eliminating the most serious form of violence, they were apparently unable to eradicate interpersonal violence altogether.

Together with the London apprentices and the undergraduate population of Oxford and Cambridge, the junior members of the inns were notorious for their violent behaviour outside the societies; William Harrison, writing in 1577, claimed that 'the younger sort of them abroad in the streets are scarce able to be bridled by any good order whatsoever'.[21] Clashes with groups of townspeople and noblemen's servants were commonplace throughout the sixteenth century, and the 1610s and '20s also saw an outbreak of assaults on officers of the courts making arrests at or near the societies and 'rescues' of their prisoners.[22] Acts of external violence were not usually recorded in the bench minutes and their frequency is thus even more difficult to establish than that of incidents within the societies. But the traditional propensity of the junior members for extramural violence seems to have waned perceptibly during the latter part of our period. The last major reported incidents were a Fleet Street riot involving 'souldiers, Templars and other innes of court men' in July 1629, which resulted in half a dozen deaths and the arrest of more than sixty participants, and an assault on a Star Chamber messenger some two months later by thirty Lincoln's Inn members. Both were investigated by the privy council at the king's command, and in September 1629 Lord Keeper Coventry and the judges were ordered to consult with the benchers about preventing the recurrence of such 'disorderly accidents . . . whereby the auncient and laudable government of the same societies hath bin much impugned and made contemptible'. While the sole apparent result of these deliberations was the reissue of the 1614 judges' orders, no further outbreaks of large-scale collective

---

[21] *Description of England*, 76.
[22] Harleian 980, f. 130; *BB*, i. 63, 135; *GIPB*, i. xxv–vi; *The Diary of Henry Machyn*, ed. J. G. Nichols (CS, 42, 1848), 65; Stone, *Aristocracy*, 232; W. H. Overall and H. C. Overall, *Analytical Index to the series of records known as the Remembrancia* . . . A.D. *1579–1664* (1878), i. 449; *APC, 1580–81*, 37; *Tudor Proclamations*, iii. 60; *St. Ch. Reps.*, 315; *The Court and Times of James the First: illustrated by authentic and confidential letters* . . ., comp. Thomas Birch, ed. R. F. Williams (1848), i. 167; W. Le Hardy, ed., *Middlesex Sessions Records, New Series* (1935–7), ii. 326, iii. 13, iv. 187, 192; *CSPD, 1611–18*, 514; *APC, 1613–14*, 26; *MTR*, ii. 529; PRO St. Ch. 8/13/16; D'Ewes, 'Secret Diary', 247; *The Court and Times of Charles the First* . . ., comp. Thomas Birch, ed. R. F. Williams (1848), i. 23–4; N. E. McLure, *The Letters of John Chamberlain* (Philadelphia, 1939), i. 347.

violence are known to have occurred either before or after the Civil War.[23]

The real significance of these developments is somewhat difficult to assess when we know so little about patterns of violence in society at large during this period. According to Stone, interpersonal violence of all kinds among the peerage showed an absolute decline between the late sixteenth and the early seventeenth centuries. At the inns the decline seems to have been qualitative rather than quantitative; while armed assaults and collective external violence virtually disappeared, the total incidence of interpersonal violence probably remained constant and may even have increased up to 1640. On the other hand the overall decline of violence after 1640 is perfectly clear, and the frequency of unarmed and unspecified assaults within the societies during the last three decades of our period may perhaps be regarded as an anomaly which modifies but does not contradict the overall trend.

The range of defiance

In 1663 Edward Waterhous, a perceptive if somewhat erratic social observer, published his annotated translation of Fortescue's *De Laudibus Legum Angliae*. Waterhous provided a particularly long gloss on the passage in which Fortescue depicts the inns as havens of peace and tranquillity where 'scarcely any turbulence, quarrels or disturbances ever occur'. This Waterhous interpreted as a specific assertion about the absence of conflict between the rulers of the societies and their subordinates.[24] Since Fortescue says nothing whatever about the form of the inns' government, it seems equally likely that he wished merely to contrast their peaceful communal life with the notorious brutality and rowdiness of medieval universities. Indeed he could hardly have shared Waterhous's preoccupation with clashes between the benchers and the junior members of the societies, for the simple reason that acts of collective resistance to the authority of the bench were virtually unknown before the early seventeenth century.

In 1533 a group of Inner Templars withdrew from commons 'and seyd that they wold sette uppe another house of court'; this was the same tactic used at Lincoln's Inn in 1555 to challenge an order against the wearing of beards. But these actions set no immediate precedent.

[23] Birch, *Charles I*, ii. 23-4; HMC, *12 Rep.*, App. 1. 389; A.R., *The Practice of Princes* (1630), 19; *CSPD, 1629-31*, 29, 34, 76; Overall, *Remembrancia*, 456; *APC, 1629-30*, 145. Cf. Max Beloff, *Public Order and Popular Disturbances 1660-1714* (1938), *passim*. The Temple riots against the lord mayor's pretended jurisdiction during Charles II's reign seem to have occurred inside the houses and with the full support of the bench: Williamson, *Temple*, 478-1, 527-8; *ITR*, iii. xix-xxiii, 66-7.
[24] *Fortescutus Illustratus*, 537.

The failure of the Lincoln's Inn barristers to dance at the Candlemas revels in 1610 was also an isolated event, and it is not clear whether their offence was deliberate or accidental.[25] However, a major rebellion over the enforcement of apparel regulations at the Middle Temple in 1617 inaugurated an era of collective defiance and disobedience which continued, with a break during the Civil War and Interregnum, until the end of the seventeenth century.

While hardly identical, these incidents, or at least those which occurred during our period, do display some broad similarities. Except at the Middle Temple, where groups of barristers staged protests against the compulsory observance of fast days in 1619 and the high rate of vacation commons in 1640, the participants were drawn almost exclusively from below the bar. This was so even at Gray's Inn in 1629 and Lincoln's Inn in 1635, where a barrister's suspension from commons provided the immediate precipitant of rebellion. The predominance of the junior members is reflected by the immediate issues at stake; the right to wear hats at the Middle Temple in 1617, the right to hold Christmas commons with gaming at the two Temples during the 1630s, the punishment of individual members at Gray's Inn in 1629 and 1638, at the Middle Temple in 1631 and at Lincoln's Inn in 1635. Academic and professional grievances were not raised at all and straightforward economic issues played a very minor part. Unfortunately, we cannot tell what proportion of the total resident population under the bar took an active part in these disturbances, since except in two instances only the names of a few ringleaders are known.

Most outbreaks of student rebellion were touched off by the benchers' rejection of appeals for the redress of some specific grievance. Thus in Trinity term 1617, four Middle Temple students petitioned the bench for permission to wear hats in hall; when their request was formally and predictably denied, the four nevertheless continued to appear in hall and the Temple Church with hats. John Dowle, the 'cheefe stirrer of mutiny', had meanwhile gathered 'a catalogue or scrowle of names of divers other gentlemen of the house that have with him resolved to continue the wearing of hats and boots and spurres both in the Temple Church and the Temple Hall'. This list was presented to the governing body when Dowle and his three confederates were called up to explain themselves; they appeared before the bench still wearing hats and stated that, with their supporters, they had determined to stay out of commons until the benchers granted their request. The latter responded by expelling the four spokesmen and ordering another forty-six members who 'because they could not be suffered to weare their hats in the Temple hall . . . putt themselves out of commons and dyett themselves som in their chambers and others at victualing howses in the towne', to submit within the first week of Michaelmas term or

25 *ITR*, i. 102–3; *BB*, i. 275–6, 312, ii. 131.

lose their chambers. At the same time the barristers of the house were warned neither to wear hats in the public buildings of the society themselves, nor to permit students to do so during vacations in the absence of the bench.[26] This uncompromising reaction seems only to have strengthened the rebels' cause, for three weeks later a petition of grievances 'exhibited on the behalf of the gentlemen of the Middle Temple whereof they desire reformacon for the societie' was signed by sixty members.[27]

Although the original document survives in the Middle Temple archives, this petition was evidently intended for presentation not to the bench, but to some external authority, perhaps the judges. Only one of its six articles deals directly with the original issue; this complains that the benchers had unfairly rejected two previous petitions for 'the lybertie of hatts, which ys no more than hath bene thought reasonable by the governours of other societies' (an unlikely but not impossible claim), and then, 'without any contempt comytted against them', discommoned all the petitioners. The second asserts that the benchers have subverted the ancient 'glorye of this societie' by admitting attorneys to membership; the third attacks the admission of the benchers' 'owne livery servants' on the same grounds; the fourth laments at great length the lack of encouragement given to 'exercises and disports of gentlemen wherewith the courts of our former princes have not disdayned to be entertayned', asserting that while in the past those who 'bestowed their charges in these exercises to the honour of the howse' were 'crowned with the garlands of the profession by being called to the barre as well as the most serious students', now 'others both to the dishonour of the house and contempte of the profession being advanced to that degree, they are onely remembered by waye of penaltye, yf they doe butt weare a hatt, boots or a yellow band, habits in other societies esteemed indifferent'; the fifth accuses the benchers of permitting servants to buy and sell their places; and the sixth complains that despite great increases in the rate charged for commons, the benchers still allow no more than 2s. 6d. each for their clerks in commons 'and burden the gentlemen with the rest, whereby commons growe to so high a rate that gentlemen find it better chepe to lyve out of commons'.

The fate of this petition is unknown and it is not clear how the dispute which engendered it was resolved. But some compromise must have been reached, for two years later students were evidently wearing hats in hall during the mean vacation before Trinity term. On this occasion a message was sent commanding the barristers in commons to warn students that the benchers intended to return and they were therefore to change back into caps. The barristers twice refused to pass

---

[26] MT MS, Minutes C, ff. 116v–117; *MTR*, ii. 615–17.
[27] MT MS, unclassified 'Articles exhibited on the behalf of the gentlemen . . .'.

on the warning and were accordingly fined £2 each for 'contempt'.[28] Their non-cooperation was probably motivated as much by resentment at interference with the customary delegated right of the bar to rule the house when no benchers were present, as by sympathy with the sartorial aspirations of the students.

Later the same year nine barristers were put out of commons for ordering flesh to be served in hall on St Matthew's Eve, 20 September, at the end of the summer vacation, which was supposed to be kept as a fasting night. This sounds like a typically puritan act, and there can be little doubt that John Puleston, one of the two 'principal commanders' had well-developed puritan sympathies. But his confederate Robert Ashley is less easily categorised; best known as the putative founder of the Middle Temple library and a translator from the French, Italian and Spanish, Ashley's career reveals no marked religious interests or tendency of any kind.[29]

Two separate accounts exist of the 1635 rebellion at Lincoln's Inn, one in the benchers' minutes and another in the diary of the student John Greene, a bencher's son.[30] The immediate background to the uprising was the discommoning of Edward Heron, a barrister, for assaulting the porter and giving 'some ill words to the bench'. This was on Thursday 11 June, and according to Greene the next day was 'pretty quiet'. But on Saturday,

> all the gentlemen almost, very few excepted, only benchers' sons and barristers, went up to the benchers [at dinner in hall] . . . to have them put Mr Heron, barrister, in commons . . . The bench took time and Coe, Garland and some more of the chiefs were warned to come to the councell at night. At night when the councell was sitting Mr Scroope and three others went up which were not warned. Mr Scroope had a great hand in the business and spoke much at the councell, but the councell differed it a little longer. That night after councell, the bench table was broke and the benches by some, but they were mended by Sunday dinner.

The benchers' own account, while mainly concerned to condemn the outrage, tallies very closely; it puts the number going up to plead for Heron's readmission as '20 at least' and states that they had previously 'confederated themselves' to come up together, 'upon the breakinge of a pott'. The confrontation at the council meeting is more fully described; besides the students who had been specifically ordered to appear, 'divers of those who were not warned did presse in, and then alsoe (as they had before done in the hall) did with great earnestness in a very bould manner, urge and retain the councell to restore Mr Heron'. When the benchers replied that they would 'take time to con-

28 *MTR*, ii. 637–8.
29 *MTR*, ii. 640–1; *DWB*, s.v. Puleston; Robert Ashley, *Of Honour*, ed. V. B. Heltzel (San Marino, 1947), 1–17; Sloane 2131, ff. 16–20.
30 Green, 'Diary', 387; *BB*, ii. 327–9.

sider thereof', the students continued to press their case, until the council adjourned and the benchers left the room.

Shortly after which time there ensued a notorious misdemeanour comitted in the hall, by breaking the bench table, tressels and formes, and by removing parte of the benche itself from the wall, and in tearing the lyneings from the bench and the formes.

At this the judges intervened, led by Sir John Bramston, chief justice of the King's Bench; Heron, Coe, Garland and Scroope were summoned to Serjeant's Inn and committed to the King's Bench prison, while the benchers expelled six more.

The Gray's Inn episodes of 1629 and 1639 are less well documented; the first is known solely through a passing reference in a contemporary letter, while the only surviving account of the second comes from the benchers' minutes.[31] In June 1629 Sir George Gresley told his correspondent Sir Thomas Puckering of an incident in the Court of Chancery, after Sir John Finch, a bencher and former treasurer of Gray's Inn, had requested that a previously enrolled order be amended; when this was refused, Finch announced his intention of complaining to the king. Sir John Salter, a master in chancery, retorted that Finch had better make haste, before Salter himself told the king of his 'insolent carriage towards a court of justice':

Whereupon some of Gray's Inn, being by, cried out 'Degrade, degrade', by reason that by his persuasion a barrister of Gray's Inn was fairly put out of commons; and so the gentlemen of the house are in a rebellion and invite this barrister to dinner and supper every day, as their guest, to one mess or another.

The incident ten years later was also occasioned by a suspension from commons, this time of six students who had not paid their commons debts; the usual punishment for a very frequent offence. In response, 'divers gentlemen . . . in a factious and mutinous manner put themselves out of commons without paying their dues'. At the same time, or perhaps a few days later – the record is not clear – 'a great number of gentlemen' came into the hall in cloaks, armed with swords, and held a 'cupboard' (normally an informal meeting of the bench at the table below the high table), 'affrontinge the orders and government of that society and the readers of the same'. On hearing of this 'outrageous insollencie and miscarriage' the king himself, out of 'his princely care for the well ordering and government of that and the rest of the houses of court', commanded the judges that 'an exemplary course be held for punishing and correcting the said abuses and insolencyes'. On 25 November three of the mutineers were sent to the

31 Birch, *Charles I*, i. 22; GI MS, Order Book, f. 420; *GIPB*, i. 337–8. There may be allusions to the 1629 stirs in a privy council letter to Coventry, quoted in part above (p. 99) and in Finch's farewell speech of 1633; *APC, 1629–30*, 145; Sloane 1455, f. 10v.

Fleet, while all those who had put themselves out of commons were ordered to return and seek the benchers' pardon, on pain of losing their chambers and undergoing 'such other punishment beyond the censures of the house as we [the judges] shall find agreeable to the lawes of the realme'.

The most serious and sustained challenge to the authority of the bench came with a series of conflicts about Christmas commons at the two Temples during the 1630s. Christmas celebrations at the inns had once purported to combine instruction and recreation. Henry VIII's commissioners reported that at a 'solemn' Christmas certain members would be appointed as officers,

> which officers for the most part are such as are exercised in the king's highness house and other noble men, and this is done onely to the intent that they should in time come to know how to use themselves . . . they have all manner of pastimes, as singing and dancing, and in some of the houses ordinarily they have some inter- lude or tragedy played.

The importance of the educational element was underlined by the obligation of members under two years standing to be in commons during the three weeks of Christmas, as they were supposed to be dur- ing the two learning vacations.[32] But all this had changed by the early seventeenth century. Christmas was no longer a compulsory vaca- tion;[33] the officers for Christmas were elected by the students who stayed in commons, not appointed by the bench; the traditional dances had grown unpopular with the young gentlemen; and while a lieuten- ant or prince was still chosen to preside over the proceedings, the main activity, expressly sanctioned by the judges in 1614, was gaming at cards and dice.

The new style of Christmas was not much welcomed by the benchers. Gaming inevitably attracted 'unworthy persons', despite orders for- bidding the admission of all strangers except 'of good sorte and fashion'. Moreover, as a Middle Temple bencher complained, 'suche sports are in base use in common innes and alehouses, and are not fitt for theire [members'] nourishinge and embracinge, being noble, ver- tuous and noblie descended, for . . . it brings a scandall to the place'.[34]

---

[32] *DBC*, 546; *BB*, i. 1; *ITR*, i. 232, 262; *MTR*, i. 239; *OJ*, 194.

[33] Gray's Inn had no vacation requirements for junior members and there is no indication that Christmas was kept as a compulsory vacation at the Inner Temple during our period: cf. *ITR*, ii. 27–8. Christmas seems to have ceased being kept as a compulsory vacation at Lincoln's Inn late in James I's reign, the last fines being levied in 1619: LI MS, Black Book VII, f. 30; the Middle Temple abolished compulsory Christmas vacations in 1607, then reintroduced them, probably as a disciplinary measure, in 1637, but no action was taken against those who forfeited their vacations and the order seems to have lapsed: *MTR*, ii. 478, 831.

[34] MT MS, Minutes B, ff. 82, 266; *ITR*, ii. 33, 173; Brerewood, 81; cf. *Cal. Wynn Papers*, 207; J. A. Manning, *Memoirs of Sir Benjamin Rudyerd* (1841), 13; *The Diary of Samuel Pepys*, ed. H. B. Wheatley (1904), vii. 245–6.

There were also moral and religious objections to the gaming, the drinking of healths, the unrestrained use of tobacco and the general 'excess' of diet and entertainment which characterised what Prynne termed 'disorderly, bacchanalian Grand Christmasses'. Simonds D'Ewes professed to be deeply shocked when he came into commons at the Middle Temple on New Year's day 1623 and found 'a lieutenant chosen and all manner of gaming and vanity practised, as if the church had not at all groaned under those heavy desolations which it did'.[35] Benchers who did not necessarily share his religious outlook found equal cause for concern in the depredations of lords of misrule and the accumulation of unpaid bills for food and wine consumed by Christmas commoners.[36]

In November 1630 the benchers of Lincoln's Inn and the two Temples ordered that, owing to an outbreak of plague, commons were not to continue after the end of Michaelmas term or over the Christmas period.[37] While fear of the plague was almost certainly the main reason for this decision – the Autumn readings had been cancelled for the same cause – by now the benchers may well have been glad of any excuse to put off Christmas commons. At the Middle Temple however, these orders were disobeyed by a number of students and barristers, who stayed in commons after term had ended and committed the steward to the stocks when he refused to serve them. They also set up a parliament of their own, with a minute book and a clerk to keep it; this was common practice at the Inner Temple, but a complete innovation at the sister house – or so the benchers claimed.[38]

At the first parliament of Hilary term 1631 the ringleaders were fined and put out of commons; the students then came up to the bench table in hall to protest this sentence, and on being rebuffed 'hasted down tumultously, and calling for pots threw them at random towards the bench table and struck divers masters'. The benchers immediately informed Sir Nicholas Hyde (the chief justice and a former Middle Templar), of this 'notorious outrage, the like whereof had not formerly bin knowne in anye other inn of court'. Hyde put two barristers in the King's Bench prison and bound two students over to good behaviour; the benchers wanted to expel all four, but they were

---

[35] William Prynne, *Histrio-Mastix* (1633), sig. i; D'Ewes, *Autobiography*, i. 233, but cf. his 'Secret Diary', 103–9, where it appears that D'Ewes was actually elected lieutenant himself and prevented from serving only by his father's refusal to bear the cost.

[36] Cf. MT MS, Minutes B, f. 220; *MTR*, ii. 856–7, 880; *ITR*, ii. 167, 187, 195, 203, 223–4.

[37] *BB*, ii. 299; *ITR*, ii. 177; *MTR*, ii. 770.

[38] Cf. IT MS, Christmas Account Book 1614–1682, ff. 32, 61. However in his 'Annals' Bulstrode Whitelocke recounts his speech at a Middle Temple Christmas parliament in 1629, where the 'proceedings were as much as they can [*sic*] in imitation of the House of Commons . . .': Additional 53726, f. 46.

eventually received back in the house. Nevertheless their parliament book was consigned to the fire, and it was declared that in future any person claiming authority in the house, other than as a delegate of the bench, would be automatically expelled. The benchers clearly saw the whole incident as a direct challenge to their authority, 'incroached upon by some younger gentlemen . . . to the disturbance of government and increase and maintenance of disorder under pretence of liberty at this time'.[39] A new schedule of regulations for Christmas commons, drawn up in November 1631, provided that the house was to be in charge of the utter-barristers, if any were in commons, or else the eight most senior members under the bar. Commons were to last no longer than three weeks; there was to be no gambling during divine service, no healths drunk in hall, and none but men of quality admitted to the gaming. But neither these, nor the similar regulations promulgated simultaneously at the Inner Temple were obeyed.[40]

At the Middle Temple a Christmas parliament of juniors met once again and decided 'in special cases to drinke healthes in hall with loude musicke'. Once more two utter-barristers and two members below the bar were singled out as ringleaders and suspended from commons. Exactly what happened at the Inner Temple is unclear, but when the benchers returned to commons in January 1632 a committee was set up to investigate the 'great disorders' over Christmas. Fear of further insubordination led the Middle Temple bench to cancel Christmas commons for 1632 and keep the hall locked up throughout the Christmas period; these precautions were effective and no more serious trouble was encountered at the Middle house until the end of the decade.[41]

But at the Inner there were 'great and insufferable misdemeanours' during the Christmas of 1633, and despite the cancellation of commons for the Christmas of 1634 a number of junior members, 'having associated with them divers persons, as well strangers as others that were discontinuers or formerly expelled', broke into the hall and kept commons for five weeks, two more than the maximum even when commons were permitted. Henry Chomley and William Hare, students of six and eight years standing respectively, were expelled and two others discommoned and fined. After this episode matters rested in uneasy peace for five years, while attempts were made to negotiate a *modus vivendi* with the students.[42]

The benchers were in an awkward position; they claimed no desire to abolish Christmas commons altogether, but their attempts to keep some measure of control over the situation were hampered by the divided loyalties of the servants and the fact that the gamesters could

[39] MT MS, Minutes B, ff. 56, 60; *MTR*, ii. 771, 773–4.
[40] MT MS, Minutes B, ff. 81–2; *MTR*, ii. 787–8; *ITR*, ii. 193.
[41] MT MS, Minutes B, ff. 86–7; *MTR*, ii. 791, 802; *ITR*, ii. 195.
[42] *Ibid.*, ii. 213, 219–21, 225, 232.

count on a measure of covert backing from the court. An Inner Temple bencher grumbled in 1634 of

> the offence of the two puisne butlers . . . in serving at Christmas commons the last Christmas, contrary to command, order and act of the bench. And though afterwards thought fit to pass over that matter of the Christmas so kept by the gentlemen in silence, by reason of some intimations from court, & other respects, yet the fault of the officers herein not to be forgotten.[43]

No explicit condemnation of Christmas disorders was elicited from the crown, the privy council or the judges until the very end of our period; the 1614 judges' orders noted that 'disorders in the Christmas time may both infect the minds and prejudice the estates' of gentlemen students, but then went on to permit gaming, although it was only three years since the last bench order against dicing and card play at Christmas had been issued. Moreover, although the 1630 orders otherwise largely duplicated those of 1614, they contained no reference to gaming or Christmas commons. In 1633 Charles I strongly condemned 'excesse of entertainment' during the Lent readings, but the excess of Christmas commons entirely escaped official disapproval.[44]

So it is no wonder that further trouble was encountered before the Civil War brought the life of the inns to a standstill. In 1638 'base, lewde and unworthie people' were admitted to the gaming at the Middle Temple, which ran on two weeks longer than permitted in the 1631 regulations (reissued in 1637), despite the intervention of the treasurer, William Conyers, and another bencher. At the first parliament of the new year one barrister was expelled, a student discommoned, the steward dismissed for supplying the revellers with provisions and a butler fined twenty nobles for his co-operation with the delinquents.[45] In November 1639 the benchers decided to lock up the hall and forbid commons altogether. Again their orders were flouted, for 'divers gentlemen of this societie with their swords drawne in a contemptuous and riotous manner assembled themselves and did by violence breake open the dores of the hall, butterie and kitchin and did sett up comons and playe'. A juniors' parliament also met, and commons continued until Chief Justice Sir John Bramston (another former bencher of the society) intervened on the king's command, calling the ringleaders before him and ordering them to break up immediately. Eleven chief offenders were fined and discommoned, while the kitchen servants who had assisted them were also punished.[46]

The climax at the Inner Temple also came in 1639. Debts incurred for Christmas commons had been mounting steadily since 1635 and conferences with the young gentlemen had apparently been quite un-

43 IT MS, Miscellanea 31, p. 50.
44 *OJ*, 318, 320–1; *MTR*, ii. 533; *BB*, ii. 308.
45 MT MS, Minutes B, f. 206; *MTR*, ii. 876–7.
46 MT MS, Minutes B, f. 221; *MTR*, ii. 887–8.

productive. So on 24 November 1639 the benchers decided to ban Christmas commons for that year, stating as their justification that in the past commons had continued beyond the permitted three weeks, and

> also for the manner thereof hath been extremely contrary to the ancient orders and good government of this house, to the great offence of Almighty God, the dishonour and scandall of this society, the most dangerous infection and corruption of the civill company and the members thereof, and the manifest prejudice to the house in divers respects, tending to the ruin and subversion thereof if it not be timely prevented.

In reply, the young gentlemen got together a petition to the privy council, which asserted that

> the government of our society consisteth of three parts, viz. masters of the bench, masters of the bar and gentlemen under the barre. That our government and all our priviledges are grounded onely upon ancient custome which wee conceave to be a law, and by that custome the benchers have usually governed in the terme tyme, the barristers in the vacation and the gentlemen in the Christmas.

They further claimed that the benchers had acknowledged their rights on previous occasions and therefore asked the council to intervene in order that Christmas commons might be held as usual.[47]

This petition was, not surprisingly, unsuccessful; no formal reply from the council is preserved, but the king, 'having taken speciall notice of the many disorders and outrages committed in the innes of court and the insufferable contempts there against government . . . did give direct command that there should be a present forbearing of commons and play in both the Temples'. Charles also ordered that the chief dissidents and mutineers should be punished in the Star Chamber and Christmas commons suspended until the benchers had devised effective means of control.[48] This long-delayed intervention was completely successful and the problem of Christmas commons did not recur until after the Restoration.

Authority and revolt

The incidents discussed above were neither mere rags, nor outbreaks of random disorder. In every case the rulers of the inns were confronted

[47] *ITR*, ii. 254; IT MS, Petyt, Letters to treasurers and benchers, 75; SP 16/441/46.
[48] SP 16/205/9: draft, copy, no signature, n.d., contemporary endorsement, 'Reference for the innes of court prohibiting the use of several unlawful recreations'. The catalogue dating '1629?' is followed by a reference to W. Herbert, *Antiquities of the Inns of Court and Chancery* (1804), 201, evidently on the assumption that the document relates to the 1629 disorders discussed above (p. 99). However, since Christmas commons were held as usual at the two Temples in 1629, this seems impossible and the only other feasible date is 1639.

with deliberate resistance directed towards concrete ends, frequently in a form which explicitly challenged their supremacy. The young gentlemen of the Middle Temple held parliaments which passed orders directly contradicting legislation enacted by the governing body. Christmas parliaments were tolerated by the Inner Temple benchers, but the students there went a step further in claiming an absolute right of self-government over the Christmas period. In 1639 the gentlemen of Gray's Inn set up a cupboard to debate their grievances; and at Lincoln's Inn the verbal and physical protests of the junior members in 1635 were held by the judges to tend to 'the distruction of the government of the inns of court'. No doubt these fears were exaggerated; commenting on a Middle Temple rebellion after the Restoration, Roger North claimed that at such times 'the ill-bred, sour part of the bench will be as ridiculously in earnest, and like state politicians, argue for their own government'.[49] This sounds like an early description of the Grayson Kirk syndrome; [50] but in pre-Civil War England, as any other society obsessed with the maintenance of the established order, even the most tentative defiance of authority could not be lightly disregarded.

Yet while the bench may have feared insurrection, the junior members showed no desire to overturn the existing constitutional structure. The Inner Temple petition of 1639 made the radical assertion (cast as an appeal to 'ancient custome'), that bench, bar and students each had full powers of governance during term, vacation and Christmas respectively; but there is no indication that the petitioners appreciated the full implications of their claim, which could well have derived from a genuine misunderstanding of previous practice, or that they wished to exploit it for purposes beyond their immediate ends. It is instructive to compare this document with another petition drawn up by a committee of grievances at the Middle Temple in 1694.[51] The latter is a comprehensive indictment of abuses in the government of the society, many of which might equally well have been attacked before the Civil War: for example, calls of unqualified men to the bar by favour of the bench, the benchers' 'extravagant eating and drinking' subsidised by the rest of the society, their hypocrisy in compelling attendance in commons when there was 'sometimes but two, sometimes one, sometimes nere a bencher in the hall'. But its theoretical basis is quite different; while sharing the same premiss as the 1639 petition (that the inns of court are voluntary societies), it goes on to argue, in a Lockean manner, that orders of the bench were therefore 'enlicensed and en-

[49] *Lives of the Norths*, iii. 47–9.
[50] 'Kirk told Paterson that Columbia had to stand firm as an example to other schools. . . . Each side viewed the university as a miniature version of full-scale national revolution': Jerry Avorn *et al., Up Against the Ivy Wall* (New York, 1969), 72.
[51] MT MS, unclassified, 'Resolution of the Committee for Grievances', 1694; cf. *MTR*, iii. 1431.

spirited by the general concurrence, submission and consent of the society'. Without the benefit of such ideological underpinning, the Inner Templars fifty years before could only protest that their society was a kind of balanced polity, each part of which had a limited share in the power of government, rather as the parliamentary opposition to the early Stuarts envisaged an ideal constitution where King, Lords and Commons worked in harmony together.

Student militancy at the inns of court in the early seventeenth century was quite possibly as complicated a phenomenon as student militancy in America and Europe today. Yet the events discussed above seem to have had no overt political content and to have been entirely isolated episodes, without parallel at Oxford or Cambridge for example. The historian's task is further simplified by the sparseness of the surviving evidence; so little can be discovered about participants or precipitants that attention must be concentrated on long-term causes, even at the risk of exaggerating their relative importance.

By the middle of our period the 'mutual consent and . . . order of common understanding', which Edward Waterhous regarded as fundamental to the very existence of the inns, was clearly under considerable strain.[52] The rapid growth of the societies during the second half of the sixteenth century must have tended to depersonalise relations between their junior and senior members. Although the Elizabethan and early Stuart inns of court are often depicted as 'collegiate' institutions, the cohesiveness of their corporate life is easily exaggerated and insufficient attention paid to the high incidence of non-residence, the widespread habit of eating out of commons and the use of the societies as casual lodgings by 'knights and gentlemen, forrainers and discontinuers'. The colleges of Oxford and Cambridge still effectively dominated their provincial settings, while the inns were only part of a large metropolitan complex. They demanded very little of their members, whose behaviour and life styles were moulded largely by the outside world rather than the societies themselves.[53] It seems likely that there was a marked increase in the proportion of 'amateur' to 'professional' entrants after the mid-sixteenth century and that the former tended to coalesce into a distinct subgroup, following their own pursuits with little interference or supervision from the governing bodies.

The consolidation of the benchers' authority within the houses was, as we have seen, a long-drawn out process. Their internal supremacy had probably been substantially achieved before the end of the fifteenth century, but they were still gathering in some minor prerogatives over a hundred years later. As the powers of government accumulated in their hands, the benchers set themselves apart from

[52] *Fortescutus Illustratus*, 526.
[53] Cf. Sheldon Rothblatt, *The Revolution of the Dons* (1968), 183–4, 187–9, ch. 7, *passim*.

their subordinates behind a screen of self-appointed privileges and exemptions,[54] while attempting to bolster up their authority over a much larger body of junior members by imposing apparel regulations and undertaking a concerted drive against casual violence. That the most serious outbreaks of rebellion occurred in reaction to the enforcement of dress rules and efforts to regulate the disorders of Christmas commons is hardly coincidental; but there are also some hints of a general decline in respect for the status and authority of the bench during the early seventeenth century.[55] It has recently been suggested that Stuart Englishmen envisaged all relations of inferior to superior in terms of a patriarchal model founded on the Fifth Commandment.[56] Within a school or college, the master or tutor might well play the role of father to his students, but at the inns there were too many 'fathers' and insufficient personal supervision of the 'sons' for such a concept to work to the benchers' advantage. The Middle Temple petition of 1617 could easily be read as a filial denunciation of the benchers' failure to fulfil their paternal duties to the society.

The outbreaks of protest and rebellion at the inns between 1617 and 1640 were therefore closely related to some of the institutional changes examined in previous chapters. But besides the internal conflicts and tensions there was an important external factor. An age gap between rulers and ruled could hardly be avoided; indeed the fact that Middle Temple benchers were slightly older than their colleagues elsewhere may help to explain why this society experienced more frequent and serious student disorders than any other house.[57] Yet the age differential was nothing new; the more important differences were those of attitude and outlook. The young men who came up to the inns during the 1620s and '30s were from the generation born and brought up after James I's accession, whose representatives in the Long Parliament showed as decided a preference for the royalist side as their seniors displayed for his parliamentary opponents. The reasons are not entirely clear, but would seem to stem from a basic ideological change around the middle of James I's reign, a general reaction against the whole scheme of values associated with Elizabethan Calvinism, manifested no less at the inns by the new-style Christmas, with its gaming and drinking, than at the universities by the rise of Arminianism and neo-scholasticism.[58]

The divergent attitudes of benchers and students towards masques and revels would seem to be another aspect of the same generational

---

54 See above, p. 84.

55 Cf. Manningham, 'Diary', 36; *OJ*, 318, 321; IT MS, Miscellanea, 31, p. 37.

56 G. J. Schochet, 'Patriarchalism, politics and mass attitudes in Stuart England', *Historical Journal*, 12 (1969), 413–41.

57 The median ages of benchers at call between 1590 and 1639 were: GI–44 years; IT–43.5 years; LI–44 years; MT–47 years. (Calculated from those whose birth dates are known, between 35–45 per cent of the total).

58 Cf. Kearney, *Scholars and Gentlemen*, 169–70.

gulf. Except in 1613 and 1634 the masques presented at the early Stuart inns were financed and organised solely by the members below the bar; hence the complaint of the Middle Templars in 1617 that 'these exercises to the honour of this howse' received no support from the masters of the bench. Yet in 1631 we find the Middle Temple benchers complaining that Christmas 'was wont to be employed in more praise-worthy purposes, as revels, barriers, arraignments, and other manly and ingenious exercises'. Their notion of suitable forms of recreation evidently excluded not only gaming, but also the mixed French and country dances which had become popular since Charles I's accession.[59] The students still elected masters of revels and continued to learn and practise dancing,[60] but the formal 'grave measures' danced around the hall by men alone, which constituted the traditional revels, seem to have lost favour and were soon to disappear altogether. Hence the complaint of an anonymous Middle Temple bencher that 'the measures were wont to be trulie danced, it being accounted a shame for any inns of court man not to have learned to dance, especially the measures. But nowe their dancing is tourned into bare walking'. Worse yet, 'the yonger gentlemen, ignorant of the auncient and usuall formes', showed no qualms about entertaining ladies at their festivities.[61]

Finally, it may be that the declining level of violence and the rise of protest and rebellion in the early seventeenth century were linked causally as well as chronologically. Stone's peers sublimated their violent drives in litigation and the pursuit of electoral influence. Junior members of the inns may have transferred their aggressive energies from acts of expressive, interpersonal violence to acts of instrumental, collective opposition, whereby implicit resistance to authority became conscious and articulate. Such a transition could be regarded as analo-gous to the gradual development of political consciousness among the landed classes in the later sixteenth and early seventeenth centuries. But resistance to the benchers' government before 1640 cannot be cor-related precisely, either in terms of issues or personnel, with resist-ance to the king's government after 1640. The benchers may have acted as agents of the central authorities in the drive against casual violence and disorderly dress, yet their efforts to regulate Christ-mas commons were hindered rather than helped by the court. It is interesting to note that among the known participants in the pre-Civil

[59] Cf. *Table Talk of John Selden*, ed. Frederick Pollock (1927), 64.
[60] See below, pp. 154, 163. Dancing lessons remained a standard 'extra' for junior members as late as the 1720s, although professional law students may have felt little need for them: cf. *Lives of the Norths*, i. 19; Edward Hughes, *North Country Life in the Eighteenth Century* (1952), 82. The author of the Brerewood MS grumbled that even 'Post-revels, performed by the better sort of young gentle-men . . . with galliards, corantoes and other dances . . . have been disused, here and at the other innes of court, to the great impairement of theire honor and reputation': Brerewood, 16.
[61] *BB*, ii. 291, iii. 137; *GIPB*, ii. xviii; MT MS, Minutes B, ff. 60, 87; Brerewood, 15.

War disturbances at the inns were no less than three future regicides, as well as a parliamentarian judge and a recruiter M.P.;[62] they also included the royalist officer Sir Adrian Scroope and the royalist governor of Holt castle in Denbighshire, Richard Lloyd.[63] This is hardly surprising, for it would obviously be absurd to portray the inns of court revolts as so many dress rehearsals for the Great Rebellion. On the other hand, it does not seem entirely fanciful to class them among both the causes and effects of that 'de-legitimation' of established authority which helped make revolution possible.

[62] Augustine Garland, Nicholas Love (both LI); William Saye (MT), John Puleston (MT), John Pickering (GI), Nicholas Lechmere (MT). Sources: *Al. Ox.*; *Al. Cant.*; *DNB*; *DWB*.

[63] Sources as above.

VI

Learning
the Law

The inns of court are frequently described as 'the third university' of Elizabethan and early Stuart England.[1] But although the inns displayed certain characteristics of a university – enrolling students, providing instruction and granting a degree equivalent – we must not overlook their other activities or assume that they were educational institutions first and foremost.

Maitland described the medieval inns as 'associations of lawyers which had about them a good deal of the club, something of the college, something of the trade union'. In our period the societies were at once both more and less than a university. Even Coke merely claimed that the inns of court and chancery together constituted 'the most famous university, for the profession of law only, or any one humane science, that is in the world'.[2] Their formal academic activities were confined to the common law, barbarous by definition, lacking

---

[1] Its original source is probably Sir George Buc's *The Third Universitie* in Stow's *Annales*, ed. Howes (1615); Buc claimed that the inns alone would be sufficient to qualify the metropolis for this title: *ibid.*, 965. Harrison, Stow and Covell had earlier described the inns as a university, but only in a metaphorical sense, or with the qualification apparent even in Coke's famous boast (see n. 2 below): *Description of England*, 70; *Survey*, i. 76; W(illiam) C(ovell), *Polimanteia . . . Whereunto is added a letter from England to her three daughters, Cambridge, Oxford, Innes of Court . . .* (1595), sig. P2. Noy's assertion in 1632 that 'every inn of court is an university of itself' (Harleian 980, f. 81) was part of an elaborate demonstration (echoing *DLLA* ch. 50) that the ranks of barrister, bencher and reader were equivalent to the university degrees of bachelor, master and doctor. Cf. this professional chauvinism with a parent's reference in 1648 to 'what some call a third university, the inns of court': *Memorials of the Great Civil War*, ed. Henry Cary (1842), i. 384.

[2] *Selected Essays*, 125; *Le Tierce Part des Reportes . . .*, sig. Divv.

any respectable classical pedigree and hence rigidly excluded from the curricula of Oxford and Cambridge. On the other hand, 'those free and honourable innes (as they are called, colleges by their use)',[3] could introduce students to a far wider range of informal cultural and intellectual pursuits than the two universities, isolated in their provincial market towns, were able or willing to provide. Yet despite their collegiate pretensions, the educational functions of the inns were not an integral part of their original constitution and continued existence, but had rather accumulated over the years by a still obscure process of chance and circumstance. At the universities learning and teaching were from the very beginning, in theory and to a large extent in practice, essential and paramount concerns. The importance of this distinction will become more apparent in the course of the following chapter.

Methods of aural instruction

Students at the inns acquired their law in various ways, for only one of which the societies took any formal responsibility. This system of aural instruction was similar to and doubtless modelled on the scholastic exercises of the medieval universities. As much method as metaphysic, scholasticism did not disappear from Oxford and Cambridge at the end of the middle ages; the formal teaching of both universities and inns continued to be grounded on disputatious aural exercises throughout the sixteenth and seventeenth centuries.[4]

As Hastings Rashdall observed, these exercises were a particularly effective way of training lawyers, since they tended to cultivate 'a dexterity in devising or meeting arguments and a readiness in applying acquired knowledge . . .'.[5] Being graded in complexity and difficulty, they also helped to define an internal membership hierarchy and provided the main formal mechanism for promotion from one rank to the next. The essence of the inns' exercises was the formulation and debate of a hypothetical case or set of circumstances involving one or more controversial questions of law; just as in disputation the university undergraduate maintained a thesis by argument from philosophical and theological authorities, so in 'case-putting', bolts and moots, the inns of court student sought to justify his interpretation of the law by citing the maxims, precedents and principles which were the authorities of his craft. The university declamation, a rhetorical setpiece designed to test the student's fluency and familiarity with classical authors, was roughly equivalent to the memorisation and recitation of pleadings drawn up to the cases argued in moots. The most ad-

[3] Joseph Hall, *The Works . . .* (1625), 671.
[4] W. T. Costello, *The Scholastic Curriculum at Early Seventeenth-Century Cambridge* (Cambridge, Mass., 1958), *passim*.
[5] Rashdall, *Universities of Europe in the Middle Ages*, i. 25n.

vanced exercise at the inns was the reading, which corresponded more or less to the university lecture; readings were essentially devoted to the exposition of a statute or part of a statute, but also provided the opportunity for a good deal of case argument.[6] The form of the individual exercises, especially the number and rank of participants and the sequence of their performance over the course of the academic year, varied considerably from one inn to the next.[7] However there were three main types – simple case arguments, moots and readings. The most elementary exercise – 'case-putting' or 'keeping the case' – was open to every member, regardless of rank or seniority. At the Middle Temple cases were argued every weekday during term, after the midday meal in hall:

> One of the benchers . . . puts a short case, consisting of two or three difficult questions in the law, of his own invention. The case being put from one mess to the other throughout the table, they divide themselves by three into a company that argues it.

The same procedure was followed down the hall by the utter-barristers and students, 'which kind of exercise doth both whet their wits and strengthen their memory'. Case-putting may not have been regarded as an official exercise at Gray's Inn, but it was the profession's distinctive mode of discourse, practised at all four societies in one form or another and even carried by lawyers into the House of Commons. Students and barristers were bound to discuss problems with their colleagues and to find, in Coke's words, that 'conference with others . . . is the life of studie'.[8]

Normally the first formal exercise in which students participated would be a moot, which was essentially a more elaborate case argument in the form of a mock trial, with two or three utter-barristers or benchers sitting as judges and two students or barristers acting as opposing counsel. There were various kinds of moot – petty and grand, chapel, house, term, hall and library – but while participants, place, time and standard of argument differed, the general principle was the same. The formulation of moot cases (except perhaps for grand moots at the inns of chancery during vacations),[9] was the joint responsibility of the two barristers or students who were to present them, and

---

[6] R. J. Schoeck, 'Rhetoric and law in sixteenth-century England', *Studies in Philology*, 50, (1953), 110–27; cf. the discussion of moots as 'a shadowe or figure of the auncient rhetoricke' in Sir Thomas Elyot, *The Boke named the Gouernour*, ed. H. H. Croft (1883), i. 148–9.

[7] Each house had its own detailed rules and traditions for the allocation of exercises in term and vacation: cf. *OJ*, 289–90; LI MS, Black Book VI, ff. 531–2; IT MS, Miscellanea 28, f. 3v.

[8] T. F. Plucknett, *Early English Legal Literature* (Cambridge, 1958), 80–90); *OJ*, 22; Neale, *Elizabethan House of Commons*, 20; Edward Coke, *The First Part of the Institutes of the Lawes of England* (1628), sig. qq².

[9] Gareth Jones, *History of the Law of Charity 1532–1827*, (Cambridge, 1969), 238; cf. D'Ewes, *Autobiography*, i. 218; *OJ*, 203.

this task seems to have been at least as demanding as the actual debate itself. After the Restoration several collections of ready made cases were published, 'to oblige the students of the law ... with quaeres and mootpoints for their exercises, the want thereof is so generally lamented', but only one such printed compendium was available during our period. Cases were supposed to contain at least one arguable point of law and those which did not could be overruled or 'failed' by the adjudicators.[10] So serious students undoubtedly took pains in drawing up their cases; Simonds D'Ewes, for example, spent more than a fortnight preparing the cases for his first house moot at the Middle Temple in 1622. Most cases recorded in students' notebooks and the printed compendia dealt with fairly complicated questions of real-property law. A typical example is this moot case, argued at the Middle Temple in Lent vacation 1612:

> [A man has] a bastard elder son and a younger daughter who is within age. The bastard dies having had issue. His father dies. The bastard's issue enters and grants a rent charge. The grantee distrains and has the return 'irreplevisable'. The bastard's issue dies, never having been interrupted in seisin. The daughter being within age, enters. The grantee of the rent charge distrains upon the daughter. The daughter makes a rescue and the grantee brings the assize.
>
> The points:
>
> 1. Whether the issue of the bastard, being in without interruption, shall bar the woman who is within age.
> 2. If such a judgement, that is to say when the grantee has the return 'irreplevisable', amounts to a seisin upon which the other can bring an assize.[11]

At the appointed time the two men who had prepared the case, with two students who were to recite the appropriate pleadings for and against the action concerned, took their seats on a bench facing the three adjudicators. The pleadings, which had also been drawn up by the two 'moot-men', were first recited from memory 'in homely law french';[12] then the first mootman rose as counsel for the plaintiff to address himself to the law-points at issue, which were agreed upon beforehand between the two disputants. Contemporary accounts give

[10] *Les Quaeres Del Mounsieur Plowden*, (n.d. [?1620]); John Clayton, *Topicks in the Laws of England* (1646); H.B., *Critica Juris Ingeniosa: or Choice Cases in the Common-Law* (1661); *idem, Plowdens Quaeries: Or, a Moot-Book of Choice Cases* ... (1662); William Hughes, *Hughes's Quaeries: or, Choice Cases for Moots* (1675); Anon, *Certain Select Moot-Cases Intituled, Les Cases de Greys-Inn* (1680). *OJ*, 106.

[11] D'Ewes, 'Secret Diary', 97–101. CUL MS, Dd. v. 14, f. 6. (I am indebted to Mr A. W. B. Simpson for help with this translation). For an inn of chancery case on mercantile law argued in 1647, see Lansdowne 1115, f. 1.

[12] Harvard Law School MS, 130 (Turner), unfoliated, contains the pleadings and defendant's speech from a New Inn moot written out fair in English, presumably before the exercise. *DBC*, 545; *OJ*, 314.

the impression that adjudication followed immediately after the main speeches for the plaintiff and defendant, but the notes taken at the Middle Temple moot cited above show at least nine other individuals besides the two mootmen advancing arguments, usually by citing year-book cases bearing on the disputed points. Finally the mooters presented the judges with a slice of bread and a mug of beer and the exercise was over.[13]

This is a composite account patched together from a variety of sources and takes no account of slight differences in the procedure at each house. The Inner Temple, for example, had a much more complicated and lengthy exercise known as the imparlance, which seems to have continued for the course of a full term, while members of Gray's and Lincoln's Inn took part in bolts, or moots without pleadings, at which 'the sufficiency of the matter in law of some case then putt is for the most part questioned onelie'.[14] However the essential element was always the formulation and elucidation of cases and the participation of junior and senior members, the former doing most of the argument, the latter adjudicating, explaining and commenting on their efforts.

Both contemporary and later writers tend to concentrate on the readings, which were the most ceremonious and sophisticated exercises, as well as being composed and delivered by recognisable individuals. But it must be remembered that the less glamorous case-argument exercises were the student's daily fare; readings were a twice-yearly luxury, and perhaps a somewhat indigestible one at that. While relatively few readings from our period have found their way into print, many original drafts and student summaries exist in manuscript. Surprisingly little use has been made of this unpublished material, although it provides much biographical information about leading members of the legal profession, as well as a potentially rich source of data on the evolution of legal doctrine.[15]

Professor Thorne has shown that in the early fifteenth century readers were expected to do little more than repeat the work of their predecessors. Readings consisted of standard short lectures which, over an eight- or ten-year period, covered a cycle of the most important 'old' statutes – that is, those enacted before Edward III :

> Since the reading thus remained substantially the same, it made little difference who the particular reader was. It was rather more important for a hearer to note the names and arguments of those

[13] *OJ*, 206–7; CUL MS, Dd. v. 14, ff. 6–7v.

[14] Bodl. MS, Rawlinson B. 374, ff. 50–2; IT MS, Barrington 78, ff. 13v–18; LI MS, Baildon transcript, p. 127; *GIPB*, i. 102.

[15] Cf. *HEL*, v. 497–9; C. H. Williams, 'Early Law Readings', *BIHR*, 3 (1925–6) 96–101; B. H. Putnam, *Early Treatises on the Practice of the Justices of the Peace in the Fifteenth and Sixteenth Centuries* (Oxford, 1924), chs. v–vi. R. G. Usher's study of sixteenth and early seventeenth-century readings, announced by Putnam, (*ibid.*, 168, p. 7), apparently never materialised.

who disagreed with the reading and any new points they might make . . . This pattern of substantial repetition had begun to disappear by the middle fifteenth century, though perhaps first only in lectures by second readers.[16]

By the mid-sixteenth century the situation was completely reversed. A reading was no longer one of a series of texts recited at regular intervals. It is true that some sixteenth and early seventeenth-century readings did acquire an authoritative status, circulated widely in manuscript, and occasionally came into print. John Denshall's Lincoln's Inn reading on 4 Hen. VII, c. 24, delivered in 1524, appears alongside summary reports of King's Bench cases from the early years of James I in the notebook of Eusebius Andrewes, who entered Lincoln's Inn in 1600, and died soon after his election to the bench in 1629; Denshall's reading was eventually published in 1662.[17] Robert Callis's reading on Henry VIII's Statute of Sewers, delivered at Gray's Inn in 1622, was published as the authoritative work on the subject in 1647, supplementing several manuscript copies authenticated by the author which were already in circulation.[18] Another highly regarded reading from our period, which did not however come to the press, was James Whitelocke's treatment of 21 Hen. VIII, c. 13 (plurality of benefices) at the Middle Temple in 1619.[19]

But the value of these readings depended on their ingenuity and lucidity as expositions of a statute or branch of law, rather than their place in a traditional canon. The reader was now free to choose whatever statute he wished as the basis for his reading, within the bounds of political discretion and his own capabilities. In general readers avoided legislation enacted in the current reign,[20] and few readings were delivered on pre-Tudor statutes, with the exception of Magna Carta, Merton and Westminster II; Westminster II was chosen by Francis Bacon for his double reading at Gray's Inn in 1601 and again

---

[16] Thorne, *Readings and Moots at the Inns of Court*, lxvii–lxviii.

[17] Harleian 3209 (Pt. 47a), ff. 2, 17, 19v; *Le Reading del Monsieur Denshall Sur l'Estatute de Finibus* . . . (1662). Other MS copies of Denshall's reading include Ellesmere 481a and Nottingham Univ. Library MS, Mellish XVI. 3, ff. 33–62.

[18] Robert Callis, *The Reading . . . upon the Statute of 23 Henry VIII cap. 5, of Sewers* . . . (1647). Cf. CUL MS, Dd. v. 3; Harvard Law School MS, 1053; Hargrave 91, ff. 1–163.

[19] Cf. Bodl. MS, Ashmole 1150; Harvard Law School MS, 1077; CUL MS, Ee. vi. 3, ff. 192–226v; LI MS, Law 14 (Cupboard I. i.); Hargrave 91, ff. 196–295v; Hargrave 237, ff. 5–95v; MT MS, Rare Book Room, 'James Whitelocke's Reading'. Cf. his son's boast that 'the professors of the law . . . so generally have commended and desired copying' these lectures: Additional 53726, ff. 8–8v.

[20] The only examples of readings delivered on a statute passed under the reigning monarch noted by the present writer are Thomas Wade's lectures on the Elizabethan Statute of Fraudulent Conveyances, given at Gray's Inn in 1590 and James Altham on 21 Eliz. I, c. 9, also at Gray's Inn in 1600: Hargrave 398, ff. 159–161v; *The Journal of Sir Roger Wilbraham*, ed. H. S. Scott, *CS Miscellany*, 10 (1902), 36.

by Richard Keble for his first reading at the same house in 1638.[21]

Readers by and large confined themselves to land law and the law of spiritual jurisdictions and persons; few lectures on penal statutes have been identified and none at all on the great constitutional legislation of the sixteenth century.[22] Since disputes about land inheritance and tenure were the main professional concern of common lawyers, this emphasis (which was common to the lesser case-argument exercises) is entirely understandable. Nor is it difficult to see why lawyers should have been disinclined to meddle with, say, the Elizabethan Acts of Supremacy and Uniformity. But readings were not necessarily devoid of political content. Any statute which related to the temporal jurisdiction of the Church provided an obvious vent for anticlerical polemic, while the Lincoln's Inn lectures of the royalist Robert Holbourne, delivered in Lent 1642, were issued by the printer to Oxford University as a contribution to the propaganda battle which accompanied the outbreak of the Civil War.[23]

A reader's academic duties commenced from the date of his election, which was normally at least six months before the reading took place; he was required to sit as an adjudicator at all term moots and vacation exercises until the week before he read. When an utter-barrister or bencher received less warning, usually because of the death or incapacity of one of his seniors next in line to read, he was sometimes offered special inducements to prepare the lectures in time.[24] During the week before his reading, the reader-to-be 'absented himself out of commons . . . in which time he seldome comes abroad, that his entrance may be with more state'. On the preceding Sunday he made his solemn first appearance at the church or chapel of his inn, attended by 'twelve or fourteen servants at the least in one livery', and taking precedence over all other members and strangers, as he would do until the reading concluded. Next morning, at 7 a.m. in summer and 8 a.m. in winter, the reader formally proceeded to the head of the hall and recited the oaths of supremacy and allegiance. His statute was then read out by the sub-lector, a gentleman of the house selected by the reader to carry his books. The reader then rose to deliver an

---

[21] Stowe 324, ff. 145–50; Bodl. MS, Rawlinson C. 207, ff. 184–5. For other examples see Prest, 'Some aspects of the inns of court', 197, n. 3.

[22] Eusebius Andrewes read on 5 Ed. VI, c. 16 (Sale of Offices); John Barkesdale on 21 Jac. I, c. 19 (Bankrupts); Aegremont Thynne on 13 Eliz. c. 8, (Usury): Additional 25231, ff. 60–68v; LI MS, Maynard 57, ff. 1–84; Hargrave 91, ff. 320–9. In 1662 William Prynne delivered a course of readings on the Petition of Right: Hargrave 96, ff. 31–55v.

[23] Robert Holbourne, *The Reading in Lincolnes-Inne . . . Feb. 28 1641 upon the Stat. of 25 E.3. cap. 2 being the Statute of Treasons* (Oxford, 1642); cf. the reader's speech of John Wilde at the Inner Temple in 1630 on 3 & 3 Ed. VI, c. 13: CUL MS, Dd. v. 8, ff. iv–x. For Edward Bagshaw's anti-clerical reading in 1640, see below, pp. 214–15.

[24] SP/16/257/51; *BB*, ii. 87; cf. National Register of Archives, Report 0615 (Lenthall MSS), 88; Hargrave 398, ff. 143, 151v.

introductory speech in English, which by tradition 'must first disparage himself'. This rhetorical set-piece usually included an acknowledgement of the reader's gratitude to his colleagues and patrons, as well as a digression on the financial and intellectual effort which his task entailed, 'too great', claimed Arthur Turner, reader at the Middle Temple in 1629, 'when I looke uppon mine owne wants and imbecillity'.[25]

Having tendered his devotions and excuses, the reader would then normally explain his choice of statute. John Barkesdale told his audience at Lincoln's Inn in 1627 that he had first hoped to read upon the Elizabethan act of 1585 concerning hue and cry, but found this too difficult and could make no better progress with 28 Hen. VIII, c. 11 (First Fruits); so finally 'considering this declining age, wherein trades and tradesmen so much decay, I betook myself to that of bankruptcy', the statute 21 Jac. I, c. 19. Readers often emphasised the importance and relevance of their statute for students and practitioners; thus George Browne claimed that no act was 'more generall or of larger extent or of greater use' than his statute, 2 & 3 Ed. VI, c. 8, while Edward Littleton said he had chosen 27 Ed. III, c. 17 because it was 'a law of continual and frequent use, with which he himself had often been concerned' and one which 'was rarely, if ever, mentioned in the printed books of the common law, although there are many excellent cases relevant to it in the records at the Tower, and elsewhere'.[26]

Finally the reader would turn to the text of the statute, reciting the title, preamble and the clauses with which he would be concerned and expounding the 'main contents, importance, purveyance and drifte of the law itselfe'. This discussion was frequently accompanied by a detailed account of the origins and purpose of the act.[27] However readers rarely if ever attempted to expound a whole statute. Thus Henry Sherfield's Lincoln's Inn reading on the Statute of Wills (32 Hen. VIII, c. 1) and the supplementary Act (34 Hen. VIII, c. 5), was not concerned with wills in general, as treated by those statutes, but with only 'one part of the lawe, which is what shall be said an act executed within this lawe and what not'. The emphasis of the reading was clarified by the reader's 'divisions' or heads, each of which referred to a particular problem of interpretation. Sherfield's four divisions may be roughly paraphrased as follows:

25 *OJ*, 206; Whitelocke, *Lib. Fam.*, 70; Hargrave 206, f. 3; MT MS, Rare Book Room, 'James Whitelocke's Reading', f. 3. Harvard Law School MS, 123 (Turner), unfoliated.

26 LI MS, Maynard 57, f. 2; Hargrave 402, f. 67; Hargrave 372, f. 54 (my translation).

27 Cf. Stowe 424, f. 127, Coke's first lecture on the Statute of Uses, Inner Temple, 1592: 'I shall demonstrate today what a use is, the varieties of uses, why uses were invented, their necessary adjuncts and corollaries . . .' (my translation).

1. What categories of conveyance come within the compass of these acts?
2. (*a*) In what form should such conveyances be executed, (*b*) How does the seignory of the lands transferred affect the application of the act?
3. Under what conditions are lords entitled to receive a third part of the land conveyed?
4. How should this portion be calculated? [28]

Although the separate divisions might be analysed in general terms, their main function was to provide a common theme for the case discussion which took up the greater part of each day's lecture. Having announced his divisions, the reader then presented his first list of cases, each provided with a solution in order to illustrate and support his interpretation of the law. The number of cases, like the number of divisions, was left entirely to the reader's discretion. Only one (the 'reader's case') was dealt with in the lecture; but this was the subject of an elaborate point-by-point analysis, designed to clarify the relationship between the provisions of the statute and potentially conflicting principles of common law.[29] When this exposition finished, the junior cupboardman (one of the barristers assigned to attend the reading) took up the argument on a case, not necessarily the same one that had been expounded by the reader himself. The debate was continued by the other barristers present:

> and the antient bencher or the antientest of the judges then present, who are to argue the reader's cases (if they will) may put the utter-barrister appointed that morning, to any other of the reader's cases; after whom the judges and benchers argue according to their own antiquity, the puisne bencher beginning first; and so everyone after another till the antientest . . . and lastly the reader is to answer the objections made against his conclusion, to show his opinion of his case . . . and so concludes that morning's reading.[30]

Even granting the ability of early Stuart congregations to sit through three-hour sermons, the reader's audience must have been close to exhaustion by this time. When Dr John Hoskyns attended his brother's reading at the Middle Temple in 1619, he wrote to his wife that 'Mr Reader going to the hall at seven of the clock cannot conclude his matter until allmost two . . . they say preachers are long, but sure the law is very tedious'.[31]

Nevertheless a further bout of argument followed dinner, with another barrister taking another of the reader's cases, and debate continuing on the same lines as in the morning. This procedure was

[28] Stowe 424, f. 39.
[29] Cf. *Lives of the Norths*, i. 151; T. F. Plucknett, *The Legislation of Edward I* (Oxford, 1949), 16–17.
[30] *OJ*, 160, 206; *DBC*, 544–5.
[31] *Life, Letters and Writings of John Hoskyns*, 50.

repeated on Monday, Wednesday and Friday for the next two or three weeks. On the last day the reader gave another 'house speech', thanking members for their attendance and attention, followed by a resumé or 'brief repetition in the manner of an index, of the most substantial heads of his statute'. After a short formal bout of argument, the proceedings concluded and the reader was escorted for the first stage of his journey out of town by 'the young students and many others ... with great state and solemnity'.[32]

The state of the learning exercises to 1640

Although scholastic exercises continued to be performed at the universities throughout our period, undergraduate education was increasingly effected by private reading under the supervision of college tutors. At Cambridge 'hidden flaws in the scholastic structure had become gaping cracks' by 1640; the performance of academic acts and exercises was markedly more perfunctory than forty years before and the formal requirements for attendance were no longer scrupulously enforced. According to Holdsworth the aural learning exercises at the inns had also run into difficulties by this date, and for similar reasons. The growth of a printed legal literature gave students a short cut to knowledge previously attained primarily through an extended course of aural instruction; so, from the mid-sixteenth century onwards, the whole system declined, being maintained only with 'increasing difficulty' under the early Stuarts, and collapsing altogether during the Civil War. Attempts to revive it after the Restoration proved fruitless and by 1700 no more than a few educationally insignificant vestiges survived.[33]

An interesting variant of Holdsworth's thesis has recently been advanced by Mr Kenneth Charlton, who points to the fact that Holdsworth accepted without question various highly favourable sixteenth-century accounts of the learning exercises, while failing to notice that fines for academic delinquencies are recorded in the bench minutes of Lincoln's Inn from the late fifteenth century. On this basis Charlton concludes that the decline of the system was already well advanced by Henry VIII's reign, which was thus far from being the 'Golden Age' that Holdsworth imagined.[34]

Yet decline is a relative term; once it is accepted that the learning exercises flourished during the fourteenth and fifteenth centuries, while finally disintegrating at the end of the seventeenth century, the intervening period is too easily seen as one of inevitable deterioration.

32 Callis, *The Reading*, 219; *OJ*, 207–8.
33 Costello, *Scholastic Curriculum*, 4; *HEL*, vi. 478–85; Maitland, *Selected Essays*, 120–1; H. G. Hanbury, *The Vinerian Chair and Legal Education* (Oxford, 1958), 5–10.
34 Kenneth Charlton, *Education in Renaissance England* (1965), 177–86.

Holdsworth deplored the consequences of the cessation of the learning exercises, both for the legal profession and the inns themselves. He therefore tended to regard every change from what he took to be a well-established and entirely successful medieval system as necessarily a change for the worse, a harbinger of total collapse. On the other hand, examples of mid fifteenth-century exercise delinquencies have no significance in themselves – educational institutions rarely work as smoothly in practice as the glowing accounts of old boys and friends in high places might suggest. They can only be used as evidence of decline on the supposition that such defaults were previously rare or unknown; but in fact failures to moot and attend learning vacations are recorded in the earliest Black Book, when the learning exercise system was certainly in its infancy.[35] Detailed obligations for compulsory attendance at learning vacations were not finally worked out at Lincoln's Inn until the mid-fifteenth century, and there is a world of difference between the few surviving readings from this period and the highly individual productions of the sixteenth and early seventeenth centuries. So whatever kind of legal instruction the inns may have provided before the early fifteenth century, it evidently had little in common with the complex exercise system which had evolved by the beginning of the Tudor period, and no meaningful comparison between the two is possible.

If the learning exercises were not declining from an ideal but mythical medieval excellence, were they nevertheless showing the same signs of weakness and decay as their university cousins? One simple way of answering this question would be to count the number of recorded defaults in their performance; if the annual total rose progressively over a given period, then there could be little doubt that decline had set in. Unfortunately insufficient evidence is available for a comprehensive statistical analysis of the learning exercise system at any point before the Civil War, and the data which does survive provides no consistent or useful conclusions.[36] However, it is still necessary to examine the arguments which Holdsworth advanced without recourse to statistics. He claimed that the extent to which the vigour of the exercise system had diminished during the second half of the sixteenth century could be appreciated by comparing the joint benchers' orders of 1557 with the judges' orders of 1591. Thus the fifth clause of the 1557 orders seems to illustrate excessive zeal on the part of readers and benchers, whose enthusiasm for the exercises led them into arguments too erudite for the average student to follow: 'That the mote-cases in every of the houses of court, for the vacation time, do not contain above two points argumentable . . . [and] none of the bench shal argue above two points'. By contrast

[35] Cf. *BB*, i. 3, 21.
[36] Cf. W. R. Prest, 'The learning exercises at the inns of court, 1590–1640', *J. of the Soc. of Public Teachers of Law*, 9 (1967), 302–5.

the 1591 orders, which are wholly devoted to regulating the minimum length and maximum expense of readings, stand as an indictment of the senior members' growing indifference towards the educational function of the exercises.[37]

However the fifth clause of the 1557 orders is concerned not with inns of court readings, but with grand moots at the inns of chancery. Holdsworth unfortunately copied this clause from Dugdale, whose transcription of the original orders omits the phrase 'in every of ther inns of chauncery' after the words 'houses of court' in the passage quoted above. Holdsworth's reference to the zeal of the 'readers and benchers' which the 1557 orders supposedly sought to curb is also based on a misunderstanding; the relevant portion of the 1557 clause states 'that none *of the benche* shall argue about ii poyntes' (my italics). It seems clear that inns of court benchers were not the subject of this order, but rather the two 'learners' or students from each inn of court who accompanied the inn of chancery reader and 'sitting as benchers (do in court at their motes) hear and argue such motes as are brought in' by students of the inns of chancery.[38]

What of the 1591 order, which states that whereas inns of court readings 'have time out of mind continued . . . by the space of three weeks at the least, till of late years . . . to the great hindrance of learning', readers have ended their course of lectures 'in farr shorter time'. There can be no denying that the length of readings decreased quite substantially during our period. The 1591 order required single readings to continue for at least three full weeks; but in 1614 readers were permitted to end on the Wednesday of the third week and in 1628 the minimum was further reduced to two weeks. 'Heretofore the reading continued by the space of a month; afterwards three weeks and now latelie not a fortnight', said the compiler of the Brerewood MS in the early 1630s; and a contemporary account from the Inner Temple states that 'the reader at the first weekes end, or fortnights end, do end his reading'.[39]

The tendency is quite clear, but it cannot be regarded as incontrovertible evidence of decline. By the end of the sixteenth century printed books were playing a major part in legal education; readers may well have found that a long exposition of their statute was no longer demanded, so a reduction in the length of readings would not necessarily diminish their educational value. Moreover each day's lectures and discussion now lasted all morning at least, whereas according to Henry VIII's commissioners two hours was then the normal duration of a day's reading.[40] The view that the standard of readings declined as their length diminished is also open to question, although it has been endorsed by Professor Thorne and appears to gain some support from the strictures of Bacon and Coke (on this

[37] HEL, vi. 481–3.   [38] OJ, 311; BB, i. 320; ITR, i. 192; MTR, i. 557; DBC, 545.
[39] OJ, 313, 318, 319; Brerewood, 20; OJ, 160.   [40] DBC, 545.

subject the two were for once united). Coke noted in the first volume of his *Institutes* (1628) that Littleton could cite 'ancient readings for proofe of the law, but new readings have not that honour, for they are so obscure and dark'. The main problem was that the cases presented by readers were 'long, obscure and intricate, full of new conceits, like rather to riddles than lectures, which when they are opened they vanish into smoake'. Bacon said much the same at somewhat greater length in the introductory speech to his double reading in 1601, where he proclaimed his intention to 'revive and recontinue the ancient form of reading . . . being of less ostentation and more fruit than the manner lately accustomed . . . not to stir concise [*sic* ? conceits] and subtle doubts, or to continue tedious and intricate cases . . . to open the law upon doubts, and not doubts upon the law'.[41]

These condemnations of 'the manner lately accustomed' need not be taken at face value. The main reason that some old readings (by no means all) could be cited as authorities was precisely that they were old. A few Jacobean and Caroline readings also attained authoritative status and even got into print, but usually not for at least a generation after they were delivered. While the actual readings of the fifteenth century may have been concise, there is no evidence that the arguments between the reader and his audience were any less complex than these provided by readers' cases in the late sixteenth and early seventeenth centuries.[42] In this period the reader's task was complicated by the great bulk of Tudor legislation, while the widening range of legal literature which became available in the sixteenth century must have increased the level of competence among the reader's audience, enabling him to pitch his arguments at a higher level than was possible when learning was mainly acquired by aural means.

Given the complexity of early-seventeenth-century law, it is difficult to judge whether students found readings delivered at this time as baffling and obscure as Bacon and Coke alleged. The fashion for presenting a great many intricate cases, often bearing only slight relation to the statute itself, seems to have waned after the turn of the century. Most of the readings from the 1620s and '30s examined by the present writer do not exceed more than ten cases per division, a substantial reduction from the twenty to twenty-three cases presented by Coke on each division of his reading at the Inner Temple

---

[41] Thorne, *Readings and Moots*, xvi; Coke, *First Part of the Institutes*, 280–1; *The Learned Reading of Sir Francis Bacon . . . upon the Statute of Uses* (1642), 2–3. Cf. *A Discourse upon the Statutes*, ed. S. E. Thorne (San Marino, 1942), 172, for a less critical account of the typical approach, c. 1565.

[42] Cf. Thorne, *Readings and Moots*, lxvii–lxviii; Putnam, *Early Treatises*, 166, 169–70: 'Marowe's chief . . . pride, lay in subtle legal analysis, and in the exercise of great ingenuity in imagining all possible cases . . . To the modern reader the method often seems both confusing and pedantic . . .'. (Thomas Marowe's reading *De Pace* was delivered at Gray's Inn in 1503).

in 1592.[43] A few readers may have continued to seek the applause of their colleagues rather than the enlightenment of students; in his autumn reading at Lincoln's Inn in 1626, Nicholas Franklin cited ten cases on each of his ten divisions, full of 'poyntes not obvious to every view nor to the apprehension of every capacity, and yet to such as sought them out with diligence dyd appere delightful'.[44] But others were well aware of the dangers of perplexing their audience with extraneous learning. Introducing the case at his first lecture, James Whitelocke claimed that he had

> indeavored hereafter to comprehend variety yet with propriety to the matter of my statute that as much as may be we may ... apply ourselves to debate that thoroughly which we have in hand, then wander upon matters of another nature and I take it rather to belonge to me *legere et docere* than *arguere*.[45]

Edward Littleton echoed the same concern in his reader's speech at the Inner Temple in 1632: 'he wished mainly to apply himself to his statute, having no other common-law points than those which served by way of introduction'.[46] The reader's dilemma was that of any teacher, to instruct without confusing, to stimulate without going beyond his pupils' range. A 'dull and easy' lawyer was just as unsuccessful as the reader who pitched his arguments above the students' heads.[47]

Nor were readings breaking down due to the difficulty of recruiting readers. To be sure, double readings disappeared during our period, despite the judges' strenuous efforts to preserve them. But double readings were squeezed out by single readings, and the greatly increased numbers of benchers and barristers who were eligible to read for the first time. The disappearance of double readings had no detrimental effects on the instruction of students; indeed because double readings usually lasted for a week or less, the substitution of single readings in Lent vacations meant that the amount of instruction provided was actually increased. The larger pool from which readers could be drawn also helped offset the diminishing professional advantages of performing a reading. Nor can it be assumed that the cost of the lavish entertainment expected from the reader was a general deterrent; in an age of conspicuous consumption, many lawyers relished the opportunity to display their wealth, munificence and influential

---

[43] Stowe 424, ff. 128–132v.   [44] CUL MS, Dd. v. 57 (2), f. 71.

[45] MT MS, Rare Book Room, 'James Whitelocke's Reading', f. 4.

[46] Hargrave 372, f. 54; cf. Barkesdale's announced intention to 'keep me close to my statute, not to decline from the text like wandring prechers ... I shall be forc't to argue poynts upon the statute rather than poynts at common law, least I leave the statute in the same case I found it; I shall use short conclusions and playn, rather than long and intricate': LI MS, Maynard 57, f. 2. Cf. Bacon, *Learned Reading*, 3–4, and Jones, *History of Charity*, 245–6.

[47] D'Ewes, *Autobiography*, i. 241: 'Mr Warde the reader ... being but a dull and easy lawyer ... gave little satisfaction to his auditors'.

connections.[48] While the difficulty of persuading men to read may occasionally have induced the benchers to cancel readings at the least hint of plague or to wink at readers who ended their lectures prematurely, on no occasion during our period was any inn compelled to go without a reading because a reader could not be found.

It is true that the inns of chancery readings delivered during term-time by barristers appointed from the 'parent' inns of court were virtually defunct by 1640. Although the inns of chancery had been forced to accept the visitatorial jurisdiction of the inns of court during the later sixteenth century, all other ties between them were frayed or broken. The proportion of entrants to the major inns who came up from the inns of chancery fell precipitously in the early seventeenth century; rather than being 'preparatory colleges for freshmen', the inns of chancery were increasingly monopolised by members of the lower branch who had no intention of ever graduating to an inn of court.[49]

TABLE 15 *Percentage of non-honorific entrants from inns of chancery, 1590–94 and 1635–39*

	Gray's Inn	Inner Temple	Lincoln's Inn	Middle Temple
1590–94	24·2	63·1	22·6	25·7
1635–39	4·3	4·9	0·6	2·3

(For more detailed figures see Prest, 'Some aspects . . .', 394.)

Lectures on 'some chapter of Littleton or some statute law' were unlikely to be of much interest or use to these embryonic pettifoggers, and an inn of chancery readership was no longer regarded as a mark of distinction for a rising young barrister. Although a few still performed their duty conscientiously, most read perfunctorily, by deputy, or not at all. The attitude of their audiences was hardly encouraging; in 1628 and 1630 no readings at all were delivered at Furnival's Inn, because the principal and students of the house absented themselves, 'upon a misconceyted wrong to be done them by theire reader, that he remembered them not with such benevolences as other the readers of that house had used to doe'.[50] Nevertheless the decline of the inns

[48] See above, pp. 60–3; *HEL*, iv. 484–5; cf. Henry Chauncy, *The Historical Antiquities of Hertfordshire* (1826), ii. 433. Cf. Whitelocke, *Lib. Fam.*, 74–6; Williamson, *Temple*, 470–6; Jones, *History of Charity*, 242; Essex R.O., Bramston Papers, Bundle A(10); *Lives of the Norths*, i. 98.

[49] *Fortescutus Illustratus*, 526; Carr, *Pension Book of Clements Inn*, xvi–xxvii; see also A. W. B. Simpson, 'The source and function of the later year books', *LQR*, 87 (1971), 100–118.

[50] *BB*, ii. 265, 281, 293. Published inns of chancery readings from our period include John Doddridge, *A Compleat Parson . . .* (1630); Charles Calthorpe, *The Relation between the Lord of a Mannor and the Coppy-Holder his Tenant*

of chancery readings was an independent development which had no direct effect on participation by inns of court students during vacations in the grand or inn of chancery moots, which still formed part of the qualifications for call to the bar.

While Francis Moore stated in his reader's speech at the Middle Temple in 1607 that 'this exercise of readinge is the chiefest wee have for attayning learninge', the lesser case argument exercises were actually the foundation of the inns' educational system. Students in the early seventeenth century still continued to attend moots and found it worth while to take notes of the arguments at these and lesser exercises. Although one can hardly judge the standard of the exercises from such brief summaries, their very existence suggests that the lesser exercises still fulfilled a serious educational purpose, and had not yet degenerated into mere formal rituals, performed 'perfunctorily . . . by way of *opus operatum*, as for tale and not for weight'.[51] In 1592 Sir Thomas Lucas, a bencher of the Inner Temple, had his son admitted to clerks commons in his own house with the hope that 'he wyll indevvor him selfe according to the place to bringe in some moote or case in the tyme of this graunde vacaycon'. It was not only anxious parents who took the case exercises seriously; in 1611 Heneage Finch apologised for having left a letter from his father unanswered because of 'an exercise of the house, where I was to instruct some young gentlemen, from which without great necessity . . . I could not conveniently spare any tyme'. Again in 1626, Simonds D'Ewes writing to Sir Martin Stuteville from the Middle Temple claimed that 'my head hath been soe fulle of mootes as I scarce had time in the better part of a weeke to visite my father'.[52] Of course these excuses may not have been true, but they were evidently felt to be plausible.

Writers before and after the Civil War fully accepted the value of aural learning exercises. William Fulbecke recommended students 'by domesticall moots to exercise and conform themselves to greater and weightier matters'; Michael Hawke emphasised 'what a laudable and difficult taske it is to argue a case accurately upon a quare or demurrer in law', while as late as 1667, in his scheme for legal study published as the preface to Rolle's *Abridgement*, Sir Mathew Hale advised the student to undertake certain preparatory reading to 'fit

---

(1635); Robert Callis, *The Case and Argument against Sir Ignoramus of Cambridg* (1648). Cf. Carr, *op. cit.*, xxx–xxxii, for inn of chancery exercises in the eighteenth century.

51 Jones, *op. cit.*, 245; *Lives of the Norths*, i. 39. Cf. Hargrave 398, ff. 172v seq.; Harleian 1225; CUL MSS, Dd. xi. 7, Dd. xiii. 24; IT MSS, Barrington 55, 66, 78; LI MSS, C. 4 (Bevir), I.i (Robertson), and references above, pp. 117–19.

52 IT MS, Petyt, Letters to treasurers and benchers, 38; HMC, *Finch*, i. 39; D'Ewes, *Autobiography*, ii. 188. Cf. Harleian 379, f. 14, Simonds to Paul D'Ewes, 9 Apr. 1623: 'what with daylie studie, dinner cases, supper discourses, evening mootes, the whole time & minde are filled with law . . .'.

him for exercise, and enable him to improve himself by conversation and discourse with others'.[53]

The collapse of the exercise system

Yet while the exercises continued on the whole to be taken seriously and performed conscientiously during the early seventeenth century, their significance in the total context of legal education had undergone a major change. Students had always learnt their law by attending the courts and studying in private, as well as by public argument and discussion. Observing the manner in which actual trials were conducted was a time-honoured means of legal self-education; the earliest year books show judges occasionally interrupting counsels' arguments to clarify an abstruse point for the benefit of students sitting in the body of the court. Like Quarter Sessions in the counties, Westminster Hall during term time was a fashionable venue, and it cannot be assumed that all the students who went there or occupied places set aside in the Star Chamber for young gentlemen 'towardes the lawe' did so solely to improve their legal knowledge. The Star Chamber was particularly popular because it offered an opportunity to see and hear the great lords of the Council, occasionally even the king himself, at relatively close quarters, while laymen must have found its cases intrinsically more interesting and its procedure less technical than those of the common-law courts. The Star Chamber's jurisdiction was also regarded as a sort of national equivalent to that exercised locally by the justices of the peace; Sir Thomas Wentworth, who was admitted to the Inner Temple in 1607, apparently continued to attend the Star Chamber even after returning from a continental tour in 1613; Sir George Radcliffe claimed that Wentworth spent seven years together in 'constant attendance' at the Star Chamber, thereby receiving 'many directions for his carriage towards the publick. This was in those days a most pleasing and useful employment for a young gentleman, who is [sic] like to have any part in the government of his country'. Simonds D'Ewes also frequented the Star Chamber before his call to the bar, but thereafter went only to the Common Pleas, 'to hear and report cases in the morning', which gave 'great increase' to his studies.[54]

The notes which a serious student like D'Ewes jotted down in court would probably be written up afterwards in his case or commonplace

[53] William Fulbecke, *A Direction, or Preparative to the Study of the Lawe* . . . (1600), 41; *Collectanea Juridica*, ed. Francis Hargrave (1791–92), i. 277; Michael Hawke, *The Grounds of the Lawes of England* . . . (1657), sig. [a5].

[54] *Year Books 2–3 Edward II*, ed. F. W. Maitland (*SS*, 19, 1904), xvi, lxxvi; Buc, *Third Universitie*, 969; *Cases in Camera Stellata*, ed. Baildon, 39; *Collectanea Juridica*, ii. 48; Additional 22 603, f. 11; *Strafford's Letters and Dispatches*, ii. 434; Egerton 2983, ff. 13–24; D'Ewes, *Autobiography*, 220, 260.

book, and collated with other material gathered from private reading and the learning exercises. The earliest systematic textbook for law students, published in 1600, advised that 'it is a profitable course under titles to digest the cases of the law . . . either heard or read' and by this time a wide range of legal literature was available, both in manuscript and print.[55] Reading and commonplacing were not novel methods of learning the law. A considerable corpus of collected writs and pleadings, statutes, abridgements and year books had circulated in manuscript during the fourteenth and fifteenth century and in Plucknett's words, much of this material 'positively reeks of chalk, duster and ink'. Lincoln's Inn had a library by at least 1474 (six years before Lettou and Machlinia brought out the first printed law book) and the same is very likely true of the other houses. Manuscripts were undoubtedly expensive (so were early printed books), but there is no reason to suppose that students did not borrow what they could not buy.[56]

However, the manuscript legal literature of the fifteenth century and before was primarily intended for reference purposes rather than sustained private study. No general treatises were in common use. Model collections of writs and the like doubtless served as admirable source-books for discussion and disputation, but could have hardly provided a satisfactory basis for a course of individual reading. Although the early printers were quick to exploit the legal market, their initial output did little more than give the old books a wider circulation. It was with the appearance of works like Fitzherbert's *Abridgement* (1514), St Germain's *Doctor and Student* (1523), and Perkins's *Profitable Booke* (1530) that the range of legal literature began to expand and diversify. By the middle of the century students were being advised that 'familiar talking, and moutyng together' was just as effective a way of learning the law as 'great booke skil, or muche beating of their braine by any close studie, or secret musying in their chamber'.[57] So whereas private reading was almost certainly no more than a supplement to and preparation for aural means of instruction before the introduction of printing, from about the 1550s onwards the position had been decisively reversed.

But a decline in the relative importance of the learning exercises during the course of the sixteenth century hardly explains their eventual collapse in the later seventeenth century. For one thing, as

[55] Fulbecke, *A Direction*, 44. Cf. Edmund Plowden, *Les Comentaries, ou Reportes* . . . (1578), sig. q. iiv; J. D. Cowley, *A Bibliography of Abridgements* . . . *of English Law to the year 1800* (1932), xvii–xviii.

[56] Plucknett, *Early English Legal Literature*, 90 and chs. 5–6 *passim*; Margaret Hastings, *The Court of Common Pleas in Fifteenth-Century England* (Ithaca, 1947), 65; *BB*, i. 59; *ITR*, i. 6; *OJ*, 197; Williamson, *Temple*, 126.

[57] H. S. Bennett, *English Books and Readers 1475 to 1557* (Cambridge, 1952), 76–95; *idem, English Books and Readers 1558–1603* (Cambridge, 1965), 156–66; *HEL*, v. 355–412, 423–93; Thomas Wilson, *The Arte of Rhetorique* (1553), f. 21.

we have already argued at some length, neither their mechanical operation nor standard of performance seems to have declined significantly before the Civil War. For another, it would be quite wrong to suppose that all aural means of instruction were made obsolete overnight by the advent of the printing press. The inns' exercises continued to serve a number of necessary educational functions as a practical complement to book learning, encouraging students to think and argue on their feet, to apply theoretical knowledge to concrete problems and to match wits with their fellows and seniors. In short, they filled much the same role as moots and case-book discussions in modern law schools. Despite the growing concern with method and system, which infected the common law no less than other branches of learning in the post-Ramist age, contemporaries were unconscious of any inherent conflict between aural and visual approaches to learning the law.[58] By 1700, when readings had ceased altogether and lesser case-argument exercises 'shrunk into mere form', students were still putting cases and arguing problems with each other in chambers, in hall and at meetings of informal dining clubs.[59] Thus what we have to explain is the collapse of a system, rather than the disappearance of the essential activity around which that system was built.

In the period before 1642 the learning exercises were weakened not by direct competition from the printed book, but by their adaptation to an institutional purpose for which they were thoroughly unsuited. The only members of the societies who could not avoid participating in exercises, by one means or another, were those seeking call to the bar.[60] During the second half of the sixteenth century, as the degree of barrister became synonymous with the minimum qualification to plead in the higher courts and the numbers seeking call increased substantially, detailed qualifications replaced the vague criteria of 'learning and continuance', which had served when call was merely an internal promotion. Besides being of seven or eight years continuance, candidates for the bar were now required to have performed house exercises during the three years immediately preceding their petition for call and to have argued a minimum number of moots and other exercises.[61] But since the exercises had lost their primacy within the whole scheme of legal education, to make them an essential prerequisite for entrance to the profession was inevitably to encour-

[58] Cf. W. J. Ong, *Ramus: Method and the Decay of Dialogue* (Cambridge, Mass., 1958), 227. Ellesmere 2885 is an agreement of the cursitors in Chancery to introduce readings on writs in their hall on week nights during term, dated 1596; cf. Lansdowne 1169.

[59] *HEL*, vi. 488–90, 497. W. B. Odgers, 'Changes in the common law, and in the law of persons, in the legal profession and in legal education', in [Council of Legal Education], *A Century of Law Reform* (1901), 32–3.

[60] Cf. Prest, 'Learning exercises', 310–11.

[61] See above, pp. 51, 54–5.

age evasion or perfunctory fulfilment of the minimum requirement.

Because continuance was coming to be interpreted in the sense of membership of the society, rather than residence in commons, it became entirely possible for students to be admitted several years before they came into residence, to serve their vacations and perform the stipulated number of exercises during the three years before call (standards of performance seem to have been immaterial, so long as the traditional forms were strictly observed), and then come to the bar. The benchers made little effort to eliminate this loophole; rather than insisting on seven years attendance 'usually in commons', they merely tried to ensure that at least the two or three years immediately before call should be spent in residence.[62]

It is impossible to tell how many students took advantage of their complacency. One was Simonds D'Ewes, whose father, a six clerk in Chancery, had him admitted to the Middle Temple in 1611 at the tender age of nine. After two years at Cambridge, D'Ewes moved to his father's Chancery Lane lodgings in October 1620 and into a chamber at the Middle Temple twelve months later. In May 1623 the benchers announced a general call to the bar and D'Ewes put his name forward as a candidate. When several days passed and no call had been announced, a rumour went around:

> that it was staied to enquire into the continuance of men in the house in commons, which troubled mee for one, for though I had been long admitted, yett I had been but a small time in commons, about twoe yeares and a halfe, so I feared divers of us might be stayed together.

Yet if an investigation was indeed held, it must have been very cursory, for D'Ewes received his call at the end of the following month.[63] That this case was not exceptional is shown by D'Ewes's reference to 'divers of us', and by the careers of Robert and Unton Croke, John Denham, John Greene, John Maynard, Gilbert Millington, George Radcliffe, Bulstrode and James Whitelocke, all of whom were called to the bar at the prescribed continuance or less, having remained for varying periods at a university after their admission to the inns.[64] For these men books were the main means of learning the law, the learning exercises at best a supplement, at worst an irritating barrier to the rich rewards of a successful legal career. While Bulstrode Whitelocke recognised the value of informal case argument, and re-

---

62 *GIPB*, i. 243, 291, 308; *ITR*, ii. 101; cf. *ibid.*, i. 423, ii. 236–7; *MTR*, ii. 540–1, 836–7.

63 *MT Adm. Reg.*, i. 97; D'Ewes, 'Secret Diary', 163–5, 176; his call is listed as of 23 May 1623 in *MTR*, ii. 682.

64 Sources: printed admissions register, *Al. Cant.*, *Al. Ox.*; Brendan O Hehir, *Harmony from Discords. A Life of Sir John Denham* (Berkeley, 1968), 7–8, 16.

commended 'constant putting of cases' to his sons as 'the best way to improve the knowledge of the law', of the other exercises he said no more than that he had performed them 'according to the orders of the society for my degree of utter-barrister'.[65]

The same attitude lay behind the reluctance of barristers to fulfil their post-call obligations, which usually included attendance at learning vacations and the performance of a number of moots for three years following call.[66] Even more serious was the occasional practice of accepting lump sum compositions for the fines resulting from such defaults, especially from men who intended to practise in Ireland or the provinces. Where made in advance, such compositions amounted to commuting an academic obligation for a cash payment, although it was emphasised on several occasions that those who missed exercises and paid fines must still make up their full quota.[67]

These ominous developments seem to have had little direct effect on the operation of the learning exercise system as a whole during the half-century before the Civil War. The decline of the scholastic exercises at the universities during this period was largely a function of the decline of the universities themselves, in relation to their constituent colleges, accelerated by the existence of an alternative channel of instruction in the form of the college tutor. No such alternative was available at the inns, and the role of aural exercises in the practical training of lawyers could not be duplicated by other means. Moreover, institutional pressure tended to uphold the system, since the exercises were common to each house, whose rulers made strenuous efforts to maintain them. The benchers had a vested interest in the system through which they had risen to authority, but they also felt a strong obligation to preserve for posterity the inheritance passed on from their predecessors. So while sufficient reasons for the decline or disappearance of the system may have existed before 1642 – a readily accessible and diversified legal literature, the use of exercises for 'probation' rather than 'institution', the increasing expenditure expected from readers, the replacement of verbal by written pleadings in the courts, the conflicting demands of professional practice, and so forth – these remained dormant or at least contained until the outbreak of Civil War.

But it was one thing to preserve the system as a going concern, quite another to revive it after a five-year break between 1642 and 1647, when no exercises whatever were performed. Their educational

[65] Additional 53726, f. 12. Cf. Roger North, *A Discourse on the Study of the Laws* (1824), 12; see also L. G. Schwoerer, 'Roger North and his notes on legal education', *HLQ*, 22 (1959), 303–19.
[66] Cf. *OJ*, 159, 312; *BB*, ii. 45, 251; *GIPB*, i. 304; *ITR*, i. 367; *MTR*, ii. 536.
[67] Cf. *BB*, ii. 25–6, 50, 81; GI MS, Ledger A, ff. 73v, 111v and Order Book, f. 223v; *ITR*, ii. 35, 237; *MTR*, ii. 574, 769. See also above, pp. 55–7.

value had hardly diminished significantly within that space of time, but even institutions primarily dedicated to the advancement of learning rarely determine policies by educational criteria alone. The financial crisis which confronted all four houses, due to the exodus of members and the drastic shrinking of admissions during the war years, was a compelling incentive for the benchers to accept the wholesale commutation of academic obligations into a source of additional revenue. The judges had insufficient power to check this process, and the second Protectorate parliament appealed in vain to Cromwell and his council 'to take some effectual course . . . for reviving the readings in the several inns of court and the keeping up of exercise by the students there'. Charles II and his ministers showed equally little willingness to meddle with the inns on this issue; although the judges' orders of 1664 contained six specific articles and a general injunction for 'keeping up of constant exercise', no serious attempt was made to enforce these statements of good intent.[68]

In 1669 William Prynne, as usual out of step with the times, beseeched his unresponsive fellow-benchers 'to encourage the declining diligent study and publicke exercises of the common law, now overmuch neglected, discontinued and perfunctorily performed'. Prynne attributed this state of affairs to 'slothfulness, selfishness, or pretended novel exemptions'. Yet while the dons of unreformed Oxford and Cambridge were hardly models of energy and public spirit, the scholastic exercises of the universities continued to be performed well into the nineteenth century, 'considered by competent critics to serve a useful, indeed a valuable [educational] purpose'.[69] The fundamental reason for the failure of Prynne's appeal was simply that the rulers of the inns, unlike their academic counterparts, had no formal educational commitments to prevent them from abdicating all responsibility for the instruction of junior members of the societies.

[68] *Diary of Thomas Burton, Esq.*, ed. J. T. Rutt (1828), ii. 313; *BB*, iii. 445–9.
[69] William Prynne, *Brief Animadversions on . . . The Fourth Part of the Institutes . . . by Sir E. Cooke* (1669), sig. A2. D. A. Winstanley, *Unreformed Cambridge* (Cambridge, 1935), 46.

VII

Legal and Liberal Education

While rapid expansion of the universities and inns of court during the century or so before the Civil War may reasonably be said to constitute a quantitative 'educational revolution', the qualitative aspects of this phenomenon remain open to debate. The previous chapter outlined the methods of legal instruction and self-education available to students at the inns and contended that the mechanical operation of the learning exercise system had not deteriorated significantly before 1640. But it did not attempt to assess the effectiveness of these methods, a task which will be attempted in the first half of this chapter, while the second will examine the broader role of the societies as fashionable academies, where young men learned to be 'somewhat more a gentleman than before'.[1] Our aim will be to discover what kind of academic and cultural nourishment was provided for the members of these 'seminaries and nurseries wherein the gentry of the kingdome and such as serve his majesty in the common wealth are bredd and trayned upp'.[2]

'The inns of court man that never was studient'[3]

The stereotype inns of court student depicted by contemporary character-writers, dramatists, moralists, poets and satirists, was an idle

---

[1] Clement Ellis, *The Gentile Sinner* (1661), quoted K. D. Bulbring ed., *The Compleat English Gentleman by Daniel Defoe* (1890), lxiv.
[2] *APC, 1629–30*, 145.
[3] Powell, *The Arte of Thriving*, 132; this and the following two sections are based in part on Wilfrid Prest, 'The legal education of the gentry at the inns of court, 1560–1640', *P. & P*, 38 (1967), 20–39.

and fairly dissolute young man, with a marked preference for 'Shakespeare's plaies instead of my Lord Coke'.[4] We should doubtless be wary of accepting this portrait at face value, both because it may be unduly influenced by the escapades of a rakish minority and because it inevitably contains an element of caricature, a straining for literary or moral effect. The considerable surviving body of biographical evidence along the same lines may also reflect the influence of the stereotype; old men often tend to exaggerate the follies of their youth, and even if their recollections are accurate, their experiences may well have been far from typical.

Yet scepticism can be carried too far. Even the most melodramatic memoirs and sensationalist journalism should not automatically be assumed to lack any factual basis, especially when both point in the same direction. Take, for example, the lurid pamphlet *An Alarum against Usurers*, published by Thomas Lodge, a former resident of Lincoln's Inn, in 1584. This depicts the grim fate of a young gentleman who is sent to the inns of court, neglects his studies, falls into debt, and into the hands of a money-lender's broker, mortgaging and eventually losing his estates. Lodge's story sounds suspiciously like a trailer for *The Jew of Malta* or *Michaelmas Term*; but in 1596 two brokers were convicted in the Star Chamber for 'coseninge' young gentlemen exactly as Lodge describes, prompting Burghley, who was sitting on the bench, to warn parents against letting their sons go to the inns without appointing 'one or two superintendentes over them, that they maye . . . certify there freindes of there manner of lyving'.[5] Moreover, as this example suggests, contemporary sources do not merely catalogue or condemn student delinquency, ignorance and laziness. They also point to its prime causes: inadequate supervision and the difficulty of the common law as a subject of study.

Blackstone thought one main reason why his contemporaries had stopped sending their sons to the inns was that 'all sorts of regimen and academical superintendence, either with regard to morals or studies, are found impracticable and therefore entirely neglected'.[6] Yet, as we have seen, control over the personal lives and extramural behaviour of members was relaxed from the mid-sixteenth century onwards, in direct response to the expansion of the societies. The lack of a tutorial system meant that parents were obliged to make their own arrangements, if they wished their sons to be placed under any kind of personal supervision. Few seem to have followed James Cleland's sound advice, that they should send their boy to the inns only in the company and under the care of his tutor. It was rather more common to enlist

---

[4] Francis Lenton, *Characterismi* (1631), sig. F4.
[5] Lodge, *op. cit.*, 2–8; *Cases in Camera Stelleta*, 47. Cf. HMC, *4 Rep.*, App. 1, 83.
[6] Blackstone, *Commentaries on the Laws of England*, i. 25.

relatives or friends in London to keep an eye on the young man.[7] While better than nothing, this makeshift expedient could rarely have been entirely satisfactory. Too much depended on the character of the chosen overseer: according to his own account, Sir John Reresby was led into 'swearing, gameing and all manner of debauchery' by a wealthy kinsman at Gray's Inn during the Interregnum. Even 'a man of discretion, fidelity and prudence' was hardly in a position to exercise the same close control which might be expected from a full-time private tutor.[8]

Senior members of the inns occasionally acted as unofficial law coaches to gentlemen students, but the practice does not seem to have been widespread. John Petre, the eldest son of a prominent Essex landholder, paid a Mr Molesworth five shillings in 1567 for 'reading law to me'. Richard Barker, who became a bencher of Gray's Inn in 1594, was chosen by Sir Nicholas Bacon 'to be an instructor for his two sonnes . . . for attaining of some knowledge in the studies of the law'; Augustine Baker acted in a similar capacity for Sir Nicholas Fortescue's son at the Inner Temple; while in 1618 the 'demeanour and instruction' of Hugh Magneisse, the eldest son of an Irish knight, was entrusted to Richard Hadsor, an Irish lawyer of the Middle Temple. Edward Hyde's father enlisted the aid of his brother, Sir Lawrence Hyde, to look after the boy when he went up to the Middle Temple in the late 1620s; but despite Sir Lawrence's comforting reports that 'your son Ned . . . studieth hard and is very orderly and frugal', Lord Clarendon later gave a very different account of his student days:

> When he reflected upon himself and his past actions, even from the time of his coming to the Middle Temple, he had much more cause to be terrified upon the reflection than the man had, who viewed Rochester bridge in the morning that it was broken and which he had galloped over in the night.[9]

The degree of supervision provided by kinsmen, family friends and acquaintances obviously varied a good deal. In 1663 Edward Waterhous printed an ambitious scheme imparted to him by 'my worthy friend Mr Langford', a member of Gray's Inn who was called to the bench in 1657:

[7] Ηρω-παιδεια, or the Institution of a Young Noble Man (1607), 96. Cf. Stone, Aristocracy, 691; HMC, Rutland, i. 195–6, 198; Life of . . . Radcliffe, ed. Whitaker, 87, 94. The two 'manucaptors' or 'sureties' required by each student at his admission were merely financial guarantors and not necessarily even members of the house.
[8] Memoirs of Sir John Reresby, 4; Harleian 4009, ff. 73–4.
[9] A. C. Edwards, English History from Essex Sources 1550–1750 (Chelmsford, 1952), 30; GIPB, i. 37; Memorials of Father Augustine Baker, ed. P. J. McCann and R. H. Connolly (CRS, 33, 1933), 66; APC, 1617–18, 181; The Life of Edward Earl of Clarendon . . . written by himself (Oxford, 1759), 67 ff.; Davies, 'The date of Clarendon's first marriage', 406.

with which he himself had profitably disciplined young gentlemen in Gray's Inn. The natural day's twenty-four hours he thus distributing.

From 5 in the morning to 6.	Ad Sacra. Begin with God by reading and prayer.
From 6 to 9.	Ad Jura. Read the law carefully and understandingly.
From 9 to 11.	Ad Arma. Carry on harmless acts of manhood, fencing, dancing etc.
From 11 to 12.	Ad Artes. Forget not academique learning, rhetorick, logick.
From 12 to 2.	Ad Victium. Eat seasonably, moderately, and allow time to digest.
From 2 to 5.	Ad Amictias. Visit civilly your friends, and repay kindnesse in kind.
From 5 to 6.	Ad Artes. Read history, romances and poetry.
From 6 to 8.	Ad Victium . . .
From 8 to 9.	Ad Repetitionem et Sacra. Repeat your parts and say your prayers.
From 9 to 5.	Ad Noctem et somnium . . .[10]

But there is nothing to suggest that Langford himself took any active part in this programme, which was probably drawn up merely to help those who asked his advice about the best way of ordering their time.

While a few fortunate youths managed to obtain some assistance with their academic problems, the majority struggled on alone. Before Augustine Baker went up to the Inner Temple in 1596, his brother, a practising barrister, helped him with law-French and loaned him a few books. This, Baker claimed,

> is usually all the help that any commen to the study of these lawes, at London, hath or well can have towardes such study from any other. For what is further therein to be done, he must do himselfe, and supply with his own industry, experience and the assistance of his fellow students.[11]

Students evidently did a good deal to assist each other; Simonds D'Ewes read Littleton with 'a young gentleman religious and honest' and took 'sweete benefitt' from discussing cases in the learning vacations, although on at least one occasion he found the arguments of more senior men so perplexing that he 'began to despaire almost of studying any further'.[12]

It has been suggested that students with problems would have had no difficulty in getting advice from senior members, 'so friendly and intimate was the truly collegiate life of the inns'. But the evidence seems rather to imply that advice and consultation were often sorely

---

[10] Waterhous, *Fortescutus Illustratus*, 151–7. [11] Baker, *Memorials*, 45.
[12] D'Ewes, 'Secret Diary', 42.

needed and rarely available, except, perhaps, for a fee. Abraham Fraunce thought it was 'the want of teachers and good discipline which is in the universities, that makes law seem harde and philosophie very easie', while an anonymous mid-seventeenth-century critique of legal education emphasised that in the absence of tutors, entrants had to be expected to arrive 'furnished with grammar [and] logicke, to direct them in perfect method . . . but wee have seen this by experience miserably to fail, the reading of the lawes left to the wandring innventions of every puisne student'.[13]

The lack of 'regimen and academical superintendence' was aggravated by the location of the societies. Unlike the universities, the inns had no powers to remove prostitutes and players from their immediate environment. With theatres on both sides of the river, Alsatia, Ram Alley and the Savoy on their door steps, young men at the inns, often with money in their purses and swords by their sides for the first time in their lives, were exposed to a wide variety of metropolitan temptations and vices. At Oxford and Cambridge the young gallant's

> Tutor was the man that kept him in,
> That he ran not into excess of sinne . . .

But coming to London and the inns of court he was 'crept from the cradle of learning to the court of liberty . . . from his tutor to the touchstone of his wits . . . he is his owne man now . . .'.[14]

The inns did not ask their junior members to make even a pretence of studying the law; entrants were accepted entirely without regard to aptitude or academic qualifications and there were no sanctions to spur the lazy, although the common law was generally admitted to be 'difficult and obscure above all other artes and sciences'.[15]

Sir Thomas Elyot's indignation was aroused by parents who set young children to the study of the law, 'the most difficult and grave learning, which hath nothing illecbrouse, or delicate to tickle their tender witts'. It was hardly remarkable that 'the more part, vanquished with tediousness . . . do abandon the lawes and . . . give themselves to gaming and other (as I might say) idle business . . .'. In our period the problem of adjustment to the tedium of learning the law was not attributable solely to the 'tender witts' of young students; at the age of twenty-two even the gifted and industrious Simonds D'Ewes 'found still the study of the law so difficult and unpleasant', that he could 'justly account the two years last past among the unhappiest days of

---

[13] Hanbury, *The Vinerian Chair*, 8; Abraham Fraunce, *The Lawyer's Logike* (1588), sig. Q; Bodl. MS, Rawlinson C. 207, ff. 245–7; John Cooke, *The Vindication of the Professors & Profession of the Law* (1646), 57.
[14] Francis Lenton, *The Young Gallant's Whirligigg* (1629), 3; *idem, Characterismi* (1631), sig. F4.
[15] Bodl. MS, Rawlinson C.207, f. 249.

my life'. Similarly Sir Henry Spelman, who was admitted to Lincoln's Inn from Cambridge in 1598, at the age of seventeen, told how:

> My mother sent me to London to learn the law; when I had saluted the threshold, I found a foreign language, a barbarous dialect, an uncouth method, a mass which was not only large, but which was to be continually born on the shoulders; and I confess that my heart sank within me.[16]

Entrants from the universities who had imbibed the prejudices of clerical, classicist dons were of course likely to be biased against the law from the start; indeed Augustine Baker claimed that students who had stayed on at Oxford or Cambridge beyond seventeen years of age could rarely adapt themselves to studying common law, 'for to wits seasoned with these pleasant studies . . . the law is more harsh and barbarous'. Richard Brathwaite entered Oriel College, Oxford in 1604, and then transferred to Cambridge, but being urged by his parents 'to tune my course of studies from these sweet academical exercises', entered Gray's Inn in 1609. He found 'these thorny plashes and places of the law' entirely repugnant after 'the fresh fragrant flowers of divine poesie and morall philosophy' and 'but lightly profited' from his stay:

> being there seated, where I studied more for acquaintance than knowledge: Nor was I the only one . . . who ran deeply into areers with time and gulled the eyes of opinion with a law-gowne. For I found many in my case who could not recompense their parents many years charge with one book-case.[17]

Yet professional lawyers also admitted, often boastfully, that learning the law was at best no brief or easy task: 'A learned man in the lawes of this realm is long in the making . . . the studie abstruse and difficult'. Nowadays the law is approached via its separate branches – contract, tort, family law, criminal law and so forth. This degree of abstraction had not been achieved three hundred years ago. A rough division existed between the law of real and personal property, criminal law and the law of actions (each internally rambling and inconsistent), but actions remained 'a reall and generall affectation scattered throughout the whole law (as the blood is through the bodie)'. Viewed as a whole the common law was a formless, confused jumble of undigested particulars, successfully resisting all efforts at simplification or systematic statement. Practitioners insisted on its status as a true science, 'full of learning and grounded upon as solid reason, as any other science vulgarly so called'. But they were forced

---

[16] Elyot, *The Governour*, ed. Croft, i. 136; D'Ewes, *Autobiography*, i. 220; R. L. Edgeworth, *Essays on Professional Education* (1809), 313.
[17] Baker, *Memorials*, 65; Richard Brathwaite, *A Spiritual Spicerie* (n.d.[1638]), 426–9. Cf. *Epistolae Ho-Elianae The Familiar Letters of James Howell*, ed. Joseph Jacobs (1890), 34.

to confess in the same breath that it had 'not yet been reduced to a scholastic method, so as to be taught systematically'.[18]

It was a truism of textbook writers that the common law was rationally grounded upon various well-known fundamentals. By this they did not mean that its detailed propositions could be deduced from certain basic premises, nor that it was a neat and symmetrical body of knowledge. The reason of the law was in fact a mystique, a professional trade secret, which could only be comprehended by those who had diligently applied themselves to its subtleties for many years. This point is brought out clearly by Coke's famous reply to James I in 1607:

> Then the king said he thought the law was founded upon reason, and that he and others had reason as well as the judges. To which it was answered by me that true it was God had endowed his majesty with excellent science and great endowments of nature, but his majesty was not learned in the laws of his realm of England, and causes which concern the life or inheritance or goods or fortunes of his subjects are not to be decided by natural reason, but by the artificial judgement and reason of the law – which law is an act [*sic*. ?art] which requires long study and experience, before that a man can attain to cognizance in it.[19]

So, as Richard Keble put it in the opening speech of his Lent reading at Gray's Inn in 1638, paraphrasing the words of Sir William Staunford seventy years before,

> this knowledge is planted soe farre off, the iorneye thereunto soe exceeding longe . . . the wayes and pathes soe rugged and unpleasant, that most choose, rather to rest in want of this knowledge than to undergoe the wearisome labour in the sadd shadowes of their studyes to find it out. And doe many tymes, turne themselves to delights of youth.[20]

Guides to method

The most formidable part of the would-be lawyer's training was to read, digest and commonplace cases from the year books and the reports. Various printed aids to this task were available; abridgements and digests which summarised cases, statutes and writs under alphabetical headings; institutional books, which aimed to provide a more or less comprehensive map of the whole body of the law or some major aspect; specialised treatises on narrower topics, such as the jurisdic-

---

[18] Sir Edward Coke, *A Booke of Entries* (1614), sig. Ai (f. 2r); Harleian 980, f. 81; Heneage Finch, *Law, or a Discourse thereof* . . . (1627), 225; Sir John Croke, preface to Robert Keilway, *Reports D'ascuns cases* (1668, 1st publ. 1602), sig. a.
[19] *Reports of Sir E. Coke* . . ., ed. G. Wilson (1777), *XII Rep.*, 65.
[20] William Staunford, *An Exposition of the Kinges Praerogative* (1607, 1st publ. 1567), sig. Aiiii; Bodl. MS, Rawlinson C, 207, f. 185.

tion of the courts, forest and mercantile law, the law for J.P.s, and so forth; and books of method, which sought to impart the techniques of studying and absorbing legal principles. The practice advocated by Coke was to begin with the institutional books – Littleton's *Tenures*, St Germain's *Doctor and Student*, Perkins's *Profitable Booke*, Finch's *Nomotechnia* and possibly Coke's own *Commentary on Littleton*, then work back from the sixteenth-century reporters – Coke, Dyer, Keilway, Plowden – to the year books. This was the approximate plan of campaign adopted by Simonds D'Ewes in the 1620s and Justinian Pagitt in the 1630s, and still being recommended by Sir Mathew Hale in 1668.[21]

But to the modern reader even the so-called institutional works are heavy going, and it is hard to believe that students in the seventeenth century found them much more congenial, even if they came prepared with some background knowledge and were accustomed to using texts which their modern counterparts would find extremely confusing, dry and poorly arranged. Littleton's *Tenures*, the cornerstone of the common law, which Coke characteristically called 'the most perfect work ever written in any humane science', went through at least sixty editions before the Civil War. Yet anyone who has grappled with this book is more likely to endorse John Cooke's assessment of Littleton as 'undoubtedly the most crabbed author to begin with of any science in the world'.[22] From the first page, a complicated table in law-French showing the different varieties of tenure, Littleton makes no concession to his reader. There seems to be no logical order in the development of each section, and while the rules of inheritance, for example, are discussed in detail with year-book citations, no attempt is made to formulate general principles.

Coke's *Commentary*, the first volume of his *Institutes*, aimed to 'institute and instruct the studious, and guide him in a readie way to the knowledge of the nationall lawes of England'. Coke's expressed hope was that the student who had previously been discouraged, 'as many are', by his struggle with 'as difficult termes and matters as in many years after', would 'have the difficulties and darknesse both of the matter and termes and wordes of the art in the beginning of his studie facilitated and explained unto him, to the end he may proceed in his studie cheerefully and with delight'. But Littleton's comparatively brief treatise provided merely the framework on which Coke built a 'painfull and large volume', the fruit of a lifetime's reading and practice. Without an index or even a table of contents, it must

---

[21] D'Ewes, *Autobiography*, i. 161–305; see below, p. 163; Hargrave, *Collectanea Juridica*, ii. 48. The older method, which began with a close study of writs and pleadings, is well illustrated by 'The autobiography of Sir John Savile of Methley . . . 1546–1607', ed. J. W. Clay and John Lister, *Yorks. Arch. J.*, 15 (1898–1900), 423. Cf. L. A. Knafla, 'The law studies of an Elizabethan student', *HLQ*, 32 (1969), 221–40.

[22] Cooke, *Vindication*, 94.

have taxed the student's concentration and diligence to the utmost; indeed Roger North maintained that Coke on Littleton 'breeds more disorder in the braine than any other book can'.[23] It was too formless and yet not sufficiently comprehensive to be regarded as an institution in the classical sense. That it could have been so widely recommended for the groundwork of legal studies is a telling verdict on the state of the law in the seventeenth and eighteenth centuries.

Another long book, which attempted to cover the whole common law, rather than just the law of real property, was the work first published in law-French as *Nomotechnia* in 1613, and in English, with some changes and omissions, as *Law, or a Discourse thereof . . .* in 1627. The first part dealt with the derivation of the common law, maxims and principles of legal construction; the second with substantive law, legal personality and the law of property real and personal; the third with 'offences and punishments' or criminal law; while the fourth and by far the largest handled writs and pleadings, the law of actions. Although often regarded as a precursor of Blackstone's *Commentaries*, as an attempt to systematise the law for beginners it was only partially successful; in more than five hundred pages, the author said very little about equity, or recent developments in the action of trespass and commercial law. Nor did he succeed in reducing the complex subject of actions to an easily handled group of fundamental elements, despite his assertion that whoever 'would take the whole body of the law before him and goe really and judicially to work, must not lay the foundation of his building in estates, tenures, the gift of writs and such like, but at those current and sound principles which our books are full of'.[24]

A few authors took another approach; instead of trying to rationalise the structure of the law, they sought primarily to improve the student's learning techniques. Both Abraham Fraunce's *The Lawyers Logicke* (1588) and Sir John Doddridge's *The English Lawyer* (1631), were intended to show that a student could acquire a knowledge of the law without great difficulty if he took advantage of the methods of formal logic. Fraunce, an M.A. of St John's College, Cambridge, was admitted to Gray's Inn in 1583, called to the bar in 1588, and afterwards practised at the council of the Marches. He is best known as a disciple of the French humanist philosopher Peter Ramus, and his *Lawiers Logike, exemplifing the praecepts of Logike by the practise of the common Lawe* represented the culmination of seven years'

---

[23] *The First Part of the Institutes of the Laws of England, or, A Commentary on Littleton, not the name of a Lawyer onely, but of the Law it self*, (1628), sig. qq 2; North, *Discourse*, 22.

[24] Cf. *HEL*, v. 399–401. I am grateful to Mr J. P. Cooper for drawing my attention to Bodl. MS, Eng. Misc. e. 476, an English text entitled 'Nomotecnia The arte of Lawe or the Lawyers Logique', which seems to be a common source for both the 1613 and 1627 editions, but is dated from Gray's Inn by Michael Pyndar, 23 Aug. 1604.

labours, beginning at Cambridge, to produce an English version of Ramus's *Dialecticae Libri Duo.*

Fraunce's main thesis was that while the lack of instruction and supervision at the inns made the common law seem 'so hard, so unsavoury, so barbarous', these apparent difficulties would disappear once the correct intellectual tools were applied: he himself had found 'the practise of law to bee the use of logike, and the method of logike to lighten the law'.[25] However Fraunce's book seems to have made no mark on the legal profession, perhaps because his attempt to apply philosophical methods to legal analysis was regarded as too abstract and impractical.

More notice was taken of Doddridge's tract, published posthumously after a pirate edition appeared in 1629. This was longer and much more comprehensive than Fraunce, with extensive introductory remarks on the 'naturall gifts and faculties the student of the law ought to be furnished withall', and the 'vertues intellectual and the liberall sciences' which he should endeavour to acquire. But the central thesis was again 'that logike is necessary for obtaining of the knowledge of the law'; and despite Doddridge's stated intention merely to inform the student of the rules of logic, 'leaving the exact knowledge thereof to the logike schoole', more than two-thirds of the book are concerned with the detailed development of this theme. It is hard to see how the beginner could have derived much benefit from this well-intentioned but long-winded discussion, although it might perhaps have helped the intellectually fastidious overcome their repugnance to the common law. After the Restoration William Phillips suggested that, if Doddridge had lived longer, he 'doubtless had produced a piece worthy of such a learned man, but therein he hath handled only, though indeed fully, one part of the study, to wit, the collecting of principles and maxims'.[26] While it was all very well to provide the student with a method of analysing cases, neither Doddridge nor Fulbecke could suggest to which cases and in what order their methods should be applied.

More down to earth with William Fulbecke's *A Direction, or Preparation to the Study of the Law* (1600), which was intended as a comprehensive guide to the first steps of legal learning. Very little is known of Fulbecke, who belonged to Gray's Inn, having taken an M.A. degree at Christ Church in 1584 and possibly practised as a civil lawyer; he also wrote a *Parallele, or Conference of the Civill Law, the Canon Law and the Common Law of this Realme of England* (1601–2), which,

25 Cf. W. S. Howell, *Logic and Rhetoric in England, 1500–1700* (Princeton, 1956), 222–8; Abraham Fraunce, *Victoria*, ed. G. C. Moore Smith (Louvain, 1906), xiv–xi; *idem, Lawyers Logike*, sig. Q.
26 Doddridge, *The Lawyers Light: or A Due Direction to the study of the Law* (1629); *idem, The English Lawyer; Describing a Method for the managing of the Lawes of this Land* (1631) sigs. A3–4, 62, 107; W. Phillips, *The Principles of the Law Reduced to Practice* (1661), sigs. A2v–A3.

like John Cowell's *Institutiones Juris Anglicani* (1605) and Sir Thomas Ridley's *View of the Civile and Ecclesiastical Law* (1607), compared and contrasted the rival codes. After the obligatory panegyric to the common law, Fulbecke discussed the 'good qualities wherewith the student of the law ought to be furnished', emphasising the necessity of diligence and powers of concentration, in view of the great number of cases which had to be read and remembered. After discussing the best time in the day for study, Fulbecke goes on to deal with other difficulties 'which are more frequent and doubtful, and are occasions, that many which doe enter this studie doe break off their course, and bid the law farewell'. These turn out to be identical with the stock criticisms of ecclesiastics and schoolmen, that the common law was a barbarous study, 'a science voide of all proper definitions, artificial divisions, and formall reasons'. The rebuttal is also along fairly conventional lines: Fulbecke asserts, for example, that 'the wordes of the law, though they be harsh in form, yet they are pregnant in sense', and claims the law is based on reason, although this reason is not common or natural, but specific to the law itself.

Moving on to the question of reading, Fulbecke gave a brief indication of the content and authority of a large number of texts, without offering any guidance as to the order in which they were to be read. Judging from the sequence in which they are listed, the learner might have supposed that he should proceed from Justinian's *Institutes*, via the commentators, to the year books. This is almost as if students coming to medieval English history were told that they would never really understand the subject unless they commenced with the chronicles and progressed to the pipe rolls. It was precisely because the year-books were so complex, with 'the most difficult cases of the lawe / as they come to hand / set out of frame and order [that] for lack of good grundes playnely expressed the same yeres / have so amased / dulled and discouraged many noble wyttes lernying the same'.[27]

In the following chapter Fulbecke expounded some elementary principles of legal construction and advised students to participate in learning exercises, 'for as a man knoweth by his books, so is hee known by his practise'. Later chapters include an exposition of the 'ende and effecte of the lawe ... in distinguishing and establishing the property and community of things' and a short glossary of legal terms and phrases. Finally he propounded a 'methode ... to bee used in handling and disposing matters of law', a technique of analysis and synthesis designed to help the learner distinguish *rationes decidendae* from *obiter dicta*, illustrated by application to a chapter of Littleton and two year-book cases.[28]

John Cooke praised Fulbecke's *Direction* as 'the most judicious that

[27] John Britten, [On the laws of England], (1540), sig. A.
[28] *A Direction, passim.*

ever was concerning this subject' and it would clearly have provided much more practical assistance to the fledgling lawyer than the works of Doddridge and Fraunce. On the other hand, Fulbecke was equally unable to solve the basic problem, the disorderly and unsystematic nature of the common law itself. The law remained 'a farrago of detailed instances, which defied any scheme of arrangement, save possibly the alphabetical'; methodisers might produce any number of secondary axioms or maxims by applying formal logic to individual cases, but the task of relating one to another and eliminating exceptions was beyond human skill. As Roger North remarked early in the eighteenth century, 'of all professions in the world, that pretend to book learning, none is so devoid of institution as that of the common law'.[29]

The difficulties of negotiating the intellectual morass of the common law are graphically described by an anonymous treatise in the Bodleian library, which on internal evidence seems to date from the late 1640s.[30] The author is clearly a Baconian-minded common lawyer, well acquainted with the literature of his profession and widely read outside it. His overriding concern is to rationalise the learning process. The need for direction is first established:

> Necessary it is, that in the reading of the lawes of England, order and method bee observed; but this order and method noe mann as yett hath endeavoured to sett downe. Neither are there any tutors appointed . . . as other arts and sciences, have in the university . . .

However, the main reason for the difficulty of the law is that students have been ill-advised:

> infinitely therefore doe they erre who direct men to read perticulers, and those perticuler controversies and also all such matters as are of totally different nature, as all our cases in the yeare bookes are . . . and mostly filled with itterated janglings, aboute pleadings and exceptions to writts etc. more than the matter it selfe.

Thus Coke's advice to commence with the 'little' books and read back from the modern reporters to the year books must be discarded, for it will 'both confound and weary the spirits, if not of all, yett of most':

---

[29] Cooke, *Vindication*, 70; Plucknett, *op. cit.*, 19–20; W. S. Holdsworth, 'Charles Viner and the abridgements of English law', *LQR*, 39 (1923), 37–9; North, *Discourse*, 1.

[30] 'Directions for the orderly reading of the law of England' Bodl. MS, Rawlinson C. 207, ff. 245–70. This large paper book contains an assortment of legal material in different hands dated between 1614 and 1663, including notes on Whitelocke's 1619 reading, Keble's 1639 reading, rules for the exposition of the statutes attributed to one of the Crews, and a draft marriage settlement of 1663. The 'Directions' are a corrected draft, and undated; they contain no reference to external events, but numerous texts are cited, the latest being Coke's *Third Institutes* (1644) and Nathaniel Bacon's *Historical Discourse of the Uniformity of England* (1647).

my selfe (for want of better), followed this course by the advise of Lord Cookes epistles, and other his scattered and broken directions ... till I had with a wearied spiritt, and almost destroyed body, read all bookes of lawe that I could find, and after that confused labour and almost lost tyme, returned too late to a more methodicall reading and studie.

Students were able neither to understand nor evaluate such confused and controversial material, 'though industry were almost infinite'. Moreover 'it was never yett the methode in any arte or science to beginne study with controversy. But with sound positive certaine rules of learning'.

The only sure way was for prospective law students first to attend university, where they could acquire some knowledge of grammar, logic, rhetoric and philosophy. They must then be told 'what authors in this lawe ... are first to be read, and in what manner and order, which to this day, as I conceive, is much wanted and much desired, there being no bookes of methodicall institution or introduction to the same'. They should in fact commence with the sixteenth-century abridgements of the year books, especially Brooke, who gives 'the case, judgment and reason'. Having read the entry under one title, the student must 'methodize by arte and rule of genus and specie', and so on with as many other entries as he may wish: 'Then to methodize these titles into that method of Bracton, such as concerne persons first, as worthiest, such as concern things next as necessariest, and such as concern actions last. And so to subdivide them.' [31]

This all seems rather familiar, except the suggestion that the abridgements should be substituted for the original year books. Commonplacing was hardly a novel technique and rules for collating miscellaneous material under subject headings were a major concern of all the methodisers. Despite his desire to develop a rational approach to legal learning based on the deductive method, the author's analysis of the problem is far more impressive than his proposed solution.

Lay and professional legal knowledge

Coke once compared learning the law to drawing water from a deep well:

As the bucket in the depth is easily drawne to the uppermost part of the water ... but take it from the water, it cannot be drawne up but with great difficulty; so albeit beginnings in this study seem difficult, yet when the professor of the law can dive into the depth, it is delightfull, easy and without any heavy burden.[32]

Another analogy which suggests itself is with the process of spiritual conversion; after dark days of confusion and struggle, the soul breaks

[31] 'Directions . . .', ff. 245, 246–7, 252, 255, 257, 259–60, 260–72.
[32] Coke, *Institutes*, i. 71a.

through to the clear conviction of the elect: just so Simonds D'Ewes recorded in his diary for 23 May 1623 that '. . . my love to the studie of the law beganne now to encrease verie much, I being reasonablie well able to command what I read; and finding dailie use of it I exceedinglie desired knowledge'.[33]

The difficulties of learning the law were obviously not insurmountable, or there would have been no legal profession at all in early seventeenth-century England. A lack of supervision and institutional incentives did not prevent ambitious and diligent young men from acquiring sufficient knowledge to be called to the bar and to practise. The minimum qualifications for call probably did not demand any highly developed legal expertise; but it is significant that while proponents of law reform frequently accused attorneys, court officers and solicitors of ignorance and incompetence, barristers were condemned for lacking morals, not learning. Reformers argued that the law need not be so complex if it were restated in plain English and accused the profession of needlessly complicating straightforward human issues of right and wrong for their own gain. In short, it was felt that barristers were too well briefed in their own sophistries, not that the public was being inadequately served by ill-trained men.[34]

But the fact that the fittest and most highly-motivated survived tells us nothing about the fate of the majority, the young gentlemen sent to the inns to acquire an elementary knowledge of law, rather than be called to the bar. No separate course of instruction was provided for amateur students, and none of the writers discussed above paid any special attention to their needs. Sir Humphrey Gilbert's scheme for an academy of young noblemen, which was designed partly for 'all those gentlemen of the innes of court which shall not apply themselves to the study of the law', envisaged the appointment of a lawyer to 'reade the groundes of the common lawes, and . . . draw the same as neare as may be into maximes, . . . for the more faire teaching of his auditory'. The duties of the J.P. and sheriff were also to be taught, 'not medling with plees or cunning pointes of the law'.

A more elaborate plan, presented to Burghley in 1592 by Thomas Bowyer, a Middle Temple bencher, was entitled, 'The seventeen partes of study of the lawes of England. Wherein every nobleman and gentleman may with great pleasure bestowe some part of his youth, and at whatever part he end become and continew able well to serve God, his prince and country'. The seventeen parts were actually branches or topics, each of which the young aristocrat was supposed to tackle in turn, from *De Verborum Significatione*, to *De Regulis Juris*. Bowyer actually prepared detailed instructions only for the first part, which

---

[33] Harleian 646, f. 69.
[34] Cf. Donald Veall, *The Popular Movement for Law Reform 1640–1660* (Oxford, 1970), chs. 2, 9; Mary Cotterell, 'Law reform during the Interregnum' (Sydney M.A. thesis, 1967), *passim*.

he thought the student would take four years to master by common-placing from a law dictionary and abridgements. At the same time he was to read over Littleton, 'to understand the tongue only, wythout regard to the matter at that his first reading'. Bowyer promised to write up the other sixteen parts, given both Burghley's encouragement and sufficient time; evidently one or both was not forthcoming, for this fragment alone has survived.[35]

In the absence of more definite directions or guides for study, we may infer that amateur students generally worked along the same lines as professionals.[36] Unfortunately, apart from John Petre's purchase of a handbook for justices of the peace, 'a booke of the later parte of henry the sixt his yeares' and a copy of Staunford's *Pleas of the Crown* (1567), we have no specific biographical evidence about the course of legal studies followed by any non-professional student during the later sixteenth or early seventeenth centuries.[37]

However, the kind and standard of legal knowledge acquired by amateur students can have borne little relationship to the professional expertise of the practising barrister. Even a thorough grounding in the institutional books like Littleton or Finch would hardly give the reader access to 'the reason of the law', that intimate, almost instinctive knowledge of substantive law and procedure in the field of real property, which the professional acquired only through a long process of reading, commonplacing, observing the courts and attending learning exercises. Gentlemen may well have been able to impress their social equals and intimidate their inferiors by recapitulating the forms of tenure; but it is doubtful whether this knowledge would have had much further utility, since the precise application of the law to any given circumstances could not ordinarily and positively be deduced from a limited number of general premises. The law's excessive formalism made it imperative for litigants to enlist expert professional advice both on strategy and tactics; those who could afford it kept a lawyer close at hand with an annual retaining fee.

A little knowledge of real property law could be a very dangerous thing. Even the most mechanical and seemingly straightforward legal procedures were fraught with perils for the unwary, as William Sheppard emphasised when he warned against 'the rash adventures of sundry ignorant men that meddle so much in these weighty matters . . . that may perhaps have some law books in their houses, but never read more law than is on the backside of Littleton'. The 'pragmatical

---

[35] *Queene Elizabethes Achademy*, 6–7; Lansdowne 98, ff. 10–12; Lansdowne 99, f. 159.
[36] Cf. the examples cited in *P & P*, 38 (1967), 25n.
[37] Essex R.O., D/DP A17, Nov. 1568, March 1569. Cf. Harrington's joke that at Lincoln's Inn, where he was admitted in 1581, he studied Littleton 'but to the title of discontinuance': N. E. McLure, *The Letters and Epigrams of Sir John Harrington* (Philadelphia, 1930), 11.

attorney', 'lawless scrivener' or 'ignorant vicar', who claimed to be able to draft a conveyance or judge a title, must have acquired his knowledge 'by education, or . . . not have it at all':

> But if they tell me that they have good precedents, I will tell them that a good conveyancer must be as well able to judge of the validity of the title, and primitive estate of him that is to convey, (which a man can never do without knowledge of the rules of law, no more than a blind man can judge of colour), as to make a derivative estate and conveyance by good precedent.[38]

Apart from land law, a country gentleman was likely to be personally concerned with the law administered by J.P.s and manorial courts. Neither of these specialised branches seems to have been much studied or taught at the inns, and both were treated at great length in numerous manuals specially designed for 'gentleman not conversant with the studie of lawes'. By the beginning of the seventeenth century few courts leet or baron were still presided over by laymen, although in any case Professor Dawson doubts whether 'the office of steward required of its incumbents an extensive knowledge of the common law', since the large role played by the freeholders' jury severely limited the steward's powers of decision.[39]

Even a cursory glance through the literature of the period will suggest that the England of Elizabeth and the early Stuarts was a society much concerned with legal forms and processes. It has been claimed that the apparent familiarity of many members of the landed classes with common-law doctrines and techniques can best be accounted for on the hypothesis that this knowledge was acquired during a period of residence at the inns of court.[40] Yet it is by no means certain that the admitted 'legal-mindedness' of the sixteenth and early seventeenth centuries was the product of a wide dissemination of legal knowledge. In many respects law then occupied much the same place in the popular mind as economics has enjoyed during the present century. Yet we would not necessarily expect our contemporaries who freely use terms drawn from the language of economics to have had any formal acquaintance with that subject; no more should we regard

---

38 William Sheppard, *A Touchstone of Common Assurances* (ed. Richard Preston, 1820, 1st publ. 1641), xxi–xxii; cf. Thomas Phaer, *A newe boke of Presidentes etc, in manner of a Register* (1543), sig. aiv: 'how great incomodities . . . aryse . . . by the negligence or rather ignorance of some . . . for lacke of good presidentes, or better, learned counsell . . .'. For examples of Chancery bills and answers rejected by the court as 'made in the country, without the advice of learned counsel', see Cecil Munro, *Acta Cancellaria . . . 1558–1624* (1847), 72, 81, 211, 216–17.

39 Cf. Putnam, *Early Treatises . . .*, 165–6; G. L. Haskins, *Law and Authority in Early Massachusetts* (New York, 1960), 167–8, 180; Michael Dalton, *The Countrey Iustice* (1618), sig. A3v; F. W. Maitland and W. P. Baildon, *The Court Baron* (*SS*, 4, 1891), 3–4; J. P. Dawson, *A History of Lay Judges* (Cambridge, Mass., 1960), 212–15.

40 Stone, *Aristocracy*, 692.

the litigious Jacobean who speaks portentously of actions, entails and fines as peculiarly gifted with an understanding of the technicalities of the common law.

Professor Harbage recently pointed out that, on the strength of some cleverly placed snippets of legal jargon, Shakespeare has been credited with a knowledge of the law which 'might have ruptured even the capacious brain of the Lord Chief Justice'. The copious scattering of legal terms and allusions through so much of the surviving evidence – correspondence, diaries, memoirs, plays, poems and treatises of all kinds – can easily mislead us into a similar assumption about Shakespeare's society at large. But we are then little more discerning than the rustics described by Abraham Fraunce, dashed 'quyte out of countenance, with villen in gros, villen regardent, and tenant par le curtesie'.[41]

So judged solely as law schools, the inns of court give little comfort to those who take an optimistic view of the quality of higher education in late sixteenth- and early seventeenth-century England. Learning the law was undoubtedly a frustrating, inelegant and tedious business, despite the efforts of textbook writers to simplify and systematise the task; little was (and perhaps could) be done by the inns to ease the professional student's labours and no distinctive methods of instruction were developed to meet the amateur's more limited requirements. No doubt some exceptionally gifted, industrious and sober youths may have acquired a modicum of legal knowledge during their stay, but the mere fact of an individual's admission to an inn certainly cannot be taken as evidence that he received there a legal education of any kind, or that he had any special familiarity with the theory and practice of the common law.

Accomplishments and the decline of creativity

Yet the inns were more than law schools. In the later fifteenth century Fortescue claimed that they could properly be regarded as 'a kind of academy of all the manners nobles learn', since in addition to the law their students were taught the courtly arts of dancing and singing. Despite a general preoccupation with classical book-learning, Tudor educational theorists fully shared the medieval enthusiasm for such non-academic outward accomplishments. Their characteristic attitude was expressed by Richard Mulcaster's rhetorical question: 'For which be gentlemanly qualities, if these be not, to reade, to write, to draw, to sing, to play, to have language, to have learning, to have health and activi-

---

[41] Alfred Harbage, *Conceptions of Shakespeare* (1966), 24; Fraunce, *op. cit.*, sig. Q3v. cf. Thomas Heywood's reference to the dull brain of a country justice, 'whose wit/Lies in his spruce clearke's standish . . .': *The Fair Maid of the West* (1631), sig. B2v, and *The Collected Papers of Frederic William Maitland*, ed. H. A. L. Fisher (Cambridge, 1911), ii. 477.

tie . . ?' Besides serving to fulfil the ideal of the balanced, well-rounded man, neither boor nor scholar, the physical graces and skills were important external symbols of gentility, and hence as much in demand by the genuine as the would-be gentleman.[42]

Fortescue does not say that the inns themselves provided any instruction outside the common law and throughout the later sixteenth and early seventeenth centuries junior members who wished to learn fencing, dancing and music – the courtly *trivium* – either patronised specialist academies or hired private tutors. John Petre, up from Essex at the Middle Temple, joined Currance's dancing school in April 1568, during his third term of residence, and in the following month was buying daggers and foils from one William Napper. William Fitzwilliam, admitted to Gray's Inn in 1594, paid almost as much for a month's dancing lessons as for his commons, while also receiving tuition in singing and attending a 'fence scole'. In the 1620s another Middle Templar paid the more modest sum of six shillings a month to be taught the viol by 'Mr Taylor, my musitian', but patronised a dancing school which exacted fifteen shillings in entrance fees and tips alone. Penurious students might wish to avoid such charges, but puritans who could afford them did so without marked scruples of conscience: Simonds D'Ewes was admitted both to dancing and fencing schools, while at Lincoln's Inn John Hutchinson 'exercised himself in those qualities he had not such opportunities for in the country, as dancing, fencing and music . . . entertaining the best tutors . . . at some expense'.[43]

The inns did little to encourage, although nothing to hinder, activities of this kind. Members had a chance to practise their dancing at the revels held every Saturday night between All Saints and Candlemas, and in the occasional masques staged by the societies. But from about the middle of James I's reign the Christmas period was devoted less to dancing than to gaming, and the production of masques also languished, despite a brief revival in the 1630s. The last masque to be written by a resident member of the society which performed it was William Brown's *Ulysses and Circe*, staged for the Inner Temple Christmas of 1614. The courtly accomplishments which the masque demanded were perhaps ceasing to be a standard attribute of the young inns of court student; it took weeks of rehearsal, with the inns 'all turned into dancing schools', before the participants in James Shirley's *Triumph of Peace*, presented by the four houses at Whitehall in 1634, were ready to play their parts.[44] This entirely professionalised

[42] *DLLA*, 119–21; Richard Mulcaster, *Positions* (1581), 208; Simon, *Education and Society in Tudor England*, 340–1, 353.
[43] Essex, R.O., D/DP/A17; Finch, *op. cit.*, 124; Bodl. MS, Eng. Misc. c. 238, pp. 12, 24; Cottonian Charter XVI. 13, ff. 11v, 12; *Memoirs of Hutchinson*, 54.
[44] Cf. above, pp. 112–13 (revels) and below, pp. 223–4 (masques). A. W. Green, *The Inns of Court and Early English Drama* (New Haven, 1931), 92–185, has a list of

production required more than three months to prepare; by contrast the *Masque of the Prince D'Amour*, staged a year later at the Middle Temple in honour of Charles Louis, the titular Count Palatine, was a very rushed job, 'devised and written in three days' by the cavalier poet Sir William Davenant, a close friend and former room-mate of Edward Hyde, although not himself a member of the society. The *Masque of the Prince d'Amour* was attended by Queen Henrietta-Maria, incognito in citizen's dress; but this first occasion on which a member of the royal family visited an inn of court was also the last on which a formal masque was presented by any of the societies.[45]

Just as the masques performed at the inns after 1614 were all written and designed by outsiders, so the plays produced there during the early seventeenth century were exclusively the work of professional dramatists, and troupes of paid actors. Indeed, after a brief but highly creative burst of dramatic activity in the 1560s, the societies seem to have relied entirely upon professionals; the only indigenous play known to have been performed between 1568 and 1640 was Thomas Hughes's *Misfortunes of Arthur*, presented at Greenwich by the gentlemen of Gray's Inn in 1589.[46] The passion for playgoing among members remained a stock literary joke, and with good reason; in a year and a half at the Inner Temple in the mid-1620s, Edward Heath attended no fewer than forty-nine plays. But this interest was entirely passive; and the action of the Lincoln's Inn benchers, who put an end to all plays and interludes in the house, foreshadowed a climate of opinion when the respectable lawyer would jeopardise his professional reputation by even attending a theatre.[47]

Dr Finkelpearl has observed that 'between Wyatt and Surrey and the appearance of Spenser and Sidney, all the poets, in fact almost all writers of any value, were connected with the inns of court . . . they were the literary center of England'. The societies lost their primacy to the new breed of professional writers during the later sixteenth century, but many members continued to circulate verse in manuscript among their friends. Indeed it has been claimed that the inns were the focal point of a major shift in poetic taste during the 1590s,

---

masques presented at the inns; also F. J. Finkelpearl, *John Marston of the Middle Temple* (Cambridge, Mass., 1969), chs. 2–6; HMC, *12 Rep.*, App. 2, 34 and *13 Rep.*, App. 2, 125.

[45] William Davenant, *The Triumphs of the Prince D'Amour* (1635), sig. A3; Alfred Harbage, *Sir William Davenant* (Philadelphia, 1935), 36; Williamson, *Temple*, 356–9, 440–1.

[46] But see F. J. Finkelpearl, 'John Marston's *Histrio-Mastix* as an inns of court play: a hypothesis', *HLQ*, 29 (1966), 223–34.

[47] F. S. Boas, *An Introduction to Tudor Drama* (Oxford, 1933), ch. 3; Alfred Harbage, *Shakespeare's Audience* (New York, 1941), 80–1; Egerton 2983, f. 24; L. C. Knights, *Drama and Society in the Age of Johnson* (1937), 229; William Prynne, *Histrio-Mastix* (1633), sig. 2v; Samuel Johnson, *Works*, ed. Robert Lynam (1825), iii. 402.

the rejection of neo-Petrarchan sonneteering for a direct and worldly statement inspired by the cynical, witty style of the Ovidian elegy. The leading figures in this literary revolution were John Donne, at Lincoln's Inn between 1592 and 1594, Thomas Campion, who entered Gray's Inn in 1586 and published his first work nine years later, although he had by then withdrawn from commons, and Sir John Davies, who joined the Middle Temple in 1588. Among their close contemporaries, fellow wits and versifiers were Francis Beaumont, John Ford, Everard Guilpin, Nicholas Hare, John Hoskyns, John Marston, Richard Martin, Thomas Overbury, Benjamin Rudyerd, John Salisbury and Edward Sharpham.[48]

The inns of court poets of the 1590s were fortunate enough to hit upon a style which neatly embodied both the rejection of an established literary convention and an approximate statement of their own social and personal attitudes. But this productive synthesis was not long maintained. William Browne's *Britannia's Pastorals* (1613–1616) was the last poetic work of any consequence written by a resident member before the Civil War. Neither the sophisticated and technically polished court verse of the cavaliers nor the devotional poetry of Crashawe, Herbert and Traherne were congenial idioms for the inns of court student. By the time Browne returned to Oxford in 1624 the poets of the 1590s had long since moved away from the inns or given up writing altogether; Donne did come back to his old house, but as a D.D. and preacher, while Campion became a doctor and Davies a judge. Many Caroline poets – among them Benlowes, Carew, Cokayne, Denham, Lenton, Suckling and Vaughan – joined an inn for fashion's sake, but produced little or nothing during their stay. To this silver age of poetry, 'the most prolific in small talents . . . that the British Isles have perhaps ever known', the inns' active membership contributed only two decidedly third-rate versifiers, Thomas May and George Wither. So Thomas Randolph had ample justification for mocking the sterility of a convention turned in upon itself:

> . . . each day I'le write an Elegy,
> And in as lamentable Poetry,
> As any Inns of Court-man, that hath gone
> To buy an Ovid with a Littleton.[49]

The slackening of creativity at the societies after the turn of the sixteenth century is apparent in other spheres. During the first half of Elizabeth's reign their members virtually monopolised the publication of translations from the classics and modern languages, but Robert Ashley and William Style appear to be the only residents who published any translations whatever between 1603 and 1640. Even histori-

---

[48] Finkelpearl, *John Marston*, 261–4, 24; Carey, 'The Ovidian love elegy', chs. 9–13.
[49] C. V. Wedgwood, *Seventeenth-Century English Literature* (1950), 75; *The Poems of Thomas Randolph*, ed. G. Thornbury (1929), 39.

cal and antiquarian research, which were closely linked with the special interests and techniques of the common lawyer, seem to have lost much of their attraction after the dissolution of the Society of Antiquaries early in James I's reign. Thereafter the leading English antiquaries and historians, with the exception of John Selden and Edward Hyde, were not lawyers or inns of court men but heralds, university dons and gentlemen of private means.[50]

So while the inns undoubtedly remained a congenial milieu for those whose ambitions and talents ranged beyond the common law, after the first decade of the seventeenth century their members contributed to the arts and sciences rather as consumers and patrons than producers.[51] This was partly a reflection of growing specialisation within the legal profession (and indeed all intellectual life), partly a symptom of the general cultural malaise which seems to have set in around the middle of James I's reign; as divisions within society and the state grew more pronounced, the energies which had previously been devoted to literature and scholarship were channelled instead towards political and theological concerns.[52] Lawyers and young inns of court men still played a major role in London's intellectual society; Edward Hyde's acquaintance 'whilst he was only a student of the law, and stood at gaze, and irresolute of what course of life he should take', included Ben Jonson, Thomas Carew, Charles Cotton, Sir Kenelm Digby, Thomas May, John Vaughan, John Selden, William Davenant and Bulstrode Whitelocke. All these, except Digby, had some sort of personal connection with the inns, but their relationship was mediated by common interests rather than institutional affiliations.[53] That sociable bachelor Selden made a special point of gathering a circle of bright young protégés around him, providing Bulstrode Whitelocke, for example, with instruction in Hebrew and general advice about his course of study; (Francis Bacon, on the other hand, made no great

---

[50] C. H. Conley, *The First English Translators of the Classics* (New Haven, 1947), 23–7; Douglas Bush, *English Literature in the Earlier Seventeenth Century 1600–1660* (Oxford, 1962), 57–75. R. J. Schoeck, 'The Elizabethan Society of Antiquaries and Men of the Law', *N & Q*, n.s. 1 (1954), 417–21; J. G. Pocock, *The Ancient Constitution and the Feudal Law* (Cambridge, 1957), 93–4; Linda van Norden, 'Sir Henry Spelman on the chronology of the Elizabethan Society of Antiquaries', *HLQ*, 13 (1949–50), 131–60; F. S. Fussner, *The Historical Revolution* (1962), 26–32, 92–100, 134–6, 275–98. The withdrawal of the common lawyer from historical studies is even more noticeable after the Restoration: cf. D. C. Douglas, *English Scholars* (1939), 104–5, *et passim*; *The Diary and Correspondence of John Evelyn*, ed. William Bray (n.d., [1906]), 717–18.

[51] Cf. Alfred Harbage, *Shakespeare and the Rival Traditions* (New York, 1952), 53–7; I. A. Shapiro, 'The Mermaid Club', *Modern Language Review*, 45 (1950), 6–17; G. M. Young, 'Shakespeare and the Termers', *Proc. of the British Academy*, 33 (1947), 81–99.

[52] Cf. Hill, *Intellectual Origins*, 9–13, *et passim*.

[53] *Life of Clarendon*, 59–61.

effort to encourage wits and writers from Gray's Inn.) [54] But the fact remains that, with few individual exceptions, resident members of the inns became increasingly spectators and talkers, rather than active scholars and writers. It would be surprising if the societies had not produced some poets, playwrights and scholars during our period, since they drew their members predominantly from the relatively small leisured, literate élite and because London provided unique facilities for the development of potential talent. Yet for many whose interests lay outside the law the inns must have been simply a convenient place to lodge while surveying the field and seeking out a patron. Writers who had left the houses many years before often continued to identify themselves as members, but it would be naïve to suppose that their work therefore represents an indigenous inns of court movement or school. [55]

Varieties of learning

According to their learned preacher William Crashawe, the two Temples offered 'the most comfortable and delightful company for a scholler that (out of the universities) this kingdome yeelds'. In a later sermon Crashawe admonished the benchers of Gray's Inn to 'hold up learning in yourselves, help it forward in others, and shame them that say, law and learning cannot live together'. [56] The intellectual life of the inns was not however confined within rigid scholastic boundaries. Some indication of its diversity may be gained from the titles of books dedicated to the collective membership of the houses before 1640. These include, besides the inevitable law texts and sermons, the revised edition of Richard Percyvall's *Spanish Grammer* (1599), the fourth, fifth and sixth editions of Gerard Legh's immensely successful heraldic handbook, *Accedens of Armory*, and the 1635 edition of Mercator's atlas, the *Historia Mundi*, which earnestly beseeched the 'virtuous and learned gentlemen of the inns of court' to

[54] R. H. Whitelocke, *Memoirs, Biographical and Historical, of Bulstrode Whitelocke* (1860), 14, 17; cf. Gilbert Burnet, *Lives of Sir Mathew Hale and John Earl of Rochester* (1829), 23–6.
[55] Thus Thomas Lodge, admitted to Lincoln's Inn in 1578, soon gave up his studies and left the house, but continued to publish as '. . . of Lincoln's Inn, gent.'; cf. Thomas Lodge, *The Life and Death of William Longbeard* (1593), t.p. The evidence for associating Thomas Jordan and Thomas Nabbes with the inns during the 1630s (cf. Wedgwood, *Seventeenth-Century English Literature*, 76), seems to be no more than their dedication of works to patrons at Gray's Inn. James Shirley is supposed to have lived and written at Gray's Inn during the 1620s, but his son, who apparently supplied Anthony Wood with this information, may well have antedated the connection, since Shirley was only admitted to membership (honorifically) after the performance of *The Triumph of Peace* in 1634; cf. R. S. Forsythe, *The Relations of Shirley's Plays to the Elizabethan Drama* (New York, 1914), 25–6; *GI Adm. Reg.*, 202.
[56] William Crashawe, *Romish Forgeries and Falsifications* (1606), sig. q3; *idem*, *The Parable of Poyson* (1618), sig. A2.

Let none Henceforth be
Your mistresses, but fair Geographie. . . .[57]

John Minsheu's eleven-language dictionary, *The Guide into the tongues* (1617), was printed with the aid of contributions solicited from individual benchers and junior members of Gray's Inn, Lincoln's Inn and the Inner Temple, despite the rejection of Minsheu's requests for support from the official funds of the societies.[58] Young university *alumni* like Edward Hyde kept up their classics as a relief from the tedium of the law; students were frequently advised that humane studies were an indispensable basis and complement to legal learning. Moreover, while the inns were never major centres of scientific activity, we do know that individual members studied astronomy, anatomy, geography, history, mathematics and a wide range of foreign languages in their own time.[59]

If playgoing was the inns of court man's favourite recreation, listening to sermons and political gossip came a close second. Besides supporting their own preachers, the inns invited 'strangers' to deliver occasional sermons; members also went to hear sermons preached at Paul's Cross, the City churches and the court, although Sir John Harrington hinted that lawyers who went to court on Sundays were less interested in hearing the sermon than in lobbying for preferment.[60] It was inevitable that members should have taken a close interest in political questions and public affairs. Many lawyers served as M.P.s, the Westminster courts were only a few steps away from St Stephen's chapel and Commons' committees frequently met in the halls of the inns and the Temple Church. Lawyers who acted as stewards for country gentlemen, were landholders themselves and rode on circuit to the assizes were bound to notice the state of feeling in the country and carry a two-way news traffic between London and the shires. The law was so intermeshed with politics that students could hardly have been exposed to one without the other. Fleet Street was already the news centre of the country; the inns were strategically placed between City and court, ideally situated to pick up the latest rumours about

[57] F. B. Williams, *Index of Dedications and Commendatory Verses in English Books before 1641* (1962), 223.
[58] *Idem*, 'Scholarly publication in Shakespeare's England: a leading case', in *Joseph Quincy Adams Memorial Studies*, ed. J. G. McManaway *et al.*, (Washington, 1948), 755–73.
[59] *BB*, i. 398; D'Ewes, *Autobiography*, i. 230; E. R. Taylor, *Mathematical Practitioners of Tudor and Stuart England* (1954), 104, 118, 137, 162, 173, 175, 262; *idem*, *The Original Writings and Correspondence of the Two Richard Hakluyts* (*Hakluyt Soc.*, 2nd. ser., 7b, 1935), i. 3–7; Sir Gilbert Burnet, 'The Life and Death of Sir Mathew Hale', in Mathew Hale, *Contemplations Morall and Divine the Third Part* (1695), 13–15; W. B. Rye, *England as seen by Foreigners* (1865), 103. See also B. J. Shapiro, 'Law and science in seventeenth-century England' *Stanford Law Review*, 21 (1969), 736–7.
[60] Sir John Harrington, *Epigrams* (1615), sig. D2v.

Continental wars or Whitehall scandals: as D'Ewes put it, 'London, like Africa *semper aliquid novi parens*'.

A vivid impression of the lively gossip market at one inn is provided by an anonymous poem of 1628, dedicated to the 'Peripatetique College-Errant of Novellists, Rumourists, Buzzists and Mythologists of this Age, incorporated in Grayes Inne walkes':

> Freinde, sette not heere, unless thou bee
> a sectary of Noveltye,
> sworne to the Colledge, and profess't
> a ceremoniall Nouelliste:
> stuffed with Ballades, Masques and Rymes,
> Of Malice smarting at the Tymes
> with fictions, rumours, buzzes, fables,
> or voyder newes from Nobles tables
> Gazetts, Corantos of affayres,
> whole Annales of the fighting Stares,
> Intelligence from euery state,
> Or dragons seene in Sussex late . . .
> . . .
> But if thou all these talents wante,
> doe not these sacred shadowes haunt.[61]

Accounts of book purchases and library inventories further illustrate the breadth of interests represented at the inns. Sir Roger Wilbraham, a bencher of Gray's Inn who returned from Ireland to become a master of Requests in 1600, drew up at this time a list of intended reading: apart from numerous professional texts he included the *oblectamenta historiae* of Caesar, Livy, Pliny, Sallust, Comines, Lipsius, Camden and Holinshed, as well as Sebastian Verro's Aristotelian epitome of natural philosophy, *Physicorum Libri X* (1581) and Jean Fernel's *Universa Medecina* (Frankfurt, 1581).[62] A more conventional balance between ancients and moderns appears in an inventory of the books of William Smith, the eldest son and heir of an East Anglian landed family, who was admitted to Gray's Inn from Cambridge University in June 1608 and died the following year. Smith left at Gray's Inn works by Catullus, Cicero (*De Oratione*), Livy, Plutarch (*The Lives*), Seneca (*Flores*), Suetonius and Tacitus; he also possessed a copy of Spenser's *Faerie Queene*, Gerard Mercator's *Atlas* (available only in continental editions until 1635) and an unspecified work by

---

[61] D'Ewes, *Autobiography*, ii. 185; Bodl. MS, Rawlinson Poet. 166, ff. 89–90; cf. P. L. Ralph, *Sir Humphrey Mildmay: Royalist Gentleman* (New Brunswick, 1949), 154.
[62] *The Journal of Sir Roger Wilbraham*, xxi. Wilbraham also lists three '*Sacris Libris*': John Rainolds, *The Summe of the Conference betweene John Rainoldes and John Hart* (1588), plus two unidentified titles, '*Controversiae Ambarum Ecclesiarum Beza, et Textus Proverbiorum Novumque Testamentum*'. (Note that for all books listed in the text only the date of the first known edition is given.)

the German mathematician and philosopher Johannes Magirus.[63]

Three near-contemporaries at the Middle Temple, Simonds D'Ewes, William Freke, and Justinian Pagitt, kept extensive records of their literary acquisitions and pursuits. D'Ewes began his career as a bibliophile at the Middle Temple, where he arrived from Cambridge in Michaelmas term 1620. His purchases up to the year 1626, when his interests turned almost exclusively to antiquarian research, were concentrated in the fields of law, current politics and theology, heraldry, history and genealogy. He bought no classics, other than an English selection from the *Odes* of Horace, no romances, plays or verse apart from a contemporary edition of Sidney's *Arcadia* and no mathematical or scientific material, except among some two dozen manuscripts acquired from the library of the astrologer John Dee, none of which D'Ewes seems to have prized very highly.[64]

William Freke was the sixth son of a Dorset squire; he entered the Middle Temple from Oxford in 1622 and came into commons at once, although he was not formally admitted to a chamber until 1626. William kept detailed notes of his expenses, from which it is possible to trace his book purchases, and hence, presumably, his reading.[65] His first year's acquisitions included two devotional works, Lewis Bayly's *Practice of Pietie* (1613) and Christopher Sutton's *Godly Meditations upon the Sacrament of the Lord's Supper* (1601), the pseudo-Aristotelian 'Problemata' (presumably the English translation first published in 1595), John Indagine's *Briefe Introductions ... unto the Art of Chiromancie, or Manuell Divination, and Physiognomy* (1558), an unidentified work of Albertus Magnus, Robert Record's *The Ground of Artes* (1542), Thomas Hill's *The Art of Vulgar Arithmeticke* (1600), an English Littleton and 'a booke of flowers and beastes'. During the next year Freke invested in Thomas Lodge's popular romance *Rosalynde: Eupheus Golden Legacie,* which ran to eleven editions between 1590 and 1640, Samuel Daniel's *The Collection of the historie of England* (1612–17), George Sandys's travel book, *The Relation of a Journey begun an. Dom. 1610* (1615), 'a french bible', Shakespeare's *Othello* and Thomas Thomkis's academic play, *Lingua or the Combat of the Tongues* (1607).

In 1625 Freke bought Francis Bacon's *Apothegemes* and a ballad on the Amboyna massacre hot from the press, together with the collected works of the Elizabethan puritan Edward Dering, and 'a

63 SP 12/288/27. This undated document has been calendared in *CSPD, 1601–03,* 313. But references to books at Cambridge and to the delivery of the inventory to 'Mr Owen Smith' indicate that the owner of the property listed was William, son and heir of William Smith Esq. of Burgh Castle, Suffolk, etc. and brother of Owen, who was admitted to Trinity College, Cambridge, in 1606, to Gray's Inn in 1608, and died unmarried in 1609: *Al. Cant.*, iv. 113.
64 A. G. Watson, *The Library of Sir Simonds D'Ewes* (1966), 20–2, 226–48.
65 Bodl. MS, Eng. misc. c. 238, pp. 11–98; C. B. Fry, *Records of a Wiltshire Parish* (1935), 15–16; *MTR*, ii. 625, 709.

treatise of patience in tribulation'. Next year, besides plague bills, 'other pamphletts', 'the English Secretarie' and Marlowe's translation of Ovid's *Elegies*, he acquired a manuscript copy of Sir Henry Manwayring's treatise on seamanship, compiled towards the end of James I's reign and printed in 1644 as *The Seaman's Dictionary*,[66] Hakluyt's *Voyages and Navigations of the English Nation* and Samuel Purchas's *Posthumus, or Purchas his Pilgrimes* (1625); for Hakluyt he paid a deposit of eighteen shillings, on condition that his money would be refunded, less a shilling, if the books were returned before Christmas. Freke's interest in maritime exploration, particularly fitting for a West Country man and Middle Templar, also led him to make several expeditions with his elder brother to the anchorage at Gravesend and 'to see the Eastindia shippes at Erith'. Between 1627 and 1635, when he seems to have gone out of residence, Freke's purchases continue to reflect an extraordinary eclecticism, embracing antiquities, calligraphy, drawing, geography, history, contemporary English and European literature, medicine, natural philosophy, theology and public affairs. However, no law books appear after the Littleton bought in 1622, which, together with the fact that he remained a resident for nearly fifteen years without being called to the bar, suggests that Freke made little attempt to study law (although he might have borrowed professional texts from his brother Ralph, who was called to the bar in 1628, or his uncle Richard Swayne, a bencher of the house with whom he occasionally went on circuit).

Justinian Pagitt, the eldest son of a baron of the Exchequer, followed a somewhat more conventional career. Pagitt was admitted to Christ's College, Cambridge, in January 1627 at the age of fifteen and to the Middle Temple in October 1628. Although he did not gain formal admission to a chamber until June 1634, Justinian was keeping commons at the Middle Temple by the autumn of 1633, when his commonplace book or occasional journal begins.[67] Besides copies of personal letters, transcripts of sermons, notes and memoranda on astrology, dancing, family law suits, current political events and the state of his own body, mind and soul, this manuscript contains a series of weekly diaries in note form, running from 29 September 1633 to 10 January 1634.[68] Pagitt seems originally to have intended these to record how his time was spent in the three daily periods, from six to ten in the morning, from one to five in the afternoon and from seven to ten in the evening, which he set aside for secular reading and spiritual duties. But after the first week or so they include brief notes on

---

[66] *The Life and Works of Sir Henry Mainwaring*, ed. G. E. Manwaring (*Navy Records Soc.*, 1920–22), i. 85n, 134, 303–5.
[67] *Elias Ashmole (1617–1692)*, ed. C. H. Josten (Oxford, 1966), i. 14–15, iii. 1135; *MTR*, ii. 737, 823; R. L. Hine, *The Cream of Curiosity* (1920), 181–212; Harleian 1026.
[68] Harleian 1026, ff. 69–74.

virtually all his activities throughout the day, although with numerous missing and incomplete entries.

Sundays were usually kept free from worldly concerns, devoted to Bible-reading, self-catechism, sermons at the Temple Church or St Paul's and private meditation. Most weekdays also began with prayer and a chapter of Scripture, except on the not infrequent occasions when Pagitt records '*somnolentia peccavi*' or '*otiosus in cubiculo*'. During October and November at least two hours of reading generally followed, occasionally varied by an excursion to Westminster Hall, visits to friends and relatives, or physical recreation in the form of dancing, riding and vaulting. His afternoons and evenings did not conform to any fixed pattern, but the day ended by 9 or 10 p.m. with prayers, perhaps another chapter from the Bible and a brief self-examination and revision of the day's accomplishments.

Pagitt's legal studies, so far as they are recorded in his diaries, were not extensive. Between 29 September and 27 November he read and commonplaced Finch's *Nomotechnia* from page 273 to page 399; this, plus the first two chapters of a work identified only as Speed's Abridgement or 'Epitome' (which has not been found) and two cases from Coke's *Reports* made up the total of legal reading during the period covered by the diaries. In addition he attended a single moot in October and made several visits to Westminster Hall, besides going once to Newgate sessions and to Whitehall for the hearing of Dr Micklethwaite's case before the privy council.[69]

Pagitt's slow progress with the law was probably part cause, part effect of misgivings about the career to which his father had evidently destined him from birth, and more recently by securing for him the office of Custos Brevium in the King's Bench; at any rate he spent several whole mornings and afternoons during the month of October in '*meditaciones de lawyers life*' and '*de cursu vita meae*'. Yet despite a cryptic note implying a distaste for 'too much bookishnesse', Justinian managed to read an impressive amount of non-legal material. Most of the titles listed in the diaries are devotional and theological works; unlike D'Ewes, Pagitt had little interest in anti-catholic polemics, and the authors he favoured were mainly middle of the road protestants – Lewis Bayley, John Boys, Joseph Hall, the German scholar and textbook writer Bartholomew Keckerman, and the somewhat more radical Jacobean divine Andrew Willet.[70]

In December 1633 he noted '*Legi carmina vocat the Church Porch*',

[69] For Micklethwaite, see below, pp. 199–201.

[70] The works I have been able to identify are as follows: Lewis Bayly, *The Practice of Pietie* (1613); John Boys, *An Exposition of the Festivall Epistles and Gospels used in our English Liturgie* (1613); Joseph Hall, *Salomon's Divine Arts* (1609); Bartholemew Keckerman, *Systema SS. Theologiae, tribus libris adornatum* (Hanover, 1602), translated as *A Manduction to Theologie* (?1622); Andrew Willet, *Hexapla in Genesin, that is, a sixfold commentarie upon Genesis* (1605). Pagitt

which was presumably the first part of George Herbert's *The Temple*, published posthumously that year by Nicholas Ferrar. No other poetry is mentioned and Pagitt's secular reading seems not to have included any plays, romances, satires, history (with the partial exception of John Selden's *Titles of Honour*) or political tracts. The only purely literary work consulted was the *Thrysii Philotesii* of the Belgian humanist, Erycius Puteanus (1574–1646), a collection of Latin letters notable more for their stylistic qualities than substantive content.[71] At least three other works of contemporary European scholarship appear; these are the four-volume *Encyclopaedia* (Herborn, 1630) of the German Ramist Johann Alsted, the Dutch academician Edon von Neuhaus's *Theatrum Igenii Humani: sive de congnoscenda hominum indole et secretis animi libri II* (Amsterdam, 1633), a compendium of physiological and psychological observations, and the equally encyclopedic *Magnum Theatrum Vitae Humanae* (Cologne, 1631), by another Belgian catholic, Lawrence Beyerlinck (1578–1627), the archpriest of Antwerp.[72] The two English works listed differ sharply in approach and content; they are William Pemble's *De Formarum Origine* (1629), a brief metaphysical monograph by a Calvinist theologian from Oxford, and Francis Bacon's *Advancement of Learning* (1605), a map of the whole world of knowledge by one of the major intellectual figures of the age. Finally, in a letter to his friend James Harrington, the future author of *Oceana*, Pagitt requested as an 'especiall favour' the loan of 'Sir Kenelm Digby's Mathematicall Discourse which you once told me of' (another work which I cannot identify).[73] Pagitt's evident interest in compilations and schemes of knowledge, and his contacts with Elias Ashmole, who was at this time lodging in his parents' house, might perhaps be seen as symptomatic of the progress of popular scientific curiosity. But it is significant that the only section of Bacon's *Advancement* Pagitt read was from Book VIII, dealing with 'Negotiations and Business', and that this was consulted while he was attending a somewhat stormy series of meetings to finalise arrangements for the joint masque of February 1634.[74] While confirming the renewed influence of continental scholarship in England during

also mentions a 'History of the Bible' which might be the work of that title published at Cambridge by his namesake Eusebius Pagitt in 1603, and an unidentified 'Doctrine of the Bible'.

[71] *Bibliotheca Belgica*, ed. M. T. Lenger (Brussels, 1964), iv. 748–63.

[72] Fletcher, *Intellectual Development of Milton*, ii. 557–8; *Allgemeine Deutsche Biographie* (Leipzig, 1875–1900), xxiii. 509–10; E. de Seyn, *Dictionaire des Ecrivains Belges* (Bruges, 1930), i. 89–90; *The Catholic Encyclopedia* (New York, 1907), ii. 540.

[73] Harleian 1026, ff. 44–44v. No likely candidate appears in the bibliography of Digby's writings appended to R. T. Petersson, *Sir Kenelm Digby* (1956), 325–7.

[74] Harleian 1026, ff. 73–92; Francis Bacon, *Works*, ed. J. Spedding *et al.* (1857–74), v. 35 ff.; Bulstrode Whitelocke, *Memorials of the English Affairs* (1853), i. 55–6.

the early seventeenth century, this heterogeneous assortment of books and authors resists any easy characterisation, except perhaps as a reflection in miniature of the intellectual confusion of the pre-Civil War decade.[75]

The last surviving list was compiled for the forced sale of John Mostyn's books in 1643. Mostyn, who entered the Inner Temple in 1638 at the age of about thirty-five, perhaps as a companion to his elder brother's son Roger, sat as a member for county Flint in the Long Parliament, but joined the king in 1642.[76] This inventory includes seventeen named works and another thirty-four listed by size alone. Among the former were six or seven religious and theological titles, including Nathaniel Brent's translation of Sarpi's history of the Council of Trent, a volume of Lancelot Andrewes's sermons, *A Paraphrase on the Divine Poems* (1638) by George Sandys, Thomas Fuller's *The Historie of the Holy Warre* (1639) and Richard Montagu's *Appello Caesarem* (1625), some of which were perhaps acquired during Mostyn's service with Bishop John Williams during the 1620s. The secular books include an English Tacitus, the collected works of Ben Jonson, a 'Guiccardini old', an edition of Daniel's *History of England*, de Rojas' play, *The Spanish Bawd* (translated by James Mabbe in 1631), John Speidall's *Breefe Treatise of Sphaericall Triangles* (1627), Edmund Gunter's *De Sectore & Radio* (1623), an unidentified work by the arithmetician Robert Record, Rastell's *Termes del Ley* and a 'Guide of the french tongue'. If these fifty-odd books represented Mostyn's entire library, and not just that part which he kept in London, it was a small collection by contemporary standards; Sir Edward Coke's library at Holkham Hall contained more than 1,200 volumes, the portion of John Selden's library which was acquired by the Bodleian included over 8,000 separate items (mainly classics, history, science, law, theology, and Oriental literature), while in 1641 Robert Ashley of the Middle Temple bequeathed to the society a collection of more than 5,000 works covering nearly every branch of learning, but particularly strong in civil and canon law, geography, history, mathematics, medicine, politics and theology.[77]

---

[75] Two entries remain unidentified: on 15 or possibly 16 November 1633, Pagitt notes 'Legi Cassanru. (?) in Bibliotheca Westmon. de Advocatis'. I cannot place the 'Bibliotheca Westmon.', unless, of course, it is Sir Robert Cotton's library. On 30 November Pagitt notes 'Legi Cartiludin. Logic'. No such work has been found: Harleian 1026, ff. 72, 73ᵛ.

[76] Ian Roy, 'The Libraries of Edward, 2nd Viscount Conway and others: an inventory and valuation of 1643', *BIHR*, 103 (1968), 35–46; SP 20/7/10; Keeler, *Long Parliament*, 281; Lord Mostyn and T. A. Glenn, *History of the Family of Mostyn of Mostyn* (1925), 196; *Cal. Com. Comp.*, 1200.

[77] *The English Library before 1700*, ed. Francis Wormald and C. E. Wright (1958), 7–10; W. O. Hassall, *A Catalogue of the Library of Sir Edward Coke* (New Haven, 1950), ix–xxiv, 1–98; W. D. Macray, *Annals of the Bodleian Library* (Oxford, 1890), 110–23; *idem*, *A Register of the Members of St Mary Magdalen College, Oxford* (1894–1901), iii. 100–101.

Ashley thus became the second founder of the Middle Temple library, which had effectively disappeared by the mid-sixteenth century, due to the theft and dispersal of its small professional collection. The libraries of Gray's Inn and the Inner Temple also existed in little more than name during our period; their holdings were small and evidently little used, since the rooms in which they were housed seem to have been set aside mainly for gaming sessions and learning exercises.[78] At Lincoln's Inn, however, serious efforts to build up the collection and regulate its use were made from 1602 onwards, when James Ley, then a bencher, later chief justice of the King's Bench and lord treasurer, put forward a 'project for renewing of the lybrarye'. A committee report to the council 'concerninge reforminge of the librarye to his [sic] right use and storinge the same with bookes' recommended minor structural renovations and the appointment of a small group of senior members to solicit contributions of books. In 1609 all barristers and benchers were ordered to pay a levy on call, which would be put towards the purchase of books chosen by the newly appointed master of the library.[79] Acquisitions, mainly of legal works, continued to trickle in, but the next major initiative came with an offer from the barristers and students in November 1629, to make a regular contribution towards the purchase of books and the salary of a library keeper, if the benchers would provide 'convenient seates and presses both for bookes and studies'. Early next year council ordered 'that a common library shalbe made for the use of this society', and in February 1631 it was declared open, with Abraham Sherman, the chaplain, adding to his existing duties that of library keeper. Next year the entry fee of ten shillings in cash or one book was dropped, and 'every gentleman . . . admitted into the said librarie freely'. But the concession appears somewhat less significant in the light of the earliest surviving catalogue of the library's holdings, compiled in 1646. A total of only 224 titles is listed, under the headings of law, theology, philosophy, and history, a paltry collection indeed in comparison with the libraries of the two universities and most of their colleges.[80]

We have seen that during the late sixteenth and early seventeenth centuries the intellectual interests of inns of court members received little direct support from the societies themselves. Their main function was to bring together in London groups of men of similar social backgrounds, talents and tastes. Court and City provided the rest; congenial social contacts with like-minded individuals, books, ser-

---

[78] *OJ*, 197; Williamson, *Temple*, 125–6, 293, 381–3, 503, 648–51; *GIPB*, i. xlix–l; Douthwaite, *Gray's Inn*, 175–9.

[79] *BB*, ii. 73–5, 117, 121, 141, 230.

[80] *Ibid.*, 290–1, 292–3, 299, 303; Harleian 7363, ff. 81–5 (note however that the list may be incomplete, as f. 85, headed 'Phisicke bookes', contains only one entry and the following folios are blank). Wormald and Wright, *op. cit.*, 215, 217, 222; N. R. Ker, 'Oxford college libraries in the sixteenth century', *Bodleian Library Record*, 6 (1959), 459–515.

mons, theatres, lectures and demonstrations at Gresham College and the College of Physicians, tutors in practically every branch of human learning and skill. How many availed themselves of these opportunities and to what effect is impossible to determine. But from the book lists and other scattered evidence surveyed above, we may infer that many junior members, especially those who had no plans for a legal career, were preoccupied with acquiring the gentlemanly accomplishments of dancing, fencing and singing. Their cultural and intellectual norms tended to be aristocratic, literary and non-utilitarian, much influenced by the côterie fashions of the court and in many cases perhaps by their previous acquaintance with university scholasticism. Plotwell, the prodigal young Templar in Jasper Mayne's play *The Citye-Match* (1639), pays far more attention to 'the silk-man's book' than the law and speaks in 'queint figures' that to his city uncle Warehouse 'smell/Too much o'th'innes-of-court'. Warehouse tells Plotwell that if he intends to become a merchant he must be taught:

> ... French, Italian, Spanish
> And other tongues of traffique.
> *Plotwell*: Shall I not learne
> Arithmetick too sir, and shorthand?
> *Warehouse*: 'Tis well remembered; yes, and navigation.

But as soon as Warehouse departs, Plotwell shows his distaste for such practical learning.[81]

Many practising and student lawyers seem to have been slightly more adventurous, taking at least (and sometimes much more than) a dilettante interest in antiquities, history, languages and broadly scientific studies. In numerous individual cases law and learning clearly did go together. Of course, professional lawyers had the advantage of continued exposure to the intellectual stimuli of London throughout their working lives; but in any case the complexities of the common law demanded a high initial level of intelligence and a sustained mental activity which could easily spill over into other fields.

Achievements, failures and prescriptions

Edward Waterhous suggested three main reasons why the inns of court had become 'the Athens of the law'. First, their 'ingenious and fluid students, *viri omnium horarum*'. Second, their geographic location: 'London is near, and that being the metropolis of the nation, hath a daily flux and reflux of persons and things to it ... they may here have opportunity to buy authors that treat of all subjects and converse with proficients in all sciences'. Third, the fact that even those who 'come thither to study the law ... are not tethered or limited, but

[81] Jasper Mayne, *The Citye-Match* (1639), 3–5. Cf. Hill, *Intellectual Origins*, 95, 273.

give themselves a latitude of following that which is most congenial to them'.[82]

If we accept this explanation of the conditions which fostered the inns' rich cultural and intellectual life, perhaps adding the need felt by both lawyers and students to assert their gentility in the pursuit of activities not directly associated with the common law, it would appear that the prime institutional reason for the failure of the inns as law schools was a main cause of their success as liberal academies. The permissive discipline and lack of supervision, which exacerbated the difficulties of learning the law, equally allowed students full opportunity to further whatever extra-curricular interests they may have had. The only catch was that everything depended on the individual's initiative; such a *laisser-faire* system could be taken advantage of in more ways than one.

It must nevertheless be credited with some remarkable achievements. While the role of the inns as centres of creative scholarship and writing may have waned during the late sixteenth and early seventeenth centuries, they still continued to provide many a writer with an invaluable start to his career, both as congenial lodgings and anterooms to London's literary society. Their members were an important part of the discriminating and sophisticated metropolitan audience, while their patronage was also conferred directly upon actors, designers, musicians, playwrights and poets who contributed to the Christmas festivities, Grand Weeks and masques, as well as the architects, builders and craftsmen who constructed and adorned their halls and chapels. Finally, by exposing a large cross-section of the political nation, in their formative years, to the secular culture of the English renaissance, the inns helped to diffuse the artistic and intellectual effervescence of Elizabethan and early Stuart London throughout the land, to free the arts and sciences from the domination of court and Church (with its agencies, the universities) and hence to mould the distinctive cultural profile of England for several centuries to come.

But whether these substantial achievements justified or required a total lack of student guidance and supervision is another question. The rulers of the inns made no attempt to see that junior members used their freedom even to acquire the gentlemanly accomplishments, much less employed it for any serious academic or intellectual purpose. No doubt it was unnecessary in most cases to insist upon attendance at dancing or fencing school, and the careers of Edward Hyde, Simonds D'Ewes and Bulstrode Whitelocke fully substantiate Sir Lawrence Hyde's claim that 'divers sober fine gentlemen . . . are students and yet revellers'. Justinian Pagitt may have made little progress with the law between October 1633 and January 1634, but

[82] Waterhous, *Discourse . . . of Armory*, 131–3.

nevertheless managed to keep up his outside reading, despite such diversions as preparations for a coming masque, dancing school, gaming, singing and lute playing, conversation and visits with friends, attending the lord mayor's show and watching a play in the Middle Temple hall.[83]

Yet clearly this was not always the case. Edward Heath's accounts of his expenses at the Inner Temple between 1629 and 1631 record no literary purchases whatever, apart from ten play-books, but considerable outlays on clothes, gaming and hunting. John Greene's cryptic notes of each day's activities for the year 1635, while he was in commons at Lincoln's Inn, list numerous visits to plays at Blackfriars and the Cockpit, gaming at the Temples and Gray's Inn, attendance at dancing school, games of tennis, a trip to Greenwich and so forth; but there is no indication that Greene acquired any other benefits from his association with the house, and the only entry remotely connected with legal studies reads 'Mr bishe, Mr Lewis moote, I was there, had wine'.[84] The freedom which allowed members to follow their intellectual or literary inclinations instead of, or as well as, the law, equally permitted them merely to avail themselves of the ample facilities for dissipating time and money which London provided. We may be struck by the concentration of cultural opportunities in the capital; contemporaries like Joseph Hall saw the other side:

> The concourse of a populous citie affords many brokers of villany, which live upon the spoyles of young hopes. . . . How can these novices, that are turned loose upon the maine, ere they know either coast or compasse, avoid these rockes and shelves, upon which both their estates and soules are miserably wracked? . . . We see and rue this mischief, and yet I know not how carelesse we are in preventing it.[85]

The comments of Burghley, Fraunce, Gilbert, Lenton and the host of character-writers, moralists and satirists cited above do indeed suggest a fairly widespread recognition of this fundamental defect of the inns as educational institutions. Yet it attracted surprisingly little overt criticism either during or after our period, probably because only a handful of students actually sank on the metropolitan shoals and shelves, while most parents were ultimately more concerned with the social than the educational benefits which their sons could receive from the inns.

Only two concrete proposals for reforming the educational functions

---

[83] Davies, 'The date of Clarendon's first marriage', 405–7; Harleian 1026, ff. 70–76v.

[84] Egerton 2983, ff. 13–24; 'Diary of John Greene', ed. Symonds, 386–9 and MS original (in the possession of Sir Francis Wogan Festing, at Birks, nr Hexham, Northumberland): entry for 15 June 1635.

[85] Hall, *Quo Vadis?* (1617), in Hall, *Works* (1625), 671.

of the societies were advanced during the later sixteenth and early seventeenth centuries, both by puritan lawyers who believed that the behaviour and welfare of students should be a matter of active concern to the masters of the bench. Thomas Norton, the joint-author of *Gorbuduc*, a leading 'opposition' M.P. and Inner Temple barrister, probably compiled his draft of thirteen orders 'for the better government of the fower howses of court' during a sojourn in the Tower which immediately preceded his death in 1584.[86] Although concentrating on measures to safeguard the societies against catholic infiltration, Norton also recommended that no member should be in residence who 'shall not be and continue to be a studient, either of the common lawes of the realme, or ells of some other gentleman-like activitie, or ells doe busie himselfe in learninge the tongues and languages, and . . . give testimonie of his profiting therein'.

The 'other gentlemanlike activitie' to which Norton refers evidently did not include mere physical skills and accomplishments. The last paragraph of his draft concedes that 'the young gentlemen should be incouraged to acquaint themselves with fencing, riding, dauncing, singing', but only 'so that the said delightes be taken in christian sorte, and the better enabling of themselves to all honourable services, and not to feede themselves with the pleasure thereof'. This passage might almost be a direct quotation from Lawrence Humphrey's *The Nobles*, and that fact in itself goes far to explain why Norton's proposals received no better response from the privy council, to whom they were addressed, than from the benchers themselves.[87] Yet Norton's suggestions were not unprecedented; the 1574 judges' orders had included a clause to the effect that members who did not participate in learning exercises within three years after admission were to be excluded from commons and residence. This measure was probably aimed at checking the inns' expansion and reducing pressure on their physical accommodation; but the benchers never showed much willingness to restrict the growth of the institutions they governed and there is no sign that the order was ever implemented, although in any case it would have affected only a handful of junior members. The novelty of Norton's proposals lay in the fact that no student would have been able to follow entirely non-academic pursuits at any stage of his membership, while conversely at no stage would he be confined solely to the study of the law.

An equally far-reaching series of reforms was proposed by John Cooke in his tract *A Vindication of the Professors and Profession of*

---

86 Lansdowne 155, ff. 110v–113v. These follow immediately after and are in the same hand as 'A booke of Mr Norton's deuices' (ff. 87–110v, mainly proposals for excluding papists from the universities and inns of court); the date endorsed, August 1586, appears to be in another hand, and the word 'finis' appears only at the end of the thirteen orders (f. 113v).

87 *Ibid.*, ff. 113–113v; cf. Kearney, *Scholars and Gentlemen*, 39–43; cf. William Martin, *Youths Instruction* (1612), 95–6.

the Law, first published in 1646 and reissued in 1651. Cooke was a barrister of Gray's Inn, a republican and leading Independent spokesman; accepting the post of solicitor-general for the Commonwealth, he led the prosecution case at the trial of Charles I. His *Vindication* was intended primarily to rebut popular demands for excluding common lawyers from parliament, but some space was also devoted to a critique of legal education at the inns of court. Its main weakness, Cooke felt, was in failing to give the student sufficient help and guidance with his work : 'For truly, to put a young gentleman to study the lawe without direction is to send a barke without a steeres-man, saile or anchor into an angry sea'. However Cooke believed that the discontinuance of readings since the beginning of the Civil War presented an ideal opportunity for radical innovation. He suggested that henceforth readers should be required not to deal with statutes, 'which when the reading beginns are plaine and easie, and whereupon peradventure scarce one case shall happen in a man's life time', but rather to

> acquaint the society with the most usefull knowledge and daily occurences in actions of debt, upon the case, of trespasses and ejectments, the present law of the times . . . one juditious reader might in a fortnights space argue most of the controversall points which are now agitated, propounding 5 or 6 points a day, either about conveiances, assumpsits or words actionable, which are the daily subjects and disputes in Westminster Hall . . .[88]

Cooke's concern was not purely utilitarian; he also saw a need to heighten the moral and spiritual sensitivity of the profession, by devoting the first three years before call to divinity and theological studies. The remaining four years would then be quite sufficient to acquire a technical legal training, or at least a knowledge of

> the morall and rational part of the common law, which is the rule of speedy justice, to give every man his due with expedition, for to what purpose now should young gentlemen gravell themselves in the quicksands of villenage frankalmoigne, Quare Impedits, and such unnecessary contestations . . .

Finally, besides making the formal learning exercises more relevant to student needs and drastically simplifying the content of legal education, Cooke wished

> for the students good, that there might bee in every respective house two at the least appointed as professors of the law to direct young students in the method and course of their studies, that they may rather apply themselves to cases profitable than subtill, for the difficulty of the study discourages many.[89]

Despite what has been seen as a very widespread movement for

88 *Vindication*, 56–7, 94.   89 *Ibid.*, 55–6.

educational and legal reform during the Civil War and Interregnum, Cooke's proposals evoked as much interest and support as Norton's fifty years before – which is to say, none at all. The state of legal education during this period obviously did not bother those radicals who wished to sweep away the legal profession and the inns altogether, while advocates of limited law reform had no incentive to raise such a peripheral matter, which might well alienate conservative support for their other proposals, without gaining them any credit on the left. The main critics of the universities either took a radical position on law reform as well, or else had little knowledge of, and no particular interest in, the problems of the English common law system.[90] Neither parliament nor council of state showed any desire to challenge the autonomy of the inns on this issue, although a lengthy debate in the first Protectorate parliament, about exempting the two Temples from lay subsidies, provided ample opportunity for critics of the inns to state their case. But by this time the conservative reaction was in full swing and apart from Desborough's disparaging reference to the 'ribbons and other extravagencies' of the young gentlemen students and Henry Robinson's claim that the societies were 'fallen from their first constitution' by the cessation of readings, not a word of criticism or disapproval was uttered. Most speakers argued that any tax on the societies would be inequitable and unprecedented, an attack on law and learning; as one member put it, 'they are universities of the law, and surely ought to have the privileges of universities'. This assertion went unchallenged and the exemption of the inns was confirmed.[91]

Nor is it surprising that Cooke's appeal to the 'honoured and learned benchers of the severall societies' fell on deaf ears. There were practical administrative objections to his scheme (such as the problem of finding and paying the 'professors of the law'). And having once seen moderate proposals for piecemeal law reform escalate to radical demands for abolition of their profession, the benchers were bound to view any suggested modification of existing arrangements for legal education with deep suspicion. By his advocacy of a simplified and less specialised preparation for legal practice, Cooke impugned not only the moral standards of the profession but

---

90 Cf. Veall, *Law Reform 1640–1660*, ch. ix; R. L. Greaves, *The Puritan Revolution and Educational Thought* (New Brunswick, 1969), *passim*; *Samuel Hartlib and the Advancement of Learning*, ed. Charles Webster (Cambridge, 1970), 66–8; [Christopher Hill, 'Radical critics of Oxford and Cambridge in the 1650s', in *Universities in Politics: Case Studies from the late Middle Ages to early Modern Period*, ed. John Baldwin (Baltimore, forthcoming)].

91 Burton, *Diary*, i. 209–14. On the last day of its first session the second Protectorate parliament resolved that Cromwell and his council should be recommended 'to take some effectual course, upon advice with the judges, for reforming the government of the inns of court'; but the only concrete measures mentioned were providing maintenance for godly ministers and reviving the learning exercises: *ibid.*, ii. 313.

the professional ethos itself. Any change which would effectively decrease the difficulty of training for a legal career might threaten the material interests of those already at the bar; but Cooke's pragmatic reduction of the lawyer's craft to 'the rule of speedy justice' also challenged the concern with narrow technical expertise, the 'game' aspect of their work, which was and is a necessary part of any professional group's internal dynamics.

So when Cooke went to his death as a regicide in 1660, his proposals, to all appearances, died with him. The tide of the educational revolution was ebbing; order and stability were the watchwords, and in the interests of law and learning the unreconstructed inns of court and universities were allowed to slide undisturbed into their Augustan slumbers. Nearly two centuries passed before the inns were obliged to begin translating Cooke's programme into reality, thus reluctantly confirming his conviction that 'Time onely can demonstrate the utility of the praemised design'.[92]

---

[92] Cf. David Reisman, 'Towards an anthropological science of law and the legal profession', *American Journal of Sociology*, 57 (1951), 133–4. For nineteenth-century reforms, see *HEL*, xii. 30–2; Brian Abel-Smith and Robert Stevens, *Lawyers and the Courts* (1967), 63–76, 165–84.

VIII

Papists

Survival and resurgence

One reason 'religion attained not a perfect reducement' at the beginning of Elizabeth's reign, according to John Milton, was 'the great places and offices executed by papists, the judges, the lawyers . . . for the most part popish'.[1] The common lawyers indeed showed little initial enthusiasm for the 1559 church settlement. Despite a purge of catholic judges and law officers and the imposition of the oath of supremacy on all 'persons that have taken or hereafter shall take any degree of learning in or at the common laws', the profession remained riddled with papists.[2] In 1564 the bishops of Carlisle and Winchester both complained that assize judges on circuit in their sees encouraged popery, showing undue lenience to recusants and disfavour 'towardes any man or cause of religion'. Two years later Cecil was told that the appointment of George Bromley, a bencher of the Inner Temple, as attorney to the Duchy of Lancaster would 'win the hearts of a great many protestants, who, now discouraged, will take some hope if they may hear a protestant lawyer beareth authority in Westminster Hall'. In 1569 the duke of Norfolk could assume that the popish sympathies of the judges and common lawyers were a matter of 'eminent knolleg', while as late as 1581 a government

---

[1] *Of Reformation touching Church Discipline in England, and the Cawses that hitherto have hindred it* (1641), 13.
[2] *Statutes at Large*, 5 Eliz. I, c. 1. The privy council admitted in 1569 that 'we doe not certainly knowe' whether this oath was being rigorously enforced: *BB*, i. 370. For later comment on its general ineffectiveness see William Lambard, *Eirenarcha* (1581), 62.

spy claimed that 'amongst lawyers more papystes ther are then in all Inglande beside'.[3]

The first decade of Elizabeth's reign was characterised by a relatively lenient, almost lackadaisical attitude towards catholics; but Mary Stuart's flight to England, the Northern rising, Elizabeth's excommunication and the Ridolfi plot led the government to take a much tougher line. The first major action against papists at the inns came in 1569, when fourteen recusants and 'ill-favourers' were haled before the privy council; the benchers of their respective houses were commanded to expel the delinquents and in future to promote neither known nor suspected papists to bar or bench. Although this injunction was not entirely disregarded, official concern with the state of religious conformity at the inns mounted during the following decade.[4] In 1571 Archbishop Parker complained that the inns 'do now of late grow again very disordered and licentious in over-bold speeches and doings touching religion'. His concern was fully shared by the council, which asked Bishop Sandys and the ecclesiastical commissioners to investigate the enforcement of the 1569 edict and, together with the lord keeper and two chief justices, prepare 'some good orders for the due servyce of God in those houses'.[5] The results of this inquiry were apparently embodied in the judges' orders of 1574, which laid down that members who 'upon public admonition once given' did not attend the 'usual common prayers' were to be excluded from commons and residence. The admission of more than two persons to any chamber and the construction of new chambers were forbidden, partly to check expansion of the inns and the profession, but probably also with a view to simplifying the supervision of residents and the detection of suspicious strangers.[6] Finally, as an afterthought to a national census of recusants in 1577, the privy council ordered the Lord Keeper, Sir Nicholas Bacon, to survey the state of religious conformity at the inns. The returns submitted by Bacon's eight 'surveyors' listed 180

[3] 'A collection of original letters from the bishops to the privy council, 1564', ed. Mary Bateson (*CS, Miscellanea* 9, 1895), 2, 49, 60–2; H. N. Birt, *The Elizabethan Religious Settlement* (1907), 446–7; Lansdowne 102, f. 145; SP 12/149/184, quoted Henry Foley, *Records of the English Province of the Society of Jesus* (1875–83), iii. 721; see also Nicholas Sander, *Rise and Growth of the Anglican Schism*, translated David Lewis (1877; first publ. Cologne, 1585), 264–5, and Samuel Haynes, *A Collection of State Papers . . . 1542–1570* (1740), 588.

[4] R. W. Dixon, *History of the Church of England from the abolition of the Roman jurisdiction* (Oxford, 1902), vi. 207; Lansdowne 109, ff. 9–10v; SP 12/60/70; *BB*, i. 370–2; *ITR*, i. 252–4. Lansdowne 106, ff. 102–102v (cf. *ITR*, i. 271–3).

[5] J. Bruce and T. T. Perowne eds., *Correspondence of Mathew Parker* (Cambridge, 1853), 384–5. Lansdowne 15, ff. 158–158v (printed *BB*, i. 454–5) and John Strype, *Annals of the Reformation* (Oxford, 1824), III, i. 44–6. Strype ascribes this latter document to *c.* 1581, and M. M. Knappen, *Tudor Puritanism* (Chicago, 1939), 238, interprets it as an order against *puritan* non-conformity, but it is clearly another version of the letter dated June 1571 printed in the Parker *Correspondence*.

[6] *OJ*, 312.

catholics, which on the basis of the 1574 membership returns implied that about one member in five was a papist. However, no less than 104 of those included were either discontinuers or onetime suspects who had since demonstrated their orthodoxy. Of the remainder, thirty-nine were named as definite recusants, thirty-seven as 'church papists'. Gray's Inn and the Inner Temple had the highest proportion of known and suspected catholics (about thirteen and sixteen per cent of their respective resident membership), while the papist population of the other two houses was less than five per cent.[7]

As the council had told Bacon that they believed the inns to be 'greatlie infected with poperie', these figures may have come as a slight anticlimax. Yet they hardly provided grounds for complacency. By now the easy assumption that catholicism would die a natural death as its adherents passed away or resigned themselves to outward conformity with the established church was clearly invalid. In 1574 the first contingent of Douai-trained missionary priests landed in England. Charged with reviving the old faith and winning the country from heresy, they imparted fresh energy to Elizabethan catholicism.[8] The missionaries regarded the inns of court as a key target. Their large, virtually unsupervised student population was the embryonic ruling class of thirty years on; without support from at least a substantial minority of these future lawyers, office-holders, M.P.s, justices and country gentlemen, the hoped-for return to Rome was inconceivable.

Apart from the alluring prospect of a flood of well-born converts, the inns lay conveniently beyond the jurisdiction of city and suburban justices, while the constant traffic of lawyers, clients, students and servants helped cloak a priest's movements, particularly if he happened to be a former student himself and knew the lie of the land.[9] Their gardens and walks were a recognised rendezvous, ideally suited for clandestine conference and discussion. To the north and west lay open fields and woods, through which a priest might move with little risk of observation or make his escape with the authorities hot on his trail.[10]

---

[7] *APC*, 1577–78, 94–5; *CRS, Miscellanea* 10 (1921), 101–7. Little reliance can be placed on an earlier partial survey of the same year (*ITR*, i. 470–3) which is evidently the work of an extreme puritan, whose definition of popery embraced even such staunch pillars of the church as Edward Anderson and John Popham, presumably on account of their hostility towards separatists.
[8] Patrick McGrath, *Papists and Puritans under Elizabeth I* (1967), ch. 6, *passim*; John Bossy, 'Elizabethan Catholicism: The Link with France' (Cambridge Ph.D. thesis, 1960), 16.
[9] Cf. the 1591 proclamation warning against seminarists who 'attempt to resort unto the universities and houses of law from whence . . . they departed': *Tudor Proclamations*, iii. 91. Cf. Thomas Clancy, *Papist Pamphleteers* (Chicago, 1964), 119.
[10] Philip Caraman, *John Gerard, An Autobiography of an Elizabethan* (1951), 143; *The Parliamentary Diary of Robert Bowyer 1606–1607*, ed. D. H. Willson (Minneapolis, 1931), 89. W. T. Trimble, *The Catholic Laity in Elizabethan Eng-*

William Allen, the founder of Douai seminary, claimed in 1576 that his protégés had already made 'wonderful headway' at the inns of court, both by personal contact ('for nowhere do men lie hid more safely than in London') and 'books in the vulgar tongue, on every topic of controversy'. Only eleven priests had reached England during the mission's first two active years, so this progress report was possibly a trifle optimistic, especially as the government fully shared Fr Allen's concern that 'the gentry of almost all the nation' who frequented the inns should be 'rightly instructed'.[11] Certainly the greatest successes and failures of the missionaries came during the 1580s and '90s; indeed the year 1580 was particularly significant, both for the arrival of the first Jesuit mission and the establishment in Chancery Lane of George Gilbert's Catholic Association, a group of ardent young laymen who sheltered priests and brought them into touch with potential converts.[12]

Informers' reports and recusants' confessions provide a large, if not entirely reliable, body of evidence about catholics, lay and clergy, at and around the inns of court during the later years of the sixteenth century. Tales of priests sheltered and masses held at Gray's Inn, mysterious meetings in Lincoln's Inn Fields, books and letters sent and received across the seas, sinister figures like the 'subtill and noted papist' who 'lyeth mutch about Graies Inn' and Jesuit couriers posting to unknown destinations with news from the inns, are scattered throughout the papers of Burghley and his colleagues. Much of this was mere rumour or surmise, like Jacques Annias's confession that his fellow conspirators had 'great hopes of Sir Thomas Tresham and some lawyers in the inns of court'. During the fevered atmosphere of the Armada years the wildest stories found a receptive audience, although the alleged coining, in Sir Griffin Markham's chamber at Gray's Inn, of £1800 worth of plate stolen from Winchester Cathedral, might well have strained even Walsingham's credulity, had he still been alive to hear it.[13]

As the largest, most fashionable and most outlying of the four houses, with a strong representation from Ireland, Lancashire and

---

land (1964), 214, but see M. D. Leys, *Catholics in England 1559–1829* (1961), 29, and David Mathew, *Catholicism in England* (2nd edn, 1948), 52, 60.
[11] *CRS, Miscellanea* 7 (1907), 65.
[12] See John Stockwood's complaints about inns of court recusants in *A very fruitful Sermon preched at Paules Crosse* . . . (1579), 28–9. Richard Hopkins, himself a one-time student at the MT, dedicated both his translations of the Spanish mystic Luis da Granada to the gentlemen of the inns: *Of Prayer and Meditation* (St Omer, 1582), sig. A2, and *A Memoriall of the Christian Life* (Rouen, 1586), sig. A2. J. H. Pollen, *The English Catholics in the Reign of Queen Elizabeth* (Oxford, 1920), 342–4.
[13] *CSPD, 1581–90*, 346, 427, 553; *CSPD, 1591–14*, 228, 262, 431, 497, 534; *CSPD, 1595–97*, 59; *CSPD, Addenda 1580–1625*, 294; *APC, 1591–92*, 92; HMC, *De Lisle and Dudley*, ii. 335; *idem, Salisbury*, xii. 228–9; *idem, Var. Coll.*, iii. 89.

the backward North, it is not surprising that Gray's Inn was the most 'infected and corrupted'. Both the inn itself and the lane which ran along its eastern boundary from High Holborn, 'furnished with faire buildings and many tenements on both the sides, leading to the fildes towards Highgate and Hamsted', were favourite priestly haunts. John Colleton, the only defendant to escape with his life at the trial of Edmund Campion and his supporters in 1581, was saved by the testimony of a Gray's Inn barrister, John Lancaster, who proved that he had been with Colleton at Gray's Inn the same day that the latter was allegedly plotting treason in Rheims. Lancaster, a Somerset papist, enjoyed Sir Christopher Hatton's protection, which helped him to become an ancient in 1587 (after Hatton wrote to the pension on his behalf), reader in 1589 and treasurer of the house in 1595.[14] Among Campion's young proselytes was Henry Walpole, a well-born Norfolk student, who converted a number of fellow-members before leaving Gray's Inn to become a Jesuit himself. Another supporter was the Yorkshireman John Dolman, who left Gray's Inn for Rheims in 1582 after witnessing Campion's execution. Dolman came from a prominent recusant family: with his brother Thomas he was said to have 'lodged Thomas Aulfield a noted seaminarye . . . and heard him saye a number of masses in there chamber . . . dyvers other seaminaryes did haunte to theis too Dolmans'.[15]

In 1586 the missionary John Hambly confessed that he had celebrated Easter mass the previous year in a chamber at Gray's Inn with 'ix or x gentlemen of the innes of courte'. Afterwards he had met the owner of the chamber in 'Grayes Inne Felde . . . a place seminaries and catholikes do resorte some tymes to have conference together'. Hambly's testimony provided further justification after the event for the privy council's letter to the benchers in November 1585, which pointed out that many 'seminarie popishe priests have bene heretofore harboured in Graies Inn' and 'soe perverted divers yong gentlemen'. Admitting that 'the house is verie large & consisteth of a greate nomber', the council nevertheless emphasised that 'suche nurseries shold not be infected & corrupted, whereby noe good service may bee in other places hoped for hereafter'. The benchers were therefore ordered to conduct a census of all members and their servants; absentees from prayers, sermons or communion were in the first instance to be admonished, but if persisting in 'their undutifullnes & obstinacie . . . expelled for fear of infecting others'. Surveyors were duly appointed to search all chambers and take the names of occupants, but no sur-

14 Cf. Lancaster's reader's speech, in Hargrave 398, ff. 154–9.
15 Stow, *Survey*, ii. 87; Edmund Lodge, *Life of Sir Julius Caesar* (1827), 44; Ellis, *Original Letters*, 2nd ser., iii. 91; Philip Caraman, *The Other Face* (1960), 85; Joseph Gillow, *A Literary and Biographical History or Bibliographical Dictionary of the English Catholics* (1885–1902), ii. 91, 418, iii. 294; Richard Simpson, *Edmund Campion* (1896), 436; *GIPB*, i. 76, 83, 107.

veyors' reports have survived and the effects of this measure are unknown.[16]

Gray's Inn was the only house to be singled out for special attention by the privy council in 1585, but none of the other societies were entirely free of catholics. In 1586 John Baker, a former student of the Inner Temple, told Walsingham that after seven years studying the law he 'fell acquainted with them gentlemen papistes . . . became a papist . . . left my studye . . . and travelled to Rhemes'. Catholics at the Inner Temple during the late sixteenth century included Nicholas Hare and Andrew Gray, who became benchers in 1573, Anthony Metcalfe and Thomas Pudsey from Yorkshire, Henry Shelley of Sussex, the Cornishman Nicholas Roscarrock, Francis Throckmorton, Lewis and William Tresham, and their fellow-conspirators George and William Vavasour. Even the butlers of the house were accused of popish sympathies and making 'slanderous speeches concerning the state'.[17]

The Middle Temple does not figure prominently in the government's intelligence reports on catholic activities, although it had a considerable cadre of papists among its senior resident members. The best known was Edmund Plowden, a bencher from 1557 until his death in 1585. Some of his protestant colleagues complained to the council in 1580 that Plowden, with two or three of his 'dearest and most familiar friends', had turned the house into a papist sanctuary: 'by his practise and [the] friendship that he procureth and the severities and sinceritie of other houses the Middle Temple is pestered with papistes & not to be amended without your honours especiall ayd'. However, this was not forthcoming, despite the fact that Plowden's activities at the Middle Temple had come under official notice before; in the early 1570s the under-treasurer of the house, Thomas Pagitt, accused of having 'purposely disappointed any being of good religion from haveing of chambers in the howse', was said to owe his post to the influence of Plowden and Mathew Smith, another pre-Elizabethan bencher. The Middle Temple was the family inn of the Brownes, the Petres and the Wisemans, three prominent Essex catholic families; as late as 1594 the popish Earl of Northumberland and his brother Charles Percy were admitted to membership, together with the 'great captain' of the papists, Anthony Browne, Viscount Montagu. Pagitt himself remained a bencher until his death in 1614.[18]

---

[16] *CRS, Miscellanea* 12 (1921), 170–1; *GIPB*, i. 68–70.
[17] SP 12/217/38; Lansdowne 106, ff. 102–102v; *ITR*, i. 271, 273; Hugh Aveling, *Northern Catholics* (1966), 135. Leys, *Catholics in England*, 31; A. L. Rowse, *Ralegh and the Throckmortons* (1962), 71, 101–2; Bellot, *Inner and Middle Temple*, 126–30; *CSPD, 1581–99*, 427; *APC, 1586–87*, 304.
[18] SP 12/144/45. IT MS, Petyt 538. xlvii, ff. 342–3. These interrogaries are endorsed in a contemporary hand '. . . for removing papistes out of ye Inner Temple', but the references to Plowden, Smith and William Fleetwood (f. 342) suggest that this is a mistake. Two dates are endorsed, 1569 and 1571; the latter seems correct, as 'T[homas] P[agitt]' the under-treasurer, to whom the second

Despite its earlier connections with Sir Thomas More's circle, Lincoln's Inn probably had fewer catholics than any other house, although the Lancashire judge Sir George Walmsley, who married one recusant, fathered another and was himself a suspected papist, remained there as utter-barrister and bencher until his promotion to serjeant in 1580, while Thomas Valence, who became an associate bencher in 1596, was also probably a catholic. Many recusants lived in the vicinity of Lincoln's Inn and the fields lying on its western boundary were a favourite meeting-place for priests and lay papists; the Babington plot conspirators were executed there in 1586, 'even in the place where they used to meet and conferre of their traitorous practises'. Despite repeated prohibitions from the bench, junior members who could not get chambers in the house often lodged at Lincoln's Inn Grange, a tenement off Chancery Lane, where 'dyvers lewd and ill disposed persons, as well semynaries as other papystycall persons, have their chambers'.[19]

Quietism and survival

Between 1574, when the missionary priests began to arrive in England and 1609, when parliament imposed a new and more stringent oath of allegiance on all members of the inns over eighteen years of age, only two formal, state-authorised checks against catholics at the inns existed. These were the statutory but much-neglected requirement for utter-barristers and benchers to take the oath of supremacy, and the clauses in the 1574 and 1584 judges' orders obliging all members in commons to attend services at the chapel or church of their house.[20] During the last twenty years of the century, when the catholic threat reached its height, the government made no further attempts to check popery at the inns by regulation. However, the benchers themselves had begun to take firm action against catholics within their houses; by 1583 all inns required resident members to receive communion at least once a year, on pain of expulsion.[21] This rule seems at first to have been fairly well enforced, while at the same time the religious orthodoxy of candidates for promotion was coming under much closer scrutiny. Moreover, the measures in force by the mid-1580s – compulsory annual communion, compulsory church attendance, the oath of allegiance for senior members – were supplemented by the

interrogary is addressed, did not hold this office before 2 December 1570: *MTR*, i. 175, 342; Stone, *Aristocracy*, 732; *MT Bench Book*, 83.

[19] 'Narratives of the Days of the Reformation', ed. J. G. Nichols (*CS*, 77, 1859), 46. Foss, *Judges*, vi. 191; Anthony Kenney, 'The Responsa Scholarum of the English College, Rome', *CRS*, 54 (1962), 126 and *BB*, ii. 50; *CSPD*, 1591–94, 262, 298, 398, 417; Ellesmere 2118; N. G. Brett-James, *The Growth of Stuart London* (1935), 152; *BB*, ii. 2, 16.

[20] *OJ*, 312; *GIPB*, i. 70–2.

[21] *BB*, i. 408 (1578); *GIPB*, i. 17 (1574); *ITR*, i. 320–1 (1583); *MTR*, i. 239 (1580).

national machinery of penal statutes, informers, justices and pursuivants. It was perhaps difficult to see what more could be done, so far as the inns were concerned, by way of formal edict or legislative enactment.[22]

Apart from the notorious difficulties of enforcement, penal or restrictive measures were largely negative in effect, discouraging the open practice of catholicism, but doing nothing to inspire a strong spiritual commitment to the Church of England. By 1581, however, with the council's approval and encouragement, all four inns had appointed preachers, whose protestant fervour was intended to counteract the energetic evangelising of the seminaries. While the policy of fighting popery with radical protestantism did not long survive Whitgift's translation to Canterbury in 1583, the establishment of permanent preachers at the inns was in the long term certainly the most effective of all anti-catholic measures.

It is not easy to gauge the strength of catholicism at the inns by the end of the sixteenth century. Papists could still gain admission to the houses and a very few were even managing to be promoted to bar or bench, despite all the formal tests of orthodoxy. The ease with which these could be circumvented must have varied according to time, place and circumstance, but the catholic claim that their children were totally excluded from the inns was true only in a formal sense.[23] On the other hand, William Allen's confident expectations remained unfulfilled; the missionary contingents did not achieve the sustained impact which their masters had expected and the government feared.

The character of English catholicism and the official attitude towards papists began to undergo important changes shortly after the accession of James I. The failure of Guy Fawkes symbolised the failure of militancy. After twenty-five years badgering by their spiritual mentors and persecution by the government, most English catholics had grown tired of futile attempts to overthrow the Anglican church and its supreme governor. Despite sustained protests from the House of Commons, a kind of informal *ralliément* began.[24]

On the whole James I was prepared to meet the loyal catholic laity half-way. He had no desire for bloody religious persecution, pre-

[22] But see the abortive proposals advanced by Thomas Norton in the mid-1580s, 'For establishing true religion in the innes of court and chauncerie', mainly by more rigorous religious tests: Lansdowne 155, ff. 105–106v. In 1585 Burghley recommended that the inns should be visited and recusants expelled, but no action seems to have followed: Conyers Read, *Lord Burghley and Queen Elizabeth* (1960), 288–9.

[23] John Morris, *The Troubles of our Catholic Forefathers, related by themselves* (1872–77), iii. 25; William Babthorpe of Yorkshire was sent to Gray's Inn by his father in 1599, 'so that for some years, to escape trouble, he went to church, [but] only so little as might be . . .': *ibid.*, i. 228.

[24] This paragraph and the next draw heavily on John Bossy, 'The character of Elizabethan Catholicism', *P & P*, 21 (1963), 39–57; see also M. J. Havran, *The Catholics in Caroline England* (Stanford, 1962), vii, 134.

ferring an unofficial toleration from which only missionary priests and the malignant Jesuit were excepted. His role as defender of the faith was confined to the lofty planes of theological controversy and limited toleration was an essential element in his policy of peaceful co-existence and disengagement from continental wars. His son had even more reason to relax the enforcement of the penal statutes. Charles I's marriage treaty contained a secret clause which guaranteed freedom of worship to catholics and after the 1629 dissolution of parliament he could fulfil this obligation in a manner which satisfied both his conscience and his purse. Meanwhile Queen Henrietta-Maria's household became the focal centre of a new catholic revival and conversion to Rome the fashionable trend in court circles.

These developments inevitably impinged upon the inns of court. None of the anti-catholic measures handed down by the authorities between 1610 and 1640 were anything more than endorsements or repetitions of regulations which had previously been adopted independently by the four societies. The privy council ceased to chide the benchers for failing to purge their houses of recusants. Although several members of the Inner Temple were deeply implicated in the Gunpowder plot, no direct retaliation against inns of court catholics followed.[25] The imposition of the new oath of allegiance on all entrants from 1609 onwards was not specific to the inns but part of a blanket measure applicable to all subjects over the age of eighteen years; and according to Fuller, this oath was taken without misgivings by the majority of catholics.[26]

The 1614 judges' orders enjoined regular chamber searches for the detection of 'ill subjects or dangerous persons'; these seem to have been carried out reasonably conscientiously, as indeed they had been before that date. Whether they actually deterred priests and recusants from frequenting the inns is problematical. While Thomas Gataker was preacher at Lincoln's Inn from 1602 to 1611, 'divers popish priests . . . haunted the house and were verie busie in laboring to pevert the young gentlemen'. In 1614 the assembled members of the Inner Temple were warned by their treasurer, Elias Hele, that 'divers seminary priests and jesuits are supposed to harbour themselves here, either by receipt of their abettors, or colour of acquaintance'.[27] Nor did the inns lose their attraction as a venue for clandestine meetings; when Fr Augustine Baker was lodging close by Gray's Inn in 1621,

[25] *ITR*, ii. x–xl; *CSPD, 1603–10*, 269; HMC, *Salisbury*, xvii. 527.
[26] *Statutes at Large*, 7 Jac. I, c. 6; Thomas Fuller, *The Church-History of Britain*, ed. J. S. Brewer (1845), v. 67. An Italian merchant in Brussels reported to a correspondent in Collona on 3 February 1603 (O.S.) that in London 'the lord chief justice has given orders to purge the inns of court of all popishly affected': HMC, *Salisbury*, xvi. 85. This presumably refers to the judges' orders of January 1603/4, requiring the expulsion of non-communicants: *BB*, ii. 82; *GIPB*, i. 165.
[27] *OJ*, 317. Thomas Gataker, *A Discours apologetical wherein Lilies lewd lies . . . ave clearly laid open* (1654), 37; IT MS, Miscellanea 31, p. 23.

he took care to interview the laity only 'in the fields or in the inns of court gardens, or the Temple, or the Temple Church'. From about 1610, however, there is a marked decline in the reported cases of priests frequenting the immediate vicinity of the societies; this presumably reflects both the vigilance of the priest-hunters, and the greater influence of the Benedictines and Franciscans, who unlike the Jesuits did not see themselves as spiritual crusaders and were more concerned with ministering to the faithful than producing a sensational crop of aristocratic young converts. By the middle of James's reign there were also many substantial catholic householders in London, with sufficient influence and space to harbour priests.[28]

Orders for receiving communion and attending daily services were regularly repeated during the first fifteen years of the century, but during the 'twenties and 'thirties even the pretence of policing these rules was virtually abandoned. Between 1600 and 1611 at least twenty-nine members were expelled as papists and for refusing to attend church services; but between 1621 and 1640 only one expulsion was effected, and a second repealed by Charles I's intervention.[29] In June 1626 the benchers of Lincoln's Inn ordered the expulsion of Richard Minshall, a barrister and gentleman-in-waiting to the queen, and Andrew Browne, an Irish barrister. But Minshall's exclusion was revoked the following Michaelmas term, after a message had been received that the king wished 'Mr Minshull . . . whome the queene, his wife, had lately received into her service might continue heere as he did heretofore'. So Minshall remained a member of Lincoln's Inn, was knighted in December and shortly afterwards became a privy councillor and chamberlain to the king. Fifteen years later, in November 1641, he was the first recusant to be expelled from Lincoln's Inn by the Long Parliament.[30]

While the early Stuart governments showed little concern about the presence of catholics at the inns of court and the benchers' efforts to rid their houses of recusants tailed off during the 1620s, the old reputation of the inns seems to have remained alive in the House of Commons. Serjeant Randal Crew told his fellow M.P.s in 1621 that priests from Gondomar's residence at Ely House, only a few hundred yards to the east of Gray's Inn, 'sound a horn in Holborn to draw a great number of inns of court gentlemen' to mass. Dr Edward Floyd's connection with the inns – he was a barrister of the Inner Temple, as well as steward to the former Lord Keeper, Baron Ellesmere – may have underlined Crew's story. Further corroboration was provided by

[28] Baker, *Memorials*, 104; Stone, *Aristocracy*, 730.
[29] These figures, taken from the benchers' minutes, must be regarded with some caution. All but three of the recorded expulsions of recusants and non-communicants were from Gray's Inn; the other houses may not have normally listed such orders in their formal minutes, while a number of expulsions listed without reasons given were possibly of recusants.
[30] *BB*, ii. 262–3, 265–6; *GEC*, vii. 711–12.

another incident in the same parliament, when Thomas Shepherd, a young Lincoln's Inn barrister, was unanimously excluded from the house for attacking a bill against profanation of the Sabbath as savouring 'of the spirit of a puritan'. Shepherd, 'a base, jesuited papist' according to Simonds D'Ewes, was in trouble again two years later for slandering 'the late blessed Queene Elizabeth' while at supper in Lincoln's Inn hall.[31]

The hopes of some zealous protestants, that the accession of Charles I would see a purge of popish lawyers, were unfulfilled.[32] In the 1629 parliament both judges and crown law officers were heatedly attacked for their leniency towards recusants and Sir Francis Seymour proposed that 'the gentlemen of the innes of court should give account of what papists they have'. Other members chimed in with their agreement, adding that as well as recusant members, 'those that are harboured in those innes' should also be reported.[33] Nothing came of these proposals before Charles forced the dissolution in March 1629; but twelve years later the Long Parliament finally translated fears into action. On 9 November 1641, just over a week after news of the Irish rebellion reached London, John Pym's puritan cousin Francis Rous moved that the benchers of the inns be ordered to tender the oaths of allegiance and supremacy, 'to all Irish gentlemen, and such others as are suspected for recusants, as are within the inns of court'. The motion was carried without division, a similar resolution passed the Lords, and during the following weeks twenty-nine suspected recusants were expelled from Gray's Inn, together with at least four from Lincoln's Inn. The surviving records of the two Temples do not record any expulsions, although those from the Inner Temple may well have been minuted only in the lost book of bench-table orders, and some recusant members doubtless tried to avoid the oaths by absenting themselves from commons.[34]

Dr Bossy has described the history of Elizabethan catholicism as a progress from inertia to inertia; the same might equally be said about government attitudes towards catholicism between 1558 and 1640, both within the country generally and at the inns of court. Three main phases can be distinguished: inertia (1558–c. 1570), action

---

31 *Commons Debates, 1621*, ii. 82; *Complete collection of State Trials*, comp. T. B. Howell (1816–28), ii. 1153–60; Christopher Hill, *Society and Puritanism in Pre-Revolutionary England* (1964), 161; D'Ewes, 'Secret Diary', 173; *APC, 1623–25*, 19–20; *BB*, ii. 243, 246. The trial and execution in 1619 of a Middle Temple barrister, for publishing seditious libels against the spiritual power of the crown, would also have been fresh in members' minds: Harleian 583, ff. 6v–8; *CSPD, 1619–20*, 43–4; *State Trials*, ii. 1085–8; *MTR*, ii. 491.

32 Birch, *Court of Charles I*, i. 65.

33 Notestein and Relf, *Commons Debates for 1629*, 220.

34 *Journal of Simonds D'Ewes*, ed. W. C. Coates (New Haven, 1942), 104, 111; *Commons Journals*, ii. 307–9; *Lords Journals*, iv. 428; *BB*, ii. 360, 362; *GIPB*, i. 344–6.

(*c.* 1570–*c.* 1610) and inertia again (*c.* 1610–1640). None of these stages were entirely clearcut or homogeneous, and there might well be a case for specifying an additional hybrid phase of spasmodic action and inertia between 1610 and 1620.

During the first period the presence of catholics at the inns attracted little attention and less action. After 1570, largely on the privy council's initiative, a comprehensive range of measures aimed against catholic penetration of the societies was developed and enforced with some success. From about 1610 onwards the government's vigilance began to decline, although the benchers maintained their efforts until the mid-twenties; now the issue was being kept alive mainly by the House of Commons, which could do no more than protest against the government's inactivity. Finally, in 1641, there was a last coda of activity, initiated not by the government but by the Commons, at a stage of crisis in its rapidly deteriorating relations with the crown.

The contrast between the second and last phases, the 1580s and the 1630s, is very striking but should not be exaggerated. It is doubtful whether Elizabeth's ministers, in so far as they had a common and consistent policy, sought a total exclusion of catholics from the inns of court. Their rather more practical aim was to reduce catholic infiltration and influence among junior members of the societies. So long as catholics were permitted to remain in England at all they could not be completely excluded from the inns. It was almost impossible to do anything about occasional conformists and those who evaded or were prepared to take the prescribed oaths, while even avowed recusants often managed to obtain the protection of powerful friends or patrons; at the inns, as everywhere else, wealth and social rank were the papist's best protection against irritating or oppressive discriminatory legislation.

The proliferation of penal statutes created a growing demand for catholic attorneys and barristers to advise their co-religionists, which tended to nullify legislative attempts to debar recusants from legal practice.[35] And while many lawyers were fanatical anti-papists, their attitude to individual catholic colleagues was often tempered by corporate and professional ties. How otherwise could John Lancaster have joked about his beliefs in open court, when coming up to the Exchequer bar he found a fellow-barrister's servant holding his master's place: 'Lancaster would needs have the place, though the man would have kept it. "For", says Lancaster, "know thou not I believe nothing but the real presence" . . . and besides "could not think it corpus meum unless Mr Prideaux himself were there".'[36]

Finally, the loose organisation of the inns and their easy-going administrative arrangements, especially with regard to admissions,

[35] Cf. Aveling, *Northern Catholics*, 259–60, 263, 267, 294; Cliffe, *The Yorkshire Gentry*, 213, 225–6; *Statutes at Large*, 3 Jac. I, c. 1.
[36] John Manningham, 'Diary', 62; cf. D'Ewes, 'Secret Diary', 3.

tenure of chambers and supervision of junior members, must also have worked in the papists' favour. The situation was not unique; at the inns, as throughout the whole country, catholicism 'could not be destroyed outright, but only contained'.[37]

Having said this, it must be emphasised that, after the first ten or fifteen years of Elizabeth's reign, papists never comprised more than a small impotent minority, usually of junior rank and exerting little or no influence on the government of the societies. Those pre-Elizabethan members who remained loyal to the old faith were inevitably a diminishing force, and despite a few spectacular conversions, the missionary priests did not manage to capture a substantial following among the junior members, much less produce a whole catholic generation of common-lawyers. The missionaries' main impact was psychological; magnified by fear, rumour and suspicion, their activities (and the measures taken to counter them) reinforced old suspicions of the common-lawyers' orthodoxy. Given the inns' proximity to London's main recusant quarters (in Holborn, Covent-Garden and Drury Lane, Lincoln's Inn Fields and St Giles),[38] together with their sizeable contingents of Irish students,[39] it is not surprising that they became notorious as centres of catholic activity.

The gap between public image and reality was considerable, even in Elizabeth's reign, and it widened still further during the early seventeenth century. There are very few concrete reports of catholic priests proselytising the inns after 1610, while the growth of catholic colleges abroad now attracted many recusants' sons who would previously have sought admission to the societies. The generally more relaxed attitude towards catholics under James and Charles, which was evident not only at the inns, resulted partly from the more tolerant personal outlook of the monarchs and their ministers, but primarily from an appreciation of the fact that English catholicism no longer presented anything like so serious a threat to the safety of the realm as it had done during the days of Elizabeth. In this sense the early Stuarts, who responded to catholic quietism with leniency, were no less pragmatic than the last Tudor, who met militancy with repression. The chronic weakness of their policy was rather its failure to take sufficient account of the strength of atavistic fears of popery among a substantial proportion of the political nation, fears to which the public image of the inns of court made a small but not entirely insignificant contribution.

[37] Hugh Aveling, *The Catholic Recusants of the West Riding of Yorkshire* (Leeds, 1963), 232.
[38] Cf. John Gee, *The Foot out of the Snare* (1624), in *Somers Tracts*, iii. 90–4; Philip Caraman, *Henry Morse* (New York, 1957), 70; Leys, *Catholics in England*, 177.
[39] See Bedwell, 'Irishmen at the Inns of Court', 268–77; *Calendar of the State Papers relating to Ireland . . . 1598–1599*, ed. H. C. Hamilton (1885), 441–2; *ibid.*, *1603–06*, 233; *ibid.*, *1615–25*, 581.

IX

Preachers, Puritans and the Religion of Lawyers

The Clerical Establishment

'Whatsoever benefits we have from Christ, they are attributed to preaching', Richard Sibbes once informed his congregation at Gray's Inn.[1] His listeners had ample opportunity to acquire such benefits. Apart from the scores of sermons preached every week in the City and suburbs, all four inns had supported their own permanent preacher since the late sixteenth century. The first 'reader of divinity' at the Temple Church was appointed in 1571, to supplement the master of the Temple's Sunday sermons with thrice-weekly Latin lectures. From 1576 or slightly before Gray's Inn had its own permanent preacher, whose substantial annual stipend was raised by a compulsory levy on all members in commons, and in 1581 a 'constant preacher' was appointed for the first time at Lincoln's Inn.

Although 'strange' or visiting ministers continued to deliver occasional sermons, the formal appointment of preachers on an annual stipend soon became regular practice at Gray's and Lincoln's Inn.[2] Since the master of the Temple usually preached at least on Sunday mornings during term, the establishment of an additional lecturership

---

[1] *The Complete Works of R. Sibbes*, ed. A. B. Grosart (Edinburgh, 1861), iii. 372.
[2] Gray's Inn preachers were required to deliver two sermons every Sunday of the year: *GIPB*, i. 139, 367. Until 1610 the Lincoln's Inn preachers apparently preached twice a week during term; after 1610, when the stipend was raised from £40 to £60, they were also required to preach during readings and for part of the vacations. Between 1616 and 1621 all other vacations sermons were preached by Edward May, who had been appointed 'chaplain and vacation preacher' on a salary of £40; after May's dismissal temporary preachers were used again until 1628, when all vacation sermons became the permanent preacher's responsibility: *BB*, ii. 134, 179, 187–8, 277–8; Thomas Gataker, *Discours* (1654), 16–17, 35.

could be regarded as an expensive luxury by the benchers of the Inner and Middle Temple, especially when the master, while nominated by the crown, drew the major part of his income from the two Temple societies. There might also be difficulty in securing agreement between the two houses on a suitable preacher. Thus the lectureship at the Temple was never as securely established as those at the other two inns, and from 1586 to 1605 and again from 1628 to 1642, no permanent preacher at all was appointed.

As self-governing, extra-parochial 'peculiars', the inns enjoyed a large measure of autonomy in ecclesiastical matters, and the preachers, like the chaplains who read daily prayers and administered communion once or twice a term, held their positions entirely at the pleasure of the bench. The master of the Temple alone enjoyed security of tenure, as the incumbent of an impropriated benefice in the crown's gift. The minister of the Temple Church (who was appointed by the master, but supported mainly by the two Temples) and the chaplains of the other houses were part of the vast clerical proletariat of assistant curates, their lowly qualifications and status reflected by the large differential between their stipends and those of the preachers. Since the latter enjoyed both a high income and an influential, socially select audience, the inns could afford to exercise considerable discri-

TABLE 16   *Stipends of chaplains, preachers and masters of the Temple, 1590–1640*

	Chaplain		Preacher
Gray's Inn	£6/13/4		£66/13/4 (1590–1618)
			£80/0/0 (1618–1640)
Lincoln's Inn	£8/0/0 (to 1611)		£40/0/0 (to 1610)
	£20/0/0 (1611–1616)		£60/0/0 (1610–1632)
	£40/0/0 (1616–1621)		£80/0/0 (1632–1640)
	£13/6/8 (1621–1626)		
	£20/0/0 (1626–1640)		
	Minister	*Preacher*	*Master*
Temple Church	£30/0/0 (*c.* 1635)	£40/0/0 (1571–1586)	£189/18/0 (*c.* 1635)
		£80/0/0 (1605–1628)	£237/13/4 (1639)

Sources: Printed records; IT MS, Miscellanea 22, ff. 48–9; SP 16/406/56.
Note. In all cases board, lodging and various allowances supplemented the basic cash stipends.

TABLE 17 *Permanent preachers and masters of the Temple, c. 1571 – c. 1640*

Gray's Inn	Period	Lincoln's Inn	Period	Temple Church	Period	Masters of the Temple	Period
(Occasional Preachers)	c. 1571–c. 1575	(Occasional Preachers)	1571–1581	Antonio de Corro	1571–1581	Richard Alvey	1560–1584
William Charke	c. 1575–c. 1580			Master and Occasional Preachers	1578–1579		
		William Charke	1581–1593	Lawrence Chaderton	1579	Richard Hooker	1584–1591
Thomas Crooke	1581–1598	Occasional Preachers	c. 1593	Walter Travers	1580–1586		
		Richard Field	1594–1596	Master and Occasional Preachers	1586–1605	*Nicholas Balguy	1591–1601
		John Aglionby	1596–?				
Roger Fenton	1598–1616	Richard Crakenthorpe	?–1599			*Thomas Masters	1601–1628
		*William Pulley	1599–?				
		Thomas Gataker	1602–1611	William Crashawe	1605–1613		
		*Thomas Holloway	1613–1616	*Abraham Gibson	1614–1618		
Richard Sibbes	1617–1635	John Donne	1616–1622	*Thomas Chafin	1618–1627		
		†*Edward May	1616–1621			*Paul Micklethwaite	1628–1639
		John Preston	1622–1628	*Paul Micklethwaite	1627–1628		
		Edward Reynolds	1628–1632	Master and Occasional Preachers	1628–1640		
Hannibal Potter	1635–1642	Joseph Caryl	1632–1647			*John Littleton	1639–1642

* indicates persons not included in *DNB*. † chaplain and vacation preacher.

Note. After Corro and Travers, who preached three times a week, preachers at the Temple performed only on Thursday and Sunday afternoons. The conditions of his letters-patent did not require the master to preach, but in fact all masters normally delivered Sunday morning sermons during term and readings, as well as preaching on Easter Sunday, Whitsunday and Christmas day: *MTR*, i. 182; *ITR*, i. 312, ii. 9; IT MS, Petyt 538. xvii, f. 411v; Harleian 830, f. 159v.

mination in their choice of preachers and managed to secure the services of some of the most eminent scholars, ecclesiastical politicians and pulpit orators of the age.

The establishment of lectureships at the inns from 1571 onwards and the appointment of such leading puritan divines as William Charke, William Crashawe, Thomas Gataker, John Preston, Richard Sibbes and Walter Travers, suggests that the inns – or at least their rulers – were strongly influenced by puritan attitudes. However an examination of the circumstances in which the lectureships were set up, and the religious alignments of the men who held them during the seventy-odd years before the Civil War, indicates that the influence of puritanism at the inns was less marked than might at first appear.

The Elizabethan experiment

When John Whitgift became archbishop of Canterbury in 1583, five preachers had already been installed at the inns of court. The first was the bizarre Spanish Jew, Antonio de Corro, a former Heironymite monk who fled from Antwerp to London in 1568, served as pastor to the Spanish protestant congregation there until suspended by Grindal, then became reader of divinity at the Temple Church in 1571 with the help of Lord Burghley and Grindal's successor, Bishop Sandys, Although Corro had already been accused of deviating from orthodox Calvinism on the vexed questions of justification and predestination, his influential backers (who included the earl of Leicester, 'patron-in-chief' to the puritans), apparently had no qualms about his orthodoxy at this stage, and Corro himself repudiated the 'forward opinions of the Pelagians and self-justifiers' in a tract published with a dedication to the 'noble members of the Temple' in 1574. In the same year Richard Alvey, the puritanical master of the Temple, was asking Archbishop Parker how to deal with Corro, whom, he claimed, 'his auditory doth mislike for affirming free-will and speaking not wisely of predestination'. Yet it was not until 1578 that the benchers of the Middle Temple, with the Inner's concurrence, resolved 'that Corrano be licensed to depart without contribution or reward'. Corro was an aggressive individual, a storm-centre of doctrinal and personal controversy throughout his life. By this time he had obtained, or had high hopes of obtaining, a lectureship at Oxford, and was consequently neglecting his duties at the Temple Church. So his brusque dismissal was almost certainly for personal and professional reasons, rather than the benchers' disapproval of his heterodox theological beliefs.[3]

---

[3] The *DNB* incorrectly states that Corro's appointment at the Temple ended in 1574. Dr Williams Library MS, Morice II. 441 (4). *Correspondence of Mathew Parker*, 165; Antony Corro, *Dialogus Theologicus* (1574) and *ibid.*, *A Theological Dialogue* (1575), sig. [B vii]; *MTR*, i. 221. For all this see P. J. Harben, *Three Spanish Heretics and the Reformation* (Geneva, 1967), Part I, esp. 56–8, 64–5.

Corro was succeeded by a 'Mr Chatterton', who was probably Lawrence Chaderton, soon to become the founding master of Emmanuel College and a major influence on the lives of several generations of Cambridge puritans.[4] But nothing further is known about Chaderton's stay at the Temple, and by November 1580 the houses had made a fresh allocation of funds for a preacher, to be chosen by Richard Alvey and three unspecified members of the High Commission. The man they picked was Walter Travers, a personal friend and lieutenant of Thomas Cartwright, the ideological leader of Elizabethan presbyterianism.[5] William Charke, another presbyterian stalwart from Cambridge, was successively lecturer at Gray's Inn from about 1575 to 1580, and then preacher at Lincoln's Inn from 1581 to 1593.[6] Dr Thomas Crooke, 'that great and famous light', followed Charke to Gray's Inn; Crooke had been a member of the Wandsworth classis in 1575, and with Charke and Travers took a leading part in the London conference movement during the early 1580s.[7]

Thus four of the first five preachers were radical protestants, but these men were not appointed solely because their religious attitudes were congenial to the rulers of the inns. The most striking feature about the nomination of the first preachers (with the exception of Chaderton, the circumstances of whose appointment are as obscure as the rest of his personal life), is the exceptionally important part played by the civil and ecclesiastical authorities.

Corro's appointment at the Temple was secured by the influence of Burghley, Leicester and Sandys. Before engaging Charke on a permanent basis, the Gray's Inn benchers were careful to ensure that 'it be not otherwise myslyked by the privie councell, or the archbishopp of canterbury or the bishop of London'.[8] There were evidently no objections from either Grindal or Sandys, for Charke remained at Gray's Inn until 1580. After Chaderton and another famous puritan, John Reynolds, had both turned down offers from Lincoln's Inn, the benchers decided to approach Charke, but asked Sandys' successor, John Aylmer, for his approval. Bishop Aylmer apparently answered that while personally satisfied with their choice, he felt the privy council should also be consulted, 'that their good allowance and appro-

---

4 *MTR*, i. 224. In June 1581 Lincoln's Inn unsuccessfully approached Chaderton for their preachership: *BB*, i. 421.
5 *Ibid.*, 239.
6 The first and only reference to 'Mr Charke' in the Gray's Inn Order Book does not give a christian name (*GIPB*, i. 22); the printed calendar identifies him as the Cambridge puritan, later preacher at Lincoln's Inn, but gratuitously names him John, while the *DNB* does not connect William Charke with Gray's Inn. However, no other individual of the same surname listed by Foster or the Venns fits the dates of the Gray's Inn appointment, and the Venns tentatively identify William Clarke, fl. 1580, as the Gray's Inn preacher: *Al. Cant.*, i. 324.
7 Samuel Clarke, *A Collection of the Lives of Ten Eminent Divines* (1662), 25; Patrick Collinson, *The Elizabethan Puritan Movement* (1967), 342.
8 *GIPB*, i. 22.

bacion might concurre'. The council was positively enthusiastic about the proposal for a lectureship at Lincoln's Inn, 'considering the great hope of good to be done by such meanes in those places', and expressed their confidence in Charke 'to the furtherance of so good a service, as we hope this will be to God and hir majesty'.[9]

Charke's replacement at Gray's Inn, Thomas Crooke, was recommended to the society in January 1581 by Burghley, who stated that Aylmer had personally requested Crooke to accept the post.[10] Burghley's influence probably appears again in the election of his former chaplain Walter Travers as lecturer at the Temple; but once more Aylmer's approval was sought before the benchers ratified the appointment, which the Inner Temple confirmed only with the significant proviso that Travers should 'preach in his gown or some other decent apparel and not in a cloak'. Five months later Aylmer wrote again to the Inner Temple, praising the 'well doinge and orderly behaving' of their new lecturer and urging them 'to contynue yor good liking and favor towarde him'.[11]

Why did the bishops and the privy council encourage the creation of lectureships at the inns and permit them to be filled by known puritans? The explanation would seem to lie in the growth of official anxiety about catholic activity at the inns during the 1570s. Protestant preaching was generally and rightly regarded as one of the most effective antidotes to popery; indeed at the same time as the benchers of Lincoln's Inn were being commended for their decision to set up a lectureship, the council was pressing a reluctant city government for contributions towards the maintenance of learned men to preach twice a week in each parish of London, as part of 'a convenient order how the suppression of popery might be effected'.[12] Thomas Norton's scheme for extirpating popery from the inns included the provision that 'where preachings are established, the same be contynnued, and that the like be in the rest'. Norton envisaged no opposition from Aylmer, and even expressed the wish that 'everie bishop in England had taken paines and done their partes for religion, proportionately as he hath done'.[13] As late as 1585, when Whitgift's campaign against nonconforming ministers and preachers was well under way, the council endorsed Norton's views on the value of preaching, as a means of

---

9 Lansdowne 106, ff. 93–4, printed *BB*, i. 458–9; *ibid.*, 421, 424. Cf. Knappen, *Tudor Puritanism*, 261.

10 *GIPB*, i. 48.

11 S. J. Knox, *Walter Travers* (1962), 55–7; *ITR*, i. 311–12; IT MS, Petyt, Letters to treasurers and benchers, 5.

12 Cf. Overall, *Analytical Index to the Remembrancia*, 365–6; P. S. Seaver, *The Puritan Lectureships* (Stanford, 1970), 121–3. Cf. Christopher Hill, 'Puritans and "The Dark Corners of the Land"', *TRHS*, 5th ser., 13 (1963), 77–102; Charke was among the ministers whom Aylmer urged Burghley in 1577 to send into the far counties as protestant evangelists: *ibid.*, 88.

13 Lansdowne 155, f. 102.

ensuring 'the good bringing up of the youth and gentilite of this realme in the knowledge of God's true religion', and more specifically as a counter to the proselytising of seminary priests among inns of court students.[14]

There can be no doubt that Burghley's support was of crucial importance in securing the nominations of Charke, Corro, Crooke and Travers, more especially since Aylmer was yet another of Burghley's protégés. Corro's appointment in 1571 was an experiment, undertaken shortly after the first concerted official action against papist members of the inns; as a renegade from popery and a refugee from the Spanish empire, Corro was obviously an appropriate choice. The radicalism of the other ministers, all appointed during the period of Grindal's suspension, would hardly have perturbed Bedford, Knollys, Leicester, Mildmay, Walsingham and Warwick, the group of moderate but convinced protestants who for the time being held an ascendancy in the privy council. Although Aylmer, the herald of a new drive for clerical conformity, became bishop of London in 1577, he did not launch a frontal attack on puritan lecturers in his diocese until 1581, and his campaign lacked a real cutting edge before Whitgift's translation to Canterbury in 1583.[15] Perhaps Aylmer hoped that the sober lawyers would be a restraining influence on the radicals. Travers's attempts to remodel the communion service and introduce a rudimentary form of presbytery at the Temple Church did indeed encounter strong opposition from his congregation.[16] But even if the bishop had serious misgivings about these appointments, he wisely kept them to himself.

Richard Alvey's death in 1584 left the Temple mastership vacant, with three candidates vying for the queen's presentation. Richard Hooker was supported by Sandys, now archbishop of York; Travers, whom Alvey had wished to succeed him, naturally became Burghley's candidate, while Whitgift pushed the cause of Nicholas Bond, a reliable Oxford don. Each patron claimed his man was acceptable to the Templars, but in reply to Burghley's assertion that 'a number of honest gentlemen of the house' had solicited his support for Travers, Whitgift maintained that 'the greater and better number of both the Temples have not so good an opinion of him', on account of 'his disorderlinesse, in the manner of the communion and contempt of the prayers'.[17] This was apparently not just wishful thinking on Whitgift's part. The queen eventually plumped for the compromise candidate,

---

[14] *GIPB*, i. 68–70.

[15] Owen, 'The London Parish Clergy . . .', 540–53.

[16] Knox, *Walter Travers*, 59–60, 66. Cf. Bacon's suggestion to Buckingham in 1616, that the puritan Dr John Burgess might be given the preachership at Gray's Inn, 'for certainly we shall watch him well if he should fly forth; so as he cannot be placed in a more safe auditory': *Life and Letters*, v. 372.

[17] Knox, *Walter Travers*, 66–9, Isaak Walton, *The Life of Mr Richard Hooker*, in *The Works of . . . Richard Hooker*, ed. John Keble (Oxford, 1865), i. 26–30.

and even before Hooker's letters-patent were issued, the benchers of the Inner Temple saw their chance to get rid of Travers. In February 1585 he was told that his services were no longer required, as he had been appointed only 'at the request of Mr Alveye to supply his weaknes', and the new master would either preach in person or choose his own locum. Travers appealed to his powerful friends and the council sent off letters exhorting the benchers not to dismiss their preacher and rejecting criticism of Travers's radical views, which, they added 'moughte well have been spared to us, to whom Mr Travers is sufficiently knowen for his publique labors and paynes taken againste the common adversaries, impugners of the state and the religion'.[18]

The outcome of this interchange is uncertain; Dr Knox supposes that the Inner Temple eventually agreed to continue Travers's stipend, but no order countermanding the original decision appears in the parliament minutes.[19] Since the council had reluctantly agreed 'yet looking for better aunser from you', that the Inner Temple was perfectly entitled to dismiss Travers, so long as nothing was done to prevent him preaching in the Temple Church as a servant of the other house, it seems equally likely that the benchers held firm.

On his induction to the mastership in March 1585, Hooker took over the Sunday morning sermons, leaving the pulpit to Travers in the afternoon; so began a famous theological disputation, which attracted wide attention at the time and was still well remembered seventy years later. For a year 'the forenoon sermon spoke Canterbury and the afternoon Geneva', until Whitgift intervened with a prohibition ordering Travers to cease preaching.[20]

Hooker remained at the Temple Church, preaching 'but now and then', until 1591.[21] He was succeeded by Nicholas Balguy, but no permanent lecturer was appointed in Travers's place until 1605. Some six years after Travers had been silenced, William Charke left Lincoln's Inn, 'as was suspected, through the secret undermining of one of prime note in the house who . . . wrought with the archbishop for his removal'.[22] Only Crooke remained unmolested until his death in 1598, and his position had probably moderated considerably during his early years at Gray's Inn.[23] His successor was the scholarly Roger Fenton, chaplain to Sir Thomas Egerton, a man with little sympathy for the puritans; Fenton was eulogised after his death as 'one whom every man did know so approved for sanctity, so catholicall for profession, so conformable for unity'.[24] After Charke had left Lincoln's Inn, a

---

18 *ITR*, i. 333; IT MS, Petyt, Letters to treasurers and benchers, 12.
19 Knox, *Walter Travers*, 70–1.
20 Fuller, *Church History*, v. 188; Knox, *op. cit.*, 70–8.
21 *The Seconde Parte of a Register*, ed. Albert Peel (Cambridge, 1915), ii. 184.
22 Gataker, *Discours*, 55; this sounds like Egerton, who became attorney-general in 1592: see below, n. 24.
23 Owen, 'The London Parish Clergy', 57.
24 Emmanuel Utie, *A Motive Dedicated to the Honourable Society of the Gentry*

committee of benchers was deputed to choose four divines from Ox-
ford and Cambridge, each one to preach for three months of the year.
Although approved by Whitgift, this scheme soon lapsed, and Richard
Field, a chaplain-in-ordinary to the queen and a friend of Richard
Hooker ('the more that their judgements agreed together'), was ap-
pointed permanent preacher. Field was followed in turn by John
Aglionby, who served as chaplain-in-ordinary to both Elizabeth and
James and became principal of St Edmund Hall, Oxford, in 1601.[25]

The pattern is interesting and significant. Between 1575 and 1581
the installation of three leading presbyterians as preachers at the inns
of court had been permitted and even encouraged by Aylmer, Burghley and the council. But in September 1583 John Whitgift became
archbishop and began a determined drive against clerical nonconformity. Before the year was out he had rebuked Aylmer for allowing
Alvey and Travers to 'reform' the order of service at the Temple
Church.[26] Alvey's death next summer gave the archbishop a perfect
opportunity to intervene without encroaching upon the extra-parochial
status of the inns, for the mastership was the only preaching benefice
not controlled by the societies themselves. Although Whitgift failed
to get his own candidate in, he managed to keep Burghley's out, persuading the queen that Travers was by no means the 'learned, discreete and wise man' necessary for such a position, 'in respect of the
company there, who being well directed and taught may do much good
elsewhere in the commonwealth, as otherwise also they may do much
harm'.[27] Travers's silencing twelve months later and the failure of his
repeated appeals to the council against Whitgift's prohibition were
further evidence of the extent to which the balance of power had
shifted against the godly party since Grindal's death.

Travers might have worsted Hooker in debate, but the debate itself
seriously weakened his cause, dramatising the breach within the church
and lending credence to the view that 'to suffer one opposite to the
English discipline' to preach at the Temple (or any other house) was
'in effect to retain half the lawyers of England to be of counsel against
the ecclesiastical government . . .'. Richard Bancroft, Whitgift's chosen
agent and successor in the struggle against nonconformity, had already
pointed out the threat posed by precisians who

> thrust them selves forward by all the power of their frendes, to be as
> they terme it readers, but I feare seducers, in the innes of courte . . .
> the flower of the gentilitie of England being by that means trayned

---

in *Gray's Inne*, in Roger Fenton, *A treatise against the necessary dependence upon
that One Head* (1617), 58. For Egerton's religious views, see *DNB* and Ellesmere
466–7.

25 *BB*, ii. 28–9, 34; *Ath. Ox.*, ii. 182.

26 Peel, *Seconde Parte of a Register*, i. 206; John Strype, *The Life and Acts of
John Whitgift* (Oxford, 1822), i. 405–8.

27 Walton, in Keble, *op. cit.*, i. 28–9.

up in a disobedient mislikinge of the present estate of the churche...[28]

The national upsurge of separatism in the late 1580s and the simultaneous erosion of puritan influence on the council and at court helped to consolidate the position of those like Hatton and Whitgift, who regarded the use of puritan preachers to counter popery as a remedy no less deadly than the disease it was supposed to cure. Lincoln's Inn had become notorious as a centre of Martinist sympathisers before Charke's removal, while the separatists Henry Barrowe and Robert Lacey both proved to be former residents of Gray's Inn. The benchers, always responsive to shifts of power and policy at the centre of government, were not slow to draw their own conclusions, choosing to succeed the radicals of the early '80s either men of known discretion or no preachers at all.[29]

The initial establishment of lectureships at the inns of court and the installation of Charke and his fellow radicals had owed at least as much to official fears of popery as to the puritanical sympathies of the benchers. The religious alignments of the early preachers cannot simply be equated with those of the men who formally appointed them, for the benchers were not free agents, but acted under heavy pressures from outside, both before and after 1583. Of course this is not to say that the Elizabethan inns contained no puritans, or that their puritan preachers exercised no influence. But it is an oversimplification to suppose that puritanism was evenly diffused throughout the four houses, or that their 'impregnation' with 'the teachings of the zealous' was completed by the installation of a preacher in the last of the four houses in 1581.[30]

Moderates and radicals

Between 1600 and 1640, fifteen ministers held lectureships at the inns of court. Like their predecessors, a bare majority were puritans – radical but non-separatist protestants, inspired by the theology and practice of the Continental reformed churches, sharing 'a core of doctrine about religion and church government, aimed at purifying the church from inside'.[31] But the spiritual brotherhood did not monopolise the inns' pulpits, and their influence was not equally distributed between the four houses.

[28] Peter Heylyn, *Aerius Redivivus: or the History of the Presbyterians* . . . (Oxford, 1670), 315; *Tracts ascribed to Richard Bancroft*, ed. Albert Peel (Cambridge, 1953), 57.
[29] Collinson, *Puritan Movement*, 385–97; *The Marprelate Tracts 1588, 1589*, ed. William Pierce (1911), 355; *The Writings of Henry Barrow, 1587–1590*, ed. L. H. Carson (1962), 93, 98–9; *The Writings of John Greenwood, 1587–1590*, ed. L. H. Carson (1962), 306–7, 315.
[30] Cf. Knappen, *Tudor Puritanism*, 270.
[31] Hill, *Society and Puritanism*, 28.

Lincoln's Inn had the highest turnover of preachers (possibly because it paid a relatively lower stipend than the rest), and four of the eight ministers who served there during the early seventeenth century (Caryl, Gataker, Preston and Reynolds) were clearly puritans. But two (Donne and May) could not be so described and the religious position of the remaining two (Pulley and Holloway) is unknown.[32] Of the three preachers appointed at Gray's Inn, only Sibbes was undoubtedly a puritan. Moving to the Temple, we find again only one certain puritan (Crashawe), although Micklethwaite and perhaps Gibson displayed puritan leanings at an early stage of their careers. (Neither Nicholas Balguy nor John Littleton, masters of the Temple Church between 1591–1601 and 1639–42 respectively, ever showed any tendency towards puritanism, but Thomas Masters was certainly a puritan towards the end of his life[33] and Micklethwaite could perhaps still be classified as a sympathiser when he became master in 1628.) In short, although all four societies appointed puritan preachers, no house maintained an unbroken succession of puritans, while Lincoln's Inn alone appointed a puritan during the years of Laudian ascendancy and non-parliamentary government after 1629. These facts do not in themselves destroy the common view of the early seventeenth-century inns as hotbeds of puritanism, but they at least suggest that it may require some modification.

Further evidence pointing in the same direction emerges when we glance at relations between the inns and their preachers. Although the benchers of Lincoln's Inn lost no time in dismissing the chaplain and vacation preacher Edward May, when he published in 1621 a high-flying sermon containing bitter attacks on certain unnamed puritan members of the society, they remained on the best of terms with May's contemporary John Donne, who was certainly no puritan.[34] 'Mr Doctor Donne' was indeed the most popular and respected of all the society's preachers before the Civil War; when he resigned in 1622 to become dean of St Paul's, the benchers, 'glad of his preferment but loath wholly to part with him', resolved unanimously that their late preacher should retain his bench chamber, 'that he may at his pleasure and convenient leisure repaire to this house, being a worthy member thereof'. Two years later Donne was recalled to preach the dedication sermon at the consecration of the society's new chapel.[35]

The Temples were without a permanent preacher for nearly two decades after Whitgift's dramatic silencing of Walter Travers in 1586,

[32] Pulley may be tentatively identified as the William Puller who matriculated from Trinity, Cambridge in 1584 and died in 1645, having held livings in Kent and elsewhere: *Al. Cant.*, iii. 405. For Holloway see F. De Paravicini, *Early History of Balliol College* (1891), 332–3.

[33] *MT Bench Book*, 301; D'Ewes, 'Secret Diary', 9.

[34] *BB*, ii. 224–5; Edward Maie, *A Sermon of the Communion of Saints* (1621), sigs. A2v–3 and *passim*.

[35] *BB*, ii. vii, 229–301.

although sermons continued to be delivered by the masters and occasional visiting preachers. After Nicholas Balguy's death in 1601, several conferences between representatives of both houses considered the appointment of a preacher, but it was not until 1605 that William Crashawe accepted the post. Coming to the Temple from lectureships at Beverly and Bridlington, Crashawe found life in 'so civill, scholasticall and well-governed societies' very congenial.[36] But his relations with the Middle Temple deteriorated badly from 1608 onwards and in 1610 the house discontinued their contribution to his stipend, after a group of utter-barristers had petitioned against a proposed increase in the levy from which it was paid. They complained that Crashawe drew income from a Yorkshire benefice held *in absentia*, but while the benchers adopted this pretext to justify their action, a number of other issues were involved, including Crashawe's recent marriage, a dispute about an unauthorised building he had erected against the side of the Temple Church, and his recent brushes with the bishops and the convocation of Canterbury. The Inner Templars, on the other hand, continued to support Crashawe for three more years, until he returned to his native Yorkshire.[37]

Crashawe's successor was the young and talented Abraham Gibson, who commenced his promising career with a Paul's Cross sermon against the sin of blasphemy and rapidly became chaplain to both Sir Francis Bacon and James I, as well as preacher at the Temple. Gibson apparently got on well with the Middle Templars, who voted him a benevolence of 20 marks when he graduated B.D. at Cambridge in 1617.[38] He left to take up a living in Suffolk the following year, and his place was given to Thomas Chafin, a prebend of Salisbury Cathedral and chaplain to the courtier Earl of Pembroke, William Herbert, a leading opponent of Buckingham and the 'Spanish' party. Nothing is known of Chafin's views while he was at the Temple; in 1634, after Herbert's death, he was said to have preached a sermon at Salisbury Cathedral before Sir Nathaniel Brent, Laud's commissioner, praising Thomas Arundel (the persecutor of the Wycliffites) as a blessed archbishop, comparing him with Laud ('our little Aaron'), and beseeching God 'to deliver us from lay-parliaments'. An accusation against Chafin for this indiscretion was presented during the first session of the Long Parliament, when Simonds D'Ewes recalled that he 'had long known this man at the Temple and never tooke him to be [a] deepe scholler but to say noe worst of him a sociable man . . .'. The benchers of the Temple were evidently not averse to sociable men, for Chafin remained

---

[36] The quotation is from Crashawe's petition to the benchers of the Middle Temple, 9 Feb. 1610, one of several original documents relating to Crashawe in Middle Temple archives and as yet uncatalogued.

[37] *ITR*, ii. 54, 59, 73; *MTR*, ii. 492, 514, 516, 524; I.R., *The Overthrow of the Protestants' Pulpit-Babels* (St Omer, 1612), 4–5.

[38] Abraham Gibson, *The Lands Mourning for vaine Swearing* (1613); *idem, Christiana-Polemica, or a Preparative to Warre* (1619), sig. A 4v; *MTR*, ii. 618.

in their service until shortly after Charles I's accession, when he was dismissed in favour of Dr Paul Micklethwaite.[39]

Micklethwaite came to the Temple Church from Sidney-Sussex College, one of the centres of Cambridge puritanism, where he had held a fellowship since 1612. In 1624 he was put up by the vice-chancellor, Dr Thomas Paske, to stand against John Preston for the important town lectureship at Holy Trinity Church. Since Preston was supported by Buckingham as well as a majority of citizens, Micklethwaite's defeat is hardly surprising. However the contest was not simply a factional struggle between Arminians and puritans, as Preston's modern biographer suggests, but rather turned around the university's purported right to nominate town lecturers, a privilege previously upheld by James I and successfully challenged on this occasion by Buckingham's intervention.[40]

So the issues were confused, and Micklethwaite's stand against Preston did not put him into disfavour with the Cambridge puritans. Preston's biographer Thomas Ball, who took his M.A. from Queens' a year after the lectureship controversy, confessed long afterwards that he had been puzzled by Micklethwaite's candidacy, 'until I understood that he was set upon by the prelaticall heads, who told him it was a service acceptable to the king, and he should be rewarded for it'. The reward was substantial, if delayed.[41] In June 1627, six months after he had begun preaching at the Temple Church, Attorney-General Heath, treasurer of the Inner Temple, started a campaign to have Micklethwaite preferred to the mastership. Through Sir Edward Conway, Heath urged that Thomas Masters, the incumbent, be given a prebend in the Chapel Royal at Windsor, thus leaving the place free for Micklethwaite: 'Not myself only' (Heath claimed) 'but the whole body of both our societies are taken with him so farr, as that we much covet his settling with us'.[42]

[39] *ITR*, ii. 116, 160; *The Journal of Sir Simonds D'Ewes*, ed. Wallace Notestein (1923), 276, 419; cf. D'Ewes, 'Secret Diary', 10; A. G. Matthews, *Walker Revised* (Oxford, 1948), 371; T[homas] C[hafin], *The Iust Mans Memoriall* (1630).

[40] *Al. Cant.*, iii. 183; John Venn, *A Biographical History of Gonville and Caius College: 1349–1847* (Cambridge, 1897), i. 193; G. M. Edwards, *Sidney-Sussex College* (1899), 69, 77; Irvonwy Morgan, *Prince Charles's Puritan Chaplain* (1957), 117–24.

[41] Thomas Ball, *The Life of the Renowned Doctor Preston*, ed. E. W. Harcourt, (Oxford, 1885), 98–9. For evidence of Micklethwaite's continuing friendship with Samuel Ward,the master of Sidney-Sussex, see his letter of October 1630, Bodl. MS, Tanner 71, f. 53. In 1635 Micklethwaite named Richard Holdsworth, the moderate puritan master of Emmanuel College, as one of his executors and bequeathed a ring to Ralph Brownrigg, who succeeded Sibbes as master of St Catherine's Hall; Brownrigg was a follower of Bishop John Williams and a firm anti-Arminian: PCC 51 Coventry.

[42] SP 16/70/23, 29. Micklethwaite had moved to London in 1625, after accepting a lectureship at St Saviour's, Southwark; he held this post at least as late as December 1627, but seems to have been involved in a dispute with the vestry before he

Neither Heath nor Conway had any reputation for favouring Arminians, yet it is hard to believe that either Charles or Buckingham would have knowingly permitted another puritan to become master of the Temple.[43] However Micklethwaite was 'an eminent preacher', with sound scholarly credentials; despite his Cambridge background and continuing puritan associations, he had shown himself eager to serve the crown, so his sponsors probably found no difficulty in representing him as an orthodox, conformable minister.[44] Buckingham had broken off his flirtation with the puritans in 1626, and may have appreciated the irony of being asked to advance a man who three years before had stood against the now-discarded Preston. In any event, Masters's death in the spring of 1628 conveniently cleared the way for Micklethwaite, who received his letters-patent in August of that year. Within twelve months the new master and the benchers of both houses were embroiled in the first of a series of bitter disputes which ended only with Micklethwaite's resignation in 1639.

There had been financial squabbles between previous masters and the Temple societies, but Micklethwaite's claim to certain rents and payments was just one of the issues at stake.[45] He also demanded precedence in the halls of both houses, argued that he was entitled to receive a tithe of the fees of his 'parishioners', and suggested that his office carried 'episcopal jurisdiction and the power to excommunicate offenders'.[46] After his petitions of grievance had been referred successively to the judges, the king's learned counsel, a body of 'Lords Referees' and Attorney-General Noy, Micklethwaite finally obtained a settlement which satisfied his financial demands; but meanwhile he complained that the Temple Church was being profaned by 'the common resort of all people into the round walk and lower parts', and had the doors locked, to be opened only for services.[47] When the benchers responded by changing the locks, Micklethwaite again petitioned the crown, asking that, as the Temple was a 'church of eminency', the king would rule that it should be arranged in conformity with the

---

left; London R.O., P/92/Sav. 450, 21 Jan., 4 Feb., 22 Feb., 9 Dec., 1626, 31 Dec., 1627; SP 16/175/69.

[43] For Heath, see Aylmer, *King's Servants*, 112. In 1624 Conway had successfully persuaded Bishop Montaigne of London that John Davenport, the founder of New Haven colony, was entirely orthodox: *Letters of John Davenport*, ed. I. M. Calder (New Haven, 1937), 13–17.

[44] Thomas Fuller, *The History of the University of Cambridge*, ed. James Nichols (1840), 227; D'Ewes, 'Secret Diary', 150. In March 1624 D'Ewes unsuccessfully approached his 'good friend' Micklethwaite to accept a benefice in his gift: Harleian 379, ff. 10–11v, 28–29v.

[45] Harleian 830, f. 166; *ITR*, i. 380, 383, 386, 430, ii. 43–4; *MTR*, ii. 509; Williamson, *Temple*, 315–16, 384–96; MT MS, box labelled 'Temple Church and Master of the Temple Church'; Harleian 830, ff. 158–65; IT MS, Miscellanea 31, pp. 1–14; SP 16/54/21, 299/17, 231/66.

[46] IT MS, Miscellanea 31, pp. 8–9.

[47] *Ibid.*, p. 12; SP 16/154/21.

Chapel Royal. Charles complied, and Micklethwaite immediately had the communion table moved to the east and railed in, the pulpit removed to one side of the nave and the doors locked. Yet Micklethwaite, by now a royal chaplain-in-ordinary, did not long enjoy the fruits of victory; in April 1639 his master presented him to a rich Bedfordshire benefice where he died a few months later.[48]

Micklethwaite's cause was naturally taken up by those who stood for 'the good discipline of the church' against the common lawyers, 'who love not the church'.[49] The lawyers for their part put up only a limited resistance, fearing lest spirited opposition 'would render us much to obloquy', or that 'he should complain to the high commission court'. Some measure of their concern is indicated by the voluminous briefs and tables of precedents drawn up to counter Micklethwaite's arguments, for example that 'the master of the temple hath no place of jurisdiction here, either as pastor, or governor, or as master of a college'.[50] In the 1630s such claims had to be taken seriously. Yet at no time did the benchers indicate disapproval of Micklethwaite's preaching, or attempt to appoint a puritan lecturer to offset the master's high-church sermons.[51] Perhaps they feared giving him any additional pretext for petitioning the crown; but even after John Littleton (whom a puritan friend of John Winthrop described as 'second to none in impiety'), became master in 1639, the office of preacher remained in abeyance. It was not revived until February 1642, when Hugh Cressy, the son of a Lincoln's Inn bencher and formerly one of Wentworth's

---

48 Williamson, *Temple*, 393–4; HMC, *10th Rep.*, App. 2, 166; Anon, *Vox Borealis*; *Or, The Northern Discourse* (1641), in *Harleian Miscellany*, ed. Thomas Park (1809), iv. 427; Thomas Rymer, *Feodera* (1704–32), XI, ii. 144.

49 SP 16/175/69, Samuel Brooke to Laud, 17 Nov. 1630. Presumably because of his connections with the moderate Calvinists of Cambridge, Micklethwaite does not seem to have received any direct support from Laud; Brooke's suggestion that Micklethwaite should succeed him as master of Trinity College, Cambridge, was apparently ignored by the archbishop: *CSPD, 1629–31*, 396. For Brooke see *DNB* and H. R. Trevor-Roper, *Archbishop Laud* (2nd edn., 1962), 112–13.

50 Cf. IT MS, Miscellanea 31, pp. 6, 9, Miscellanea 32, *passim*; MT MSS in box labelled 'Temple Church and Master of the Temple Church'.

51 Micklethwaite probably remained an orthodox doctrinal Calvinist until 1635 or even later. In 1630 he delivered a sermon on predestination; John Davenant, the Calvinist Bishop of Salisbury, prepared a detailed critique which seems to have convinced Samuel Ward that Micklethwaite had not strayed into Arminianism; Bodl. MSS, Tanner 71, f. 53, Tanner 279, ff. 300–302. Thomas Gataker told Ward next year that Micklethwaite was said 'to closely deliver some of theire [the Arminians'] tenets', but added that he hoped this secondhand report was mistaken; Ward evidently informed him it was: Bodl. MS, Tanner 71, ff. 68, 92. See also the terms of Micklethwaite's will, above n. 41. Pagitt's notes of sermons at the Temple Church and Whitehall (December 1633–March 1634) show Micklethwaite defending outward reverence to God, especially bowing to the altar and the name of Jesus; in conjunction with his actions at the Temple Church, this suggests that Micklethwaite accepted the Laudian position on ceremony and church government while remaining aloof from any closer doctrinal or personal association with that party: Harleian 1026, ff. 14v–18; cf. CUL MS, Dd. v. 31, ff. 181–182v.

chaplains, was elected on the recommendation of James Ussher, the moderate archbishop of Armagh. Cressy lasted less than a year, joining the king at Oxford in 1643; he was received into the catholic church in 1646 and ended his life as a Benedictine monk.[52]

Further light is thrown on the Temple benchers' decision not to engage a permanent preacher by the situation at Gray's Inn. When Richard Sibbes died in 1635 after eighteen years service to the house, Dr Hannibal Potter, fellow and later master of Trinity College, Oxford, was elected in his place. Neither a distinguished theologian nor an outstanding preacher, Potter was however chaplain to the Arminian bishop of Winchester, Walter Curll, through whose influence as visitor of the college Potter became master of Trinity in 1643. For the first five years of his tenure Potter's relations with Gray's Inn were entirely uneventful. But in February 1641 Robert Sydney, the disaffected second earl of Leicester, reported from Paris to another puritan peer, Lord Mandeville, that he had heard some disturbing reports of Potter, who was said to have announced in a sermon in Gray's Inn chapel that 'they who suffered death for religion in Queen Mary's time were as arrant traitors as those of the gunpowder treason', and that Guy Fawkes and his fellow plotters were as much martyrs as the Marian protestants.[53]

Leicester suggested that Mandeville might wish to investigate the matter, but the benchers of Gray's Inn took no formal steps to rid themselves of Potter's presence until July. The question of electing a new preacher monopolised the agenda of a pension held on 9 July. No decision could be reached, so the matter was deferred to the following Michaelmas term, only to be held over again when pension met on 3 November. After three successive meetings on 18, 19 and 20 November 1641 it was finally ordered that 'Mr Doctor Potter is to remove and absolutely leave the lecturers place'. In February 1642 John Jackson, a presbyterian later elected to the Westminster Assembly, was chosen preacher and remained at Gray's Inn until 1645.[54]

It seems likely that after Sibbes's death the benchers of Gray's Inn were unwilling to choose another puritan to succeed him. Sibbes had

---

[52] *Winthrop Papers, 1489–1649*, ed. Forbes, iv. 195; *MT Bench Book*, 308; Cressy was recommended to Wentworth by Laud: see Laud's *Works*, ed. J. H. Parker (Oxford, 1847–60), vi. 386.

[53] Hannibal Potter is noticed in the *DNB* life of his brother Francis, which confuses him with Christopher Potter, vice-chancellor of Oxford in 1640: cf. John Nalson, *An Impartial Collection of the Great Affaires of States* (1682), i. 700 and *Oxford Historical Register 1220–1900* (Oxford, 1900), 26. David Lloyd, *Memoires . . . 1633–1660* (1668), 542; John Aubrey, *Brief Lives*, ed. Andrew Clark (Oxford, 1898), i. 173; *N.B.* however that Potter is said by Wood (*Ath. Ox.*, ii. 623) to have preached the funeral sermon of Henry Gellibrand, the Gresham professor of mathematics, for whom see Hill, *Intellectual Origins*, 57. William Montague, *Court and Society from Elizabeth to Anne, Edited from the Papers at Kimbolton* (1864), i. 364.

[54] *GIPB*, i. 342, 345–7; GI MS, Order Book, ff. 432, 434.

always been careful to avoid clashes with the ecclesiastical and secular authorities;[55] but by this time even a moderate was suspect. At the height of the Micklethwaite affair, and only a few months after Laud moved to Lambeth Palace, the benchers of each house had received a letter clearly spelling out the government's attitude to any expression of nonconformity at the inns of court.[56] Writing by the king's direction, Laud stressed the importance of ensuring that their chaplains and preachers should be not only 'learned, and able to preach well, but also discret and prudent and very obedyent'. In manner and form reminiscent of Whitgift's warnings to Elizabeth or the privy council's letter to Gray's Inn in 1585, Laud went on to emphasise the strategic importance of the inns as educational institutions for 'almost all young gentlemen', who, on returning from London to their native shires, 'steere themselves according to such principles as in those places are preacht to them'. It was thus a matter of considerable concern to 'the state both of the church and kingdome, that the preachers in those houses be both conformable men and very well grounded in theyr professions'.

The benchers were ordered to see that the ministers who officiated at daily services wore surplices and read the litany without omissions or transpositions. Preachers were to read through the whole daily service in full vestments at least four times a year, and on all occasions 'discreetly conteyne' themselves 'within those bonds which confine the doctrine and discipline of the Church of England'. No vacancy was to be filled except by men who would observe these requirements. The letter closed with an ominous warning: 'His majesty is resolved that noe one of these places shall use any pretence of privilege against governement, civill or ecclesiastical . . .'.

At a Lincoln's Inn council meeting on 27 January 1634 this letter was read out to the benchers, who were informed that both the preacher, Joseph Caryl, and the chaplain had during the previous vacation, 'conformed themselves to such orders of the church as in the said letter are conteyned'.[57] Since Caryl remained at Lincoln's Inn until 1646 the question of a conformable successor did not immediately arise. But at Gray's Inn the death of Sibbes, who must also have conformed, raised a problem for which the election of Potter, the protégé of a highly respectable Laudian bishop, was the benchers' solution.

---

[55] See William Haller, *The Rise of Puritanism* (New York, 1938), 231, and cf. Robert Jenison's complaints about Sibbes's timorousness as early as 1621: Bodl. MS, Tanner 73, f. 29.
[56] SP 16/254/49 (*CSPD, 1633–34*, 340–1) is an undated draft of this letter, in the hand of William Dell, Laud's secretary, endorsed 'The copy of the letter intended to be sent to ye Innes of Court by ye Bp. of London (1633). This lre. wth. very little alteration was sent'. *BB*, ii. 313–14 summarises the letter actually sent, which is dated London House, 16 Dec. 1633. Laud was translated to Canterbury on 19 Sept. 1633, so the letter was presumably drafted under his direction but actually sent under the name of Juxon, his successor.   [57] *BB*, ii. 313.

The Puritan lay presence

Laud's intervention in 1633 was part of a movement throughout the 1630s towards closer control and supervision of the inns by the state. But during the previous thirty years there was virtually no interference with the benchers' prerogative of appointing preachers, and certainly nothing like the strong official pressures which accompanied the installation of the first permanent preachers. Patrons from outside the societies no doubt introduced and recommended candidates, but our ignorance of the circumstances surrounding the majority of appointments suggests that they were in fact largely determined by the benchers themselves.[58] There is thus some justification for taking the views of preachers chosen by the inns during the first thirty years of the century as a rough guide to those of the benchers who appointed them. On this basis, as any other, Lincoln's Inn emerges as the real stronghold of puritanism among the four inns.

When John Cooke (a Gray's Inn man himself) wished to show that the common lawyers were as zealous in the godly cause as the members of any other calling, he cited the sufferings of 'our worthy and learned bretheren Mr Sherfield and Mr Pryn' (both of Lincoln's Inn), asking rhetorically, 'Did not Mr Greene of Lincoln's Inn suffer matirdome for it, in Queene Maries daies?' The force of Cooke's claim was hardly blunted by his last example, although the Marian martyr Bartholomew Green was actually a barrister of the Inner Temple. Such errors are the stuff on which traditions flourish; this one was sufficiently powerful for nearly all of Cromwell's early biographers to enrol their subject at Lincoln's Inn, although there is no real evidence that he was ever admitted to the house.[59]

During the late sixteenth and early seventeenth centuries men like Sir Edward Atkins and his father Richard, Samuel Browne, Richard Branthwaite, Sir Randolph Crew, Ralph Eyre, William Hakewill, Sir Henry Hobart, Richard Kingsmill, William Lambard, Sir Ralph Rokeby, Henry Sherfield, Sir Thomas Richardson, Sir John Tindall, Thomas Wentworth, Ralph Wilbraham and Sir Humphrey Wynch maintained the society's reputation as a puritan forcing-house, both by personal example and through their votes on the governing body.[60]

58 Cf. *ITR*, ii. 73–4; Gataker, *Discours*, 33–4; *DNB*, s.v. Sibbes; Dr Williams Library MS, Morice II, ff. 615 (12); Morgan, *Prince Charles's Puritan Chaplain*, 109–11.

59 Cooke, *Vindication*, 12; *DNB*, s.v. Green, Sherfield; John Foxe, *Acts and Monuments*, ed. George Townsend (1838), vii. 731; *The Writings and Speeches of Oliver Cromwell*, ed. W. C. Abbott (Cambridge, Mass., 1937), i. 32–3.

60 A. F. Pearson, *Thomas Cartwright and Elizabethan Puritanism* (Cambridge, 1935), 179, 307 (Atkins Sr., Branthwaite and Tindall); Claire Cross, *The Puritan Earl* (1966), 71 (Branthwaite); I. M. Calder, *The Activities of the Puritan Faction in the Church of England* (1957), xii (Eyre); *Documents Relating to the Proceeding Against William Prynne*, ed. S. R. Gardiner, (*CS*, n.s. 18, 1877), xxiv (Wilbraham); and *DNB* for remainder. Thomas Cartwright's brother-in-law John

The benchers of Lincoln's Inn consistently manifested far more positive concern for the spiritual well-being of members than their colleagues in the other houses.

In 1600 a special bench committee of 'censors and visitors for matter of religion and good life' was set up, charged to keep 'a vigilant
eye . . . upon the whole estate of this fellowship'; a similar body was
appointed again in 1611. At the urging of Thomas Gataker, who
came to the house as preacher in 1602, the benchers agreed to transfer
the Wednesday morning sermon to Sunday afternoon, in the hope
of deterring lawyers from interviewing clients on the Sabbath. In
1633 the hour of morning prayers was changed from six to seven,
because 'by reason of the cold winter mornings' they were 'lesse
frequented by the gentlemen of this house, and speciallie by those of
the elder sort'. Unlike the other houses Lincoln's Inn did not employ
troupes of professional actors to stage their 'lewd ungodly entertain-
ments' during the Grand Weeks; towards the end of James's reign
grand Christmasses with their dicing and toasts were abolished, and
from 1627 onwards no gaming was permitted in the hall on Saturday
nights, 'for the better preparing to keepe holy the Saboth Day'.[61]

William Prynne's *Histrio-Mastix* (1633) was dedicated to 'his much
honoured friends', the benchers of Lincoln's Inn, in recognition of
their 'former play-oppugning actions' and 'pious tender care . . . of
the young student's good'. Prynne felt that the most striking evidence
of the latter were the new chapel and library, completed in 1623 and
1632 respectively. According to a catalogue compiled in 1646, the
library then contained at least 220 separate titles, of which no fewer
than 95 were 'divinitie bookes'. The chapel, built to a distinctly old-
fashioned 'country' style, cost about £3,500, an almost 'insupportable
chardge'. But when finally completed, with its stained glass windows
by Bernard van Linge of Old Testament figures and the apostles, and
its bell supposedly taken at Essex's siege of Cadiz in 1596, the chapel
was the society's showpiece and a source of tremendous pride to the
benchers, one of whom apostrophised it as the 'moost beautiful and
moost renowned modell for ecclesiastical use and the divine worship
of Almightie God within this academy, . . . very lyke the same to
continue immatcheable to future posterity even to the end'.[62]

Lincoln's Inn chapel rapidly became a focal centre of London
puritanism; when John Preston first arrived at Lincoln's Inn the old
building could hardly accommodate the members of the house, 'but

Stubbes was an utter-barrister of LI: for his friends and influence see Ralph
Rokeby, 'Oeconomia Rokebiorum', in T. D. Whitaker, *An History of Richmondshire* (1823), i. 164, 179; Pearson, *op. cit.*, 179, 354, 307; Collinson, *Puritan Movement*, 480, n. 3.
[61] *BB*, ii. 66, 142, 287, 311; Gataker, *Discours*, 16–17.
[62] Prynne, *Histrio-Mastix*, sig. i; Harleian 7363, ff. 81–5; Roxburgh, *Origins of
Lincoln's Inn*, 6–7.

when the chappell was new built . . . the number was exceeding great, that were his constant hearers, and foundations laid, that will not be easily ruined'. According to Laud's chaplain Peter Heylyn 'it was well he [Preston] died so opportunely; Laud was resolved that there should be no more than one bishop of that city, and would have found some way or other to remove him out of Lincoln's Inn'.[63]

Preston's successor was Edward Reynolds, who had already clashed with Heylyn at Oxford before he came to Lincoln's Inn. But this was his first appointment outside the university and he did not enjoy anything like Preston's fame as a puritan leader and preacher, while his ecclesiastical position was sufficiently flexible to secure him a royal chaplaincy as well as the patronage of the Lord Keeper Thomas Coventry, who was noted for his 'assidious devotions in the sett and fixed formes' of the Anglican Church. A follower of John Prideaux, the Calvinist who clung to his regius chair of divinity at Oxford throughout the Laudian ascendancy, Reynolds sat in the Westminster Assembly, took the Covenant after some hesitation and was among the ministers chosen by the victorious parliament in 1646 to preach his old university into obedience. He was also the first inns of court preacher to be made a bishop, his elevation to the see of Norwich in 1661 being part of Charles II's abortive scheme to comprehend the presbyterians within the Church of England. Reynolds was followed at Lincoln's Inn in 1632 by Joseph Caryl, another of Prideaux's disciples, a distinguished biblical scholar and later a frequent preacher to the Long Parliament. Although there is little evidence of his views before 1640, Caryl adopted a far more radical position than his predecessor during the Civil War and Interregnum, remaining a nonconformist until his death in 1673.[64]

None of the other houses rivalled the puritanism of Lincoln's Inn, either in reputation or reality. There were certainly some puritans and zealous Calvinists among the benchers of Gray's Inn and the two Temples during the half century before the Civil War. Those who may be so identified, with varying degrees of confidence, include at Gray's Inn James Altham, Francis and Nathaniel Bacon, Sir Thomas Crew, Sir Humphrey Davenport, Sir Henry Finch, Edward Reeve, Alexander Rigby, Christopher Sherland, Francis Thorpe and Sir Henry Yelverton; at the Inner Temple Richard Aske, Edward Bulstrode, Sir George and Unton Croke, Elizeus Hele, Sir Edmund Prideaux, Henry Rolle, John Stone and John Wilde; and at the Middle Edward Bagshaw, Sir Robert Brerewood, James

---

63 Ball, *Life of Preston*, 105–7; Peter Heylyn, *Cyprianus Anglicus* (1668), 157.

64 *DNB*, s.v. Caryl, Reynolds; Seaver, *Puritan Lectureships*, 287; *Ath. Ox.*, iii. 1083; IT MS, Petyt. 538. xvii, ff. 362–362v; A. G. Mathews, *Calamy Revised* (Oxford, 1934), 103; H. R. Trevor-Roper, 'The Fast Sermons of the Long Parliament', in *Essays in English History Presented to Sir Keith Feiling*, ed. Trevor-Roper (1964), 122; Additional 4346, ff. 46–60v.

Morice, Sir Sydney Montagu, Sir Augustine Nicolls, Sir Edward Phelips, John Puleston, John White and Sir James Whitelocke.[65] Yet within their societies these men do not seem to have wielded an influence comparable to that enjoyed by their counterparts at Lincoln's Inn. The tone of zealous piety which pervades the Black Books is conspicously absent from the records of the other houses. Apart from a few orders restricting the performance of learning exercises on Sundays and various efforts to restrain the excesses at Christmas commons – which were not motivated by solely religious considerations – the corporate actions and policies of these three inns cannot be said to bear any distinctly puritan imprint.[66] Moreover, as we have already seen, Gray's Inn and the two Temples appointed considerably fewer preachers and among them fewer puritans during our period than did Lincoln's Inn.

Nevertheless, all four houses undoubtedly served as a propaganda base and general nexus for puritan clergy and laymen. Thomas Gataker's sermons at Lincoln's Inn regularly attracted members of Prince Henry's household as well as the puritan Lord Robert Rich (later first earl of Warwick), 'by reason of the vicinity of his house in Holborn'. For nearly twenty years Richard Sibbes preached the Word at Gray's Inn to young gentlemen students, 'learned lawyers of the house, many noble personages and many of the gentry and citizens'.[67] In 1631 the second Earl of Warwick, who fully inherited his father's religious views, obtained permission to build a gallery at the east end of Gray's Inn chapel, from which he and his friends could listen in comfort to Richard Sibbes's sermons. Warwick's guests must have included John Pym, the earl's near-neighbour in Gray's Inn Lane, and also a devoted admirer of Sibbes.[68] The Providence Island Company, that caucus of puritan opposition, met at Warwick's house, at Pym's lodgings, at Lord Brooke's house on the Gray's Inn Lane corner of High Holborn, or at Sir Gilbert's Gerrard's chamber in Gray's Inn, which was occupied by Sibbes when he came down from Cambridge to preach. The secretary of the Providence Company and Pym's trustee for his lands in Bermuda was another Gray's Inn resident, William Jessop. Two other Providence Company members of Gray's Inn were Henry Darley, who sat for Northallerton in the Long Parliament, a

[65] Sources: *DNB*; *DWB*; *Al. Ox.*; *Al. Cant.*; Foss, *Judges*, v. vi; Neale, *Elizabeth I and her Parliaments*, i. ii; Keeler, *Long Parliament*; Williams, *Index to Dedications*; George Yule, *The Independents in the English Civil War* (Cambridge and Melbourne, 1958); D. A. Kirby, 'The Radicals of St Stephen, Coleman Street, London, 1624–1642', *Guildhall Miscellany*, 3 (1970), 102.

[66] *GIPB*, ii. 284–5, 292; *ITR*, ii. 52, 96; *MTR*, ii. 509; and see above, pp. 105–9.

[67] Hill, *Intellectual Origins*, 219; Gataker, *Discours*, 37; Samuel Clarke, *A Generall Martyrologie* (1651), 166.

[68] *GIPB*, i. 300; Pearl, *London and the Outbreak of the Puritan Revolution*, 41. Pym's appreciation of Sibbes's preaching is recorded in Samuel Hartlib's 'Ephemerides' for 1634; I owe this information to Dr. Hill.

friend both of Pym and John Winthrop, and Christopher Sherland, who became a bencher in 1627 and was one of Sibbes's colleagues in the scheme for purchasing impropriations and establishing puritan lectureships which Laud broke up in 1633. When Sherland died in 1632 his place among the Feoffees for Impropriations was taken by Sir Thomas Crew, another Gray's Inn man, though now a serjeant-at-law, and when Crew himself died two years later, Sibbes preached his funeral sermon. Sir Nathaniel Rich, Warwick's half-brother, and deputy governor of the Providence Company, was also a Gray's Inn member and a friend of Sibbes; Rich had some influence at Lincoln's Inn and tried to persuade William Bedell, pupil of the great Cambridge puritan William Perkins, to take up the lectureship there after Thomas Gataker's resignation.[69] Oliver St John, who defended Hampden in the Ship Money case, was a barrister of Lincoln's Inn when he joined the Providence Company; three years before his chamber had been searched for seditious papers after he had circulated a manuscript to 'divers lords' (including his client Francis Russell, fourth earl of Bedford, another leading opposition peer and an associate bencher of Lincoln's Inn), 'showing the odiousness' of 'projects to get money without a parliament'; in 1639 he acted for Pym in a Chancery law suit.[70]

Yet another Providence Company member was Robert Gurdon, an Inner Temple barrister, who sat for Ipswich in the Long Parliament and was a leading member of the Eastern Association during the Civil War; Gurdon's son Robert shared his chamber at the Temple with the younger John Winthrop in 1625, until Winthrop went to lodge with his puritan uncle Emmanuel Downing. Downing and Winthrop senior, the future governor of Massachusetts, were specially admitted to the Inner Temple in 1628 as attorneys in the Court of Wards. Winthrop's business adviser and colleague in the Massachusetts Company was John White, a lawyer of the Middle Temple and also a feoffee for impropriations. His senior colleague William Whitaker was one of Pym's trustees and had stood surety when Pym was admitted to the Middle Temple; he also acted with Simonds D'Ewes as guarantor of William Drake, the son of devout puritan parents who sat for Amersham between 1640 and 1648. Moreover John White was a friend of Edward Bagshaw, who published the posthumous works and biography of his puritanical Oxford tutor Robert Bolton, whose *Discourse about the state of True happiness* (1610) was dedicated to Bagshaw's

---

[69] A. P. Newton, *The Colonising Activities of the English Puritans* (New Haven, 1914), 58, 61–2, 70; J. H. Hexter, *The Reign of King Pym* (Cambridge, Mass., 1941), 77–88; *GIPB*, i. 266; E. S. Shuckburgh ed., *Two Biographies of William Bedell* (Cambridge, 1902), 256–8; Bald, *John Donne*, 319.
[70] I owe this last information to Mr. Conrad Russell's discussion of his research on Pym's early political activity at an Institute of Historical Research seminar, February 1968.

step-father, Sir Augustine Nicolls, another Middle Temple bencher.[71]

It would be possible to continue tracing connections of this kind almost indefinitely, but the point has been made. Most of these individuals were puritans by upbringing; their religious beliefs were acquired primarily from parents, teachers and university experiences. Yet they found at the inns companions, kinsmen and mentors whose attitude and backgrounds paralleled and reinforced their own. While never exclusively puritan in membership or opinion, the societies nevertheless acted as a point of contact in London for puritan gentry and lawyers from all over England, serving to strengthen and extend the network of family and regional connections on which the lay puritan movement was built.[72]

Geographical and institutional factors obviously suited the inns for this role. But it also seems possible that the common lawyers who constituted the more stable element of the societies' membership had particular reasons to be attracted by puritanism, or at least certain aspects of the puritan programme. The traditional rivalry between the law and the church, the two oldest learned professions, must have led many lawyers to sympathise with puritan demands for curtailment of the powers exercised over the laity by church men and ecclesiastical courts.[73] Exacerbated during the later sixteenth century by the jurisdictional clashes of common-law and church courts, the jealousy and suspicion with which Whitgift and Laud regarded the lawyers was echoed by their clerical followers who, 'finding that in former times . . . many churchmen were employed eminently in the civil government . . . imputed their wanting those ornaments their predecessors wore to the power and prevalency of the lawyers'.[74]

Clerical jibes at the 'barbarity' of the common law and the 'crew of unlearned lawyers' were not unnoticed.[75] The reaction to George Ruggle's burlesque play *Ignoramus*, presented before James I at Cambridge University in 1614, indicates the sensitivity of the profession to reflections on their learning or social status. This satirical attack on the common lawyers was answered by Robert Callis in a Staple Inn reading the following year, where he illustrated the law of ecclesiastical benefices by the corrupt dealing of an imaginary clergyman, Sir Ignoramus. Callis's reading was not published until 1641; a more immediate result of *Ignoramus* was to impel John Selden to be-

---

71 *The Diary of John Rous*, ed. M. A. Green, (*CS*, 66, 1856), 46; *CSPD, 1629–31*, 98; *APC, 1629–30*, 170–1; Black, *Younger John Winthrop*, 23–7; *ITR*, ii. 169; Keeler, *Long Parliament*, 390–1.
72 Cf. Michael Walzer, *The Revolution of the Saints* (Cambridge, Mass., 1965), 243–4.
73 Cf. Hill, *Society and Puritanism*, ch. 8.
74 Edward, Earl of Clarendon, *The History of the Rebellion*, ed. W. D. Macray (Oxford, 1887), i. 404–5; cf. *The Works of John Whitgift, D.D.*, ed. John Ayre (Cambridge, 1851), i. 312–14.
75 Cf. Strype, *Whitgift*, i. 405–8.

gin his *History of Tithes,* which argued by clear implication that tithing was of human, not divine, institution.[76] The laity had every reason to fear a clerical resurgence after Charles I's accession; the lawyers had particular grounds for disquiet, as the church courts expanded their activities, bishops called judges to account, Micklethwaite waged his successful campaign against the Templars and the Arminian bishop of Chichester, Richard Montagu, laid claim to the lands and buildings of Lincoln's Inn.[77]

While anticlericalism was the most powerful force driving lawyers towards the puritan camp, various other more tenuous pressures operated in the same direction. The common law was pre-eminently a career open to talent; despite the role played by patrimony and patronage, a successful lawyer was as much a selfmade man as could be found in seventeenth-century England. Such a person would very likely find the puritan emphasis on a direct relationship between individuals and their God and the necessity of labouring in one's calling attractive. The puritan tendency to equate worldly success with spiritual election doubtless appealed to the strong sense of achievement implicit in Sir Robert Heath's boast (which comes strangely from Buckingham's former protégé), that he had been preferred to all his 'severall places . . . without my owne suit'.[78] A corollary was the stress puritans placed on preaching as the prime means of leading men to God. A lawyer could appreciate and criticise sermons on his own terms, for logic, rhetoric and argument from authority were also his basic stock in trade. The pious Sir Augustine Nicolls, whose 'forbearance to travel on the Lord's day wrought a reformation on some of his own order', was by no means the only successful barrister to favour and encourage 'plain and profitable preaching'.[79] A hard-worked lawyer's efficiency might well be enhanced if he strictly observed the Sabbath, thus gaining at least one day in seven to recuperate from the mental and physical strains of his calling. Puritans emphasised the need for lawyers to keep Sunday a day of rest and devotion: Mathew Hale found to his comfort that 'the more closely I applyed myself to the duties of the Lords Day the more happy and successful were my businesses and imployments of the week following. So that I could from the strict or loose observation of this day take a just prospect and true calculation of my temporall success in the ensuing week'.[80]

Derided for their insularity by university-trained clergymen and civilians, the lawyers undoubtedly felt a strong common cause with

---

[76] Cf. J. L. van Gundy, *Ignoramus . . . An Examination of Its Sources and Literary Influence* (Lancaster, Pennsylvania, 1906), 7, 12, 66.

[77] Cf. Roxburgh, *Origins of Lincoln's Inn,* 19–27; *BB,* ii. 332–8.

[78] *Memoir of Chief-Justice Heath,* ed. E. P. Shirley (Philobiblon Soc., Miscellany i, n.d.), 20; cf. Sir James Whitelocke's self-righteous comments on lawyers who paid cash for their preferments: *Lib. Fam.,* 44.

[79] David Lloyd, *State Worthies* (1766), ii. 245–6.

[80] Harleian 4009, ff. 45–6.

the fiercely nationalistic puritans. They could hardly rebut the charge of parochialism, but maintained that the common law was immemorially bound up with the rights and liberties of Englishmen, while the law administered by ecclesiastical and prerogative courts was valid only if sanctioned and received by the common law itself.[81] Sir James Whitelocke appealed to this notion when, asserting his right as a common lawyer to plead before the Earl Marshall's Court, he argued that the issue did 'much concern our whole order and all other gentlemen of England, that naturallie desire to submitt all their fortunes to the rule of their homeborn law'.[82] Nicholas Fuller, the Gray's Inn bencher whose campaign against the High Commission's ex-officio oath became a puritan *cause celèbre*, was described by the publisher of his speech before the Commission in 1607 as upholding 'the lawes and liberties of the land (the high inheritance of the subjects) . . . maugre the malice of the prelates'. Despite the well-known interest of Cardinals Pole and Wolsey in reforming the common law, it could hardly be represented as a bulwark against popery until the old recusant benchers of the inns had passed away. Then the claim had a certain cogency; in 1617 the puritan Richard Bernard thanked God for 'the happie policy of the civil state', resulting from the 'just and wholesome lawes of this nation; by which . . . the supremacie is given to the sovraigne authority and the bishop of Rome quite shut out'. No wonder, he added, that papists are such enemies to the common laws of England. Before Laud stopped his reading at the Middle Temple in August 1639, Edward Bagshaw had argued that the common law was more agreeable than any other to the law of God: 'it advanceth true religion and worship; and the rise and fall of one, is the rise and fall of the other'.[83]

So a combination of ideological and material forces tended to draw common lawyers into the puritan camp. But the intimacy of the association is easily exaggerated. Far from being a union, it was at best an incomplete and temporary alliance. The legal profession was not generally regarded by contemporaries as particularly sympathetic to the puritan cause.[84] Writing after the Restoration Peter

---

[81] See Pocock, *The Ancient Constitution and the Feudal Law*, ch. 2, sect. I.
[82] Bodl. MS, Smith 71, f. 59.
[83] *The Argument of Master Nicholas Fuller* (1607), sig. a; Richard Bernard, *A Key of Knowledge for the opening of Secret Mysteries* (1617), sig. A2v; Stowe; 424, f. 5.
[84] Cf. E. H. Emerson, *English Puritanism from John Hooper to John Milton* (Durham, N.C., 1968), 21. Only one pre-Civil War source which specifically identifies the common lawyers as puritan in outlook is known to the present writer. An anonymous letter of *c*. 1626–28 lists among the enemies of the duke of Buckingham 'lawyers, citizens and western men (who are most hot infected with puritanisme)': *Cabala, sive Scrinia Sacra: Mysteries of State and Government* (1654), 227; from internal evidence this is clearly a high-church production. After the Restoration John Aubrey reported that Captain Robert Pugh, the catholic-educated royalist soldier, 'was wont to say that civilians (as most learned and

Heylyn did indeed contend that the sermons of Walter Travers at the Temple Church had 'possest many of the long robe with a strong affection to the devices of Geneva and with as great a prejudice to the English hierarchy; the fruits whereof discovered themselves more or less in all the following parliaments, where any thing concerning the Church came into agitation'.[85] But Heylyn cited no evidence to support his claim about the 'Genevan' sympathies of the profession, other than Bishop Cosin's allegation that puritans drew on the technical expertise of common lawyers in framing objections to the ecclesiastical jurisdiction; moreover, he omitted Cosin's careful rider that the lawyers who rendered this service were 'in no way affected to their other fancies'.[86]

Heylyn was writing as a partisan, determined to vindicate his former master William Laud by establishing an interpretation of English church history and the 'rise of puritanism' which has held favour among historians until very recent times. He played down the Calvinist element in the Elizabethan Church, identified puritanism with presbyterianism and claimed that Laud was merely combating a subversive movement which had been allowed to rise within the church during the lax administration of Archbishop Abbot. But it is now apparent that Laud and his Arminian followers were attempting to impose new doctrinal and liturgical forms, not simply to suppress puritans unwilling to accept a well-established Anglican norm. With their capture of the episcopacy and universities in the 1620s, mere orthodox low churchmanship came to be officially reclassified as puritan dissent. The Laudian stress on rebuilding the economic and social prestige of the clerical estate further extended the definition of puritanism to all those who opposed a resurgence of clerical power, and indeed to all who differed from the Caroline government's policies in Church and state.[87]

Many who were labelled puritans by the bishops and courtiers of Charles I did not accept the title and were not so regarded by their associates and friends. Christopher Sherland of Gray's Inn claimed in 1628 that 'all good true-hearted Englishmen and christians' were now called puritans by those who told the king that 'he may command what he listeth and do as he pleaseth with our goods, lives and religion'.[88] Lord Cottington, a crypto-catholic, who gave the first judgment at the Star Chamber trial of Henry Sherfield in 1632, described Sherfield's breaking down a window in his parish church

---

gent.) naturally incline to the church of Rome; and the common lawyers, as more ignorant and clownish, to the church of Geneva': *Brief Lives*, i. 60.

[85] *Aerius Redivivus*, 313; cf. *idem, Cyprianus Anglicus*, 407.

[86] John Cosin, *An Apology for the Proceedings* . . . (1597), sig. A2v.

[87] Cf. Hill, *Society and Puritanism*, ch. 1; N. R. N. Tyacke, 'Arminianism in England, in religion and politics, 1604 to 1640' (Oxford D. Phil. thesis, 1968), 1–8, 239–40, *et passim*.

[88] Quoted Hill, *Society and Puritanism*, 20.

as the act of a puritan or Brownist; but Chief Justice Richardson, a former colleague of Sherfield on the bench of Lincoln's Inn, personally corroborated the testimony of Sherfield's witnesses, that the defendant had always shown himself conformable to the government of the church, had prosecuted separatists as a J.P., and had been observed to receive the communion kneeling. (Most of the common-law judges sitting at this trial took a lenient view of Sherfield's action, arguing that the window, which depicted God as 'a little old man in a red and blue coat', should have been removed, because it encouraged idolatry among the simpler members of the congregation; Laud and Neile however maintained that images of the Deity were not in themselves idolatrous, and represented Sherfield's offence as a very serious challenge to the authority of the church, aggravated by his rank and profession).[89]

The barrister John Mansell, Prynne's chamber fellow at Lincoln's Inn, was reported by a hostile witness from Northamptonshire in 1638 to have spoken against liturgical ceremonies and expressed the view that 'those who are called puritans are for the most part religious, conscionable, honest men'. Another Lincoln's Inn barrister, Henry Parker, ended his *Discourse concerning Puritans* (1642) with these words:

> I have said enough to make myself condemned for a puritan, . . . but verily, if thou art not an antipuritan of the worst kinde, I am not a puritan. . . . If thou thinkest some men religious which affect not the name of puritan, I thinke so; if thou too thinkest most men irreligious which hate the name of puritan, I thinke so too.[90]

Dr Pearl has described Oliver St John as 'typical of many puritan lawyers . . . a man of orthodox, Calvinist-inclined views which were as compatible with low-church Anglicanism as classical independency or presbyterianism'.[91] Sir John Bankes, a man whom Charles I evidently considered sufficiently orthodox to be entrusted with the politically sensitive office of attorney-general after Noy's death, was still prepared to stand patron to a volume of sermons published by Richard Sibbes in 1635.[92] And Sir John Finch declared before the Commons in December 1640 his hope that 'for my affection in religion no man doubteth me. . . . I lived thirty years in the society of Grayes Inne, and if one that were a reverend preacher in my tyme

[89] *State Trials*, iii. 519–42.
[90] SP 16/414/163; Haller, *The Rise of Puritanism*, 365–6; cf. Additional 53726, f. 40v, for Bulstrode Whitelocke's distinction between 'a knowne puritan or an hippocrite, and a knave puritan, one that is religious in heart as well as in profession, butt knaves reproach him with the name of puritan, bicause he will not do ill . . .'.
[91] Valerie Pearl, 'The "Royal Independents" in the English Civil War', *TRHS*, 5th ser., 18 (1968), 79–80.
[92] Richard Sibbes, *The Soules Conflict . . .* (1635), pref. ded.

(Dr Sibbes) were now alive, he were able to give testimony to this house'.[93] Religious and political divisions were by no means clearcut or coterminous in the first forty years of the seventeenth century, how-ever straightforward they may appear from later vantage points.

With a few notable exceptions, the puritanism of the inns and their common-lawyer members was conservative, erastian and moderate (differing little from the typical cast of thought among the country gentry, with whom the lawyers predominantly identified themselves). While Coke, Selden and many others attacked the church and clergy before 1640, they had no wish to destroy the fabric of ecclesiastical government and let in sectarian anarchy or presbyterian theocracy. Discussing the lawyers' animosity towards the clerical estate during the early months of the Long Parliament, Clarendon describes how 'many pragmatical spirits' gradually passed from 'the womanish art of inveighing against persons' to the belief that 'a parity in church was necessary to religion, and not like to produce a parity in the state; the suspicion of which would quickly have worn upon their divinity'.[94] Class and professional interest alike kept a firm check on the religious radicalism of most lawyers before 1640.

At the trial of Prynne, Burton and Bastwick in 1637 Laud expressed his belief that the defendants were unrepresentative of their respective professions, and claimed that Prynne might 'seek the inns of court . . . and scarce find such a malevolent as himself against state and church'. This was not mere wishful thinking: although Prynne's latest bio-grapher depicts him as a religious moderate before 1640, it is im-portant to distinguish between the content of Prynne's thought and the manner in which his views were expressed. Both Laud and the benchers of Lincoln's Inn took the openness and violence of Prynne's attack upon the bishops as evidence that they were dealing with a dan-gerous fanatic, a would-be leveller of church government, a latter-day Martinist.[95]

The reaction to Edward Bagshaw's anticlerical reading at the Middle Temple early in 1640 was significantly different. Bagshaw came from a long line of Northamptonshire puritans and had been in trouble with the High Commission the previous year. His religious sympa-thies may be gauged from a passage in his opening speech, which praised Edward III as an enemy of the papacy and 'a freinde to true religion, for he was a favourer of John Wickliffe the maintainer of the doctrine of the Lollards and Waldenses, being the same in sub-stance which protestants now possess'.[96] The whole tone of his first week's reading was strongly critical of the temporal powers of the

---

93 Nalson, *op. cit.*, i. 693.   94 *History of the Rebellion*, ii. 406–7.
95 Laud, *Works*, vi (I), 39; W. M. Lamont, *Marginal Prynne* (1963), chs. 1–2 *passim*; for the sentence disbarring and expelling Prynne, see below, pp. 228–9.
96 SP 16/437/58; Bagshaw's reading is in Hargrave 206 ff. iv, *seq.*, and Stowe 424, ff. 3–36v (the quotation above is from *ibid.*, f. 4).

church. At the beginning of the second week he advanced the proposition that ministers deprived of their benefices by the High Commission had a right of appeal to the common-law courts; the same afternoon Laud successfully requested the king to intervene and Bagshaw was ordered to cease reading. This unprecedented action 'made a loud noise throughout the cities of London and Westminster' and Bagshaw became a minor hero. The Middle Temple benchers made no attempt to discipline him and 'scarce any reader before was ever attended out of town with such a number of gentlemen of the same house'. The silencing of Bagshaw also added to Laud's unpopularity among the 'vulgar sorte', who believing Bagshaw to be a determined enemy of the bishops, elected him for Southwark to the Long Parliament, without (as he later claimed) 'my asking or seeking or stepping one foot out of my chamber in the Middle Temple to that purpose'.[97]

Yet Bagshaw sadly disappointed his radical supporters; although siding with Pym at first, he refused to present a root-and-branch petition from his constituency, voted against root-and-branch in the House and followed his patron, Lord Montagu of Boughton, to join Charles I at Oxford. Bagshaw and Prynne agreed in denouncing the usurpations of the prelates; but whereas Bagshaw expressed his views in a semi-private forum, and was careful to veil his insults in ambiguous or technical language, Prynne published his attacks to the wide world and spared no linguistic effort to drive the barbs home. Prynne lost his ears and his membership at Lincoln's Inn not so much for what he said as the way he said it.[98]

Lay high-church men are generally more difficult to track down than lay puritans, partly because they have attracted little attention from historians, partly because they were less vocal and certainly fewer in number than their opponents. But besides papists and crypto-catholics, the inns of court and the legal profession always contained some individuals whose outlook was definitely antipathetic to the puritan cause. Among them were Christopher Fulwood, William Hudson, Thomas Procter and Sir Euble Thelwall of Gray's Inn; Sir Julius Caesar, Richard Dyott [99] (the son of the bencher Anthony Dyott) and Thomas, Lord Coventry of the Inner Temple; William Austin,[1] Chris-

[97] Bagshaw, *A Just Vindication of the Questioned Part of the Reading* (1660), 2–3, 9–14; SP 16/447/30 (1); Stowe 424, ff. 6–35.
[98] Keeler, *Long Parliament*, 74; HMC, *Buccleugh*, iii. 373.
[99] University of Chicago Library MS, 196 Thomas Procter, 'The parishioner's claim for the vicar's maintenance'; Dyott defended Bishop Montagu's doctrines in the parliament of 1625 and was excluded from the Commons in 1626 for helping to block Buckingham's impeachment: Tyacke, *op. cit.*, 173.
[1] Austin, a barrister like Dyott, published in 1633 his *Devotionis Augustinianae Flamma, or Certayne Devout, Godly and Learned Meditations*, dedicated to 'Deo optimo maximo, et ecclesiae catholicae' and consisting of short devotional pieces on the saints, apostles and angels; the theological viewpoint is distinctly non-Calvinist.

topher Brooke, Sir Thomas Egerton and William Noy of Lincoln's
Inn; John Hoskyns, Robert Hyde and Richard Martin of the Middle
Temple.[2]

Even under Whitgift and Laud, the church was never without
powerful friends among the common lawyers: Whitgift regarded
Egerton as 'a constant favourer of the clergy, zealous for the established government'; the lawyer James Dalton was described by Sir
Francis Knollys in 1593, after his part in a Commons debate on church
government, as one of the 'confederates of the clergie government';
while in 1634 Laud mourned the death of William Noy, his own 'dear
friend' and to the church 'the greatest she had of his condition, since
she needed one'.[3] If we are to give the puritan lecturers their due, we
should recognise that Chafin, Donne, Fenton, Hooker, May, Micklethwaite, Potter – perhaps even Bishops Bancroft and Laud, as well
as Laud's tutor Buckeridge, all of whom served as visiting preachers –
must also have left some mark on their congregations.[4] The godly
preachers could not dissuade the societies from a strict observance
of Lent and other traditional fasts, nor did they manage to suppress
the endemic gaming and revels at Christmas and Grand Weeks. The
literary caricature (and its real life exemplars) of the inns of court
student as a roistering gallant, compulsive playgoer and indefatigable
wencher also survived their ministrations.

Even at Lincoln's Inn, spiritual imperatives were often qualified
by wordly considerations. It is just possible that George Montaigne,
an Arminian sympathiser but no rigorous disciplinarian, who occupied
the see of London when the society's new chapel was completed,
would have insisted on its formal consecration against the objections
of the bench. It seems entirely unlikely that pressure from the same
quarter impelled the benchers to issue an order forbidding members
'to sitt, leane or rest with their handes or armes . . . against the communion table, or lay their hattes or bookes upon the same'.[5] But the
most telling illustration of the practical limits of puritan influence at
Lincoln's Inn is provided by a recollection of William Prynne's. During
Prynne's student days it was customary to hold revels with 'dancing,
dicing and gaming' in the society's hall every Saturday night between
All Saint's Eve and Candlemas. According to Prynne, the festivities

[2] Sources: as above, p. 207, n. 65. See also Robert Wright, *A Receyt to Stay the
Plague* (1625), ded. epistle; IT MS, Petyt 538. xvii, f. 362v; Osborn, *Hoskyns*, 24–5.
[3] Heylyn, *Cyprianus Anglicus*, 347; Ellis, *Select Letters*, 3rd. ser., iv. 111; Laud,
Works, iii. 121, vii. 106.
[4] Wilbraham, *Journal*, 23; Laud, *Works*, iii. 157; Manningham, 'Diary', 38.
[5] *BB*, ii. 243; cf. orders against wearing hats or cloaks in the chapel, *ibid.*, 8, 281.
At his trial Laud cited the stained glass windows of Lincoln's Inn chapel, in reply
to Samuel Brown's attack on his own innovations at Lambeth Palace; but this
begged the question, as the Lincoln's Inn windows did not depict any divine person, and hence fell outside the scope of the second commandment: *Works*, iv.
200.

usually lasted until midnight and sometimes until four the next morning, not only profaning the Sabbath but also making it difficult for the revellers to stay awake through the Sunday morning sermon:

> Which being a great corasive to my spirit, grief to my heart, and scandall to many religious lawyers, students and our lecturers, I used my best endeavors to reform this long continued abuse; and by my interest in some pious benchers of Lincoln's Inne procured them by an order of council to suppress all publique gaming and dicing in the hall, with all Grand Christmasses and disorders in that abused season; and likewise to restrain the length of their revels on Saturday nights, by confining them to a certain houre; though they could not totally suppresse them, as they and I desired, *being over ruled therein by the majority of benchers, pleading long prescription, custome, and unwillingnesse to displease the revellers and young students, for their continuance.*[6]

Contemporary comment on the religious attitudes of common lawyers most frequently emphasised their secularism and indifference to spiritual matters. This was to some extent merely another item in the catalogue of moral failings traditionally attributed to the profession. But lawyers also levelled the charge against themselves; thus an utter-barrister of Gray's Inn expressed the hope that his commentary on the forty-first psalm might turn the advocate's thoughts from worldly affairs 'to sue for his owne spiritual good, with greater importunity'.[7] Augustine Baker, who gave up a flourishing practice at Gray's Inn to become a Benedictine monk, pointed out that law was 'a most terrene study, as whose subject is wordliness . . . apt to cause answerable quality of spirit in the student . . . very remote from desires or thinking of celestiall or everlasting goodnesse'. At the consecration of their new chapel John Donne warned the members of Lincoln's Inn against spiritual negligence or sloth:

> Beloved, it is not always colder upon Sunday, then upon Satterday, nor at any time colder in the chappell then in Westminster Hall . . . They that love a warme bed . . . a warme studie . . . a warme profit, better then this place, they deny Christ in his institution. . . .[8]

Again, Edward Dalton reminded the Templars that

> the greater your care is for establishing others or yourselves in terrestial endowments, the greater corasive it is to the conscience, if it be not paralleled with an equal measure of studie and endeavour to gather assurance of your owne Coelestial inheritance.[9]

[6] William Prynne, *A Briefe Polemicall Dissertation* . . . (1654), sig. A2 (my italics): Prynne's claim to have secured the abolition of gaming in hall is contradicted by an entry for 5 November 1635 in Greene, 'Diary', 389.
[7] William Bloys, *Meditations upon the XLI Psalme* (1632), sig. A3v.
[8] Baker, *Memorials*, 46; cf. Lloyd, *State Worthies*, ii. 114.
[9] John Donne, *Encaenia* (1623), 35; Edward Dalton, *Doubtings Downfall* (1624), sig. A3; cf. Cooke, *Vindication*, 12–14; Edward Bulstrode, *A Golden Chaine* (1658), sig. A2.

Practising lawyers were fully occupied with their work for most of the year, while the majority of the community, engaged in rural activities, interspersed short periods of intense labour with long intervals of near or total idleness. During term the barrister was busy with his clients and their cases at Westminster; in vacation, as one dramatist put it, 'when suits will not make them, they make suits': more fairly perhaps, there were assizes to attend, manor courts to be held, country clients to visit. Caught up in this hectic year-round tempo, a successful common lawyer might well have been hard put to find sufficient time and energy for his spiritual duties.[10] Even if the spirit were willing, the flesh was often weak; Sir Robert Heath recalled sitting in his study one Sunday afternoon, having just returned from the country, 'reading on a book of divinitie, fitt for the thoughts of that day, when I was on a suddayne overtaken with a slumber (as too often happens when our thoughts should be most fixed upon heavenly meditations)'. John Cooke admitted that 'our great practisers . . . have scarce enough time to keepe grace alive in the soule . . . spirituall zeale . . . being often quenched (if not lost) by the throng and crowd of over much temporal imployments'.[11] A popular explanation for the notoriously poor attendance of lawyers at assize sermons was that they were too busy interviewing clients; indeed the law so much preoccupied the attention of its practitioners that Bulstrode Whitelocke, even in the 'study of divine trueths . . . did not altogether neglect that of my calling; the noting of the dependence, and resemblances of some of our English lawes, with those of the Hebrewes, being part of my designe in those meditations'.[12]

This is not to deny that those active but numerically restricted circles of radical protestants, which Professor Collinson has traced through the Elizabethan countryside, had their counterparts at every inn of court and among every generation of common lawyers. From the 1520s onwards the inns had harboured small cells of doctrinaire protestants among their members; but these zealots were no more typical of the legal profession as a whole than either St Thomas More on one side or the tiny handful of lawyers among the Marian exiles on the other.[13] While few common lawyers dared oppose, and many actively assisted Henry VIII's break with Rome, an enthusiasm for the expropriation of church lands and the reduction of clerical privilege required no commitment to protestant theology. And a century later, when Laud complained that the common lawyers 'had gotten so much power over the church', or issued a challenge to Henry Sherfield 'and such of

---

[10] S. S., *The Honest Lawyer* (1616), in *Tudor Facsimile Series*, ed. J. S. Farmer (1914), sig. C5.
[11] *Memoir of Chief-Justice Heath*, 12; Cooke, *Vindication*, 13.
[12] Bulstrode Whitelocke, *A Journal of the Swedish Embassy* (1772), ii. 431.
[13] Cf. A. G. Dickens, *The English Reformation* (1964), 137; *idem, Lollards and Protestants in the Diocese of York* (Oxford, 1959), 14, 60, 132–3, 137; Christina Garrett, *The Marian Exiles* (Cambridge, 1938), 41, 83, 89, 225–6, 428.

his profession as slight the ecclesiastical law and persons', he was not talking about matters of belief or doctrinal dissent.[14] The relationship of the church to the state and society was indeed a theological question, but its temporal implications were too momentous for Laud or his opponents to suppose that it could be safely left to the theologians.

[14] *Works*, vi (I), 20, 210.

X

The Inns of Court
and the
English Revolution

The inns existed on the periphery of seventeenth-century politics. They had no formal parliamentary representation, dispensed very little patronage and expressed no corporate voice on public issues. While both lay and professional members frequently rose to prominence at court and in parliament, the course of their careers rarely had much direct connection with the societies themselves. Yet as educational institutions and professional associations, the inns could not hope to escape political involvement, at a time when law and politics were closely intertwined. While they hardly played a leading role in the conflicts which led up to the Civil War, neither were they mere supernumeraries or passive spectators.

Political education

The political significance of attitudes and beliefs imbibed by students at the inns before 1642 is obviously an important question, to which, unfortunately, no short or very satisfactory answer can now be given. It is usually assumed that the influence of the inns worked for 'country' and parliament as against 'court' and king, that they were, in Dr Wedgwood's words, 'nurseries of the legalist opposition' to the early Stuarts.[1] This assumption may well be correct but it is very difficult to test.

However strong our faith in education as an agent of personal and social change, the overall political effects of inns of court attendance

[1] C. V. Wedgwood, *The Great Rebellion The King's War 1641–1647* (1958), 615. Cf. Dodd, *Life in Elizabethan England*, 38–9; Wallace Notestein, *The English People on the Eve of Colonisation 1603–1630* (New York, 1954), 91–2.

must remain conjectural unless and until they can be demonstrated by mass-biographical research. But to discover the political alignments of even a sample of members before or during the Civil War and to distinguish the effects of their inns of court attendance from those of age, wealth, regional origins and other relevant variables would be a massive task, especially in the absence of comparative figures for other social groups. The problem might be reduced if all potential political influences seemed to point in the same direction; yet the range of religious belief represented at the houses hardly suggests that they were sufficiently monolithic or close-knit institutions to endow their members with a uniform political outlook. Nor do contemporaries seem to have been particularly impressed by their political influence one way or the other. Thomas Hobbes saw the universities, not the inns of court, as Charles I's ideological trojan horse.

Some modern commentators have emphasised the role of the inns as purveyors of legal education and values, particularly Sir Edward Coke's brand of constitutionalism, to the sons of the landed gentry.[2] We have already questioned their success in teaching law to laymen, and in any case the instruction which was provided concentrated on the *minutiae* of real property law rather than broad issues of constitutional jurisprudence. Possibly even a superficial acquaintance with some elementary texts and a casual attendance at learning exercises might have sufficed to impart something of what Professor Pocock terms 'the common-law mind' – that is to say, a deep respect for the common law as guardian of the ancient constitution and arbiter of relations between king, parliament and subject. But the common-law mind did not have an exclusively parliamentarian orientation. To cite Professor Pocock again, 'there was a common-law case for the crown as well as against it, and the former case was expressed in the same language and based on the same assumptions as the latter'.[3] The political role of the common law and lawyer in the seventeenth century still awaits proper investigation, but it certainly was not confined to an alliance with parliament in defence of the subject's rights against the arbitrary exactions of a would-be absolute monarchy. The common law remained a trusty servant of the crown, as it had been since the middle ages, and the early Stuarts never lacked expert professional advice to further what Professor Judson called their 'striving for legal absolutism'.[4]

A stay at the inns might have influenced a student's later political attitudes for reasons largely unrelated to the content and quality of

---

[2] Cf. Stone, 'Educational revolution', 78; Hill, *Intellectual Origins*, 256; D. L. Farmer, *Britain and the Stuarts* (1965), 19.

[3] Pocock, *Ancient Constitution and the Feudal Law*, 31, 55.

[4] Cf. G. E. Aylmer, *The Struggle for the Constitution 1603–1689* (1963), 36, 51; E. W. Ives, 'Social change and the law', in *The English Revolution 1603–1660*, ed. *idem*, (1968), 121–6; M. A. Judson, *The Crisis of the Constitution* (New Brunswick, 1949), 118 and ch. 4, *passim*.

the legal education to which he was exposed. It seems reasonable to assume that most young men who went up to an inn during our period returned home with more political awareness than when they left. The high level of political consciousness among members is amply demonstrated by surviving correspondence and diaries, by the circulation of 'libels' and manuscripts on politico-historical subjects and by incidents like the public toast drunk to the protestant heroine Elizabeth of Bohemia by 'thirty of the civillest and best fashioned gentlemen' at the Middle Temple Christmas of 1621. In 1623 James I specifically warned members (although without noticeable effect) to 'be wary of their discourse, not to speak of state matters and things beyond their reach; but to apply themselves to such discourses as befit their profession, as putting of cases'.[5] Attendance at any place of higher education probably tended to increase the student's assertiveness and self-confidence, perhaps also (as Professor Curtis suggests) his sensitivity to the shortcomings of the monarchy. Opponents of the early Stuarts had no monopoly of political consciousness, but the spread of an intelligent interest in public affairs undoubtedly aggravated the political difficulties of James and Charles I; so the royalist duke of Newcastle may not have been entirely off the mark when he lumped the inns with the grammar schools and universities as purveyors of education and hence of discontent with the *status quo*.[6]

Beside this general role of 'consciousness-raising', the inns maintained specific institutional and personal ties with parliament. Unlike the universities they enjoyed neither the honour nor expense of direct parliamentary representation. But the Commons always contained a substantial contingent of former and current residents, rising from just over a quarter of all M.P.s in 1563 to more than a third in 1584 and 1614 and to over half the entire House in 1640.[7] While most of these men were country squires who had long since discontinued and had never been called to the bar, there were also the practising lawyers, who formed the largest group in Elizabethan and early Stuart parliaments next to the gentry. Many lawyer M.P.s were still active residents of their inns, and thus provided the societies with a kind of informal parliamentary representation, although apparently without acting as a coherent bloc or pressure group.[8]

[5] See above, p. 159 and cf. Nichols, *Progresses of James I*, iv. 751; *Diary of John Rous*, ed. Green, 46; *CSPD, 1629–31*, 98; *CSPD, 1634–35*, 304, 342; SP 16/54/82 (I); SP 16/101/42; HMC, *Salisbury*, xvii. 162; IT MS, Miscellanea 31, pp. 25–6; D'Ewes, 'Secret Diary', 173–4.

[6] Cf. M. H. Curtis, 'The alienated intellectuals of early Stuart England', *P & P*, 23 (1962), 39–40; Peter Laslett, foreword to J. H. Hexter, *Reappraisals in History* (1961), xvii–xviii; S. A. Strong, *Catalogue of Documents . . . at Welbeck* (1903), 188, 192–3; Lawrence Stone, 'Communication', *P. & P*, 24 (1963), 101–2.

[7] Stone, 'Educational revolution', Table VIII; T. L. Moir, *The Addled Parliament of 1614* (Oxford, 1958), 57.

[8] For the proportions of barristers, see Neale, *Elizabethan House of Commons*, 301–2; Brunton and Pennington, *Members of the Long Parliament*, 5.

Since the benchers of each inn always included a number of past and present M.P.s, it is hardly surprising that no difficulty was placed in the way of Commons' committees meeting in the halls of the societies and in the Temple Church. Individual M.P.s frequently attended sermons and readers' dinners at the inns; both Houses came to the Temple Church for communion and a sermon at the opening of the 1621 session, having been refused by the dean and chapter of Westminster Abbey, and the Long Parliament assembled on several occasions to hear sermons in Lincoln's Inn chapel.[9] But it would be rash to assume that whatever opportunities for contact with 'opposition' attitudes and people these occasions afforded were generally of decisive importance, or that they signified any kind of overriding institutional commitment.

Court connections

Although historians have been impressed by links between the inns and parliament, contemporaries were probably more aware of their connections with the royal court. Parliament was at best an intermittent event, but the court exercised its attractions as arbiter of taste and fountain of preferment all the year round, not just for the gentlemen students who followed its lead in dress and deportment, but for any member who sought advancement and patronage. Courtiers no doubt disdained the mere lawyer, while the assertion of the Gray's Inn students who dedicated the published version of *The Masque of Flowers* to Sir Francis Bacon, that the inns were 'third persons with the court and the nobility in doing the king honour' seems a trifle strained.[10] Yet it was not merely their location which justified Clarendon's boastful characterisation of the societies as 'suburbs of the court itself'.[11]

The most striking affinity of the inns and the court was their mutual taste for the masque. Indeed the inns made a major contribution to the evolution of this sophisticated dramatic form through their traditional Christmas festivities, centring around a mock prince and his court; the prototype of the fully developed Stuart masque was the *Masque of Proteus and the Adamantine Rock*, presented by the Prince of Purpoole and his followers from Gray's Inn before the queen at Greenwich in 1594.[12] This was one of three masques known to have been staged by the inns during the 1590s; during James's reign two

[9] Cf. Neale, *op. cit.*, 366; *GIPB*, i. 99 and above, p. 159; *CSPD, 1619–23*, 221. The proposed House of Commons fast in 1576 was to be held at the Temple Church: Heylyn, *Aerius Redivivus*, 287. Trevor-Roper, 'The fast sermons of the Long Parliament', 320.

[10] Nichols, *Progresses of James I*, ii. 735; cf. Carey, 'The Ovidian love elegy', 345 ff.

[11] Clarendon, *Tracts*, 331.

[21] Enid Welsford, *The Court Masque* (New York, 1962), 163.

joint masques were given at Whitehall to celebrate the marriage of Princess Elizabeth in 1613, and a separate masque by Gray's Inn shortly after honoured the marriage of Somerset and Lady Frances Howard. The Inner Temple staged masques in 1614 and 1619, the Middle Temple in 1617 and 1621, and Gray's Inn again in 1618, while each inn sent ten members to perform a mock tournament or barriers at Whitehall when Charles was created Princes of Wales in 1616. After the Middle Temple masque of 1621, no more productions were attempted until Shirley's ambitious *Triumph of Peace* in 1634, which was followed a year later by the Middle Temple's *Masque of the Prince d'Amour.*

Although some props and costumes were usually borrowed from the Revels Office and any nobles in town who were willing to assist, masqueing was an expensive pastime in which only a select group of 'galant young gentlemen' [13] could afford to take part, even when the costs were subsidised by a levy on all members of the societies, as in 1613 and 1634. But the benefits were considerable, both for the masquers themselves and any senior members associated with the entertainment; when Buckingham went to the Middle Temple for supper and a masque in January 1617, John Chamberlain speculated that the occasion was intended to 'preoccupate' his favour. We do not know who invited Buckingham on this occasion, but a year later he was admitted honorifically to the Middle Temple with his brother Sir John Villiers at Walter Pye's Lent reading; Pye was by this time firmly attached to the Buckingham bandwaggon, having obtained a Welsh judgeship through his patron's influence in February 1617.[14]

Whether masques were staged at court, or like William Browne's *Masque of the Inner Temple* in 1614, 'done to please ourselves in private',[15] courtiers were sure to be among the audience, which meant the chance of advancing suits and seeking preferment. A masque presented at court was a 'service', which by convention required a reward in turn, even if only a banquet for the masquers. Bacon's contribution to the Gray's Inn masques of 1613 and 1614 represented a return of thanks for his promotion to attorney-general in October 1613.[16]

Many courtiers had paused briefly at one of the inns before their translation to higher realms, like Charles Blount, the eighth Lord Mountjoy, who 'as he came from Oxford . . . took the Inner Temple in his way to court'.[17] The houses were always eager to enroll courtiers

[13] Lansdowne 107, f. 13, and see above, pp. 154–5.
[14] McLure, *Chamberlain's Letters*, ii. 142; *MTR*, ii. 626; Aylmer, *King's Servants*, 308–10; see below, p. 225.
[15] Welsford, *op. cit.*, 261; *CSPD, 1603–10*, 187.
[16] See E. A. Honigman's introduction to the *Masque of Flowers*, in *A Book of Masques*, ed. G. E. Bentley (Cambridge, 1967), 151–4 and Nichols, *op. cit.*, ii. 591–2.
[17] Robert Naunton, *Fragmenta Regalia* (1641), quoted Alexander Croke, *The Genealogical History of the Croke Family* (Oxford, 1823), ii. 228.

and peers as honorary members, setting up their arms in chapel or hall as visible evidence of the society's honourable connections. The motive was probably less to secure additional friends than to maintain an aristocratic image; as a member put it, the 'greatest number of our nobilitie have pleased to become members . . . by which acquisition the whole body is much beautified'.[18] A particularly influential person might be made a member of more than one inn; Buckingham, for example, having been admitted to the Middle Temple in 1618, was enrolled at the Inner Temple in 1622. He had close personal connections with both societies; besides Sir Walter Pye, his clients at the Middle included Sir Anthony Benn, Sir John Hoskyns and Sir Nicholas Hyde, and at the Inner Lord Thomas Coventry, Sir Robert Heath, Sir Richard Shilton and even Sir Edward Coke.[19]

There is nothing to suggest that courtly patrons usually restricted their favours to the members of any one society at the expense of the rest; another of Buckingham's protégés was Robert Shute of Gray's Inn, who became recorder of London in 1621. However it is not clear that each house received an equal share of the available patronage throughout our period. Ten former members of Lincoln's Inn sat as judges and barons of the Exchequer between 1603 and 1625, but only two, Sir Thomas Richardson and Sir William Jones, from 1625 to 1640. (Jones is counted twice as he was appointed a puisne justice of the Common Pleas in 1621; Richardson was the only Lincoln's Inn lawyer raised to the bench during the period 1625–40, being made chief-justice of Common Pleas in 1626, then transferred to the King's Bench in 1631, where he died in disgrace after his clash with Laud over the Somerset church ales).[20] The disparity seems particularly striking if it is recalled that Lincoln's Inn consistently produced more barristers than any other house, except in the decade 1610–19, when it took second place to the Middle Temple. Perhaps Ellesmere's influence as Lord Chancellor from 1603 until his death in 1617 had something to do with the relative success of Lincoln's Inn members in the competition for promotion to the bench under James, while the house's puritan reputation may have adversely affected the career prospects of its members after Charles came to the throne. A comprehensive survey of legal promotion would need to include a much wider range of offices than the judgeships of the Westminster courts, but this is a task which awaits the historian of the early seventeenth-century legal profession.[21]

---

[18] IT MS, Miscellanea 32, 'Antiquities of the Inner and Middle Temple', f. 24.
[19] *IT Adm. Reg.*, 404; Cooper, 'Promotion and politics among the common law judges', 24, 78, 127; Menna Prestwich, *Cranfield* (Oxford, 1967), 143–4.
[20] T. G. Barnes, 'County politics and a puritan cause célèbre: Somerset church ales, 1633', *TRHS*, 5th ser., 9 (1959), 103–22.
[21] Source: Foss, *Judges*, vi, *passim*. Calls of serjeants follow a similar pattern, with Lincoln's Inn members taking a close second place to Inner Templars between 1603 and 1625, then dropping to last place between 1625 and 1640.

The most frequent occasions which brought the inns and the court together were such gargantuan gastronomic events as the banquet customarily given for newly-called serjeants in the Middle Temple hall ('counted the third feast in England after the coronation and St George's feasts', although Simonds D'Ewes found to his disappointment that 'the cheare was nothing soe great as the rumor is'),[22] the Grand Day feasts held on All Saints and Candlemas day, and the twice-yearly readers' dinners. Unfortunately, few guest lists survive from these lavish functions. It is no great surprise to find Buckingham at John Hoskyns' reading in Lent 1620, since it was through his means that Hoskyns became a Welsh judge the following year, but it would be interesting to have the names of the 'reasonable portion of lords' who also sat at Hoskyn's table.[23] Only by a casual mention in a letter to Sir John Coke do we learn that Sir Francis Windebank and the Venetian ambassador were among the guests at Robert Hatton's Middle Temple reading in August 1635. Secretary Windebank had been admitted to the Middle Temple as a young man in 1602, four years before Hatton entered, and was probably invited merely as a distinguished member of the society; Hatton himself sided with parliament in the Civil War and was rewarded with a serjeantcy in 1648.[24]

In sharp contrast to these establishment figures, the principal guest at John Barkesdale's Lincoln's Inn reading in 1628 was that 'oracle of those who were called puritans in the worst sense', William Fiennes, Lord Saye and Sele. Apart from being contemporaries at Oxford, the nature of the relationship between the reader and his guest is unknown. Barkesdale himself is a shadowy figure; a Berkshire man, he entered Lincoln's Inn in 1600 after taking his B.A. from Corpus Christi. There he had met Daniel Fairclough or Featley, Archbishop Abbot's chaplain and later a member of the Westminster Assembly, who preached at Lincoln's Inn chapel on the first Sunday of Barkesdale's reading and was admitted an honorary member of the house the same day.[25]

Sir James Whitelocke's account of his own reading at the Middle Temple in August 1619 provides the most complete surviving guest list for any reader's feast before the Civil War. Besides the Netherlands ambassador and the renegade Italian archbishop of Spalatro, Whitelocke entertained Archbishop Abbot, Bishops Buckeridge, Carleton and King, the earl of Worcester (who was both lord privy seal and a confessed papist), Sir John Davies, the king's attorney in Ireland, Sir Lionel Cranfield and 'divers knights and gentlemen'. The inclusion of Cranfield and Davies, both Buckingham followers, is indicative of the strenuous efforts Whitelocke was making to ingratiate himself

22 D'Ewes, 'Secret Diary', 223–6.
23 Osborn, *Hoskyns*, 50.
24 HMC, *12 Rep.*, App. 2, 88; *MT Bench Book*, 111.
25 LI MS, Maynard 57, f. 1; Clarendon, *History*, i. 241.

with the court and efface the unfortunate reputation which had clung
to him since the parliaments of 1610 and 1614. He had already succeeded in obtaining Buckingham's nomination to the special commissions of the peace for the liberties of Westminster and St Martin's,
but his big reward came the following year, when he was made a serjeant and then chief justice on the Chester circuit.[26]

The relationship between the inns and the court did not depend
solely upon the mutually beneficial self-interest of client and patron,
plus a certain congruity of tastes and cultural values. These ties were
supplemented and strengthened by quasi-institutional connections
between the government of the realm and the governors of the four
societies. Although the inns rarely came into contact with the state
before Elizabeth's accession, government supervision and surveillance
was extended over almost every aspect of their activities during her
reign. But there is no reason to think that the common lawyers of the
early seventeenth century 'opposed James and Charles for tampering
with the inns of court'.[27] James showed little desire to meddle; the
favours he lavished on the universities were not extended to the inns of
court, but by the same token their daily affairs were virtually immune
from the interference of the Scholar King. It is true that in 1608 the
Inner and Middle Temples received letters-patent confirming possession of the site and buildings they had occupied without formal title
since the expropriation of the Order of St John in 1540. However this
was a straightforward commercial transaction, initiated by the inns'
fears that the validity of their occupancy was about to be questioned
and concluded with the presentation to James of a gold cup worth
£666.[28]

Only one official judges' order was issued during James's reign, and
the king's few personal interventions were either disregarded or successfully resisted by the societies. The 1603 edict forbidding the admission of plebeians was never enforced and an attempt to place a royal
nominee in the Temple Church lectureship after Crashawe's resignation was quickly abandoned. Even Bacon's scheme for drafting six
hundred members into an inns of court militia (perhaps to counterbalance the puritan-dominated Honourable Artillery Company) met
with a negative response, despite James's request for the benchers'
cooperation; consultation between the four houses endorsed the Middle
Temple view 'that there is noe willingness nor ability to perform the
contents of these letters'.[29]

---

[26] Whitelocke, *Lib. Fam.*, 75–6; Prestwich, *Cranfield*, 142. Lists of presents received by readers also provide useful information about their connections and
contacts: see for example *Lib. Fam.*, 70–3, and Jones, *Charity*, 242–3.
[27] Cf. J. D. Eusden, *Puritans, Lawyers and Politics in Early Seventeenth-Century England* (New Haven, 1958), 2.
[28] Williamson, *Temple*, 260–70.
[29] *BB*, ii. 193–4; MT MS, Minutes C, f. 120.

Charles I inherited his father's notorious dislike of lawyers,[30] but not his attitude of indifference to the inns of court. Throughout the first fifteen years of Charles's reign the societies were deluged with admonitions and instructions from Whitehall on a vast range of subjects, including the Micklethwaite affair, Christmas commons at the Temples, Richard Minshall's expulsion, the St Paul's rebuilding, the conformity of chaplains and preachers, the observation of Lent, martial exercises, student riots, the sheltering of bankrupts, contributions to loans and benevolences, and a boundary dispute between the Inner and Middle Temples.[31] Yet the benchers gave no hint that they resented this massive interference; on the contrary, the government's commands were received with an unusual show of respect. When the king wrote in 1632 asking the societies to ensure that no flesh was served at readers' dinners during Lent, his letter was ordered to be transcribed into the Black Book of Lincoln's Inn, as 'testimony of their earnest desire that the gracious contentes of the said letter should in all suceeding tymes with like willingness be hereafter embraced and obeyed'.[32] Laud's letter of 1633 was also copied into the Black Book, so that all future chaplains and preachers could be informed of its contents, 'to the intent that they should in like manner conforme themselves to the same orders of the church'.[33] An equally satisfactory response greeted requests in 1638 for contributions towards Laud's projected rebuilding of St Paul's Cathedral. The official begging letter was read out in hall before the assembled society (as it was at Gray's Inn) and three benchers appointed to 'promote' donations. One was William Hakewill, Prynne's 'very good friend and acquaintance' but now a commissioner for the rebuilding (which did not deter him from taking the Covenant in 1643 or accepting a mastership in Chancery in 1647).[34] Finally, it may be noted that Prynne's expulsion from Lincoln's Inn, following his conviction for the publication of *Histrio-Mastix*, was made by unanimous vote of the bench, who took the opportunity to record their detestation of his book as

> no other than a rayling invective against his Majestie, his dearest consort . . . the magistrates and the whole present state and government of the kingdome; conteining . . . open incitements of his people to sedition . . . uncharitable and unchristian censures of all sorts of

30 William Lilly, *Several Observations on the Life and Death of King Charles I* (1656), in *Select Tracts Relating to the Civil Wars in England* (1815), i. 140; see also 'Debates in the House of Commons in 1625', ed. S. R. Gardiner (*CS*, n.s., 6, 1873), 4–5.

31 Cf. above, pp. 99–100, 109, 183, 199–201, 203, and below, p. 232; *CSPD, 1628–29*, 74, 181; *OJ*, 318–21; Williamson, *Temple*, 374–5; *ITR*, ii. lxxv.

32 *BB*, ii. 308 and cf. *GIPB*, i. 313; *ITR*, ii. 205. Edward Bysh was fined for serving flesh in Lent nearly a year *before* Charles's letter was received: *BB*, ii. 303. In 1630 the privy council singled out the inns for their exemplary observation of Lent and fish days: *APC, 1630–31*, 71–2; cf. above, pp. 215–16.

33 *BB*, ii. 313, see above, p. 203.

34 *BB*, ii. 347–8; *GIPB*, i. 331; Additional 21505, f. 20.

people except the factious and disobedient contemners of the present government.[35]

While the benchers probably had little choice but to comply with the government's dictates, their manner of compliance was not mere grudging acquiescence. Nor is this puzzling, for the legal profession was by no means united in opposition to the early Stuarts. Common lawyers were rather caught between two conflicting pulls: hostility towards the conciliar and prerogative courts may have tended to draw them into alliance with the parliamentary 'opposition' (although the extent and strength of this ill-feeling is often exaggerated), but at the same time they were led by personal ambition into the arms of the court, simply because most major law offices were in the crown's gift.[36] Indeed the conflict was frequently more apparent than real, for a prominent role in opposition was a proven route to preferment. Among the many lawyers who entered the service of James and Charles after a period of spirited opposition in the House of Commons were Lord Coventry, Sir Thomas Crew, William Hakewill, Sir Edward Herbert, John Hoskyns, Sir Edward Littleton, William Noy, Sir George Radcliffe, Sir James Whitelocke and Sir Henry Yelverton. In 1629 Charles I denounced the young lawyer M.P.s who 'take upon them to decry the opinions of the judges'; but during the following decade his government relied heavily upon the services of many men who had first come to notice for their vigorous attacks on Buckingham and the court.[37]

Nor was it entirely a matter of self-interest. Charles's dissolution of parliament in 1629 and his measures for raising extra-parliamentary revenue were soundly based on the letter if not the spirit of the law; after all, the king had no shortage of legal advice. Coke's idiosyncratic but profoundly conservative view of the common law as arbiter between king and parliament was neither binding on his colleagues nor particularly relevant to the situation of the 1630s. In the 1620s D'Ewes, Prynne and Selden had searched out precedents from the Tower to sustain parliamentary attacks on the crown's fiscal, foreign and religious policies; in the following decade Noy found his justification for non-parliamentary taxes in the same place.[38] The common law could

---

[35] *BB*, ii. 317–18; Prynne was prosecuted in the Star Chamber by William Noy, with the assistance of Robert Mason, another bencher of the house: *State Trials*, iii. 562–9. See above, p. 214.

[36] See Aylmer, *King's Servants*, 56–7; *idem*, *The Struggle for the Constitution*, 36, 51; E. W. Ives, 'Social change and the law' in *The English Revolution 1625–1660*, 120–30.

[37] S. R. Gardiner, *The Constitutional Documents of the Puritan Revolution 1625–1660* (Oxford, 1906), 93; Prestwich, *op. cit.*, 138–44; J. P. Kenyon, *The Stuart Constitution 1603–1688* (1966), 102–7.

[38] Hill, *Intellectual Origins*, 263; B. S. Manning, 'The nobles, the people and the constitutions', *P & P*, 9 (1956), 54. In 1637 Laud took delivery of a 'book of the records in the Tower, which concerned the clergy, and which I caused to be collected . . .': *Works*, iii. 228.

not provide a sure protection against the crown's encroachments on the subject's property rights, much less offer a workable compromise when king and parliament disagreed. In short it was a political tool, used for whatever advantage it might give by whoever could exploit it. However cynically we may regard the motives of those lawyers who accepted office during the 1630s, it is hardly fair or relevant to accuse them of betraying the judicial code they professed.

So there is nothing inherently improbable or mysterious about the *rapprochement* between the court and the inns during the late 1620s and 1630s, especially since the benchers of each house at this time as at any other included a number of senior lawyers who held high office under the crown: Sir John Bankes, Sir William Denney, Sampson Eure, Sir John Finch and Sir Edward Mosely at Gray's Inn; Sir Charles Caesar, Sir Thomas Gardiner, Sir Robert Heath, Edward Herbert, Sir Edward Littleton, Sir Richard Shilton, Sir Richard Weston at the Inner Temple; Sir Edward Clerke, William Hakewill Robert Mason, William Noy, Peter Mutton at Lincoln's Inn; Peter Ball, Sir Henry Calthorpe, Richard Hadsor, Sir Richard Lane, Sir Thomas Malet and Sir Walter Pye at the Middle Temple.[39]

Most of these men had been appointed specifically to advise and represent the crown; their position was closer to that of servants in the royal household, bound to their master by personal loyalty, than to the bureaucrats and sinecurists who administered the machinery of the law courts. Their offices carried authority, prestige, and often precedence over their fellow benchers; it was natural that they should have taken a leading part in promoting the event which best symbolises the close and harmonious relationship between the inns of court and the court of Charles I. This was the combined presentation by the four houses of James Shirley's masque *The Triumph of Peace*, staged before Charles and Henrietta in the Banqueting House on 3 February 1634. Bulstrode Whitelocke, who served on the organising committee, states that the production was intended as a visible repudiation of Prynne and his *Histrio-Mastix*, although the original pretext appears to have been the birth of the duke of York, later James II, in October 1633. However the project originated, it received the enthusiastic support of both 'the younger sort' and the 'grandees ... master Attorney-General Noy, Sir John Finch, Sir Edward Herbert, Mr Selden', who 'knew it would be acceptable to their master and mistress, and to all the court'.[40] The production was highly professionalized, with costumes and sets by the court architect Inigo Jones and songs by the court musician William Lawes. It was also very expensive; the costumes of the hundred main masquers, provided by themselves, were

[39] Sources: *DNB*; *Al. Ox.*; *Al. Cant.*; Foss, *Judges*; Jones, *Sessions in Wales*.
[40] Bulstrode Whitelocke, *Memorials of the English Affairs* (1853), i. 53–5; see also C. V. Wedgwood, *Poetry and Politics Under the Stuarts* (1958), 36; Williamson, *Temple*, 396–7; HMC, *12 Rep.*, App. 2, 34.

reckoned to be worth at least £100 apiece, the inns levied a total of over £6,000 from their members, and Whitelocke estimates the final cost at the huge sum of £21,000.

Shirley took as his theme 'the happiness of our kingdom, so blest in the present government', which was exemplified by the three allegorical figures of Peace, Law and Justice, united in praise of their parents, 'Jove and Themis':

> To you, great king and queen, whose smile,
> Doth scatter blessings through this isle,
>   To make it best,
>   And wonder of the rest,
> We pay the duty of our birth;
> Proud to wait upon that earth
>   Whereon you move,
>   Which shall be nam'd,
> And by your chaste embraces fam'd,
> The paradise of love.

This paean was followed by the appearance of the sixteen grand-masquers, four from each inn, 'the sons of Peace, Law and Justice':

> No foreign persons I make known,
> But here present you with your own,
> The children of your reign . . .
> These have no form, no sun, no shade,
> But what your virtue doth create,
> Exalted by your glorious fate,
> They'll tower to heaven, next which they know,
> And wish no blessedness but you.[41]

Despite a courtier's prophecy that the masquers' horses would prove better dancers than their riders, the production was a resounding success, so much so that it was repeated a few days later at the queen's request in Merchant Taylors' hall, under the lord mayor's auspices. This second performance, according to Whitelocke, 'also gave great contentment to their majesties, and no less to the citizens, especially those of the younger sort and of the female sex'. Queen Henrietta informed a delegation from the inns 'that she never saw any mask more noble . . . and desired that her thanks might be returned to the gentlemen for it', while Charles, 'with great affability and pleasingness', assured them that 'we are exceedingly pleased with the testimony they lately gave us of their great respect and affection to us'.[42] But, Whitelocke adds, 'these dreams passed and these pomps vanished'.

---

[41] *The Dramatic Works and Poems of J. Shirley*, ed. Alexander Dyce (1833), vi. 255, 277, 278–9.
[42] HMC, *13 Rep.*, App. 2, 125; Whitelocke, *Memorials*, i. 61–2.

Towards civil war

The *rapprochement* between the inns of court and the court of Charles I was never complete. Even *The Triumph of Peace* could not evade reality altogether, for it included an antimasque satirizing projectors and monopolists, 'an information covertly given to the king', (so Whitelocke claimed) 'of the unfitness and ridiculousness of these projects against the law'.[43] While his interference with the affairs of the societies may have aroused little active resentment, the benchers of the Temple had good reason to feel aggrieved by Charles's reluctance to help them suppress Christmas disorders, and their colleagues at Lincoln's Inn must have resented the privy council's lack of action against the spread of speculative building in the fields to the west of their house.[44] Despite their considerable influence and prestige, the crown law officers were a small minority among the benchers, let alone the common lawyers as a whole. Nor did the inns' rulers have the broad powers to control the thought and utterance of their subordinates which the university authorities wielded.

Little evidence of the political climate among the inns' rank and file membership during the 1630s or any other decade has survived, but reports from government spies and informers suggest a marked rise in seditious talk at the societies from about 1637 onwards.[45] The most concrete sign of dissatisfaction with the aims and methods of Charles I's government was the failure of royal appeals, in February 1639, for funds to fight the first Bishops' War. The king asked the four inns for a voluntary gift of £5,000 but only 'the four king's counsel . . . and some great practisers' contributed, together with twenty-one barristers and benchers from the Inner Temple. Considerable resistance had been encountered, especially at Lincoln's Inn, when the houses were assessed for the forced loan in 1626; in 1639 money was tight, the societies had been in financial difficulties for the last few years and the king's credit stood very low. But political hostility must also have played a part.[46]

Many common lawyers doubtless felt that the policies of Laud and Wentworth posed a serious threat to the independence and privileges of their order. The harrying and disgrace of Chief Justice Richardson and the silencing of Edward Bagshaw were only the most notorious instances of churchmen calling lawyers to account; no less ominous were Wentworth's brusque endeavours in Ireland and the North 'to buckle up these fathers of the law that use to deal with us *puros laicos*

---

43 *Ibid.*, 58, 62.
44 Brett James, *Growth of Stuart London*, 152–6.
45 Cf. *CSPD, 1637–38*, 21; *CSPD, 1638–39*, 89; *CSPD, 1639*, 152; *CSPD, 1640–41*, 40.
46 HMC, *Buccleugh and Queensberry*, i. 276–7, iii. 307–8; *CSPD, Addenda, 1625–49*, 604–5; *APC, 1625–26*, 380–1.

(as they term us) according to their own good pleasure, so great is the advantage of their profession'.[47] Intimidation of barristers in politically sensitive cases was perhaps increasing during the 1630s; an article of the Grand Remonstrance complained that 'lawyers have been checked for being faithful to their clients; attorneys and solicitors have been threatened and some punished, for following lawful suits'.[48] But it is still doubtful whether the corporate interests of the common lawyers had more than marginal significance in determining their political outlook during the eleven years non-parliamentary government.

The lawyers 'interlocked with the gentry, or were its retainers'; many lawyers were also landholders and devoted no less attention to their estates than their practices.[49] It is unnecessary to suppose that their attitude towards Ship Money and the other fiscal devices introduced during the 1630s was any different in substance or motivation from that of the political nation as a whole. There is little evidence that Coke's occasional hostility to conciliar and prerogative courts was widely shared by common lawyers, who pleaded in these courts on exactly the same basis as in the King's Bench or Exchequer. The abolition of the Star Chamber by the Long Parliament 'may be considered a phase of the general reaction against the episcopacy', although it is possible that the lawyers appointed to the committee to view the precedents of the court in May 1641 convinced the larger committees, which had previously been considering only the regulation of the Star Chamber, that total abolition was necessary. Professional hostility was more directly focused on the church courts, but it was by no means impossible for common lawyers to cooperate with the ecclesiastical jurisdiction, and the attack on these courts in the Long Parliament would seem to be fully explained by their general political role in the previous decade.[50]

The inns played little active part in the political struggles which preceded the Civil War. They were not as closely identified with the court as the Arminian-dominated universities, which came under fierce criticism almost as soon as the Long Parliament met, and entirely escaped the attentions of the Grand Committee on Religion,

[47] See Laud, *Works*, v. 335–7, vi (II), 386; *CSPD, 1629–31*, 15, 19–20, and see above pp. 209–10; C. V. Wedgwood, *Thomas Wentworth* (1961), 40–2.

[48] See R. G. Usher, *The Rise and Fall of the High Commission* (Oxford, 1913), 319; *State Trials*, iii. 715–16, 719–20; Gardiner, *Constitutional Documents*, 213.

[49] Cf. Wallace Notestein, 'The winning of the initiative by the House of Commons', *Proc. British Academy*, 11 (1924), 171–2; Osborn, *Hoskyns*, 75–7, 79; Additional 53726, ff. 81v–82.

[50] Cf. Usher, *op. cit.*, 317–21; W. J. Jones, *The Elizabethan Court of Chancery* (Oxford, 1967), 17–24 and Pt. III, *passim*; H. E. Phillips, 'The last years of the court of Star Chamber, 1630–41', *TRHS*, 4th ser., 21 (1939), 103–6, 128–31; *Commons Journals*, ii. 134; R. A. Marchant, *The Church under the Law*, 109, 239–40; Philip Tyler, 'The Ecclesiastical Commission at York', *Northern History*, 2 (1967), 33–6.

being scarcely even mentioned in debate before the outbreak of war. They continued as before to accommodate Commons committees, and on at least one occasion the whole House attended a sermon in Lincoln's Inn chapel. Clarendon claimed that the 'spirit and over-activity' of the king's legal servants had made the entire profession 'obnoxious to reproach' by 1640. But while members of the Long Parliament had every reason to regard the common law as a god that had failed, their retribution was directed against individual royalist counsellors and judges, rather than the profession as a whole.[51]

Despite these continuing parliamentary associations, the inns were by no means totally committed to the parliamentarian cause, even though Charles removed some of his ablest supporters – Bankes, Brerewood, Robert Hyde, Edward and Timothy Littleton – by promoting them as serjeants or judges in 1640 and 1641. Whatever the dictates of politics and prudence, the benchers could not control the company kept by junior members, nor their cultural and social affinities with the court, and it was inevitable that at some point efforts would be made to exploit this substantial reservoir of potential royalism.

Late in November 1641 the king returned to London from his seemingly successful expedition to buy off the Scots, confident that the time was right for a counterattack on his enemies in the English parliament. The narrow margin by which the Grand Remonstrance had just passed the Commons confirmed that the political tide was now running in his favour, as moderate men grew fearful of the constitutional and social implications of further encroachments on the royal prerogative. Throughout December London was tense with rumours of impending coup and countercoup; but while Pym and his followers feared violence from the king, Charles's greatest weakness was his lack of sufficient troops to overawe parliament and the mobs which surged around Westminster Palace. The young gentlemen of the inns were not equipped or organised as a military force, but most probably had some familiarity with weapons. While hardly a substitute for disciplined veterans, the king's military resources were so slight that their numbers and swords could not be lightly disregarded.[52]

The success of attempts to secure their allegiance, including a 'constant table' at court dispensing free food and wine,[53] was strikingly

---

[51] Coates, *Journal*, 81; Clarendon, *History*, i. 91; cf. Kenyon, *Stuart Constitution*, 105.

[52] This was not the first time that the inns had been looked to as useful allies in times of civil disturbance; see Bertie Wilkinson, *Constitutional History of England in the Fifteen Century* (1964), 12; A. R. Myers, *England in the Late Middle Ages* (1963), 204; *CPSD, 1595–97*, 129; *APC, 1600–01*, 147; above, p. 227; SP 16/101/42. For evidence of members engaging in military training see William Bariffe, *Military Discipline; or, the Young Artillery Man* (1639), commendatory verses by Andrew Wheatley and John Hayward.

[53] *The Memoirs of Edmund Ludlow*, ed. C. H. Firth (Oxford, 1894), i. 23–4.

demonstrated on December 30, 1641. After a day of particularly heavy
rioting, a band of 500 armed men marched from the inns to Whitehall, 'upon the occasion of a report brought to them that the king's
person was in danger' or, as Thomas Coke wrote to his father, Sir
John, from Gray's Inn, 'in testimony of their affections to his majesty
and . . . their service for the suppression of these tumultuous
assemblies'.[54] This 'proffer of service to his majesty in a warlike manner' did nothing to quiet the fears of the Commons, especially when
the articles of impeachment against Lord Mandeville and the five
members were taken round to each inn on 3 January by the courtiers
Sir William Fleming and Sir William Killigrew, with a message 'de-
siring the gentlemen ther to be in readines' next day, 'to come down
to the Court if they should be required'. At the beginning of the
morning session on 4 January Alexander Rigby of Gray's Inn and
William Smith of the Middle Temple reported this action to the
House. After Pym had tabled the articles against himself and the
other members, four M.P.s were chosen, one from each inn, to 'goe
to the fowre inns of court and to acquaint them that wee understood
how they had been sollicited'. They were to be informed that Killigrew and his confederates had been summoned as delinquents, that
parliament was determined to protect the king, and 'that the cause
of sending unto them is not any diffidence they have in them,
but to advise them from any practices that they shall be moved
unto'.

The reports brought back by the messengers at the beginning of
the afternoon session were to the general effect that the societies
protested their loyalty both to king and parliament, the Middle Tem-
lars adding that 'their intention to defend the king's person was no
more than they were ther unto bound by the oathes of allegiance
and supremacie; with which severall answers . . . the howse rested
exceedingly well satisfied'. These verbal assurances of neutrality were
never tested, since the king did not in fact call upon the inns for
assistance, probably because he had been forestalled by the Commons' prompt action; had he done so, the outcome of this crisis might
have been very different.[55] In the summer of 1642 Edmund Ludlow
and a group of like-minded friends from the inns began to prepare
themselves for the coming conflict by training under the direction of
a drill master at the Artillery Gardens. Most were incorporated into
the earl of Essex's bodyguard, which consisted of 'a hundred gentlemen' under the command of Sir Phillip Stapleton, an Inner Templar;
but in 1644 a whole regiment of foot was commissioned by Sir Edward

---

[54] Coates, *Journal*, 368; HMC, *12 Rep.*, App. 2, 302; in a petition presented to
Charles II *c.* 1663 Sir William Mason, who had served as a royalist officer and
was called to the bench of Gray's Inn in 1660, claimed credit for organising this
force, which he put at 400 men: *CSPD, Addenda, 1660–1670*, 688.
[55] Coates, *op. cit.*, 368, 376, 378–80, 398; *Commons Journals*, ii. 367–8.

Littleton from inns of court members who had accompanied the king to Oxford.[56]

The incidents of late December–early January 1641–2 were at best an inconclusive demonstration of loyalty, but no time was lost in exploiting their propaganda value. On 7 January Dr John Hinton, the queen's physician, presented to the Commons a petition purporting to come from the inns, although apparently drafted and presented by himself alone. Three printed versions are known, with minor verbal differences but the common aim of rallying support for the king in his new-found public role as defender of church and society against the excesses of Laudians and radical puritans alike.[57] Thus the Commons are exhorted to 'spare the poore protestants . . . a distraction in religion', to 'qualify the exorbitances of the separatists and disorderly persons, that thereby the city of London and suburbs may be disburthened from their continuall cares and feares', and to 'serve God's true anointed, his immediate vicegerent, our true and lawfull sovraigne lord the king . . . without any impeachment of his regality'. On examination by an understandably hostile committee of the House, Hinton admitted that the piece was entirely his own work; there is no way to tell how many resident members might have endorsed its general sentiments.

When hostilities between king and parliament broke out some six months later the allegiance of the inns was dictated simply by their location. Control of the societies passed to those benchers who remained in London or could come up for infrequent bench meetings; not all these men were parliamentarians and substantial contingents of out-and-out royalists may be identified among the benchers of each house, except Lincoln's Inn. No doubt more would have swung to the crown if the inns and law courts had been located in a part of the country which was under royal control when the fighting began. But in any case the parliamentarian benchers were little more than caretakers, as admissions shrank to a handful, learning exercises ceased altogether and the houses were virtually deserted between the sum-

---

[56] Ludlow, *op. cit.*, i. 38–9; Robert Steele, *Tudor and Stuart Proclamations 1485–1714* (Oxford, 1910), ii. 2568.

[57] (i) *The Humble Petition Of The Peacefull Obedient and Honest Protestants of this kingdome, presented unto the Honourable House of Commons By the Gentlemen Of The Foure Innes of Court* (1642): Wing H3567; (ii) *The Humble Petition Of The peacefull, obedient, religious, and honest Protestants . . . presented unto the Honourable House of Commons, in their behalfe, by Doctor Hynton, 1642. With an Answer to the severall Objections proposed against him concerning the Protestants Petition, by a Committee . . . of Commons* (1642): Wing H3568, H3569; (iii) *The two petitions of the County of Buckingham . . . Together with the Petition of the Foure Innes of Court* (1641): Wing P1795. The wording is substantially the same in each, but (ii) includes a 4 page summary of Hinton's examination before the Commons' committee meeting at the Guildhall on 8 January 1642. For Hinton's later account of his part in preparing the petition, see Ellis, *Select Letters*, 3rd ser., iv. 297–8.

TABLE 18   *Political alignment of benchers in the first civil war*

	Parliament	Crown	Neutral/Unknown
Gray's Inn	14	10	8
Inner Temple	14	9	12
Lincoln's Inn	23	6	7
Middle Temple	10	9	6
Total	61	34	33

Note. This table includes all full benchers elected before August 1642 who are not known to have died before that date. Those who appear to have remained in residence for any substantial period after 1642 are counted as parliamentarians unless positive evidence to the contrary has been found.

mers of 1642 and 1646. As throughout the previous half-century, ambiguity and a lack of total commitment in any direction remained the dominant political characteristic of the inns during the Civil War.

The war itself helped end the education boom; henceforth, admissions to the inns dropped steadily towards their mid-Hanoverian low, while the importance and prestige attached to education by the national economic and political élites declined very rapidly. But since the bar was well on the way to achieving its uniquely aristocratic standing among the learned professions, the inns could afford to dispense with the reflected glory which the sons of the ruling class had brought them for most of the sixteenth and early seventeenth centuries. The disruptions of the 1640s gave the learning exercise system its quietus; any slim chance of reviving and remodelling it was effectively blocked by the conservative backlash against radical attacks on the legal structure during the Interregnum. Finally, the breakdown of gild and trading company monopolies foreshadowed under the Commonwealth and carried through in the later seventeenth century did not disturb the benchers' control over admission to the upper branch of the legal profession. By 1660 it was clear that the future development of the societies would be as professional associations, clubs, lodgings and offices. Only the collegiate rhetoric, architectural and literary, has survived to the present day.

Glossary

Ancient:	rank of membership between barrister and bencher (GI, MT).
Bench:	governing body of senior members (the masters of the bench or benchers).
Continuance:	length of membership, sometimes length of residence.
Council:	formal benchers' meeting (LI).
Inner-barrister:	most junior rank of membership, student.
Learning exercise:	aural disputation, as bolt, moot, imparlance, reading, etc.
Learning vacation:	two periods, between Hilary and Easter, and Trinity and Michaelmas terms, when learning exercises, especially readings, conducted.
Parliament:	formal benchers' meeting (IT, MT).
Pension:	formal benchers' meeting (GI).
Reading:	series of lectures presented during learning vacations at inns of court, or during term at inns of chancery.
Utter-barrister:	rank of membership above student, below bencher.

Note: D. S. Bland, *The Vocabulary of the Inns of Court* (Liverpool, duplicated monograph, 1964) discusses the etymology and usage of these and other terms peculiar to the inns.

Note on Archival Sources

The archives of the four inns are preserved in widely differing states of repair, completeness and accessibility. Each society has published calendars of its benchers' minutes for this period; these are of uneven quality and must be used with caution, but for the reader's convenience they have been cited in preference to the originals wherever possible.

The titles given below follow the usage of the respective libraries, where most of the documents are housed and all are to be read.

GRAY'S INN

There is no handlist of the MS records of Gray's Inn; A. J. Hopwood, *Catalogue of the Ancient Manuscripts Belonging to ... Gray's Inn* (1869) covers literary and legal MSS acquired by gift or purchase.

Library

Book of Orders Vol. i. 1569–1669 (Pension Order Book). Calendared (many mistakes and omissions) as *GIPB*, i.

Admittance Book I, 1581–1649. Calendared in *GI Adm. Reg.*, with pre-1581 admissions from Harleian 1912, ff. 4ᵛ–84.

Treasurer's Office

Ledger A. Mainly accounts, plus some pension lists and copies of official letters to the bench from the late sixteenth through the late seventeenth centuries; extracts in *GIPB*, i. 461–94.

INNER TEMPLE

There is a brief handlist of Inner Temple archives in *ITR*, i. vii–viii. W. D. Macray catalogued the Barrington and Petyt MSS in HMC, *11 Rep.*, App. vii, 227–308, and a complete catalogue of the society's MSS. by Dr J. Conway-Davies is in the press. (I am grateful to the Librarian, Mr W. W.

Breem, for permitting me to consult the typescript 'Summary of Lists of Inner Temple Manuscripts Collection', prepared by Dr Conway-Davies).

Library

Acts of Parliament, 1589–1638, 1638–1687, calendared *ITR*, i, ii.

Admittances, 1571–1640 (see below)

Accounts Book, 1606–1648 (Stewards' and treasurers' accounts)

Christmas Accounts, 1616–1682 (part-calendared in *ITR*, ii.)

Chamber Admissions, 1615–1667

Inner Temple, Miscellaneous MSS (cited above as IT MS, Miscellanea 22, etc.).

22. Clerk's Book (cf. *ITR*, ii. lxxxix)
29. Pamphlet on Rules, etc. . . . 1520–1670
31. A Treatise on the Duties of the Officers and Members (actually a chronicle of house affairs *c.* 1630–34 by the bencher John Wilde: cf. p. 11)
32. Antiquities of the Inner and Middle Temple. This volume was acquired in 1931 from Lord Mostyn's library: cf. HMC, *4 Rep.*, App. i. 353.

'A volume of 84 original letters etc. to the Treasurers and Benchers of the Inner Temple 1570–1679': this important collection, catalogued among the Petyt MSS by Macray and cited above as Petyt, Letters to treasurers and benchers, has been reclassified by Dr Davies as Inner Temple Miscellaneous MS 30.

A major deficiency in the published records of the Inner Temple is the lack of a reliable transcript of the original admissions registers. A three-volume copy and translation with index by L. Rees Lloyd was completed some years ago, but is at present available for consultation only in the Librarian's office. (Vol. i, 'Admissions to the Inner Temple to 1659' [1954] is cited above as *IT Adm. Reg.*). The publication of this work would be a great service to scholarship and one may hope it will not be long delayed.

LINCOLN'S INN

Joseph Hunter, *Lincoln's Inn Library: Catalogue of the Manuscripts* (1838) lists the society's legal and literary MSS; an annotated version with supplementary material covering later accessions is available in the Librarian's office.

Steward's Office

Black Books, vols. i–vii (1422–1660), calendared with some omissions in *BB*, i, ii.

Calendar of Admissions, i–vi (1573–1657), transcribed by Joseph Foster as

Library

LI *Adm. Reg.*, i.

Vacation Commons 1629–1635 (Stewards' accounts and lists of commoners).

Red Book, 1598–1691 (Chamber admissions and transactions).

MIDDLE TEMPLE

In addition to bench minutes, admissions records and fragmentary accounts, the Middle Temple possesses a large quantity of miscellaneous domestic records. Cataloguing commenced in 1964 and is still in progress. Meanwhile the only guides to the Middle Temple archives are the cursory list in *CMTR*, and a card-index which covers most of the material in the muniments and rare books rooms.

Library

Minutes of Parliament, D (1551–1610); C (1610–1626); B (1626–1658) (Translations and summaries in *MTR*, i & ii, and *MT Adm. Reg.*).

A booke of Accounts Anno Domini 1638. (Record of treasurer's expenditure, 1637–1638, 1638–1639).

The fifty boxes of papers mentioned by Hopwood in 1903 were removed from the Muniments Room in 1967. (This material is cited above as MT unclassified MSS). Although mostly dated after 1660, it also includes some valuable earlier items, including papers of the under-treasurers Richard Baldwin and John Bayliffe, original letters to the bench, documents relating to masters of the Temple, particularly Paul Micklethwaite, and the list of grievances prepared by junior members in 1617.

While not technically archives, two early seventeenth-century MSS presented by Lord Reading in 1910 must be briefly mentioned. Known as the 'Brerewood MS' and the 'History of Lincoln's Inn', these descriptions of the customs and government of the Middle Temple and Lincoln's Inn were evidently part of a larger work intended to deal with all four societies.

The Brerewood MS begins with the words 'Now as I have before spoken of the Inner Temple . . .' (p. 3), and a passage on p. 82 commending the old forms of public revels appears almost word-for-word on f. 23ᵛ of IT MS, Miscellanea 32, 'Antiquities of the Inner and Middle Temple', although this is in a different hand and follows a more strictly chronological plan of arrangement. None of these MSS is signed. The Brerewood MS bears the pencilled name of Sir Robert Brerewood, who was elected to the bench of the house after his reading in Lent 1638, but this is probably not contemporary. However, on p. 37 the author apologises for a long account of the form of a reading on the grounds that he himself has just been elected reader, and the last name on a list of benchers '*ibidem nunc vel nuper in vita scilicet tempore huius editionis Anno 1638*' is that of Brerewood. Other internal evidence (pp. 32, 50, 72, 75) suggests that the work was compiled between 1631 and 1638.

The 'History of Lincoln's Inn' is in the same hand as the third MS in the Reading Donation, a volume entitled 'Legal Antiquities', which also contains internal evidence that it was part of a larger treatise on the inns of court (f. 22). I have used a copy of the Lincoln's Inn MS by W. P. Baildon, now in the Lincoln's Inn Library, citing it as LI MS, Baildon transcript. R. F. Roxburgh provides a description of the contents in his *Origins of Lincoln's Inn*, 2–13, and makes a somewhat unconvincing attempt to attribute to William Hakewill. Portions of the Brerewood MS were reprinted in Dugdale's *OJ*, but none of the others have been published.

Appendix 1

Total admissions 1422–1650

Lincoln's Inn

1422	12	1442	12	1462	9	1482	17
1423	12	1443	14	1463	16	1483	14
1424	16	1444	16	1464	3	1484	9
1425	0	1445	10	1465	8	1485	21
1426	0	1446	9	1466	11	1486	20
1427	8	1447	0	1467	17	1487	3
1428	22	1448	0	1468	8	1488	11
1429	9	1449	4	1469	5	1489	20
1430	9	1450	5	1470	19	1490	5
1431	5	1451	10	1471	7	1491	3
1432	10	1452	6	1472	7	1492	7
1433	13	1453	20	1473	6	1493	16
1434	10	1454	16	1474	21	1494	22
1435	5	1455	22	1475	16	1495	5
1436	3	1456	11	1476	23	1496	14
1437	11	1457	13	1477	12	1497	9
1438	0	1458	12	1478	9	1498	4
1439	6	1459	11	1479	7	1499	14
1440	5	1460	8	1480	7		
1441	5	1461	3	1481	4		

	Gray's Inn	Inner Temple	Lincoln's Inn	Middle Temple
1500	0	0	4	0
1501	0	0	10	3
1502	0	0	8	13
1503	0	0	15	12
1504	0	0	13	9
1505	0	34	16	19
1506	0	10	16	9
1507	0	26	13	5
1508	0	12	15	7
1509	0	16	16	7
1510	0	22	9	12
1511	0	12	11	9
1512	0	8	15	16
1513	0	9	7	8

242

	Gray's Inn	Inner Temple	Lincoln's Inn	Middle Temple
1514	0	21	11	14
1515	0	17	17	6
1516	0	12	18	19
1517	0	8	14	25
1518	0	18	10	10
1519	0	16	9	13
1520	0	24	17	16
1521	21	19	8	8
1522	20	14	20	11
1523	9	11	15	6
1524	15	12	16	9
1525	16	16	6	0
1526	9	13	13	0
1527	27	11	4	0
1528	30	10	21	0
1529	18	8	22	0
1530	22	8	10	0
1531	31	5	13	0
1532	26	14	14	0
1533	30	18	17	0
1534	22	16	20	0
1535	13	13	14	0
1536	25	8	18	0
1537	43	20	15	0
1538	0	2	21	0
1539	29	18	17	0
1540	26	5	11	0
1541	31	7	23	0
1542	24	6	17	0
1543	22	5	12	0
1544	47	5	20	0
1545	0	6	16	0
1546	29	23	22	0
1547	26	37	23	0
1548	21	16	8	0
1549	17	27	16	0
1550	15	33	20	0
1551	31	24	12	12
1552	43	18	29	27
1553	48	26	5	17
1554	32	26	4	16
1555	40	43	22	29
1556	36	49	41	18
1557	18	32	31	29
1558	0	29	26	22
1559	25	34	35	19
1560	21	69	52	69
1561	51	76	54	28
1562	28	73	43	32

	Gray's Inn	Inner Temple	Lincoln's Inn	Middle Temple
1563	59	39	30	14
1564	38	43	45	20
1565	39	47	27	54
1566	35	57	25	38
1567	66	27	37	40
1568	56	52	18	29
1569	26	22	19	9
1570	40	11	27	16
1571	69	35	30	59
1572	46	35	37	48
1573	67	33	38	32
1574	33	25	26	39
1575	39	20	41	34
1576	46	42	42	42
1577	55	20	38	41
1578	53	30	35	34
1579	44	51	56	72
1580	95	43	54	84
1581	61	48	61	36
1582	76	33	52	47
1583	65	58	52	85
1584	87	41	46	54
1585	67	51	46	66
1586	69	41	52	45
1587	57	33	36	34
1588	74	26	29	34
1589	67	37	31	43
1590	60	46	39	37
1591	65	44	30	61
1592	77	20	29	26
1593	64	45	18	41
1594	122	66	58	87
1595	85	53	60	79
1596	70	35	46	50
1597	47	48	41	69
1598	111	48	46	68
1599	79	30	40	44
1600	84	38	40	59
1601	77	26	39	55
1602	75	34	52	66
1603	44	17	20	26
1604	72	43	45	69
1605	102	63	53	74
1606	87	54	61	84
1607	89	61	41	91
1608	141	52	49	86
1609	100	66	41	66
1610	100	63	64	88
1611	119	59	52	70

	Gray's Inn	Inner Temple	Lincoln's Inn	Middle Temple
1612	101	55	78	60
1613	94	53	56	85
1614	93	52	80	73
1615	111	42	60	46
1616	97	53	57	59
1617	122	44	54	60
1618	171	39	54	60
1619	162	45	46	40
1620	188	54	60	61
1621	192	53	38	42
1622	135	39	50	47
1623	93	37	47	36
1624	126	42	36	48
1625	72	23	30	26
1626	82	54	65	53
1627	130	46	56	64
1628	111	31	42	66
1629	111	43	46	63
1630	46	32	36	29
1631	146	54	75	67
1632	106	57	63	52
1633	161	49	61	58
1634	135	40	51	61
1635	115	54	67	48
1636	63	24	24	26
1637	115	66	51	65
1638	186	54	77	75
1639	128	49	70	49
1640	146	42	61	52
1641	205	42	60	59
1642	105	33	39	41
1643	21	13	3	7
1644	39	15	12	11
1645	51	25	21	20
1646	80	51	45	43
1647	168	64	49	71
1648	115	53	47	80
1649	87	29	40	46
1650	154	47	25	44

Sources: *GI Adm. Reg.* (commences 1521); *IT Adm. Reg.* (commences 1505); *LI Adm. Reg.* (commences 1420); *MT Adm. Reg.* (commences 1501, interrupted 1525–51).

Appendix 2

Residence Requirements under the Bar

GRAY'S INN

(i) *Vacations* – Nil.
(ii) *Chambers* – 1612: Owners or tenants to be in commons for 8 weeks each year, during term (*GIPB*, i. 198).

INNER TEMPLE

(i) *Vacations*[1] – pre-1666 and *c.* 1700: 4 to be served after admission (*OJ*, 158; IT MS, Miscellanea 29, f. 11).
(ii) *Chambers* – 1610, 1612: Owners to forfeit if absent more than 2 years without reasonable excuse (*ITR*, ii. 49, 66).
  – 1620: Owners to be personally in commons for 8 weeks each year (*ITR*, ii. 122).

LINCOLN'S INN

(i) *Vacations*[2] – 1442: Christmas, Lent, Autumn to be served for 3 years after admission (*BB*, i. 12).
  – 1537: Students to keep first 4 vacations together (*BB*, i. 251).
  – 1565: Students to keep 4 mean vacations after admission (*BB*, i. 349).
  – 1578: Student pardoned keeping Christmas and vacations within first three years (*BB*, i. 408).
  – *c.* 1625–30: Obligation to keep Christmas as vacation apparently removed (*BB*, ii. 192, 256, 268, 275, 299).
(ii) *Chambers* – 1595, 1608: Owners to be personally in commons for 4 months each year or forfeit, unless special admission to chamber or reasonable excuse (*BB*, ii. 40–1, 78).

MIDDLE TEMPLE

(i) *Vacations*[3] – *c.* 1540: 2 Lent, 2 Summer, 2 Christmas vacations to be served after admission (*OJ*, 194).
  – 1596: 6 vacations, 3 weeks Christmas, 5 weeks Lent, 4 weeks Summer, after admission (*MTR*, i. 361).
  – *c.* 1635: Vacations to be kept for 2 years after admission (*OJ*, 202).

246

(ii) *Chambers* – 1568: Owners to be personally in commons for 4 weeks each year or forfeit, unless reasonable excuse (*MTR*, i. 166).
– 1631: 'ancient order' for owners to be personally in commons for 8 weeks each year or forfeit, revived (*MTR*, ii. 777).

Notes:

1. In the early sixteenth century IT students were fined for failing to keep mean vacations (e.g. Baynerd, adm. 1519, fined for loss of mean vacation 1520: *ITR*, i. 50, 52). An early seventeenth-century account states that special admissions freed entrants from 'personall attendance in the grand vacations' and since an order of 1630 refers to special admissions as releasing members from all vacation requirements, it seems likely that mean vacation attendance was no longer compulsory (IT MS, Miscellanea 32, f. 17; *ITR*, ii. 203). Christmas was not a compulsory vacation during our period (*ITR*, ii. 27–8).
2. The 1442 order refers to mean rather than learning vacations. It is not clear whether students were still required to keep mean vacations by the early seventeenth century, but fines were levied only for absence from learning vacations.
3. Christmas was abolished as a compulsory vacation at the MT in 1607 and reintroduced as a disciplinary measure in 1635; but no action was taken against those not attending and the order seems to have lapsed (*MTR*, ii. 478, 831, 843).

Index